The Historiographical Jesus

The Historiographical Jesus

Memory, Typology, and the Son of David

Anthony Le Donne

BAYLOR UNIVERSITY PRESS

© 2009 by Baylor University Press
Waco, Texas 76798

All Rights Reserved. No part of this publication may be reproduced, stored in a retrieval system, or transmitted, in any form or by any means, electronic, mechanical, photocopying, recording or otherwise, without the prior permission in writing of Baylor University Press.

All Scripture is the author's own translation in consultation with the New Revised Standard Version Bible. NRSV copyright 1989, Division of Christian Education of the National Council of the Churches of Christ in the United States of America. Used by permission. All rights reserved.

Cover Design by Joan Osth

Library of Congress Cataloging-in-Publication Data

Le Donne, Anthony, 1975-
  The historiographical Jesus : memory, typology, and the Son of David / Anthony Le Donne.
     p. cm.
  Includes bibliographical references and index.
  ISBN 978-1-60258-065-7 (hardback : alk. paper)
  1. Jesus Christ--Historicity. 2. Theology--Methodology. 3. Memory. 4. Typology (Theology) I. Title.
  BT303.2.L39 2009
  232.9'08--dc22
                                                         2009003708

Printed in the United States of America on acid-free, minimum 30% pcw recycled paper.

לשרה

Contents

Abbreviations		ix
Preface		xiii
1	Introduction	1
2	Hermeneutics and History	17
3	History and Memory	41
4	Memory and Typology	65
5	Son of David and Typology	93
6	The Therapeutic Son of David	137
7	Jesus' Temple Procession	191
8	The "Son of David" Question	221
9	Concluding Analysis	259
Bibliography		269
Scripture Index		297
Author Index		306
Subject Index		309

Abbreviations

AB	Anchor Bible
AGJU	Arbeiten zur Geschichte des antiken Judentums und des Urchristentums
AnBib	Analecta Biblica
ANRW	*Aufstieg und Niedergang der römischen Welt*
ASTI	*Annual of the Swedish Theological Institute*
AUSS	*Andrews University Seminary Studies*
BBR	*Bulletin for Biblical Research*
BETL	Bibliotheca ephemeridum theologicarum lovaniensium
Bib	Biblica
BIS	Biblical Interpretation Series
BJRL	*Bulletin of the John Rylands University Library of Manchester*
BKAT	Biblischer Kommentar, Altes Testament
BR	*Biblical Research*
BTB	*Biblical Theology Bulletin*
BZNW	Beihefte zur Zeitschrift für die neutestamentliche Wissenschaft
CBQ	*Catholic Biblical Quarterly*
CBQMS	Catholic Biblical Quarterly Monograph Series
ConBOT	Coniectanea biblica: Old Testament Series
CGTC	Cambridge Greek Testament Commentary
DJD	Discoveries in the Judaean Desert
DSD	*Dead Sea Discoveries*
ExpTim	*Expository Times*
FOTL	Forms of the Old Testament Literature

FRLANT	Forschungen zur Religion und Literatur des Alten und Neuen Testaments
HB	Hebrew Bible
HNT	Handbuch zum Neuen Testament
HTKNT	Herders theologischer Kommentar zum Neuen Testament
HTR	*Harvard Theological Review*
ICC	International Critical Commentary
ITQ	*Irish Theological Quarterly*
JAAR	*Journal of the American Academy of Religion*
JAOS	*Journal of the American Oriental Society*
JBL	*Journal of Biblical Literature*
JJS	*Journal of Jewish Studies*
JNES	*Journal for Near Eastern Studies*
JQR	*Jewish Quarterly Review*
JSHJ	*Journal for the Study of the Historical Jesus*
JSHRZ	*Jüdische Schriften aus hellenistisch-römischer Zeit*
JSJ	*Journal for the Study of Judaism in the Persian, Hellenistic, and Roman Periods*
JSJSup	Journal for the Study of Judaism, Supplement Series
JSNT	*Journal for the Study of the New Testament*
JSNTSup	Journal for the Study of the New Testament, Supplement Series
JSOT	Journal for the Study of the Old Testament
JSOTSup	Journal for the Study of the Old Testament, Supplement Series
JSPSup	Journal for the Study of the Pseudepigrapha, Supplement Series
JTC	*Journal for Theology and the Church*
JTS	*Journal of Theological Studies*
L.A.B.	*Liber Antiquitatum Biblicarum*
LCL	Loeb Classical Library
LXX	Septuagint
MT	Masoretic Text
NovT	*Novum Testamentum*
NT	New Testament
NTOA	Novum Testamentum et Orbis Antiquus
NTS	*New Testament Studies*

OT	Old Testament
OTNT	Okumnischer Taschenbuchkommentar zum NT
RB	*Revue biblique*
RevExp	*Review and Expositor*
RevQ	*Revue de Qumran*
SBLDS	Society for Biblical Literature Dissertation Series
SBLMS	Society of Biblical Literature Monograph Series
SBLSP	Society for Biblical Literature Seminar Papers
SBT	Studies in Biblical Theology
SF	*Social Forces*
SHBC	Smyth & Helwys Bible Commentary Series
SNT	Studien zum Neuen Testament
SNTS	Society for New Testament Studies Monograph Series
SR	*Studies in Religion*
STDJ	*Studies on the Texts of the Desert of Judah*
StudNeot	Studia neotestamentica
SUNT	Studien zur Umwelt des Neuen Testaments
TDNT	*Theological Dictionary of the New Testament*
TTZ	*Trierer theologische Zeitschrift*
TynBul	*Tyndale Bulletin*
TZ	*Theologische Zeitschrift*
VT	*Vetus Testamentum*
WBC	Word Biblical Commentary
WUNT	Wissenschaftliche Untersuchungen zum Neuen Testament
ZAW	*Zeitschrift für die alttestamentliche Wissenschaft*
ZNW	*Zeitschrift für die neutestamentliche Wissenschaft und die Kunde der älteren Kirche*
ZTK	*Zeitschrift für Theologie und Kirche*

Preface

This book was originally completed for my Ph.D. at Durham University. That said, it might not read like your standard thesis. I have been told that the standard thesis takes a well-discussed subject, reframes it, and then slightly readjusts it. This book does not do that. Rather I have taken four related topics and built from the broad to the narrow: historiography, memory theory, typology, and Jesus. Each of these has been necessarily reframed simply by drawing out the relationship between them. But it should be said that while some of these subjects (e.g., Jesus) have been discussed at length by scholarship, others are relatively new subjects (e.g., memory theory). Moreover, because the present work has had to cover so much ground, I have not included the obligatory history-of-interpretation chapters that are common to most theses. For instance, you will find no survey of the history of historical Jesus research in this book. You will also find that my survey of historiographical thought is by no means comprehensive. To permit the space required for such surveys would have distracted from my overall thesis. Instead, I have attempted to introduce a very broad subject matter by jumping right into discussion with the voices most relevant to my own interests.

How to use this book if you do not intend to read it cover to cover: I am well aware that most academic works are not read in their entirety by researchers. Here are a few suggestions for such readers. This book is primarily about historical theory and method. If your interest in this book is historiographical, you might want to look more closely at chapters 1–4. Readers who are more interested in my treatment of the title "Son of David" might want to look more closely at chapters 5–8. The latter group should keep in mind that these exegetical chapters are the outworkings of my theoretical and methodological arguments. Thus, while the exegetical work done in these chapters has focused on a particular topic of historical Jesus research, I have used this topic as a work table to display my historiographical thesis. My thesis is put forth most clearly in chapter 4, so if you are interested in skipping right to the heart of my work, you will find it there. Having said that, I highly recommend that such readers begin at least with chapter 3, as my thesis will presuppose this discussion.

This work represents a honing of my thoughts, many of which took shape in conversations with mentors, good friends, and family. Indeed, it is now difficult to tell who belongs in which category. First and foremost are my doctor-fathers James Dunn and John Barclay. Professor Dunn's excessive generosity went well beyond what any student should expect. So much of what I have written is either an extension of or reaction against his keen insights. Professor Barclay's guidance has been invaluable. To my benefit, he is always two steps ahead of me and reminding me of the bigger picture.

I am also grateful for my many conversations with Mark Almlie, Rob Barrett, Stephen Barton, Chad Carmichael, Matt Curtis, Joel Lohr, Edward Peacock, Tim Stafford, Loren Stuckenbruck, Jason Swain, and William Telford. Each has contributed in important ways to this work. Stephanie Schultz, Alejandro Sotres, and Michael Widmer helped a great deal with language instruction. Markus Bockmuehl, Craig Evans, James Dunn, Alan Kirk, Loren Stuckenbruck, and Archie Wright have been kind enough to provide me with copies of forthcoming publications. This work would not have been possible without the continued support of my parents, Gary and Patricia Le Donne. Special thanks to my father for helping with indexing. More importantly, their larger sacrifices and hard work are ever-present in my mind. I will never be able to repay what they have invested in me. Finally, I cannot express enough my gratitude to my wife Sarah, to whom this work is dedicated. Without her, I would not have any frame of reference to translate חסד.

1

Introduction

What is history? For the Jesus historian, asking this question is precarious and the hope of an answer is elusive. It involves loosing the foundation on which we stand in order to see what lies beneath. To do so is always a precarious endeavor. It is elusive because the root of the problem is always just under the next layer of presuppositions. The problem of interpretation stems from the problem of language, which stems from the problem of perception, which leads to the concerns of epistemology, psychology, neurology, and so on. One can easily get lost down the hole of theory and never find one's way up again to apply the method. And there is the added danger of digging in earth that belongs to other disciplines. As Caird put it, "A prudent expert cultivates his own garden, not wasting time in looking over the fence at what his neighbours are doing."[1]

So, for my own sake, I approach the problem of historiography from the perspective of a biblical exegete. As it happens, I am fortunate from the start. Many of the most influential voices in historiography have also entered this discussion with biblical history in mind. This perspective not only allows me to interact with several important voices in historiography, but it also serves to focus the scope of this book. So not only am I in good company, but by focusing on the historical Jesus, I make provisions for the return journey. In unearthing the philosophical foundations of history, I necessarily explore hermeneutics, presuppositions, and theories. Upon my return to the surface I build my proposed method with a specific exegetical topic: the title "Son of David." This title provides a unique window into the Jesus tradition and has received remarkably little attention in biblical scholarship.

My goal is that the latter half of this book will provide a visible example of my primary thesis. After all, I hope to make a positive contribution to

---

[1] G. B. Caird, *The Language and Imagery of the Bible* (Grand Rapids: Eerdmans, 1997 [1980]), ix.

historiography and in doing so move historical Jesus research past the pitfalls of historical positivism. In this way, I have two aims: (1) I will build my historiographical thesis by applying it to Jesus, and (2) I will use my historiographical thesis to make Jesus visible to historical inquiry.

The Problem of New Testament Types

When engaging in historical study of Jesus, the historian recognizes that much of Jesus' New Testament portrayal was modeled after scriptural precedents. Scriptural models, prophetic fulfillments, and overarching narrative grids are so much a part of the New Testament that scholarship has been forced to question how much these texts actually contribute to history proper. Indeed, how does one distinguish history from typology?[2] Different solutions to this question have resulted in extremely different approaches to historical Jesus research. Those who presuppose that typological storytelling betrays wholesale invention inevitably conclude that when typology is employed in a biblical account, the historicity of this account is tenuous. In his study on Acts, Goulder's first two criteria for historicity illustrate this:

(1) Where [. . .] we find passages with no apparent root in symbolism, or with unimportant traces of types, we shall be justified in assuming that St. Luke was setting down a factual story. . . . This will be our first criterion: *where there are no types, Acts is intended to be factual.*

(2) [W]here an incident or passage can be accounted for wholly, or almost wholly, on typological grounds, we shall have to be very wary indeed of giving it weight as history. This gives us a second criterion: *the thicker the types, the less likely is the passage to be factual.*[3]

Here Goulder presupposed a dichotomy between typological story and factual history. When the historian applies this dichotomy to historical Jesus research, much of the biblical accounts of Jesus must be deemed "ahistorical."

More recently, Gerd Lüdemann has put forth a portrait of the historical Jesus that is built upon only those historical facts that he considered to be

---

[2] The definition of typology offered by K. J. Woollcombe is helpful: "Typology, considered as a method of exegesis, may be defined as the establishment of historical connexions between certain events, persons or things in the Old Testament and similar events, persons or things in the New Testament. Considered as a method of writing, it may be defined as the description of an event, person or thing in the New Testament in terms borrowed from the description of its prototypical counterpart in the Old Testament" ("The Biblical Origins and Patristic Development of Typology," in *Essays on Typology* [ed. Lampe and Woollcombe; SBT 22; London: SCM, 1957], 39–40). This definition will serve as a preliminary gloss until the present study can more fully discuss the nature of typology in chaps. 2 and 3.

[3] M. Goulder, *Type and History in Acts* (London: SPCK, 1964), 181, 182.

"authentic," meaning episodes of the Jesus tradition that betray no evidence of redaction. While "scriptural appeals by the evangelists" is not one of his five stated "criteria for inauthenticity,"[4] he often excludes material on this basis. For example, he considers Mark 9:11-13[5] to be inauthentic because the evangelist seems to have associated John the Baptist with Elijah and Jesus with the Danielic Son of Man.[6] Moreover, he argues, this saying is juxtaposed with an account that bears affinity to the account of Moses on Sinai.[7] Such affinities lead Lüdemann to conclude that the sayings associated with this episode are the products of invention. Lüdemann structures his study throughout by separating material that has been interpreted from material that is historical. Notice here the dichotomy between history and interpretation.

A similar dichotomy between scriptural appeals and historicity is the driving force behind much of John Dominic Crossan's work. Crossan argues that the NT accounts of Jesus are mostly fiction based upon scriptural precedents. In his *The Birth of Christianity*, Crossan assesses the Passion Narratives in this way:

> The individual units, general sequences, and overall frames of the passion-resurrection stories are so linked to prophetic fulfillment that the removal of such fulfillment leaves nothing but the barest facts . . . biblical models and scriptural precedents have controlled the story to the point that without them nothing is left but the brutal fact of crucifixion itself.[8]

Because of this, Crossan describes the gospel narratives as "Prophecy Historicized," an imagined genre that is more typological than historical. This presumed dichotomy between typology and history is pervasive in Gospels scholarship. Both Goulder and Crossan forthrightly adhere to this

---

[4] G. Lüdemann, *Jesus after 2000 Years: What He Really Said and Did* (London: SCM, 2000), 4.

[5] They asked him, saying, "Why is it that the scribes say that Elijah must come first?" And he said to them, "Elijah does first come and restore all things. And yet how is it written of the Son of Man that he will suffer many things and be treated with contempt? But I say to you that Elijah has indeed come, and they did to him whatever they wished, just as it is written of him." (Unless otherwise noted, scripture quotations are author's own translation.)

[6] Lüdemann, 59. Incidentally, it should be noted that it is much more likely that this saying was incorporated into Mark's narrative in association with the story of Elijah's appearance that immediately precedes this saying. Thus, Lüdemann is incorrect to conclude that Mark has John the Baptist in mind in this context. It is much more probable that the association with John the Baptist (which Lüdemann intuitively observes) has carried over from the pre-Markan tradition.

[7] Lüdemann, 60–61; cf. also comments on the association between Jesus and Isaiah's suffering servant (idem, 105).

[8] J. D. Crossan, *The Birth of Christianity: Discovering What Happened after the Execution of Jesus* (Edinburgh: T&T Clark, 1998), 521.

dichotomy; however, many others, like Lüdemann, betray this tendency in less obvious ways.

In his *The Historical Figure of Jesus*, E. P. Sanders includes a chapter titled "Two Contexts."[9] Sanders describes what he calls the "theological context" of Jesus and distinguishes this from what he calls the "context of Jesus' own career." The former of these sets Jesus within the salvation history of Israel. This first context places Jesus alongside great figures such as Moses and Elijah. In this way, the Gospels portray Jesus as a type of Moses (et al.), thus allowing Jesus' traditional predecessors to illuminate his role. The second of Jesus' contexts, writes Sanders, is the immediate social and political climate in which Jesus lived. This context has more to do with the history of the first century (e.g., John the Baptist and the emerging Christian church) and less to do with Israel's salvation history. Sanders points out the difficulty that this creates for historical study:

> There are no absolutely certain signs that tell us when a passage in the gospels has been invented as a parallel to an earlier stage of the history of salvation, when it has been recast to emphasize an actual parallel, and when Jesus himself (or John the Baptist) intentionally created a reminiscence.[10]

Thus Sanders (unlike the scholars cited above) acknowledges that the historian cannot simply attribute a passage framed in theological context to the early church "since Jesus himself was a theologian."[11] On the other hand, Sanders rightly suspects that the evangelists have imposed their own theology upon Jesus. Therefore, distinguishing the evangelists' theology from Jesus' theology becomes hazardous. Sanders writes:

> The more parallels there were between Jesus and characters or prophecies in Hebrew scripture, the more likely Matthew, Mark and Luke were to invent still more. They may have reasoned that if there were six similarities, there probably had been a seventh. I think that there is no doubt that they did invent some, though the possibility of overlaps, or of Jesus' own conscious imitation of scriptural types, means that we must often be uncertain.[12]

Here Sanders places his finger on the central problem of relating typology with history. But while his description of the problem hits the mark, his conclusion must be challenged. If it can be granted, as Sanders does, that Jesus did evoke scriptural types during his life, such typologies might have

---

[9] E. P. Sanders, *The Historical Figure of Jesus* (London: Penguin, 1993), 78–97.
[10] Sanders, *Historical Figure*, 90.
[11] Sanders, *Historical Figure*, 97.
[12] Sanders, *Historical Figure*, 85. I agree with much of Sanders' assessment, so it is with great respect that I offer the following critique.

been further developed by those who remembered him and told stories about him. In this way, Sanders aptly describes how interpretations of historically significant figures are gradually distorted according to changing contexts of memory over time. Where Sanders errs is his assessment of "two contexts," as if there are only two available to historical inquiry. This dichotomy is simplistic and misleads the discussion.

No, there are not only two contexts; there is a long continuum of many historical contexts that stand between Jesus and the Gospels, each connected and continuous with the others. By placing the typological discussion in a different category than the context of "Jesus' own career," Sanders has *created* two contexts and thereby bifurcates his historical portrait of Jesus.

This is not to say that there are no discernable differences between the typological imagination of the early church and the typological imitations of the historical Jesus. The opposite is true. No doubt, such interpretations evolved over time, sometimes with dramatic implications. However, rather than speaking of two contexts, I argue here that the model of a continuum is more suitable. By placing typological appeals to Israel's salvation history (most often) in a separate category than Jesus' own career, Sanders has underestimated how inseparable history and typological interpretation are from one another.

I contend that typological appeals to salvation history are to be expected along each stage of the Jesus tradition. All history, whether salvation history or otherwise, borrows language, categories, and types from previous eras. For this reason, the model of a continuum is to be preferred, one that places early typological interpretations of Jesus and the interpretations of the early church along the same trajectory.

Historiography: Where to Begin?

In both of the above quotes from Sanders, he voices his "uncertainty." This uncertainty stems from the recognition that Jesus' typological imitations are difficult to distinguish from the Gospels' typological portraits of him. Here Sanders probably falls back on the old notion of historical positivism[13] that an *ideal* historical inquiry is one that can subtract interpretation from history, leaving only the "actual" description of the past. When he laments that this cannot be done, he voices his uncertainty. Two recent studies have made

---

[13] Historical positivism is the theory that history is the task of employing rational or empirical methods, in an objective and value-neutral way, to accurately determine what happened in the past. Cf. D. R. Hiley, J. F. Bohman, and R. Shusterman, eds., *Introduction to The Interpretive Turn: Philosophy, Science, Culture* (Ithaca, N.Y.: Cornell University Press, 1991), 2–3.

similar observations concerning Crossan's hermeneutics,[14] and Lüdemann is particularly vulnerable to this criticism.[15] I should clarify at this point that I do not intend to lump all of the above scholars into a single category. Since no current scholar (that I know of) claims historical positivism, it is more accurate to say that many betray tendencies toward historical positivism. If anything, my critique of Crossan, Lüdemann, and Sanders suggests that historical positivism is the default position for much of New Testament scholarship, even among those whose approaches and conclusions vary widely. Consider the following statement of Ben Witherington:

> Much that is true about the historical Jesus is not historically demonstrable because the evidence is meager. Thus, the readers must content themselves with the fact that the historically demonstrable truths about Jesus and early Christianity are at best only a subset of what was historically true about these matters.[16]

Much like Sanders, Witherington makes an earnest attempt to move away from historical positivism. Witherington states very clearly that "there is no such thing as uninterpreted history." He concludes that "we have no ancient sources about Jesus and early Christianity from 'neutral' observers."[17] In both these statements, I wholeheartedly concur. But when Witherington's first (block) quote is examined closely, a certain historical positive lapse is evident. Here he makes a distinction between "historical truth" and "historically demonstrable truth." In his mind the latter is only a subset of the former. By describing "historically demonstrable truth" as a meager subset of the more comprehensive "historical truth" that is no longer available to the historian, Witherington's default conception of history surfaces. Perhaps not in every case, but certainly in the quote provided, what Witherington means by "his-

---

[14] H. Childs, *The Myth of the Historical Jesus and the Evolution of Consciousness* (SBLDS 179; Atlanta: Society of Biblical Literature, 2000), 21–58; D. L. Denton Jr., *Historiography and Hermeneutics in Jesus Studies: An Examination of the Work of John Dominic Crossan and Ben F. Meyers* (JSNTSup 262; London: T&T Clark, 2004), 57–78, esp. 77. Denton does well to distinguish the "early Crossan" (18–42) from the "later Crossan" (43–56). Much of Denton's criticism is directed toward the "early Crossan," but he maintains that Crossan's early faults have not been corrected but merely tempered in recent years.

[15] After removing all of the redacted material from the historical material, Lüdemann regularly concludes with a summary one-word judgment as to a text's historical value, e.g., "Nil," "Unhistorical," "Worthless." This is normally followed by a brief (one-paragraph) assessment of the historically valuable (i.e., unredacted) material. Cf. G. Stanton, review of G. Lüdemann, *Jesus after 2000 Years: What He Really Said and Did, JTS* 54 (2003): 422.

[16] B. Witherington, *New Testament History: A Narrative Account* (Grand Rapids: Baker, 2001), 17.

[17] Witherington, *New Testament History,* 15.

torical Jesus" is Jesus as he existed independently of historical memory. But by Witherington's own principles such a history does not exist.

So while Sanders voices uncertainty and Witherington voices probability, both assume a similar stance with regard to what the historian is trying to accomplish. It must be stated in no uncertain terms that historical truth has no subsets. There are not subsets of historical truth; there are only degrees of probability.[18] There is no historical truth that is not projected on the basis of evidence (or to use Witherington's term, "demonstrable"). The only thing that stands behind such historical truth is the forgotten past, and what has been forgotten about the past is not available for analysis. *The "historical Jesus" is the figure that becomes plausible on the basis of the historical evidence; there is no other.* If Jesus historians are ultimately hoping to glimpse a long-forgotten past, the evidence is doomed to be seen as meager, and the impossibility of analyzing the past will block us at every turn.

In contrast, I do not see historical probability as a barrier to the historian. All truth is simply measured in degrees of probability. To say that historical truth is always only probable does not distinguish it from any other kind of truth.

To be fair, I have no doubt that Witherington and Sanders had intended to move in a similar direction. Furthermore, I should acknowledge that a great deal of excellent exegesis has been done under the watch of historical positivism. I consider myself fortunate to rely on more than two centuries of historical-critical methodology. What my critique brings to the fore is the need for further clarification as to what exactly the task of history entails.

Historical Jesus research has only begun to scratch the surface of the issues being discussed in contemporary historiographical circles. But once this need has been felt, where does one begin? In answering this question, Keith Jenkins writes that

> while most historians would agree that a rigorous method is important, there is a problem as to which rigorous method they are talking about. [. . . W]ould you like to follow Hegel or Marx or Dilthey or Weber or Popper or Hempel or Aron or Collingwood or Dray or Oakeshott or Danto or Gallie or Walsh or Atkinson or Leff or Hexter? Would you care to go along with modern empiricists, feminists, the Annales School, neo-Marxists, new-stylists, econometricians, structuralists or post-structuralists, or even Marwick himself, to name but twenty-five possibilities? And this is a short list![19]

---

[18] The idea of "subsets" of truth betrays the idea that there is historical truth that is a priori.
[19] K. Jenkins, *Re-thinking History* (London: Routledge, 1991), 15.

Add to this list all those emerging branches that have budded since Jenkins wrote in 1991.[20] While methodological variety is not necessarily a problem for the postmodern mind, it is a problem for the author who hopes to survey these methods, do justice to the contributions of each, and then have space left over to say something of his own. With this in mind, I answer the question in this way: the best place to begin is to identify some key deficiencies with a particular discipline and seek out a particular historiographical discussion that attempts to speak to these most directly.

So rather than attempting to provide a comprehensive survey of contemporary historiography, I narrow my discussion to a branch of historiography that recently has taken seriously the problem of hermeneutics, the relay of tradition, and typological interpretation. I refer to a historiographical discussion that has emerged (for the most part) in the past twenty years called social memory theory. In my estimation, this focus (1) provides an entry point into many key hermeneutical concerns shared by many contemporary approaches to historiography and (2) serves as an apt departure point from which to apply these concerns to historical Jesus research.[21]

Before doing so, I would be remiss not to acknowledge a handful of studies that have previously attempted to bridge the gap between historiography and historical Jesus research, and admirably so. Perhaps no name in contemporary research is more associated with Jesus and historiography than Ben F. Meyer. In introducing the work of Lonergan to historical Jesus research,[22] Meyer established critical realism as the most appealed-to alternative to what I have referred to as the default setting of historical positivism. Meyer presents Lonergan's "cognitional theory" as if it comprehensively represents the more general theory of critical realism. For Meyer, critical realism specifically denoted Lonergan's cognitional theory.[23] This theory attempts to combat the "naive" realists' conception of knowing as "seeing." Rather, Lonergan emphasized a more complex process of knowing which involved the interaction between experience, understanding, and judging.[24]

---

[20] Lest we adopt a caricature of postmodernity, it is necessary to point out that not every new contribution breaks away from the pack; many attempt to refine the discipline and have been helpful to this end.

[21] This will be the focus of chaps. 3 and 4.

[22] B. F. Meyer, *Critical Realism and the New Testament* (Princeton Theological Monograph Series 17; Allison Park, Pa.: Pickwick, 1989). For a good first step into Lonergan's thought, see B. Lonergan, *Insight: A Study of Human Understanding* (New York: Harper and Row, 1978).

[23] Cf. Denton, 81–82.

[24] For a concise treatment of this theory, see B. Lonergan, "Cognitional Structure," in *Collection: Papers by Bernard Lonergan* (Toronto: University of Toronto, 1988), 205–21.

Perhaps Meyer's greatest influence was felt indirectly through the adaptation of critical realism by N. T. Wright.[25] Wright acknowledges his debt to Meyer and proceeds to adapt this theory to his own concerns for what he calls "the essentially 'storied nature' of human knowing."[26] Meyer and Wright both emphasize that there must be a reciprocal relationship between the real object (which exists independently from the knower) and the mind that knows the thing. Both seek to contextualize the knowing process within the knower's perspective and worldview. Wright's contribution to this discussion is his emphasis on the important role that stories play in creating a worldview and the way that the knower is inclined to understand his own story within the framework of larger stories. This requires that personal stories be arranged in narrative form; it also suggests the possibility that personal narratives are shaped by metanarratives. For Wright, the act of writing history is not dissimilar to the way that personal stories almost intuitively take shape. Therefore, in his view, there is no great gap between events that have occurred in time and stories created about those events. Thus history "is neither 'bare facts' nor 'subjective interpretations,' but is rather *the meaningful narrative of events and intentions.*"[27]

In my opinion, critical realism has been a worthwhile corrective. If one thinks of (naïve) realism as one extreme and idealism as another, critical realism could be thought of as that force of gravity that pulls back on the pendulum swinging toward idealism. It now serves the same correcting purpose against the momentum toward poststructuralist and deconstructionist thought (i.e., the denial of any form of realism). But as is often the case with such correctives, their countermomentum tends to pull back further than need be.

One deficiency of critical realism that the present study attempts to correct is its underemphasis on subconscious interpretation. The concept of "judging" (which is seen as the culmination of experience and understanding to form knowledge) connotes a process that moves toward conscious thought, which suggests that understanding is a process that involves *intentional* cognition. Indeed, Lonergan and Meyer begin by assuming that the knower is "aware of an object."[28] I have no problem with this description of the interplay between

---

[25] N. T. Wright, *The New Testament and the People of God* (Minneapolis: Fortress, 1992), 30–80, esp. 32–37.

[26] Wright, *New Testament*, 45.

[27] Wright, *New Testament*, 82. More recently, Denton (*Historiography*, 168–92) has endeavored to refine this concept and use it as a guiding principle in the analysis of historical data. He calls his adaptation "narrative intelligibility." Much in Denton's work moves this discussion forward and will be revisited in my own discussion of narrativization. Emphasis added.

[28] Meyer, 8. Lonergan writes: "Just as operations by their intentionality make objects

the knower and act of intentional knowing. Indeed this aspect of knowing is an apt description of the interaction between written history and the historian who intentionally attempts to understand the intended sense of the text.[29] But it must be said that much of knowledge (that does not come via textual transmission) comes to us intuitively and unawares. In my discussion of memory theory, I emphasize the idea that the interplay between memory and perception most often happens on a subconscious level.

Wright hints in this direction when he discusses how often and swiftly we process the perceived past, "selecting tiny fragments of our lives and arranging them into narratives."[30] When thought of in this way, judging might occur on a more intuitive level. However, this process is generally underemphasized by adherents of critical realism. It is precisely this aspect of memory that I emphasize in my discussion of memory refraction. Otherwise, the reader will probably find that my theoretical arguments and models cohere in large part with critical realism but are not reliant on them.[31] Conversely, I do not draw directly from the overt tenets of critical realism, and so the reader does not need to be well versed in Lonergan or his adherents to follow my theoretical argument.[32]

A recent representative from the other side of the pendulum is Hal Childs. Childs describes himself as a postfoundationalist, by which he means that he considers rational or objective foundations for knowledge to be unachievable.[33] Childs aims to undermine the entire enterprise of historical-critical scholarship and redefine history as myth. Childs' theory and method rely heavily on Heidegger's interpretation of Jung. Within this program, the quest for the historical Jesus is only valuable if it takes on a "psychological-archetypal" aim. Childs avers that the idea that Jesus is a separate historical entity from the historian is a carryover from positivism; rather, Jesus Christ is the archetype that constitutes the psyche of the Christian West.[34] He argues that the historian projects his own ego and the collective subconscious of his culture onto the historical Jesus in order to see "the reflection at the bottom of the well [which] reveals previously unknown aspects of the 'face of

---

present to the subject, so also by consciousness they make the operating subject present to himself" (*Method in Theology* [London: Darton, Longman and Todd, 1972], 8).

[29] Meyer, 27; cf. Lonergan, "Cognitional Structure," 222–27; Lonergan, *Insight*, 271–78.

[30] Wright, *New Testament*, 83.

[31] For example, I (like the adherents of critical realism) discuss the "hermeneutical circle" and adapt the concerns presented in this discussion to my own historiographical theory and method. But I do so through interaction with Schleiermacher, Dilthey, Heidegger, et al., and not through any interaction with Lonergan.

[32] For a fuller treatment of critical realism and historical Jesus research, see Denton.

[33] Childs, *Myth*, 99.

[34] Childs, *Myth*, 221.

God' that desires incarnation."[35] According to Childs, the value in historical Jesus research is found in the process of projection so that the subconscious has a means to become conscious.[36]

In stark contrast to critical realism, Childs' approach to historical Jesus research is defined by his conception of the subconscious interpretation. While my approach also emphasizes Heideggerian thought and the role of subconscious interpretation, it has very little else in common with Childs' approach. I presume that while standing in relationship to history, the historian does indeed have a basis for relative individuation. Moreover, while I grant that certain historical events and figures can take on mythic and archetypal significance, I do not think that all history can be equated with myth. Thus, part of my own method involves the distinction between memory and invention. Because Childs' method resists the idea that these two can be separated, one must seriously question whether his method even aims at historical inquiry.

Finally, I must acknowledge my debt to the recent work of James Dunn.[37] After providing a more detailed survey of hermeneutics and historiography than do most contributions to historical Jesus research, Dunn aligns himself with critical realism. While I do not assume such a stance, much of my theoretical argument hinges on the concept of memory. This concept was brought to the fore of historical Jesus research through the publication of Dunn's *Jesus Remembered*. Dunn argues more forthrightly than his predecessors that historical Jesus research should not be an attempt to describe what actually happened but an attempt to account for the initial impact of the earliest memories of Jesus. "The only realistic objective for any 'quest of the historical Jesus' is Jesus *remembered*."[38]

I take this for granted over the course of my book, but it should be asked whether Dunn has departed from critical realism at this point.[39] The aim of a critical realist history, according to Meyer, is to establish "man as he was"—that is, "History studies historical reality."[40] It seems that in order for Dunn to maintain his association with critical realism, he has to redefine historical reality in terms of historical memory. My own study attempts to do just that; I argue that history is primarily defined by the limits of memory. However, I have no intention of redefining critical realism on the basis of my findings.

---

[35] Childs, *Myth*, 98.
[36] Childs, *Myth*, 125.
[37] J. D. G. Dunn, *Jesus Remembered* (Grand Rapids: Eerdmans, 2003), esp. chap. 6.
[38] Dunn, *Jesus Remembered,* 882. Emphasis added.
[39] Cf. B. Holmberg, "Questions of Method in James Dunn's Jesus Remembered," *JSNT* 26 (2004): 451–53.
[40] Meyer, 27.

Dunn's way into the concept of memory is through his emphasis on the oral character of the Jesus tradition.[41] Indeed, oral tradition presumes the process of memory, and a particular kind of memory at that. By examining the method of transmission, Dunn offers a theory of how the initial memories of Jesus were transmitted and took synoptic shape.[42] Central to his thesis is the notion (common among oral historians) that oral tradition is a balance between variance and stability. While the details are expected to vary, the core substance of the tradition is expected to remain stable. While the discussion of orality and the New Testament precedes Dunn's treatment,[43] his work has gained for the discussion a much wider exposure than had been formerly enjoyed. Moreover, his work firmly places historical Jesus research within this discussion and reenvisages Jesus' relationship to the synoptic tradition in light of this. I consider his work to be a significant advance in historical Jesus research in this regard.

What Dunn does not offer in *Jesus Remembered* is a theory of memory that interacts with recent historiographical discussions of memory theory. Most notably, Dunn's work has been vulnerable to questions raised by social memory theory (mentioned above).[44] This deficit recently has been remedied,[45] but Dunn does so by distancing his concept of formative memory from social memory.[46] This is the departure point for my own study.

---

[41] Cf. J. D. G. Dunn, "Jesus in Oral Memory," in *Jesus: A Colloquium in the Holy Land* (ed. D. Donnelly; London: Continuum, 2001), 84–145; J. D. G. Dunn, *A New Perspective On Jesus: What the Quest for the Historical Jesus Missed* (Grand Rapids: Baker Academic, 2005).

[42] See also T. Mournet, *Oral Tradition and Literary Dependency: Variability and Stability in the Synoptic Tradition and Q* (WUNT 195; Tübingen: Mohr Siebeck, 2005).

[43] E.g. B. Gerhardsson, *Memory and Manuscript: Oral Tradition and Written Transmission in Rabbinic Judaism and Early Christianity* (Lund: Gleerup, 1961); W. Kelber, *The Oral and the Written Gospel: The Hermeneutics of Speaking and Writing in the Synoptic Tradition, Mark, Paul, and Q* (Philadelphia: Fortress, 1983); S. Byrskog, *Jesus the Only Teacher: Didactic Authority and Transmission in Ancient Israel, Ancient Judaism, and the Matthean Community* (Stockholm: Almqvist and Wiksell, 1994).

[44] I provide an extensive discussion of social memory theory in my third chapter. But see also A. Kirk and T. Thatcher, "Jesus Tradition as Social Memory," in *Memory, Tradition, and Text: Uses of the Past in Early Christianity* (Semeia 52; ed. Kirk and Thatcher; Leiden: Brill, 2005); A. Le Donne, "Theological Memory Distortion in the Jesus Tradition: A Study in Social Memory Theory," in *Memory and Remembrance in the Bible and Antiquity* (ed. L. T. Stuckenbruck, S. C. Barton, and B. G. Wold; Tübingen: Mohr Siebeck, 2007).

[45] J. D. G. Dunn, "Social Memory and the Oral Jesus Tradition," in *Memory and Remembrance in the Bible and Antiquity* (ed. L. T. Stuckenbruck, S. C. Barton, and B. G. Wold; Tübingen: Mohr Siebeck, 2007).

[46] In Dunn's view, Jesus' initial impact decisively formed the memories of him and provided a stabilizing force for the oral transmission of these memories. I revisit this discussion in subsequent chapters.

In what follows, I largely align my approach with the key tenets of social memory and critically adapt these to the unique concerns of historical Jesus research. Because social memory is a relatively new field (having only gained momentum since the 1980s) and almost completely new to historical Jesus research (having only been introduced in 2004[47]), this book is the first large-scale adaptation of social memory to historical Jesus research.[48] Moreover, this study is among the first to approach New Testament studies from the standpoint of social memory that does not take the form of a general introduction to the field.[49]

In contrast to Dunn, I consider social memory to provide the Jesus historian with a theoretical and methodological way forward that is a welcome middle ground between critical realism and postfoundationalism. Having said this, my study modifies social memory in a few fundamental ways. Because it is a relatively new approach to historiography in general and historical Jesus research in particular, there is ample room for redefinition.

Thesis and Delimitation

Jesus can be examined and discussed as a historical figure as long as history is thought of in terms of *memory refraction*.[50] This statement is not intended to be concessionary. I argue that all perception is bent in the mnemonic process and that historical memory is best understood in this way. Building from this argument, I suggest that the multiple (and sometimes contradictory) interpretations of Jesus found in the Gospels allow the historian to chart trajectories of memory refraction that have been propelled forward by the initial perceptions of Jesus by his contemporaries.

---

[47] Here I refer to the newly inaugurated (2004) Society of Biblical Literature section, "Mapping Memory."

[48] Deserving mention is G. M. Keightley, "The Church's Memory of Jesus: A Social Science Analysis of 1 Thessalonians," *BTB* 17 (1987): 149–56. To my knowledge, her study was the first to introduce social memory to New Testament studies. It was another fifteen years before social memories attracted wider interest among biblical scholars.

[49] However, see the early advances made by R. A. Horsley, "Prominent Patterns in the Social Memory of Jesus and Friends" and H. Hearon, "The Story of the Woman Who Anointed Jesus as Social Memory: A Methodological Proposal for the Study of Tradition as Memory," in *Memory, Tradition, and Text: Uses of the Past in Early Christianity* (Leiden: Brill, 2005), 79–97.

[50] Memory refraction (à la memory distortion) is defined and illustrated in the following chapters.

In order to demonstrate how distortion trajectories can be charted, I focus on typological interpretation. I argue that typology is a particular manifestation of memory refraction and that it provides an apt example of how memories are propelled forward by certain patterns of interpretation that evolve over time and (re)consideration. Central to this thesis is the concept of mnemonic continuity; I argue that memory refraction (most often) is a gradual and imperceptible process that renders past perceptions intelligible to the continually shifting contexts of the present. Because of this, refraction trajectories can be charted backward and the historian can postulate the most plausible historical memories that best account for these refractions.

My thesis is argued from the broad to the narrow. I begin with a discussion of historiography and memory, narrow this discussion to typology, and then focus my theoretical model onto a specific issue of historical Jesus research. The bulk of this book involves historical and exegetical questions concerning the title "Son of David." This topic provides a work table for my historiographical thesis. In this way, I hope to avoid an overly long treatise on theoretical models and abstract concepts. Such discussion is confined to my first four chapters, where I directly discuss the theoretical and methodological issues pertaining to history, memory, and typology. Thereafter, the reader will be able to observe my primary historiographical thesis as it is applied to a particular group of texts, ideas, and historical developments. So while my primary aim with these latter chapters is to demonstrate how my thesis plays out in historical Jesus research, my secondary aim is to shed new light on the title "Son of David" and how it was applied to Jesus. Specifically, I emphasize more so than previous studies on this topic the role that David and Solomon typology played in the application of this title.[51]

Given that my primary thesis is theoretical, my treatment of Son of David is limited to texts that specifically manifest this phrase. It occasionally is necessary to relate this small group of texts to the larger spheres of Davidism, messianism, Christology, and so on. But I limit my discussion of these to the specific points of overlap with the title "Son of David." This book is not primarily about these larger concepts and does not attempt to provide a comprehensive study on Davidism, messianism, or Christology. In this way, my study is different from previous treatments of Son of David.

My chapters proceed as follows: In this chapter, I have introduced what I consider to be a fundamental deficiency of historical Jesus research: the misunderstanding of the relationship between history and typology. I believe that this misunderstanding is a product of the tendency to want to separate historical fact from interpretation. I have suggested that greater attention to

---

[51] See my introductions to chaps. 5 and 6.

historiographical discussions outside biblical studies might serve to remedy this false dichotomy. In the next chapter, I situate my interests in historiography and memory theory within a survey of several important contributors to hermeneutical theory. In chapter 3, I survey the development and key theorists of social memory theory and suggest how this historiographical discussion might be of use to historical Jesus research. My fourth chapter constitutes my primary thesis concerning the relationship between history, memory, and typology. I illustrate my theoretical model and lay out my historiography that is an outworking of this model. Chapters 5 through 8 demonstrate my theory and method via exegesis. The introduction of chapter 5 serves as an introduction to these chapters. I refer the reader to that secondary introduction for an overview of my exegetical aims.

2

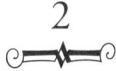

Hermeneutics and History

In this chapter I follow a particular thread of ideas about hermeneutics and history as they have developed in historiography. For the sake of space and focus, I highlight a selection of important shifts in this development: My first section (1) examines the historiographical presuppositions of Benedict Spinoza, (2) compares the dichotomies at work in the thinking of Gotthold Lessing and Leopold von Ranke, (3) discusses the hermeneutical circle and the key contributors to this concept, including Schleiermacher and Heidegger, and (4) critiques the conception of history in the work of Rudolf Bultmann. In this way, I aim to set the stage for chapter 3, which discusses contemporary memory theory.

Over the course of this book, I assume three premises. In this chapter, I discuss these with an aim to build from this foundation in the chapters that follow:

A. If perceptions are to be remembered then they will inevitably be interpreted, subconsciously, consciously, or both.
B. Perceptions that contribute to historical memory are thus always interpreted along each stage of the tradition that they inhabit.
C. The historian is never able to interpret an uninterpreted past.

My most central thesis is not addressed in full until chapter 3. Therefore I have listed these three positions as premises rather than conclusions. However, as with all premises, each could be seen as a conclusion in its own right—hence the necessity of the present chapter. Because this chapter is largely a survey of selected historiographical ideas, I do not attempt to structure what follows into three neatly contained sections that coincide with each of my three premises. Rather, I tease out the issues related to my three premises as I work through this survey.

Interpreting Interpretation

The reader will notice that premise C employs the word "interpret" twice. I here grant that the historian's primary role is that of interpreter. This, of course, is an uncontroversial position among contemporary historiographers. What I aim to emphasize is that the ancient perceivers of events and figures were themselves interpreters. As such, historical memory is from the very beginning the product of interpretation. While this point is often acknowledged, ultimately historiographers have been preoccupied with the nature of their own task. Historiography since Collingwood and Trevelyan[1] has increasingly centered on the theories and methods employed by the contemporary interpreter.[2]

I view the self-reflection of historians on their roles as interpreters to be essential and have no desire to undermine this progress. Rather, I wholeheartedly agree and refocus my own discussion onto the role that interpretation played for the first perceivers of history, on whose memories historical data were first based. Thus, to fill out premise C, I take for granted that historical memory exists first in the interpretations of the ancient perceivers and only then in the subsequent interpretations of historians. With this in mind I begin with Spinoza.

Spinoza and Scripture

Benedict (Baruch) Spinoza (1632–1677) provides a window into the early concern for biblical hermeneutics,[3] and by inference, the philosophy of history. The chief aim of Spinoza's *Tractatus Theologico-Politicus* was to combat what he considered the abuse of Scripture at the hands of the church.[4] Spinoza accused the church of using the Bible to justify doctrine and thereby attributed to the Holy Spirit "every result of their diseased imagination" (7:7).[5] His solution to this problem was to study Scripture by the same principles as one studies nature, with pure intellect and without emotion. Spinoza writes:

---

[1] R. G. Collingwood (1889–1943) and G. M. Trevelyan (1876–1962).

[2] This was prefigured by Dilthey's notion that perceptions of the past are filtered through the historian's worldview (H. A. Hodges, *Wilhelm Dilthey* [London: Routledge and Kegan Paul, 1969], esp. 228). See the discussion in R. C. Solomon, *Continental Philosophy since 1750: The Rise and Fall of the Self* (Oxford: Oxford University Press, 1988), 106.

[3] By "early" I mean that Spinoza's work was an antecedent to the hermeneutical concerns of the Enlightenment and thereafter.

[4] And thereby undermine the church's use of Scripture for political sway. See S. Preus, *Spinoza and the Irrelevance of Biblical Authority* (Cambridge: Cambridge University Press, 2001), 1–33, esp .4–6.

[5] Translation from B. Spinoza, *The Chief Works* (New York: Dover, 1951).

> By working in this manner everyone will always advance without danger of error—that is, if they admit no principles for interpreting Scripture [. . .] and will be able with equal security to discuss what surpasses our understanding, and what is known by the natural light of reason. (7:11)

In other words, Spinoza advances the idea that Scripture ought to be read as "historical narrative"[6] and not as a proof text for dogma.

While Spinoza's hermeneutic foreshadows the divorce of faith and history that finds fruition in modern biblical criticism,[7] it most loudly bespeaks Spinoza's conception of historical inquiry as akin to natural science. The foundational assumption on which Spinoza's historiography was built was that history, like nature, can be objectively studied, categorized, and understood. Of course, contemporary, postmodern critics will question whether nature can be observed in this way, but what concerns the present study is Spinoza's analogy. It is obvious that he took for granted that the natural world could and should be studied with "pure intellect" and devoid of prejudice. What would have been more controversial to his contemporaries was that the historical narratives of Scripture should be objectified in the same way. Spinoza argued that Scripture can only be fully understood when it is studied in and for its historical and literary context. As he provides exegetical examples for his method, we witness the anticipation of modern historical criticism if not the very birth of it.[8]

Spinoza held that all Scripture fell into one of two categories: revelation and historical narrative. His hermeneutic toward historical narrative most interests the present study. But the simple delineation between these two genres demonstrates Spinoza's conception of history. This categorization demonstrates that Spinoza considered history to be something other than revelation. So a brief word on his conception of revelation is warranted. He considered revelation to be the product of the prophet's imagination, and that knowledge deriving from revelation was much less reliable than that derived from the observation of nature (2:16). This was not due to the lack of divine influence, but due to the fact that "God adapted revelations to the understanding and opinions of the prophets" (2:125). Spinoza argued that in order

---

[6] Spinoza claims that biblical Scripture "is chiefly made up of historical narratives and revelation" (7:21). The Gospels fall into what Spinoza attributes to the former category.

[7] G. W. Dawes provides a helpful treatment along these lines as he discusses both Spinoza and Troeltsch ("Introduction," in *The Historical Jesus Quest: A Foundational Anthology* [Leiden: Deo Publishing, 1999], 2–3); cf. M. Rae, *History and Hermeneutics* (Edinburgh: T&T Clark, 2006), 4–21, esp. 7–8.

[8] H. G. Gadamer, *Philosophical Hermeneutics* (Berkeley: University of California Press, 1976), 47; C. Norris, *Spinoza and the Origins of Modern Critical Theory* (Oxford: Basil Blackwell, 1991), 155.

for God's message to the prophet to have been intelligible, it would have had to condescend to the limitations of the ancient mind.[9] As such, revelation does "reveal" the divine, but it is more representative of the ignorance and conflicting opinions of the prophets. "It therefore follows that we must by no means go to the prophets for knowledge, either of natural or of spiritual phenomena" (2:126).

Spinoza considered historical narrative to be less tainted by the revelatory process, but acknowledged that a similar process takes place in certain episodes of historical narrative. In the instance of Job, the "historian" gave an account of a revelation from God. In such cases, the ancient historian represents the same sort of limitations that hindered the prophets. Consider the following passage with special attention to Spinoza's parenthetical comment:

> The reasonings by which the Lord displayed His power to Job (if they really were a revelation, and the author of the history is narrating, and not merely, as some suppose, rhetorically adorning his own conceptions), would come under the same category—that is, they were adapted to Job's understanding. (2:132)

Spinoza's parenthetical comment betrays his understanding of history as something other than rhetoric that embellishes the author's "own conceptions." To do so was to extend beyond simple narration, and thereby the narration would cease to be history. It is thus evident that Spinoza's notion of history had little tolerance for the interpretive agendas of the ancient authors. Spinoza's main argument deals with the revelatory process, arguing that any adaptation to the ancient person's understanding renders the text suspect. In both comments, Spinoza betrays the idea that the filter of ancient human perception and understanding hinders an otherwise straightforward process. His parenthetical comment betrays his distrust of conscious agendas, and his main argument betrays his distrust of implicit worldviews. Spinoza concluded:

---

[9] Spinoza wrote, "So also did the revelation vary, as we have stated, according to individual disposition and temperament, and according to the opinions previously held [by the prophets]. It varied according to disposition, in this way: if a prophet was cheerful, victories, peace, and events which make men glad, were revealed to him; in that he was naturally more likely to imagine such things. If, on the contrary, he was melancholy, wars, massacres, and calamities were revealed; and so, according as a prophet was merciful, gentle, quick to anger, or severe, he was more fitted for one kind of revelation than another. It varied according to the temper of imagination in this way: if a prophet was cultivated he perceived the mind of God in a cultivated way, if he was confused he perceived it confusedly. And so with revelations perceived through visions. If a prophet was a countryman he saw visions of oxen, cows, and the like; if he was a soldier, he saw generals and armies; if a courtier, a royal throne, and so on" (2:3237). . . . "Each doubtless saw God under the form in which he usually imagined Him" (2:54).

> We have now more than sufficiently proved our point, that God adapted revelations to the understanding and opinions of the prophets, and that in matters of theory without bearing on charity or morality the prophets could be, and, in fact, were, ignorant, and held conflicting opinions (2:125). . . . We can come to no different conclusion with respect to the reasonings of Christ, by which He convicted the Pharisees of pride and ignorance, and exhorted His disciples to lead the true life. He adapted them to each man's opinions and principles. (2:133–34)

Interestingly, Spinoza likened the speaking of Christ to his contemporaries to the speaking of God to humanity.[10] In his view, Christ's speech condescended to the "opinions and principles" of his ancient audience when he spoke of angels and devils.[11] Accordingly, Spinoza believed these references to the supernatural did not give insight to Christ's understanding of reality, but rather gives insight into the worldview of the historical audience and the historian himself.[12] Spinoza picked up this line of reasoning again in chapter 7, this time in regard to "historical narrative":

> . . . the narratives generally contain miracles—that is, as we have shown in the last chapter, relations of extraordinary natural occurrences adapted to the opinions and judgment of the historians who recorded them. (7:12)

Crucial to understanding Spinoza on this point is his commitment to rationalism and his subsequent rejection of the supernatural.[13] Spinoza defined this view of reality in the first part of his *Ethics*. Spinoza held that there is only one infinite substance in the universe, and he called this substance God.[14] Because of this, Spinoza held that God and Nature were one and the same. Moreover, God does not act in ways contrary to his own nature.[15] Therefore, according to Spinoza, things perceived as supernatural are simply natural occurrences that have been misunderstood due to the limited perceptions of the historian.[16]

---

[10] Perhaps this is indicative of a high Christology on his part, or at least on the part of his readers. This is interesting considering his objection to a "personal" God in favor of a pantheistic conception of God within Nature. Cf. F. Copleston, *A History of Philosophy* (New York: Doubleday, 1963), 4:262–63.

[11] Spinoza was of the opinion that Christ did not himself believe in angels and devils, but spoke of these in order to be understandable to his ancient audience (2:135–37).

[12] Cf. Spinoza's comment on the "historian" who wrote the book of Joshua (2:68).

[13] Copleston, 261–62.

[14] See *Ethics*, propositions 11 and 14.

[15] See *Ethics*, proposition 17; cf. discussion in T. J. J. Altizer, "The Self-Saving of God," in *The Blackwell Companion to Postmodern Theology* (ed. G. Ward; Oxford: Blackwell, 2006 [2001]), 436–37.

[16] "Further, as nothing happens in nature which does not follow from her laws, and as

At this point Spinoza's treatment of the historical narratives is of particular interest to my study. Spinoza granted that certain supernatural accounts were tainted by the worldview of the ancient perceiver. But he did not appeal to this process in instances that did not invite doubt by rationalist standards.[17] While Spinoza admits that "the narratives are in great measure adapted to the prejudices of each age," he was inclined to see most narrative as "perfectly plain" while others were "more speculative." The latter description was only used of those passages that recorded the supernatural, whereas the most common kind of passage simply demonstrated "their real meaning" (7:67). Where biblical accounts did not seem incongruous with his understanding of nature, Spinoza made little appeal to the "speculative" process of ancient perception. He believed that history was more reliable when the perceptions of the historian were less recognizable.

One has to conclude that the closer the historian's perceptions were to Spinoza's own perceptions of reality, the less inclined he was to recognize them as tainted. For this reason Spinoza not only provides a window into early hermeneutical concerns, but also an apt springboard for the present study's interest in the interplay between perception and historiography.

Three observations are pertinent: (1) Spinoza's aim was to reinvent biblical interpretation in the form of scientific objectivity. While it is easy to criticize Spinoza with the hindsight of postmodernity, he should be praised for his initial pushing of the pendulum toward historical criticism. (2) Spinoza was correct to recognize that the ancient historians' perceptions of natural events were tainted by their respective worldviews. In hindsight, we can apply this recognition to all perceived events, whether they are understood to be supernatural or otherwise. (3) It follows from the first two observations that Spinoza took history as straightforward narrative when the ancient historian was as objective as possible and the modern interpreter was equally objective. If either of these "ends" seemed influenced by subjective interests, Spinoza considered the history compromised and therefore less likely to convey knowledge of the past.

Lessing and Historical Testimony

Gotthold Ephraim Lessing (1729–1781) represents a period where historical consciousness came to prominence with dramatic implications. In several

---

her laws embrace everything conceived by the Divine intellect, and lastly, as nature preserves a fixed and immutable order; it most clearly follows that miracles are only intelligible as in relation to human opinions, and merely mean events of which the natural cause cannot be explained by a reference to any ordinary occurrence, either by us, or at any rate, by the writer and narrator of the miracle" (6:21).

[17] Preus fails to take this into account (Spinoza, 32).

ways, Lessing considered himself a disciple of Spinoza.[18] I limit my focus here to Lessing's concept of historical truth.

In a short essay written in 1777, Lessing lamented that there was an insurmountable gap between historical truth (which is always, at best, accidental[19]) and experiential certainty (which, via reason, cannot be doubted), thus leading to his famous dictum, "The accidental truths of history can never be the proof for the necessary truths of reason."[20] Recent treatments of Lessing have emphasized the gap he saw between certainty and faith.[21] While there can be no doubt that this is the overall emphasis of Lessing's essay, the immediate argument that gave rise to this quote has to do with the general uncertainty of historical truth regardless of its faith claims. As such, Lessing provides a window into his historiographical stance. I now take a closer look at Lessing's general concept of history and how he saw this to relate to the "truths of reason."

Lessing began from the premise that miracles and fulfilled prophecies were once realities (i.e., in the NT period), but are no longer. This point was important for him as he was also committed to the idea that faith in Christ must come as the result of the "proof of the spirit and of power," by which he meant the proof of Jesus' mighty deeds, his fulfillment of prophecy, and his resurrection from the dead. He states repeatedly that he has no doubt that these did in fact take place,[22] but that he cannot believe these on the basis of mere testimony.

> The problem is that this proof of the spirit and of power no longer has any spirit or power, but has sunk to the level of human testimonies of spirit and power.
>
> The problem is that reports of fulfilled prophecies are not fulfilled prophecies; that reports of miracles are not miracles. These, the prophecies fulfilled

---

[18] For a discussion of Spinoza's more general influence upon Lessing, see H. E. Allison, *Lessing and the Enlightenment* (Ann Arbor: University of Michigan Press, 1966), 121–22.

[19] In contrast to "necessary truth," accidental truth should be thought of in terms of contingency. See discussion in R. C. S. Walker, "Contingency," in *Routledge Encyclopedia of Philosophy* (London: Routledge, 1998). This article rightly grounds the concepts of necessary essence and accidental extension in the thought of Spinoza and Leibniz to which Lessing was philosophically attracted.

[20] Lessing, "On the Proof of the Spirit and of Power," in *Lessing's Theological Writings* (ed. H. Chadwick; London: William Clowes and Sons, 1956), 53.

[21] G. Theissen and D. Winter, *The Quest for the Plausible Jesus: The Question of Criteria* (Louisville, Ky.: Westminster John Knox, 2002), 226–34; J. D. G. Dunn, *Jesus Remembered* (Grand Rapids: Eerdmans, 2003), 68ff.; Rae, *History*, 10–13.

[22] Echoing L. P. Wessel, it is difficult to determine whether Lessing was stating his true opinion in this respect (Wessel, *G. E. Lessing's Theology: A Reinterpretation* [The Hague: Mouton, 1977], 45).

> before my eyes, the miracles that occur before my eyes, are immediate in their effect. But those—the reports of fulfilled prophecies and miracles, have to work through a medium which takes away all their force.[23]

It is clear that Lessing's gap was a product of the idea that historical truth is less certain than truth arrived at by experience. He continues:

> Or is it invariably the case, that what I read in reputable historians is just as certain for me as what I myself experience?
> I do not know that anyone has ever asserted this. What is asserted is only that the reports which we have of these prophecies and miracles are as reliable as historical truths can ever be. And then it is added that historical truths cannot be demonstrated: nevertheless we must believe them as firmly as truths that have been demonstrated.[24]

Lessing cannot bring himself to do so. There is an implicit empiricism in Lessing's thinking. Certainty comes by way of demonstrating and through personal experience. If a truth cannot be demonstrated in his own experience, he does not feel obliged to view it as anything more than one possibility among others, however probable it might be.[25] But it cannot be doubted that Lessing also betrays his dependence on rationalism as well. This is evident in Lessing's dictum:

> If no historical truth can be demonstrated, then nothing can be demonstrated by means of historical truths. That is: *accidental truths of history can never become the proof of necessary truths of reason.*[26]

Here we see the idea of the importance of building truth upon a priori reason. Two points of clarification are warranted. The first involves the conception of "demonstration." *Demonstrieren* was a technical term used in the Leibniz-Wolffian school of philosophy, referring to the process of proving the truth of a proposition with absolute certainty.[27] While Lessing favors the term *beweisen*, he specifies elsewhere that he defines it along these lines. He defines *beweisen* in this way: "The access to any truth is displayed with other recognized and undisputable truths. . . ."[28] According to Lessing, historical

---

[23] Lessing, "Proof," 52.
[24] Lessing, "Proof," 53.
[25] He is much less inclined to build his religious life around such uncertainty. His commitment to logic did not allow him "to jump with that historical truth to a quite different class of truths" and form all of his "metaphysical and moral ideas accordingly" (Lessing, "Proof," 54).
[26] Lessing, "Proof," 53 (Chadwick's emphasis).
[27] Wessel states that the method employed in mathematical proofs was the ideal model (*Lessing's Theology*, 111). Cf. Lessing ("Proof," 55–56), where he appeals to the example of a mathematical "truth."
[28] G. E. Lessing, *Gesammelte Werke* (Rilla; Berlin: Aufbau Verlag, 1954–1958), 8:193.

truths are not indubitable and therefore cannot serve as the foundation for any higher class of truth. This, of course, hints toward a dependence upon rationalist thought that prioritizes different truths according to class.

This leads to the second concept that Lessing employs: reason. Recent treatments of this passage have overlooked the importance of Lessing's appeal to the "necessary truths of reason." Indeed, the recent studies noted above simply apply the value of faith to this juxtaposition, arguing that it is "history vs. faith" that is at issue. While such an association is not entirely misleading (considering the larger aim of the essay), it fails to account for Lessing's local argument upon which he introduces a key ideal of the Enlightenment, that being "reason." It is important to recognize that Lessing's immediate juxtaposition is between history and reason. Cassirer suggested that perhaps "no other century is so completely permeated by the idea of intellectual progress as that of the Enlightenment." Such progress involved "all the various energies of the mind," which are "held together in a common center of force." He explained that "when the eighteenth century wants to characterize this power in a single word, it calls it 'reason.' 'Reason' becomes the unifying and central point of this century, expressing all that it longs and strives for, and all that it achieves."[29]

Cassirer's assessment aptly contextualizes Lessing's appeal to reason.[30] Lessing earnestly wanted to be able to subject historical propositions to the same rigor and scrutiny that was demanded by the truth of reason. But in the end he was forced to concede that historical truth would always defy such analysis. This is most evident in Lessing's list of rhetorical questions on the subject of historiography:

> What does it mean to accept an historical proposition as true? to believe an historical truth? Does it mean anything other than this: to accept this proposition, this truth as valid? To accept that there is no objection to be brought against it? To accept that one historical proposition is built on one thing, another on another, that from one historical truth another follows? to reserve to oneself the right to estimate other historical things accordingly? Does it mean anything other than this?[31]

The process outlined here does not contain any truth that can be accepted a priori. It always begins with an accidental truth and therefore must always (only) work toward tenuous conclusions. So as much as he wished he could be certain of the "reports" about Jesus, Lessing could not. He laments that this uncertainty "is the wide ugly ditch, over which I cannot come, however

---

[29] E. Cassirer, *The Philosophy of the Enlightenment* (Boston: Beacon, 1951 [1932]), 5.
[30] Wessel, 47.
[31] Lessing, "Proof," 53–54.

often and earnestly I have tried to make the leap. If anyone can help me over, please do it. I ask, I implore him."[32]

Lessing seems to be comfortable employing both rational ideas and empirical ideas simultaneously. Indeed, this further supports the recent move away from the oversimplified distinction between rationalism and empiricism in contemporary philosophy.[33] But in either case, Lessing was at a loss. Historical data were not firsthand and therefore not scientifically testable and neither could they be considered a priori knowledge.

Spinoza's early attempts at studying history as if it was engaging in natural science set in motion an idea that historical truth could be obtained once all interpretation had been accounted for and bracketed. The desire to do so lies at the heart of Lessing's dilemma. Ultimately, however, Lessing's theory of reasonable truth demanded data that had not been passed through the filters of human testimony. History simply could not provide such data.

Ranke and Empiricism

While Leopold von Ranke (1795–1886) has had a significant impact on historiography, he wrote very little on the subject. Georg Iggers has collected a series of essays written by Ranke that speak most directly to the theory behind his method. The following section critiques Ranke's views on historiography as represented in these excerpts.

Throughout each of his essays, Ranke is vehemently opposed to the notion that the disciplines of philosophy and history should ever overlap. In Ranke's mind, the two were irreconcilable, which is most clearly seen in Ranke's conception of philosophy. Ranke was reacting to a particular school (self-designated as students of the "philosophy of history") that had argued for a teleological ideal of history.[34] According to Ranke, this school has conceived history in terms of progressive epochs wherein humanity boosts itself closer to perfection with each successive era. Finding such a notion absurd, Ranke attacks not only this notion but also the discipline of philosophy in general. He avers that only two epistemological means are available to human knowledge. The first of these is "through the perception of the particular," while the second is "through abstraction." He attributed the former to his-

---

[32] Lessing, "Proof," 54–55. For an outside perspective of Lessing's angst, see the comments of E. B. Pusey, *An Historical Enquiry into the Probable Causes of the Rationalist Character Lately Predominant in the Theology of Germany* (London: C. and J. Rivington, 1828), 51.

[33] P. Strawson represents a wide consensus of thought when he surveys Descartes, Leibniz, Hume, Kant, and others and concludes, "Perhaps empiricism and perhaps rationalism too . . . are matters of degree with more or less of each tendency to be found in each philosopher" ("The Incoherence of Empiricism II," *Proceedings of the Aristotelian Society* 66 (1992): 140).

[34] Here Ranke mentions Fichte as his key opponent within this school; however, it becomes clear later that he also has Hegel in mind.

torical research and the latter to philosophical research and states that these two epistemological forms must be kept in separate camps.[35] Here Ranke clearly shows his inclination for empiricism over and against rationalism. Ranke considered historians who sought to philosophize about history to be departing from scientific investigation.

Ranke defined philosophy as an inquiry into the unknowable, while history was epistemologically straightforward. Ranke's main objection to philosophical inquiry was his aversion to abstract thought in general. In his mind, such preoccupations robbed history of its distinctly objective nature. We see here the fruition of Spinoza's vision for historiography, not in his philosophy but in his hope that history could be treated in the same way as natural science. As discussed, Spinoza argued that with a more objective approach to history, historical certainty could be attained. This simply required a straightforward approach both by the first perceivers of the events and the contemporary historian. Ranke, for his own part, does his best to achieve objectivity on the latter end of the equation—that is, as a latter-day historian attempting to divorce himself from all subjectivity. Ranke's ultimate objective was to apply empiricism to history. He argued that historical method is that which "imposes conditions and is subject to empiricism."[36] While Ranke perhaps represents an extreme outworking of Spinoza's notion, the connection between them is undeniable, and thus a specific trajectory of historiographical theory is recognizable.

Ranke argues that the historian must remain "free from prejudice"; by this he means "not the lack of interest, but rather an interest in pure cognition undulled by preconceived notions."[37] In this way, Ranke is much like Lessing; both considered true science to involve a thorough testing in order to verify the truth with certainty. Where they differed was that Lessing had no confidence that historical data could be the object of science, whereas Ranke did. In contrast to Lessing, Ranke was much more optimistic about the historian's ability to examine historical data empirically (like mathematics[38]). He was very confident about what the historical scientist was able to accomplish if the data in question could be demonstrable. Iggers observes:

---

[35] L. von Ranke, *The Theory and Practice of History* (ed. G. G. Iggers and H. von Molke; New York: Bobbs-Merrill, 1973), 30.

[36] Ranke, 34.

[37] Ranke, 40. However, we should avoid here the common caricature of Ranke that associates him with a strictly fact-and-date approach to history. Rather he, like Humboldt, was interested in the forces and purposes that drive these events in their interconnectedness. Indeed, Ranke (48ff.) openly critiques the fact-and-date approach. Cf. D. L. Denton Jr. *Historiography and Hermeneutics in Jesus Studies: An Examination of the Work of John Dominic Crossan and Ben F. Meyers* (JSNTSup 262; London: T&T Clark, 2004), 168.

[38] Ranke (30) himself makes the analogy between the science of history and mathematics.

Ranke held a relatively simple theory of knowledge. He assumed that the past spoke directly to the historian who would honestly listen to it. In a sense, far from placing history on scientific foundations, Ranke in fact excluded the study of the past from scientific analysis and reserved an important place for intuition and subjectivism in the interpretation of historical processes.[39]

By this Iggers means that because Ranke was unaware of his own hermeneutic, he unwittingly bled much more of his own intuition into his presentation of the past than he was aware. In this way, Ranke's rejection of abstract thought toward his discipline became the source of his own bias.

The "Hermeneutical Circle"

In Friedrich Schleiermacher (1768–1834), we witness the narrowing gap between historical truth and absolute objectivity. Schleiermacher's hermeneutical circle was born out of an attempt to explain the interpretive process that takes place in the relationship between grammar, text (i.e., supposed author), and reader. This model most often has been celebrated for its circular movement from the "part" to the "whole" of a text, whereby the particular detail interprets the larger context and vice versa.[40] But, closer to my present interests, Schleiermacher extended his model to a wider spectrum of what he called "psychological" hermeneutics. Beyond his explanation of understanding as a linguistic and grammatical process, he aimed into the mind of the author and described the inner networks of the author's thought world in terms of circularity as well. Because of this, Schleiermacher is often credited as the first to adapt Herder's ideas on interpretation beyond the interpretation of texts to a more general concern for human understanding.[41] While contemporary literary critics question Schleiermacher's goal to "understand the author better than he understood himself,"[42] his argument for the interconnectivity between interior thought and manifested language

---

[39] G. G. Iggers, "Introduction," in *The Theory and Practice of History* (ed. G. G. Iggers and H. von Moltke; New York: Bobbs-Merrill, 1973), lxviii.

[40] H. G. Gadamer, *Truth and Method* (New York: Continuum, 2004 [1960]), 190–92. It is noteworthy that this idea was also discussed to a lesser extent by W. von Humboldt, "On the Historian's Task," in *The Theory and Practice of History* (ed. G. G. Iggers and H. von Moltke; New York: Bobbs-Merrill, 1973), 6, 16ff.

[41] W. Pannenberg, "Hermeneutics and Universal History," *Journal for Theology and Church* 4 (1967): 127–28.

[42] F. D. E. Schleiermacher does qualify this idea by speaking of intuitively imagining the author as a "general type." In this way the author's distinctive traits are to be measured against what is generally known of those with similar characteristics (*Hermeneutics, the Handwritten Manuscripts* [Missoula, Mont.: Scholars Press, 1977], 150–51). Cf. Humboldt's emphasis upon the historian's application of empathy (23).

is still in play in contemporary theory.[43] Where the present discussion finds Schleiermacher's circle especially helpful is in his discussion of *Vorverständnis* or "pre-understanding."

Schleiermacher argued that in order for something to be understood, it must be associated with an already understood category. He gives the example of a child learning a new word through the process of comparison. In his view, children are only able to understand a new word by relating the meaning of that word with a previously established category of meaning. He thus concluded that "every Child arrives at the meaning of a word only through hermeneutics."[44] Gadamer further unpacks this concept by explaining that, when a new word is learned, one must assimilate an alien category into a limited sphere of significance, and this process initially alters the word's "original vitality."[45] The process becomes circular because one's grammar (or language[46]) is in constant interaction with the acquisition of new words. This is what Schleiermacher termed the "grammatical" aspect of hermeneutics.

In expansion of this circle to general categories of perception, he claimed that nothing can be understood that a person "cannot perceive and construct as necessary. In accordance with this maxim, understanding is an unending task."[47] We see here the outworking of Schleiermacher's second definition of understanding: "Nothing is understood that is not construed."[48] This idea of the construal of perceptions is very close to my own interests and is revisited below.

---

[43] W. Iser adapts the hermeneutical models of Schleiermacher, Gadamer, and Ricoeur (et al.) and explains, "In hermeneutics the circle is employed to interrelate the explicit with the implicit, the hidden with the revealed, and the latent with the manifest. It basically sets out to recover what an author has not been aware of when writing, or what lies beyond the historical material to be observed in the present, . . . that is, the author's subconscious, a historical past, or the buried telos of the fractured self—is what structures this type of interpretation" (*The Range of Interpretation* [New York: Columbia University Press, 2000], 8).

[44] F. D. E. Schleiermacher, *Hermeneutik, Nach den Handschriften neu herausgegeben und eingeleitet von Heinz Kimmerle* (Heidelberg: Karl Winter Universitätverlag, 1959), 40.

[45] H. G. Gadamer, "The Problem of Language in Schleiermacher's Hermeneutic," *JTC* 7 (1970): 72; cf. A. C. Thiselton, *The Two Horizons: New Testament Hermeneutics and Philosophical Description with Special Reference to Heidegger, Bultmann, Gadamer, and Wittgenstein* (Exeter: Paternoster, 1980), 103–4.

[46] K. Mueller-Vollmer, *The Hermeneutics Reader* (New York: Continuum, 1985), 10.

[47] Schleiermacher, *Hermeneutics*, 41.

[48] As quoted in Mueller-Vollmer, *Hermeneutics Reader*, 8; set together the two-part definition reads: "Everything is understood when nothing nonsensical remains. Nothing is understood that is not construed." Gadamer (*Philosophical Hermeneutics*, 7) rightly places the first part of this definition within the context of historical romanticism and questions its usefulness for contemporary interpreters.

The hermeneutical circle was picked up and given definition by Wilhelm Dilthey (1833–1911). Dilthey was indebted to Schleiermacher's psychological application of hermeneutics but saw in Schleiermacher's thought a flaw that needed correcting. He judged that Schleiermacher's attempt imaginatively to "become the author" of the text presupposed a certain universality of human perspective.[49] Dilthey argued that the interpreter's worldview separated him from the thought worlds of those who hold and held a different perspective.[50] This, of course, served to distance the contemporary historian from the ancient perceiver in that their worldviews were fundamentally different. Both the contemporary historian and the ancient perceiver were embedded within their respective historical circumstances and, in this way, always alienated to some degree.

For Dilthey, the hermeneutical circle meant that "all understanding always remains relative" because the interpreter was always moving to and fro from part to whole and vice versa. And because he was always moving to and fro from the projection of his own perspective to the assimilation of the novum, interpretation was ever being modified. Thus it "can never be completed."[51] The interpreter is able to reach provisional conclusions, but ultimately the fact that such conclusions are always subject to revision made Dilthey's circle a vicious one.

This is addressed by Martin Heidegger's (1889–1976) contribution to the subject.[52] Heidegger's use of the hermeneutical circle allowed him (reminiscent of Schleiermacher) to speak in terms of "*Vorhabe, Vorsicht und Vorgriff*"[53] and the essential roles that these play in assimilating new perceptions. As is

---

[49] This had been the conclusion of Hume (1711–1776), who spoke in terms of the sameness of mankind "in all times and places" (*An Enquiry Concerning Human Understanding* [Oxford: Oxford University Press, 1961], 8.1).

[50] Dilthey argues that our worldviews are products of our lived experience, and because experiences vary from person to person, culture to culture, so do worldviews (Hodges, 31). Cf. discussion in S. J. Grenz, *A Primer on Postmodernism* (Grand Rapids: Eerdmans, 1996), 99–103.

[51] W. Dilthey, "The Development of Hermeneutics," in Dilthey, *Selected Writings* (ed. H. P. Rickman; Cambridge: Cambridge University Press, 1976), 258–59.

[52] In his *Being in Time*, Heidegger often raises objections to his own arguments to further the discussion. One question that he raises concerns the problem of understanding. His goal was to put forth a means of understanding *Dasein* (i.e., the person who lives responsibly and authentically in the midst of his "thrown-ness" into existence). He grants that in order to do so, one must already have at least a vague understanding of what "being" is. Recognizing the circularity of this, he argues that all understanding is circular in that we always project possibilities onto the world around us. This is the larger context of his application of the hermeneutical circle. See discussion in R. Polt, *Heidegger: An Introduction* (London: Routledge, 1998), 30–31, 70–71.

[53] M. Heidegger, *Sein und Zeit* (Tübingen: Max Niemeyer, 1961 [1927]), 150–51.

Heidegger's tendency, his use of these terms stretches the German language in uncommon ways. For our purposes, the general idea might be thought of in terms of "fore-conception."[54] He argued that the interpretation of a new thing requires a fore-conception of what one might perceive. Therefore, not only is interpretation colored by preconceived points of view but it is prefigured by them. "Any interpretation which is to contribute to understanding must already have understood what is to be interpreted."[55] Heidegger is careful to qualify this circularity:

> But if interpretation must in any case already operate in that which is understood, and if it must draw its nurture from this, how is it to bring any scientific results to maturity without moving in a circle, especially if, moreover, the understanding which is presupposed still operates within our common information about man and the world? Yet according to the most elementary rules of logic, this *circle* is a *circulus vitiosus.* If that be so, however, the business of historiological interpretation is excluded *a priori* from the domain of rigorous knowledge. In so far as the Fact of this circle in understanding is not eliminated, historiology must then be resigned to less rigorous possibilities of knowing. Historiology[56] is permitted to compensate for this defect to some extent through the "spiritual signification" of its "objects." But even in the opinion of the historian himself, it would admittedly be more ideal if the circle could be avoided and if there remained the hope of creating some time a historiology which would be as independent of the standpoint of the observer as our knowledge of Nature is supposed to be.
>
> *But if we see this circle as a vicious one and look out for ways of avoiding it, even if we just "sense" it as an inevitable imperfection, then the act of understanding has been misunderstood from the ground up.*[57]

Heidegger thus moves away from the idea that knowledge (here historical knowledge) is lamentably uncertain because of the inevitable subjectivity of perception. As long as we do not allow our "fore-having, fore-sight and fore-conception to be presented to us by fancies and popular conceptions" the task of analyzing historical knowledge will be no less rigorous than "the most exact sciences" (like mathematics). He argued that the historian's correct move "is not to get out of the circle but to come into it in the right way" because the "circle of understanding is not an orbit in which any random

---

[54] Later Ricoeur would attempt to lessen the paradoxical nature of "fore-conception" by describing the circle in terms of "guess" and "validation" (*Interpretation Theory: Discourse and the Surplus of Meaning* [Fort Worth: Texas Christian University Press, 1976], 79).

[55] M. Heidegger, *Being and Time* (London: SCM, 1962 [1927]), 194.

[56] Polt (101) describes historiology (*Historie*) as "scientific study of the past." Other commentators view this term as a synonym for historiography.

[57] Heidegger, *Being and Time,* 194 (translator's emphasis).

kind of knowledge may move"; rather, it exists properly to structure perceptions and make them meaningful to the person who exists in the world authentically.[58]

Thus Heidegger here clarifies two key points that are picked up later in my discussion of memory: (1) The inherent subjectivity of perception is not to be lamented or circumvented by the historian; (2) the interpretation of new perceptions naturally involves the recycling of previously known interpretations.[59]

A fuller treatment would have to discuss the work of Boeckh, Gadamer, and Ricoeur. But for the sake of space and focus, I add here only that Gadamer's utilization of the hermeneutical circle serves to emphasize that the circle works on the level of the subconscious, and thus it is impossible to always enter it "in the right way." In a decided modification of both Schleiermacher and Heidegger, Gadamer commented:

> The prejudices and fore-meanings that occupy the interpreter's consciousness are not at his disposal. He cannot separate in advance the productive prejudices that enable understanding from the prejudices that hinder it and lead to misunderstandings.[60]

In sum, Schleiermacher's circle (and Heidegger's adaptation of it) demonstrates how a new perception can attract a significance that has been prefigured (or "fore-conceived") in a similar type of category. Following the lead of Schleiermacher, one might describe all understanding in terms of the hermeneutical comparison between typical thought categories. Following the lead of Heidegger, one might describe all understanding in terms of the projection of typical significance. Perhaps the process of interpretation actually anticipates familiar types of significance. This discussion is revisited in the next chapter as I introduce typology. But more immediately, this discussion sets the stage for the discussion of memory theory in the latter part of the present chapter. Before doing so, it will be helpful to see how some of the themes evidenced above find an outlet in the thought of Rudolf Bultmann.

Bultmann, Hermeneutics, and History

Heidegger's influence on the theology and exegetical career of Rudolf Bultmann (1884–1976) has been well documented.[61] Heidegger's treatment

---

[58] Heidegger, *Being and Time*, 195.

[59] This, of course, is not the end of Heidegger's interpretive process. Gadamer (*Truth and Method*, 267) sums up Heidegger's model by stating that "interpretation begins with fore-conceptions that are [eventually] replaced by more suitable ones." Such "more suitable" conceptions are then projected as fore-conceptions of meaning onto subsequent perceptions.

[60] Gadamer, *Truth and Method*, 295.

[61] E.g., D. Fergusson, *Bultmann* (Collegeville, Minn.: Liturgical Press, 1992), 50–73,

of the hermeneutical circle is especially seen in Bultmann's famous essay, "Is Exegesis without Presuppositions Possible?"[62] The point of Bultmann's essay was to convince modern historians to acknowledge their own presuppositions as they attempt to translate ancient and alien languages and worldviews. Here Bultmann emphasizes that historians must be critically aware of, but not ultimately controlled by, their presuppositions. In this way, Heidegger's admonition for the historian to enter critically into the hermeneutical circle can be seen in this essay. Bultmann argued that historical science [*die historische Wissenschaft*] cannot verify acts of God; it can only verify that certain people believed that God had intervened in history.[63] We perhaps see in this statement Heidegger's move away from the Rankean notion that the historian is simply a passive observer of the past.

At first glance, it seems that Bultmann has echoed the sentiment that history is ultimately concerned with interpretations of the past and not the actual past. But it is also possible that, like Spinoza, Bultmann was more inclined to employ this distinction when the ancient interpreters referenced acts of God.

In English, the semantic range of the word "history" has two primary facets. History can simply denote time sequence, as in the phrase "over the course of history." History can also denote a specific discipline, as in what is written down about the past. The German *Geschichte* has a similar semantic range. *Geschichte* can simply denote the continuum of time. On the other hand, it can denote "story" and carry all the connotations of this range (i.e., report, account, narrative, tradition, etc). It is therefore not surprising that Bultmann employed the word *Geschichte* in both ways.

While there was another term for "historical" available to him [*historisch*], Bultmann most often preferred the phrase "*geschichtliche Jesus.*"[64] Bultmann

---

90–93; G. Jones, *Bultmann: Towards a Critical Theology* (Oxford: Polity Press, 1991), 63–125; J. Painter, *Theology as Hermeneutics: Rudolf Bultmann's Interpretation of the History of Jesus* (Sheffield: Almond Press 1987), 11–116; Thiselton, *Two Horizons*, 143–292, esp. 176–80.

[62] See especially his use of "pre-understanding" (R. Bultmann, "Is Exegesis without Presuppositions Possible?" in *The Hermeneutics Reader* [ed. K. Mueller-Vollmer; Oxford: Basil Blackwell, 1985], 246).

[63] Bultmann, "Is Exegesis," 244.

[64] Perhaps the best place to start this discussion is by mentioning how the English loan word "Historie" is sometimes set against "*Geschichte.*" In fact, Bultmann's teacher, Martin Kähler, introduced the distinction between these words by speaking in terms of *der historische Jesus* and *der geschichtliche Christus* [the historical Jesus and the historic/traditional Christ]. This is most evident in the title of M. Kähler's *Der sogenannte historische Jesus und der geschichtliche, biblische Christus* (Munich: Deichert and Leipzig, 1896). For Kähler, this distinction was born out of a polemic against modern historicism, which endeavored to establish (without presuppositions) objective facts. Thus the term Historie connotes the interest in the brute facts of history while *Geschichte*, in this context, carries the idea of impacting tradition. That is, *Geschichte* is

did, in one work, draw a distinction between these terms in an attempt to distinguish fact from event in saying that the cross was "a historic [*geschichtliche*] fact originating in the historical [*historisch*] event" of the crucifixion.[65] Painter rightly points out that, in this context, the "historic [geschichtlich]" fact of the cross is a fact of eschatological significance which is paradoxically manifested in the "historical [historisch]" event of the crucifixion.[66] It is the former that carries existential value. Painter also points out that a similar distinction is sometimes made in Bultmann's commentary on John.[67] Yet most often, Bultmann used these terms interchangeably and does so throughout his career.[68] This may be due to Heidegger's influence in that Heidegger was inclined to use both *Historie* and *Geschichte* in terms of existential-historical possibilities.[69] Regardless, Bultmann's use(s) of these terms must be understood from within their local semantic context(s).

In Bultmann's introduction to Jesus, he devoted attention to the nature of history and the task of the historian.[70] It should be noted that his understanding of the historian's task is, in at least two ways, remarkably parallel to

---

seen through the eyes of personal interest (or perhaps, the eyes of dogma). With this in mind, one wonders whether, in the context of Kähler's dichotomy, "geschichtliche Christus" is not best rendered as "traditional Christ." In a very helpful introduction to Kähler, Carl Braaten discussed this nuance and decided to translate *historische* as "historical" and *geschichtliche* as "historic." Yet Bultmann does not seem to follow Kähler's lead in respect to his terminological distinction. The issue is further complicated when one notices that Bultmann does not use the term Historie with any frequency or consistency. While such a distinction is valuable for Kähler, Bultmann avoided the phrase "historische Jesus" in favor of the phrase "geschichtliche Jesus." NB: I extend my thanks to Michael Widmer and Ron Hermes for their insight on this topic. My personal correspondence with both has helped me to hone my own analysis. See also C. E. Braaten, "Introduction" to *The So-called Historical Jesus and the Historic Biblical Christ*, by M. Kähler (Philadelphia: Fortress, 1964), esp. 21.

[65] R. Bultmann, *Kerygma and Myth* (London: SCM, 1953), 37.

[66] Painter, *Theology as Hermeneutics*, 79–80.

[67] R. Bultmann, *Das Evangelium des Johannes* (Göttingen: Vandenhoeck and Ruprecht, 1941).

[68] E.g., R. Bultmann, *Jesus* (Berlin: Deutsche Bibliothek, 1926), 16; R. Bultmann, *Theologie des Neuen Testaments* (Tübingen: Mohr Siebeck, 1948), 2; R. Bultmann, *Die Geschichte der synoptischen Tradition* (Göttingen: Vandenhoeck and Ruprecht, 1961), 1, 282, 297.

Therefore, while Bultmann's conception of history should at times be seen against the backdrop of Kähler's, it will not suffice simply to appeal to the same distinction that Kähler made between *Historie* and *Geschichte*.

[69] In this case, "existential" history is history that discloses the possibilities of authentic humanity and is thus more concerned with future application than it is with the past [J. Macquarrie, *An Existentialist Theology: A Comparison of Heidegger and Bultmann* (London: SCM, 1965 [1955]), 171]. Cf. the discussion of Heidegger in Polt, 100–102.

[70] Bultmann, *Jesus*; more popularly known as R. Bultmann, *Jesus and the Word* (New York: Scribner's, 1934 [1926]).

that of R. G. Collingwood (1889–1943).[71] Although Collingwood is widely celebrated as the bridge builder between history and philosophy, Bultmann is due more credit in this regard than is normally given.

In a full turn away from Spinoza, Bultmann thought it crucial to recognize the distinction between history and the natural sciences.[72] In his view, man perceived nature as something other than himself; natural scientists were able to separate themselves from the object of their inquiry.[73] According to Bultmann, no such objectification can be made by historians since they are "a part of history" themselves, and thus the task of the historian requires "considering a living complex of events in which he is essentially involved."[74] Collingwood would later give full voice to this distinction between history and natural science.[75] Also, Collingwood runs parallel to Bultmann in his idea that the past "is not a dead past. By understanding it historically we incorporate it into our present thought and enable ourselves [. . .] for our own advancement."[76] This understanding of historical understanding is similar to Bultmann's notion of "encountering" history, which is discussed in what follows.

This notion of the subjectivity of the historical task is of crucial importance to Bultmann's method. The aim of his task hinges on this notion. Bultmann argued that

> the examination of history is no neutral orientation about objectively determined past events, but is motivated by the question how we ourselves, standing in the current of history, can succeed in comprehending our own existence, can gain clear insight into the contingencies and necessities of our own life purpose.[77]

---

[71] I say "parallel" because Collingwood's most influential work, *The Idea of History*, was not published until 1945 (posthumously). Furthermore, even Collingwood's earliest publications (which may have been accessible prior to the writing of Bultmann's *Jesus*) contain arguments that substantially differ from Bultmann's. For example, in his first monograph, Collingwood argued, "To speak of studying the mind of Jesus from within may seem presumptuous; but no other method is of the slightest value" (R. G. Collingwood, *Philosophy and Religion* [London: Macmillan, 1916], 42–43). In contrast, one of Bultmann's primary aims was to avoid any attempt to "render Jesus as a historical phenomenon psychologically explicable" (Bultmann, *Jesus*, 6).

[72] This, of course, was first championed by Dilthey. See the selected passages provided by Hodges, esp. 142.

[73] It is worth noting that Bultmann, like Spinoza, considered natural science to be an objective and detached discipline.

[74] Bultmann, *Jesus*, 3.

[75] This is a distinction that runs throughout many of Collingwood's publications. It is given full treatment in his *The Idea of History* (Oxford: Oxford University Press, 1956), esp. 5, 213–15.

[76] Collingwood, *Idea*, 230.

[77] Bultmann, *Jesus*, 10; cf. "die Befragung der Geschichte keine neutrale Orientierung

As such, historical inquiry is only valuable as an existential (or self-involving[78]) enterprise; history is not to be "viewed" but to be "encountered." This, the key tenet of his method, should be chiefly commended for its insightful criticism of modern historiography. I do not take lightly the importance of this contribution to historical Jesus research and to historiography in general. So it is with great irony that some of Bultmann's most unfortunate weaknesses are found in his commitments to a modern mind-set.[79]

In the quote provided above, Bultmann argued that "history is no neutral orientation about objectively determined past events." It is then surprising that only pages later he undermined this notion in his assessment of the ancient interpreters:

> Of course the doubt as to whether Jesus really existed is unfounded and not worth refutation. No sane person can doubt that Jesus stands as founder behind the historical movement whose first distinct stage is represented by the oldest Palestinian community. But how far that community preserved an objectively true picture of him and his message is another question.[80]

For the modern historian, Bultmann urges "encounter" and "dialogue."[81] Bultmann described the historian's task in terms of existential self-involvement. History was not an objective accounting of facts; it was a subjective endeavor. According to Bultmann, the historian stands in the current of history and is personally affected by it and (in turn) projects this subjectivity back onto his understanding of the significance of this history. According to Bultmann, the historian properly approaches history by internalizing and projecting his interpretation of history.

But in his assessment of the writers of the New Testament, Bultmann notices these very same "subjective" characteristics and concludes that they were not interested in history(!). Rather, such characteristics demonstrate only their interest in their faith experiences (as if experience and history should be dichotomized). This point must be underscored as it is Bultmann's fatal flaw.

über objektiv feststellbare Vergänge in der Vergängenheit ist, sondern von der Frage bewegt ist, wie wir selbst, die wir in der Bewegung der Geschichte stehen, zur Erfassung unserer eigenen Existenz gelangen, d. h. Klarheit gewinnen können über die Möglichkeiten und Notwendigkeiten unseres eigenen Wollens" [Bultmann, *Jesus*, 13].

[78] A. C. Thiselton, *New Horizons in Hermeneutics* (Grand Rapids: Zondervan, 1992), 272ff.

[79] The balance of this section critiques such weaknesses, yet I do so with the greatest respect and fully aware that I am able to do so with the benefit of a postmodern context, of which Bultmann was a forerunner.

[80] Bultmann, *Jesus*, 13; cf. "Aber wie weit die Gemeinde das Bild von ihm und seiner Verkündigung objektiv treu bewahrt hat, ist eine andere Frage" (Bultmann, *Jesus*, 16–17).

[81] Bultmann, *Jesus*, 4, 12.

Bultmann did not allow the ancient interpreters to employ the same hermeneutic that he himself professed. Because the gospel writers are existentially involved with their subject matter, they must be doing something other than history.

I do not think that Bultmann considered this a double standard. It is more probable that he was previously committed to the idea that the Jesus tradition was mythical by virtue of genre. As such, the authors of this tradition were not trying to be existentially involved historians; they were existentially involved mythmakers. On this point, Macquarrie's masterful treatment of Bultmann still provides the best assessment. Macquarrie, whose *An Existentialist Theology* is largely sympathetic to Bultmann's theology, examines what he considers a presupposed undercurrent in Bultmann's conception of myth. Macquarrie concludes that Bultmann was apt to classify a New Testament narrative as myth

> (a) what might be called myth proper, the representation of the divine and other-worldly in human and this-worldly terms; (b) everything in the New Testament which implies those first-century concepts which now belong to a world that is no longer, and are not acceptable or intelligible to the modern mind.[82]

Macquarrie grants that there is myth contained in the New Testament and therefore Bultmann was justified in applying the first classification. But Macquarrie criticizes the latter classification:

> The truth is that at this point we perceive in Bultmann's thought not the influence of existentialism but the hangover of a somewhat old-fashioned liberal modernism. He is still obsessed with the pseudo-scientific view of a closed universe that was popular half a century ago, and anything which does not fit into that tacitly assumed world-picture is, in his view, not acceptable to the modern mind and assigned to the realm of myth.[83]

What needs to be distinguished here is the difference between historical narrative interpreted through the glasses of a mythological worldview and the genre of myth.[84] As Macquarrie rightly concludes, the two are given to overlap in the New Testament. But it cannot be presumed a priori that a narrative that betrays a particular worldview coincides with a particular genre.

---

[82] Macquarrie, 167.
[83] Macquarrie, 168.
[84] This is a distinction that is sorely lacking in Bultmann's influential "New Testament and Mythology," in *Kerygma and Myth* (ed. H. Bartsch; New York: Harper and Row, 1953). In this essay, he correctly argues that the worldview of the NT is mythological. But one is hard-pressed to determine when he is speaking of the narrative world of the NT and when he is speaking of the general worldview of the first preachers of the kerygma.

Macquarrie concedes that Bultmann was inclined to assign the genre of myth much too readily and often unjustifiably so.

If Macquarrie is correct that we should expect much more narrative in the Gospels that represents an interest in historical narrative, we should also expect that all of this narrative would betray a mythological worldview to some extent.[85] No doubt evidence of an ancient worldview will become most recognizable to post-Enlightenment eyes in cases where the narrative looks most alien to our own worldview. But it is irresponsible only to appeal to the author's worldview in cases where the narrative seems alien to our sensibilities. This critique can be aptly applied to Spinoza and Bultmann alike.

I would contend that Bultmann was correct in his description of history as an existentially subjective endeavor. The hermeneutical circle requires that we project our own worldview and prejudgments on to our perceptions of history. I would also contend that we should expect the same of the ancient interpreters of history.

Preliminary Observations

Recalling my initial premises, I summarily revisit each in light of the above survey.

The first is *If perceptions are to be remembered, then they will inevitably be interpreted—subconsciously, consciously, or both*. We see the beginnings of this concept in Spinoza, who recognized that the biblical authors tended to color their perceptions of historical narrative with a mythological worldview. But for Spinoza this coloring was not comprehensive; he tended to recognize this "coloring" when the subject matter involved acts of God. One of Bultmann's advances was to reject Spinoza's conception of history as objective science.

The second is *Perceptions that contribute to historical memory are thus always interpreted along each stage of the tradition that they inhabit*. This idea is shared by Lessing and Ranke. Lessing lamented that because history is filtered through secondary testimony, it can neither be approached rationally nor empirically. On the other hand, Ranke optimistically endeavored to see beyond interpretations to the objective "history" beneath. Both also are naively optimistic about the scientist's ability to obtain truth objectively by way of empiricism. The crucial difference is that Lessing did not regard history as an appropriate subject matter for scientific inquiry while Ranke did. Bultmann, like Lessing, did not regard history to be scientifically objectifiable but did not lament this fact. That historical memories have to be interpreted gave Bultmann the occasion to enter into existential dialogue with history.

---

[85] Or perhaps more accurately, we should expect that all of the New Testament's narratives would betray apocalyptic and/or eschatological worldviews to some extent.

The third is *The historian is never able to interpret an uninterpreted past*. The beginnings of this idea are evidenced in Schleiermacher's hermeneutics. The idea that a text or perception is only understood subjectively and that this understanding is ongoing led Dilthey to concede that all understanding is incomplete and inescapably circular. Heidegger followed the lead of Schleiermacher but refused to resign historical understanding to the realm of defeatism. Heidegger acknowledged that interpretation was ongoing and encouraged the historian to embrace this subjectivity and, in doing so, enter the hermeneutical circle on the right foot. While Bultmann admirably returns to the biblical texts from this vantage point, a fatal flaw emerges in his historiography. While Bultmann encourages the subjectivity of the modern historian, he fails to recognize the hermeneutical circle at work in the perceptions of the ancient historians.

3

History and Memory

In the last chapter I surveyed several well-known post-Enlightenment philosophers who have impacted historiography. In this chapter I introduce several memory theorists and historiographers who are not as well known but who have made considerable advances upon the theories already surveyed.[1]

This chapter discusses the historiographical implications of social memory theory, its beginnings, and the contributions of its contemporary adherents. The first section introduces and critiques the father of social memory theory. The second section focuses on the specific features of memory theory. In the third section I introduce a concept called memory distortion and its implications for historiography. Finally, I offer a few points of critique and caution to the theory in general and set the stage for my own adaptation of memory theory in chapter 4.

Social Memory Theory

Halbwachs and the Roots of Social Memory

Sociologist Maurice Halbwachs (1877–1945) is widely considered the father of a theory called social memory. His 1925 monograph[2] married the ideas of Henri Bergson, who was interested in the relationship between memory and time, with those of Emile Durkheim, who was interested in the relationship between society and the individual.[3] Halbwachs' groundbreaking work had

---

[1] A segment of this chapter's research was published in a different format as A. Le Donne, "Theological Memory Distortion in the Jesus Tradition: A Study in Social Memory Theory," in *Memory and Remembrance in the Bible and Antiquity* (ed. L. T. Stuckenbruck, S. C. Barton, and B. G. Wold; Tübingen: Mohr Siebeck, 2007), 163–77.

[2] M. Halbwachs, *Les Cadres sociaux de la mémoire* (Paris: F. Alcan, 1925).

[3] L. A. Coser, "Introduction" to *On Collective Memory*, by M. Halbwachs (Chicago: University of Chicago Press: 1992), 3–7.

two key aims. The first was to argue "that the past is not preserved [in the memories of individuals], but reconstructed on the basis of the present."[4] The second was to demonstrate that cognitive reconstruction of the past is fundamentally spurred and constrained by "social frameworks."[5] In keeping with his first aim, Halbwachs began his study by exploring aspects of individual (personal) memory. His description of "the mnemonic process" suggested that memories are products of the present and not preservations of the past.[6]

Halbwachs' analysis moved from individual memories to group memories and what he called the "social frameworks of memory."[7] By moving from individual memory to the social frameworks of memory, Halbwachs studied the cohesion and interdependence of these two spheres. He examined this relationship in the context of dreams, family, religion, and social class. Halbwachs' conclusion can be narrowed to three main points: (1) Memory is the reconstruction of the past based on the needs of the present; (2) Collective memory is that which is articulated into social communication;[8] (3) All memories are conceived within social frameworks.[9]

As this summary indicates, Halbwachs was concerned with societal effects upon individual memory and not initially interested in the ways that his approach to memory could aid contemporary approaches to history. From here, Halbwachs becomes a highly paradoxical character in the history of his-

---

[4] M. Halbwachs, *On Collective Memory* (trans. L. A. Coser; Chicago: University of Chicago Press, 1992), 40.

[5] Halbwachs (*On Collective Memory*, 48) wrote, "Most of the time, when I remember, it is others who spur me on; their memory comes to the aid of mine and mine relies on theirs. . . . [My memories] are recalled to me externally, and the groups of which I am a part at any given time give me the means to reconstruct them, upon condition, to be sure, that I turn toward them and adopt, at least for the moment, their way of thinking."

[6] Halbwachs (*On Collective Memory*, 40) does soften his first point by saying, "Clearly, I do not in any way dispute that our impressions perdure for some time . . . after they have been produced. But this 'resonance' of impressions is not to be confused at all with the preservation of memories."

[7] This concept is further unpacked in the next section as I introduce Halbwachs' concept of "localization."

[8] The terms "social memory" and "collective memory" have slightly different nuances: Halbwachs used the qualifier *sociaux* to describe the ways that group ideologies inform individual memories. Collective memory, rather, was used to connote memories shared and passed down by groups. As these concepts are given to overlap, the terms "collective" and "social" are often used synonymously in current discussions. In fact, they are currently used synonymously with such frequency that their nuances vary from author to author. Of late, another term, "cultural memory" has gained considerable currency. The implied distinction here simply broadens the scope of collective memory and implies a long-term cultural tradition; this should be contrasted with "communicative memory," which implies a short-term orally communicated memory (meaning within three generations).

[9] A more detailed account of Halbwachs' work is provided in the next section.

toriography. At the University of Strasbourg, Halbwachs was a close colleague of Marc Bloch and Lucien Febvre, yet he resisted their expanding definitions of history. As the innovators of the "history of mentalities" approach, Febvre and Bloch were beginning to implement interdisciplinary tools for historical research that reached beyond historical positivism.[10] In contrast, Halbwachs maintained a more conventional positivist understanding of the historian's task.[11] This is to say that Halbwachs considered memory to be a fluid and active process while history was a more rigid discipline that required the historian to maintain an objective distance from his or her subject matter.

In 1941 Halbwachs undertook a project that put his theory of memory to work in the field of topographical commemoration.[12] Halbwachs used Palestine's commemorated (or enshrined) landscape as an example of collective memory. He endeavored to show how many traditional points of reference on Israel's landscape were first conceived in the imaginations of European Christians in the Middle Ages. From the fourth century onward, pilgrims who had imagined the topographical setting of Christ's life sojourned to the Holy Land to visit the sites made famous by the Gospels. Certain images of the biblical setting had become so engrained upon their mind's eye that upon arrival it was inevitable for them to "discover (invent)" locations to anchor their imaginative conceptions. Halbwachs explained how these pilgrims superimposed an imagined Holy Land upon the physical landscape of Palestine. On these topographically significant sites were built religious shrines and churches to commemorate events from Christ's life. Halbwachs' conclusion was that these commemorative sites were valuable for tracing collective memory[13] and of no value to historians interested in the historical events behind these commemorations. Simply put, Halbwachs argued that collective memory was an unreliable source for history.

Before going further, we should note that Halbwachs' study was seriously deficient in several ways. The first is that he relied heavily upon the account

---

[10] Cf. the discussion of Bultmann and Collingwood in chap. 2.

[11] P. Hutton provides a valuable survey of Halbwachs', Bloch's, and Lebvre's relationship in *History as an Art of Memory* (Hanover, N.H.: University Press of New England, 1993), 73–77.

[12] "The Legendary Topography of the Gospels in the Holy Land," in Halbwachs, *On Collective Memory*, 193–235; trans. of M. Halbwachs, *La Topographie des Evangiles en Terre Sainte. Etude de mémoire collective* (Paris: Presses universitaires de France, 1941).

[13] Thus it becomes clear that Halbwachs' conception of collective memory is not necessarily derivative of individual memories. This is demonstrated as he makes a distinction between "collective memory" and "actual memories" (*On Collective Memory*, 212). One might seriously question whether the term "memory" doesn't become a misnomer in this case. Halbwachs seems to use "collective memory" in the same way that others use the term "tradition." However, in order to understand Halbwachs' work, it must be noted that collective memory is sometimes derivative of individual memories, but not always.

by pilgrims of Bordeaux and neglected any part that Constantine played in the localization of holy sites.[14] Also, he inexplicably presupposed that the Synoptic Gospels took written form in the second century and perhaps over a century after the events to which they attest.[15] This poorly defended position was foundational to Halbwachs' conclusion that the Gospels are mostly invented and fictive in nature.[16] Halbwachs also misrepresented (and oversimplified) the relationship between Jewish and Christian religious belief. Halbwachs was under the impression that Christianity was "drastically opposed" to Judaism and therefore understood the belief systems of the two religions to be "sharply contrasted."[17] This is unfortunate because it consequentially weakens his otherwise insightful comments on the correspondence between Jewish topography and Christian commemoration.

However, despite these shortcomings, Halbwachs' employed method became the prototypical model for later historians of tradition. In Patrick Hutton's assessment, this work "has come to be regarded as something of a model in the field. Halbwachs showed historians how to write a history of the politics of memory, and it is especially for this accomplishment that they pay him homage today."[18] This homage is not due to Halbwachs' expertise on Christian origins, nor is it due to his conclusion that collective memory is of no use to history. In fact, Halbwachs' conclusion has been largely rejected; many since have seen the enormous debt that historiography owes to the study of memory.[19] Essentially, Halbwachs' work is celebrated for his recognition that the analysis of commemoration provides a window into the thought world of the commemorators themselves. In other words, how a society chooses to remember her origins betrays a great deal of information about her current stage of development.

However, it was through the posthumous publication of *La Mémoire collective* that Halbwachs' historiographical conclusions became known.[20] It became clear that Halbwachs saw a rigid distinction between collective memory and history.[21] For Halbwachs, history was an objectively written

---

[14] Eusebius, *Vita Constantine*, 2.46; 3.30–32. Constantine's wife Helena is also reputed to have traveled to Bethlehem and Jerusalem to establish monuments at the place of Jesus' birth and at the Mount of Olives. See H. Lietzmann, *From Constantine to Julian: A History of the Church*, vol. 3 (London: Lutterworth, 1950), 147.

[15] Halbwachs, *On Collective Memory*, 209.

[16] Halbwachs, *On Collective Memory*, 213.

[17] Halbwachs, *On Collective Memory*, 202.

[18] Hutton, 75.

[19] This linkage is explained later in this volume.

[20] M. Halbwachs, *The Collective Memory* (New York: Harper and Row, 1980).

[21] J. Assmann, "Collective Memory and Cultural Identity," *New German Critique* 65 (1995): 125–33.

science that took place once collective memory had disappeared.[22] Yet his overt objection to the application of memory studies to historical inquiry was not enough to deter the impact that his implied method would eventually have.[23]

It was not until Jacques Le Goff's series of essays in 1977[24] that Halbwachs' conception of memory was given full voice within the discourse of historiography. However, much like Halbwachs, Le Goff distinguished between oral memory and written history.[25] This dichotomy has not deterred Nathan Wachtel from arguing that Halbwachs' study of collective memory provided a valuable method for analyzing oral tradition.[26] Yet, while Wachtel's essay had significance for oral historians, the implications that social memory had for national, political, and cultural histories had not yet been realized. It was Pierre Nora who finally debunked the false dichotomy between history and memory.

Nora's most celebrated work, *Les Lieux de mémoire*, undertakes a French history via the "sites of memory" of France.[27] This work was considerably influenced by Halbwachs' study of the Holy Land. Nora and his collaborators map France's past onto its present geography, architecture, and festivals. This multiauthored work was the first and remains the fullest application of social memory to a national history.[28] Nora's work demonstrates a conception of collective memory that transcends both oral tradition and written history. Nora's conception of history sets memory at center stage. Yet Nora's most overt contribution to the historiographical discussion is found in his article, "Between Memory and History."[29] This piece promotes a view of memory and history that is distinct from that of his predecessors.

---

[22] Cf. Coser, 23; L. Weissberg, "Introduction" to *Cultural Memory and the Construction of Identity* (ed. by D. Ben-Amos and L. Weissberg; Detroit: Wayne State University Press, 1999), 15.

[23] At this point, it must be made clear that the present study does not intend to propose a "Halbwachsian" approach to historiography. Halbwachs' importance should not be seen in his work alone; rather it is the influence that his work had on subsequent historiographers that makes his work important for the present study.

[24] J. Le Goff, *History and Memory* (New York: Columbia University Press, 1992 [1977]).

[25] Le Goff, *History and Memory*, 58ff.

[26] N. Watchel, "Memory and History," *History and Anthropology* 2, no. 2 (1996): 207–24; Also see J. Vasina, *Oral Tradition as History* (Madison: University of Wisconsin Press, 1985).

[27] P. Nora, *Realms of Memory: Rethinking the French Past* (New York: Columbia University Press, 1996); trans. of P. Nora, *Les Lieux de mémoire* (Paris: Gallimard, 1984).

[28] So Weissberg, 17–19. For a methodologically similar study see B. Schwartz, "The Social Context of Commemoration: A Study in Collective Memory," *SF* 61, no. 2 (1982): 374–402. Schwartz acknowledges his debt to Halbwachs as well.

[29] P. Nora, "Between Memory and History: Les Lieux de mémoire." *Representations* 26 (1989): 7–25.

As mentioned above, Halbwachs understood memory as a fluid series of reconstructions while history was associated with solidified objectivity. Le Goff's view had not deviated from this substantially. Le Goff argued that "memory, on which history draws and which nourishes it in return, seeks to save the past in order to serve the present and the future."[30] Thus, Le Goff takes Halbwachs' conception of memory and argues that history is built upon this process of subjective reconstruction.[31] But, at the same time, Le Goff seeks to describe history in terms of objective scientific methods[32] that can, in some sense, "save [or preserve] the past." Nora takes the opposite stance, arguing that memory is "absolute, while history can only conceive the relative." Nora holds that memory's fluidity is precisely what makes it reliable. "It remains in permanent evolution," ever upholding the completion of the present. According to Nora, history is "always problematic and incomplete."[33] Therefore he promotes a theory of "real memory" that is "unviolated" as long as it remains in the realm of the subconscious.[34] Nora laments that the scientific methods of historians, in their attempt to establish critically a "true" memory, can only distort memory. Contrary to Le Goff, who understood memory as merely a building block on which to construct history, Nora argues that collective memory is the essence of historical inquiry. Moreover, Nora argues that collective memories are most active on a subconscious level, continually upholding continuity with the present. History, in contrast, is the intentional reconstruction of memory.[35]

Nora's work paved the way for historiographical interest in social memory in the 1980s and thereafter.[36] And while Nora's conception of collective memory seemingly won the day, most historians who implement social

[30] Le Goff, *History and Memory*, 99.
[31] Le Goff, *History and Memory*, 106–10.
[32] Le Goff, *History and Memory*, 179–216.
[33] Nora, "Between," 9.
[34] Nora, "Between," 8.
[35] For a particularly scathing critique of Nora's conception of collective memory, see N. Gedi and Y. Elam, "Collective Memory—What Is It?" *History and Memory* 8 (1996): 30–50. Their criticism is revisited below.
[36] E.g., J. Assmann, "Ancient Egyptian Antijudaism: A Case of Distorted Memory," in *Memory Distortion* (ed. D. Schachter; Cambridge, Mass.: Harvard University Press, 1995), 365–78; P. Burke, "History as Social Memory," in *Memory: History, Culture, and the Mind* (ed. T. Butler; Oxford: Blackwell, 1989), 97–114; J. Fentress and C. Wickham, *Social Memory* (Oxford: Blackwell, 1992); M. Kammen, "Some Patterns and Meanings of Memory Distortion in American History," in *Memory Distortion* (ed. D. Schachter; Cambridge, Mass.: Harvard University Press, 1995), 329–45; D. Lowenthal, *The Past Is a Foreign Country* (Cambridge: Cambridge University Press, 1985); M. Schudson, "Dynamics of Distortion in Collective Memory," in *Memory Distortion* (ed. D. Schachter; Cambridge, Mass.: Harvard University Press, 1995); Y. Zerubavel, *Recovered Roots: Collective Memory and the Making of Israeli National Tradition* (Chicago: University of Chicago Press, 1995).

memory theory fall somewhere in between Le Goff and Nora. The balance of this study draws upon the work of these authors with attention to their conceptual contributions and not necessarily to the chronological order of their work.

From Memory to Social Memory

It is common for introductions of social memory first to point out that even the most basic form of memory (individual or personal memory) is a combination of past recollection and present imposition.[37] The present study follows suit in the hope that this discussion will introduce some of the central interests of social memory.

Halbwachs' conception of memory was hinged on the process of "localization." In this process, mental images associated with the past are anchored to specific mental frames of reference. By themselves, these images (which carry only a residue of the past) are abstract and incomplete until they are set firmly within a context of meaning. These contexts, or frames, of meaning form fragmentary ideas into complete and cohesive memories. The purpose of this process is to reinforce images associated with the past by localizing them within imaginative contexts wherein these ideas are meaningful and intelligible to the present state of mind. Patrick Hutton summarizes, "Remembering, therefore, might be characterized as a process of imaginative reconstruction, in which we integrate specific images formulated in the present into particular contexts identified with the past."[38]

Hutton aptly describes Halbwachs' conception of imaginatively localized memories. But it should be added that Halbwachs conception of "the past" is inconsistent. He vacillates between a past that can be represented by present states of mind and a past that is largely unknowable. Such inconsistency is mirrored in Hutton's summary. One may question whether the term "reconstruction" (borrowed from Halbwachs) is helpful to describe the process of localization. Such a metaphor connotes an entity that has become disjointed and can be reassembled.[39] Yet this seems incongruous with Halbwachs' argument that mental images associated with the past are fragmentary at the start. Perhaps, then, the concept of "reinforcement" (also used by Halbwachs) is more helpful to describe the part that imagination plays in this process.

In order for images associated with the past to make sense in the present state of mind, the localization process must reinforce memories with plausibility and integrity. Since the actual past cannot be conjured up to verify such

---

[37] E.g., Assmann, "Ancient Egyptian Antijudaism," 366; Le Goff, 99; Lowenthal, 210; Schwartz, 396; Weissberg, 10.

[38] Hutton, 78.

[39] I offer my thanks to James D. G. Dunn for this insight via personal correspondence.

reinforcements, the imagination is held in check by the combined memories of the social group of which it is a part. If a particular individual memory is not rendered plausibly in social dialogue, it will be corrected and in some cases rejected. Therefore, as an individual memory becomes a collective memory through this dialogue, it is corrected and completed by established collective memories. Social groups, therefore, stabilize individual memories by providing parameters for their formation. As Halbwachs conceived it, collective memory is an intricate complex of social norms, interpretations, and attitudes that spur and constrain this imaginative process. Thus, collective memory creates "social frameworks" in which individual memories must be localized if they are to have meaning.

To introduce the complexity of memory, Halbwachs used the example of an adult who happens upon a book familiar from childhood. He describes the probable reminiscence and nostalgia that the book evokes. Yet he also describes the inevitable feeling of incompleteness:

> This is so because we feel a gap continues to exist between the vague recollection of today and the impression of our childhood which we know was vivid, precise, and strong. We therefore hope by reading the book again to complete the former vague memory of our childhood.[40]

In this example, the adult's present cognitive state is reliant upon a past perception. This much may be obvious, yet this example also demonstrates that the adult's cognitive state imposes a present perception upon a former perception. Specifically, the incomplete recollection of the artifact (i.e., the book) is completed by the present perception of the artifact. Thus, the memory is reinforced: both past and present perceptions are fused to create the present cognitive state. Furthermore, the past perception is swallowed by the present so completely[41] that the adult is no longer able to distinguish comprehensively between the two perceptions.[42]

The above example is a valuable introduction in that it suggests a scene laden with potential reminiscence. In such a circumstance the adult is intentionally given to reflect upon past experience. Yet one may imagine a more complex case in which an individual memory and collective memory are conflated. Such instances are manifold within family memories. In some cases family memories are so entirely social in nature that distinguishing them

---

[40] Halbwachs, *On Collective Memory*, 46.
[41] Cf. Lowenthal, xvii.
[42] One could question whether an example so far removed from the present is helpful to the discussion of recent memories. While this particular example of reinforcement does not intend to speak to this, the present study later provides more apt examples of recent memory.

from individual recollections is all but impossible.[43] Fentress and Wickham cite the case of an adult who remembers an episode from his childhood. In this episode he recounts how he destroyed his parents' fine china in a jealous reaction to the birth of his younger sibling. Yet in this account, the adult confesses his inability to distinguish his own memory from that of his parents. He was uncertain "whether the memory of the incident was real or whether it was merely the memory of the incident as he had reconstructed it in his childish imagination after hearing the story repeated by his parents."[44]

Here the memory has not only been reinforced, but it has been socially reinforced.[45] Moreover, it has been socially reinforced to such an extent that the memory has become entirely social in nature. It is imperative that this position is not misunderstood. The memory in question is "entirely social" not at the expense of the child's individual memory, but in conjunction with the individual memory. Fentress and Wickham's example aptly demonstrates the phenomena of social memory as first conceived by Halbwachs. In his words,

> [T]he greatest number of memories come back to us when our parents, our friends, or other persons recall them to us. [. . .] I]t is in society that people normally acquire their memories. It is also in society that they recall, recognize and localize their memories.[46]

Halbwachs' statement is perhaps extreme; he is probably overstating his case. Even so, the key role that family members, friends, and co-workers play in reinforcing memory should not be understated either. People often rely on social dialogue to reinforce forgotten data. This is likely social memory's most recognizable manifestation. Yet Halbwachs' conception of social memory ran far more deeply. Halbwachs argued that the individual's relationship to society is so innate that it affects individual memories even before they enter social dialogue. One could say that there is also an internal social dialogue that parallels the external. This has led to the argument that every memory, be it private or communal, is social in nature. In Michael Schudson's assessment,

> [E]ven where memories are located idiosyncratically in individual minds, they remain social and cultural in that (a) they operate through the supra-individual cultural construction of language; (b) they generally come into play in response to social stimulation, rehearsal, or social cues [. . .]; and (c) there are socially structured patterns of recall.[47]

---

[43] Le Goff, 4.
[44] Fentress and Wickham, 22; cf. R. Wollheim, "On Persons and Their Lives," in *Explaining Emotions* (ed. R. Rorty; Berkeley: University of California Press, 1980), 299–321.
[45] Cf. Le Goff, 4.
[46] Halbwachs, *On Collective Memory*, 38.
[47] Schudson, 347.

As Schudson's first point indicates, the social framework of language shapes memory on such a foundational level that memories are, to some extent, social from the start. And in line with Halbwachs, Schudson's subsequent points (b and c) emphasize how pervasive social and cultural frameworks are within individual reinforcement. Yet before it is possible to examine how frameworks like language and articulation shape memory (and, in turn, history), it will be necessary to introduce a key feature of social memory and of the present book: memory distortion.

Memory Distortion and Memory Refraction

The study of social memory presupposes that memory is not merely the cognitive preservation of past events. Rather, "memory is a process of encoding information, storing information, and strategically retrieving information, and there are social, psychological, and historical influences at each point."[48] Borrowing from the fields of neurology and psychology, social memory theorists use the term *distortion* to delineate the difference between *memory of the past* and *past actuality*.[49] Memory distortion is most often utilized by historians to show the relationship between social memory and political power.[50] Undoubtedly, political regimes have been and are in the business of the intentional distortion of the past as a means of controlling public opinion. Yet memory distortion is not necessarily malevolent,[51] nor does it always need to be consciously strategic in nature.[52] Revisionist history is only an extreme form of memory distortion, and is by no means distortion's most prevalent manifestation.[53]

One needs to shake the negative connotations from the word "distortion" in order to understand its necessary and beneficial function. Distortion is, most commonly, a natural and benign function of memory selection.

---

[48] Schudson, 348; cf. Fentress and Wickham, 1–40.

[49] D. Schachter, "Memory Distortion: History and Current Status," in *Memory Distortion* (ed. D. Schachter; Cambridge, Mass.: Harvard University Press, 1995), 1–46.

[50] E.g., Assmann, "Ancient Egyptian Antijudaism"; Fentress and Wickham, 127–37; Kammen, 329–37; J. Miller, *One, by One, by One: Facing the Holocaust* (New York: Simon and Schuster, 1990); Zerubavel, *Recovered Roots,* 9; Nora, *Realms,* 616–18.

[51] Kammen, 329.

[52] Schudson, 351.

[53] The designation "memory distortion" may also conjure notions of false memory that have been made famous by cases of false allegations of child abuse. In these extreme cases, hypnosis and suggestive role-play spurred false memory. Aside from demonstrating how influential external contexts can be on memory, these extreme cases should not be appealed to as common representations of distortion. For a study of this nature, see S. J. Ceci, "False Beliefs," in *Memory Distortion* (ed. D. Schachter; Cambridge, Mass.: Harvard Univeristy Press, 1995), 91–125.

Matters of emphasis, perspective, and interpretation are the very basis for memory's existence. It is simply impossible to know every detail about any object; put another way, it is impossible to see an object from every vantage point. In the same way, it is equally impossible to recollect an object without emphasizing certain details, or to recall an object without perspective or interpretation. With this in mind, Kammen admits, "[We] do not know where veracity ends and distortion begins."[54] Yet this statement perhaps betrays a certain false dichotomy between veracity and distortion. *Memory is distortion*, regardless of any claims to veracity. If the criteria for veracity were defined by a given memory's lack of distortion, all discussion about the past would be rendered futile. Schudson aptly describes the issue at stake: "The notion that memory can be 'distorted' assumes that there is a standard by which we can judge or measure what a veridical memory must be."[55] Similarly Assmann posits, "[T]he notion 'distorted memory' seems to presuppose that there is something like "undistorted memory.""[56] Schudson argues that such a standard is nonexistent since "[d]istortion is inevitable. Memory is distortion since memory is invariably and inevitably selective."[57]

I say again for emphasis: *All memory is memory distortion*. This point is important for two reasons. First, contemporary memory theorists aim to debunk previous conceptions of memory that are overly passive, objective, or simplistic. Moreover, previous conceptions of memory (e.g., consider the phrase "memory bank") are entrenched in popular culture. The word *distortion* serves to resist such models and sufficiently jar sensibilities. The second reason that this point needs to be emphasized is that memory distortion is an essential feature of memory and does not necessarily denote "unreliable" memory or "invented" memory.

Still, I have found that no matter how much I emphasize this point (in academic dialogue and elsewhere), the term *distortion* carries too many negative associations. In order to avoid unnecessary baggage, I thus employ here

---

[54] Kammen, 341.

[55] Schudson, 346.

[56] Assmann, "Ancient Egyptian Antijudaism," 366. Yet, the term is necessary due to the pervasiveness of the "passive recall" model (discussed below). Unless the theorist qualifies the term "memory" with "distortion," the hearer will likely think of memory in terms of passive recall.

[57] Schudson, 348. However, Schudson (361) rejects the notion that such a position demands an agnosticized approach to memory (or history). Rather he asserts, "If interpretation were free-floating, entirely manipulable to serve present interests, altogether unanchored by a bedrock body of unshakable evidence, controversies over the past would ultimately be uninteresting. But in fact they are interesting. They are compelling. And they are gripping because people trust that a past we can to some extent know and can to some extend come to agreement about really happened."

the concept of *refraction* in place of the word distortion. I discuss my model for memory refraction in the following chapter. There I use the model of a telescope to discuss what happens to light when it is localized within the convex shape of a lens. My contention is that memory is similarly refracted in order to be remembered. Until then, the reader may simply associate the term "refraction" with "distortion" as I have defined it here.

Moving forward, it is necessary to examine further the types and roles of refraction (distortion) in memory and history. Schudson suggests four categories of distortion (refraction):[58]

(1) *distanciation*: the tendency for memories to become vague or for details to be forgotten;[59]
(2) *instrumentalization*: the tendency for memories to be reinterpreted to serve the present better;
(3) *conventionalization*: the tendency for memories to conform to sociotypical experiences; and
(4) *narrativization*: the tendency for memories to be conventionalized through the constraints of storytelling.

I would add a fifth, *articulation*: the tendency for memories to conform to language conventions. As the latter two of these have the most importance for the present study, the following section is appropriately devoted to issues of articulation and narrativization.[60]

Articulation and Narrativization

As my discussion of distortion has suggested, memory is not passive recall of the past. The "past can never be preserved in a pure, complete, and authentic form but must always be reconstructed from the viewpoint and within the semantic frames of a changing present."[61] The "semantic frames" to which Assmann refers are perhaps the most influential of Halbwachs' previously mentioned social frameworks, because memories are most often localized within language conventions. As Fentress and Wickham state, "memory can be social only if it is capable of being transmitted, and, to be transmitted, a

---

[58] Schudson, 348.

[59] This is similar, though not identical, to Ricoeur's treatment of literary/hermeneutical distanciation ("The Hermeneutical Function of Distanciation," *Philosophy Today* 17, no. 2 [1973]: 129–41). The concept is perhaps best summed up by Nietzsche, who stated that the human animal's default position is that of forgetfulness but, by breeding memory into humanity "forgetfulness can be suspended in certain cases" (F. Nietzsche, *The Genealogy of Morals* [ed. W. Kaufman; Garden City, N.Y.: Doubleday Anchor Books, 1956 (1887)], 39).

[60] Yet, as one might expect, these spheres also have a tendency to overlap. Thus I do not wholly neglect the first three types in what follows.

[61] Assmann, "Ancient Egyptian Antijudaism," 366.

memory must first be articulated. Social memory, then, is articulate memory."[62] Yet articulation can be manifested in many forms. Some memories are given expression through ritual, such as a religious observance or commemorative calendar.[63] Another common form of articulation is through art, such as a monument commemorating a particular event or person.[64] But in most cases, the articulation of memory requires verbal or written language as its central medium.[65]

It is necessary to recognize that when the memory is translated into language, this articulation must conform to the accepted semantic frameworks of its context. Thus, issues of vocabulary, syntax, grammar, metaphor, and genre act as social frameworks.[66] (One may at this point recall the previous chapter's discussion of the hermeneutical circle.) The very nature of communication demands that memory is rendered intelligibly. Truly, "every time a tradition is articulated, it must be given meaning appropriate to the context, or the genre, in which it is articulated."[67] In this way, the transition from memory to language involves not only translation, but also interpretation. Thus, the meaning or significance of the memory is formed (and reformed) by the context(s) of articulation.

Moreover, as we delve more deeply, it becomes apparent not only that the early stages of articulation aid a memory's reception into society, but that language also acts as a hermeneutic for the memory's conveyor. Along these lines, Halbwachs recognized the essential interdependence between memory, perception, and language. For Halbwachs, being able "to give names to objects and to distinguish one from the other by means of their names" is an integral part "of understanding their significance."[68] Simply put, "Speech is

---

[62] Fentress and Wickham, 47.

[63] Assmann examines Deuteronomy and deciphers seven ways to remember: "making conscious" (Deut 6:6; 11:18); "education and conversational remembering" (6:7); "making visible" (6:8); "storing up and publication" (27:2-8); "festivals of collective remembering" (16:3; 16:12); "oral transmission [via poetry and song]" (31:19-21); and "canonization" ("Collective Memory," 18–19).

[64] As mentioned previously, Nora, *Realms*, esp. 611–37, was foundational in demonstrating this point.

[65] In fact, it is very rare for either of the former media to emerge without the accompaniment of language, to some extent; cf. Fentress and Wickham, 47.

[66] This list is by no means comprehensive. On this point see J. Lyons, *Language, Meaning, and Context* (London: Fontana, 1981). Lyons concludes that "no word can be fully understood independently of other words that are related to it and delimit its sense. Looked at from a semantic point of view, the lexical structure of a language—the structure of vocabulary—is best regarded as a large and intricate network of sense-relations: it is like a huge, multidimensional spider's web, in which each strand is one such relation and each knot in the web is a different lexeme."

[67] Fentress and Wickham, 85.

[68] Halbwachs, *On Collective Memory*, 45.

an instrument of comprehension."[69] "Hence verbal conventions constitute what is at the same time the most elementary and the most stable framework of collective memory."[70] When articulating memory into a social setting, unconsciously, memory conforms to patterns familiar to the present group.[71] Gedi and Elam helpfully draw out a passage from Tolstoy's *War and Peace* to demonstrate this very point:

> [Rostov] described the Schoen Graben affair exactly as men who have taken part in battles always describe them [. . .], as they have heard them described by others, and as sounds well [. . .]. He began his story with the intention of telling everything exactly as it happened, but imperceptibly, unconsciously and inevitably he passed into falsehood.

Tolstoy goes on to explain that the story that Rostov conveyed was exactly what "his listeners expected to hear."[72] Granted this is a fictive example, but the implication is that the articulation of memory is also subject to narrativization.

The narrativization process forces both the storyteller and the audience into stereotypical patterns. Indeed, stereotypes "are an indispensable part of our cognitive mechanism, rational patterns according to which our impressions are modeled."[73] Narrativization not only shapes our memories as we retrieve them in storytelling, but also provides a grid by which we interpret our environment and our role therein. The grid provided by narrativization is most prevalent on a subconscious level.[74] Lowenthal insightfully writes that "stories appear to us as just a natural way of thinking about things, a way of ordering our knowledge [. . .] and representing them in our minds." He continues:

> The fact that we assimilate stories so readily, accepting them as representations of reality (even when we know that they are fictions), renders their function as containers of memories all but imperceptible. When we listen to a story, or when we fantasize, memory is just there. We rarely need to make an effort. Yet the function of memory in stories is all the more important for being so largely invisible. Stories do more than represent particular events in a general fashion. Stories provided us with a set of stock explanations which underlie our predispositions to interpret reality in the ways that we do.[75]

---

[69] Halbwachs, *On Collective Memory*, 44.
[70] Halbwachs, *On Collective Memory*, 45.
[71] Cf. Assmann, "Collective Memory," 127.
[72] L. Tolstoy, *War and Peace* (London: Harmondsworth, 1971), 279; cf. Gedi and Elam, 45.
[73] Gedi and Elam, 46.
[74] Cf. Nora, "Between," 8.
[75] Lowenthal, 223.

As such, pasts worth remembering are so because they bear resemblance to interesting plots, characters, and settings in our mind's eye. These resemblances function as "mnemotechniques," or "vehicles for memory." Fentress and Wickham explain:

> [A] plot functions as a complex memory image, and learning a repertoire of plots is equivalent to learning a large-scale mnemotechnique that permits the ordering, retention, and subsequent transmission of a vast amount of information. Remembering in visual images, syntactically linked and articulated in causal and logical relations, we make up little stories. This is a "mnemotechnique" we constantly use without being aware of it. [. . .] To be remembered and transmitted at all, the facts must be transformed into images, arranged in stories. Internal contexts, such as narrative genres, exist as the typical patterns in which we experience and interpret events of all kinds. Accommodating remembered facts into predisposed internal contexts may impose a radical reordering of that memory at the outset.[76]

Narrativization is therefore highly refractive (i.e., has the capacity to distort) but also highly mnemonic and therefore functionally vital.

With this in mind, the impact that metanarratives and archetypes have on perception is paramount in their distortive and mnemonic capabilities. *The climactic moments of our lives are measured against, and interpreted by, the climactic moments of great stories and, indeed, history itself.*

Peter Burke observes, "In early modern Europe, many people read the Bible so often that it had become part of them and its stories organized their perceptions and their memories." Burke's first example of this provides a compelling instance of typological cognition.

> Johann Kessler was a Swiss Protestant pastor of the first generation. In his memoirs he tells the story of how, as he puts it, 'Martin Luther met me on the road to Wittenberg.' He and a companion stayed the night in the Black Bear at Jena, where they shared a table with a man who was dressed as a knight but was reading a book—which turned out to be a Hebrew psalter—and prepared to talk about theology. 'We asked, "Sir can you tell us whether Dr Martin Luther is in Wittenberg just now, or where else he may be?" He replied, "I know for certain that he is not at Wittenburg at this moment." [. . .] "My boys," he added, "What do they think about this Luther in Switzerland?"' The students still don't get the point until the landlord drops a hint. My own point, however, is that consciously or unconsciously, Kessler has structured his story on a biblical prototype, that of the disciples who met Christ on the road to Emmaus.[77]

---

[76] Fentress and Wickham, 72, 73–74.
[77] Burke, "History," 103.

Burke also points out that the autobiography of John Bunyan "made use of schemata; Bunyan's account of his conversion is clearly modeled, consciously or unconsciously—it is difficult to say which—on the conversion of St. Paul as described in the *Acts of the Apostles*."[78]

At this point my book moves in the direction of typology. I do not give a full treatment of typology until the next chapter but I need to mention it here as I will argue that typology can be manifest in the form of narrativization. This can be seen most recognizably in the influence of metanarratives. Metanarratives are stories that are so culturally significant and so well known that they become standards of significance, by which all similar stories are measured and interpreted.[79] This interpretive process elevates certain key characters of such stories to the status of archetypes.[80] Typology is a means of interpreting the roles of relatively new characters (in the narratives of story and history) by the great characters of metanarratives.

In the cases of Bunyan and Kessler the narrativization of their personal stories were localized within, and given meaning by, the legendary stories of their religious heritage. Here we witness the marriage of individual memories to historical narratives. As seen previously, the localization of individual memories into social frameworks is facilitated by imaginative reinforcement. Such frameworks allow certain fragmentary images to be rendered meaningful and intelligible to the present state of mind. Remembering is a process of imaginative reinforcement that integrates specific images evoked in the present into particular frames associated with the past.[81] As this study has suggested, the remembering process most commonly disguises such frameworks. Narrativization is most commonly unnoticed. However, as in the examples of Kessler and Bunyan, the climactic moments of personal stories often require uncommon and "grand localizations" in order to give appropriate meaning to these memories. At such times, the metanarratives of our collective memories are manifested much more recognizably. The narrativized gridlines are laid bare, and beg to be recognized. This is the function of "typology"—a recognizable appeal to the metanarratives and archetypes that have shaped our collective memory.

Zerubavel has recognized a similar typological manifestation in times of national/political crisis. She points to an episode in Israel's history (1920) where accounts of the battle at Tel Ḥai had immortalized a one-armed mili-

---

[78] Burke, "History," 103.

[79] I here emphasize the plural: metanarratives.

[80] The reader may recognize that I have avoided an overly Jungian definition of archetype.

[81] Hutton, 78.

tary hero named Yoseph Trumpeldor.[82] Zerubavel explains that Israel's collective political identity was so weak, and her projected outlook was so bleak, that her collective identity was in a state of crisis. In this context, a group of settlements in northern Galilee were under siege but successfully defended by a small band of soldiers led by Trumpeldor. The small victory was so welcomed by the public that "the outpouring of oral and written literature that began soon after the [battle]—speeches, articles, poems, and songs—reveals the frequent use of the term *aggada* (legend) and *aggadati* (legendary)."[83] Moreover,

> the oral and written literature about Trumpeldor often created a link between him and the famous Jewish heroes of Antiquity. Trumpeldor was called the "great-grandson of the ancient heroes" and described as "a soldier in Bar Kokhba's army who has come to us from previous generations." [. . . It was written that] "there is not much difference between two thousand years ago—Judah and Maccabee and Bar Kokhba, and one year ago—Yoseph, the one armed."[84]

Zerubavel cites and evaluates many such associations with ancient lore.

> Trumpeldor's presentation as the modern reincarnation of the ancient heroes elevated him beyond the immediate historical situation and assured him an honorable position in the pantheon of Jewish heroes. The "legendary framework" served to legitimize the chronological incongruity of condensing two periods, historically separated by two thousand years, into a single heroic lore.[85]

In such a case, when a national identity is downtrodden with foreign occupation, exile, or servitude, a society will choose to commemorate a tradition more remote from the present. By reaching further back in the society's history, commemorators are able to promote a more noble identity based on the society's "golden age."[86] Since societies are often more open to the reinterpretation of more remote traditions, commemorators can weave themes of peace, political dominance, and affluence into these golden ages with less resistance. So doing, remembrancers can spur their societies toward more desirable ideals with typological appeals to noble traditions.

---

[82] Y. Zerubavel, "The Historical, the Legendary and the Incredible: Invented Tradition and Collective Memory in Israel," in *Commemorations: The Politics of National Identity* (ed. J. R. Gillis; Princeton: Princeton University Press, 1994), 105–25.
[83] Zerubavel, "Legendary," 107.
[84] Zerubavel, "Legendary," 109.
[85] Zerubavel, "Legendary," 109.
[86] Lowenthal, 21–25.

As seen in the case of Trumpeldor, a similar manifestation of such typology can also be applied to contemporary heroes. If a certain contemporary figure is perceived as particularly instrumental in his attempt to regain formerly golden ideals, this individual may indeed be typologically narrativized with legendary language. This may include accounts of the deeds of an individual bearing resemblance to archetypal figures of the society's golden age. Insightfully, Zerubavel writes:

> [T]he line separating "history" from "legend" is neither that clear nor necessarily consistent. This ambiguity does not stem only from the historical dimension of the legend, but may also result from the literary qualities of the historical narrative. When history is rendered in a story form that follows the structure of the legend, the classification of the narrative can easily become open to negotiation.[87]

As Zerubavel has alluded, the conflation of tradition (or legend) with contemporary history does not only run in one direction. The association of sacred texts with contemporary events can create a powerfully refractional lens when interpreting the traditions themselves. When Trumpeldor's generation evoked Bar Kokhba to interpret his character, they inevitably reinterpreted Bar Kokhba in light of Trumpeldor. Israel had to reinvent her tradition (however slightly) to accommodate for the new addition of Trumpeldor. However, as Zerubavel argues, the invention of tradition is not free from the constraints of the older tradition(s). The successful invention of tradition requires a close proximity to the older tradition so that its reception into the society is a smooth one. If an invention is too radical it will be largely rejected. An invented past will fail if the "society becomes aware of [its] fabricated character. Such awareness may lead to doubts about the appropriateness and validity of [the invention's] commemoration of the past."[88] Thus, depending on how central a collective memory is to a cultural identity, the conditions by which a tradition can be reinvented are particularly narrow. Innovative reinterpretation of tradition is only successful to the extent to which it is accepted.

In addition to Zerubavel's comments, it should also be pointed out that the typological appeal to Bar Kokhba and others reinforced a heroic memory into Israel's contemporary consciousness. Inversely, the memory of Trumpeldor was localized into the more established collective memory of Israel's heroes. The memories of both figures were thus reinforced by this typological conflation.

---

[87] Zerubavel, "Legendary," 105.
[88] Zerubavel, "Legendary," 106.

The example of Trumpeldor is an apt demonstration of the role of social memory in historiographical discussion. As seen previously, Halbwachs' two main objectives were summarized: (1) to show that the past is not preserved in the memories of individuals, but imaginatively reconstructed[89] according to the needs of the present; and (2) to show that the cognitive reconstruction[90] of the past is fundamentally spurred and constrained by social frameworks. When applied to the present historical discussion, we may assert that (1) the memory of Trumpeldor was created by way of imaginative reinforcement, and (2) this reinforcement was both spurred and constrained by the social frameworks of Israel's collective memory. What Halbwachs first conceived as an application for individual memory has become a highly effective methodological aid when applied to history.

By surveying the cases cited over the course of this section, it becomes clear that collective memory often survives by being articulated in narrative form. In Fentress and Wickham's example, the adult conflated his own memory with the story that his parents told. Tolstoy's Rostov unwittingly conflated his own account with stereotypical accounts familiar to his social group. Burke's accounts of Kessler and Bunyan show that they conflated their own stories with religious metanarratives. And finally, Zerubavel demonstrated that contemporary political histories can be conflated with historical archetypes.

In all of these cases it can be strongly argued that the typological conflation between personal narratives and social narratives are conceived within a short time frame and often within the life of personal memory. Most of these narrative conflations were imagined by the individual rememberers themselves and not by mythmakers generations later. There is no evidence that Trumpeldor himself appealed to the legendary figures to which he was appended. However, in his case, these typological connections were clearly made within months of his historical act. In light of this evidence, it can be argued that typological narrativization is often a means of remembering itself and not necessarily a literary device employed in a far-removed context. Moreover, the recent work on social memory has introduced a methodological approach to history that can aid the navigation through social narratives that conflate history with myth and legend. As such, I purpose to examine the historiographical value of specific typological conflations conceived by memories contemporary and near contemporary with the historical Jesus.

---

[89] As the reader may recall, the present study prefers the term "reinforcement" instead of "reconstruction." Therefore, a modified version of Halbwachs' thesis is applied.

[90] Zerubavel, "Legendary," 106.

Memory versus Commemoration

If social memory is to be of value to Jesus historians, it must be acknowledged that there are two distinct applications of this theory.[91] One of these deals more directly with the social constraints upon personal memories; the other deals more with the commemorative activity of communities. The former explores the ways in which present cognitive states evoke, constrain, and distort a person's perception of his or her personal past (i.e., Halbwachs' original conception of the theory). The latter explores the ways that present social contexts influence the collective memories of groups. To avoid confusion, I henceforth refer to the former as "memory" and the latter as "commemoration."[92]

Both applications of social memory emphasize the role of the contemporary interpreters over that of the original perceivers of the event(s). But this feature is even more exaggerated in the latter: commemorative analysis. It is commemorative analysis that has become more common in contemporary historiography. The simple reason for this is that social memory most often examines how history is commemorated in far-removed contexts, by which I mean a period measured by multiple generations. In such cases, literal, personal memory does not factor into the constraints of the commemoration. This can be seen most clearly in the work of Nora and Schwartz.

When Nora examines the ideological and political motives behind the planning of France's bicentennial celebration, his aim is to speak of an imposed national memory—in other words, a politically charged and strategic commemoration.[93] Nora is ultimately interested in the French national

---

[91] There are several subsets. For a summary of these, see A. Kirk, "Social and Cultural Memory," in *Memory, Tradition and Text: Uses of the Past in Early Christianity* (Semeia 52; ed. A. Kirk and T. Thatcher; Leiden: Brill, 2005). My concern is with the two most basic aims of social memory.

[92] Unfortunately, this semantic distinction is not common to social memory. Elsewhere I have argued that social memory theorists often confuse literal memory with memory as a metaphor for tradition; see my "Memories of the Temple-Saying: A Critique and Application of Social Memory." In *Jesus in Early Christian Memory: Essays in Honor of James D. G. Dunn* (ed. S. McKnight and T. Mournet; New York: Continuum, forthcoming). There I argue that social memory theorists most often consider memory as metaphor the same as commemorative activity. I would not disagree. But, in the conflation of these semantic spheres, memory's denotative value (and its importance for historiographical discussion) often goes underappreciated. However, see the similar delineation made by A. Assmann, *Zeit und Tradition: Kulturelle Strategien der Dauer* (Beiträge zur Geschichtskultur 15; Köln: Böhlau, 1999), 64. For this reason, I would contend that words like "tradition" and "commemoration" are ultimately more helpful to speak of memory as metaphor. On this point, cf. also Gedi and Elam, "Collective Memory," 30–32. But, contrary to Gedi and Elam, I do see value in the implied metaphor. Thus I often use *commemoration* and *tradition* synonymously, but I hereafter employ the term *memory* only when I refer to the word's denotative value.

[93] Nora, *Realms*, 611–37.

identity as it stands two hundred years after the revolution. Similarly, when Schwartz examines the changing significance of the national monuments in Washington D.C., his aim is to speak of how later generations utilized perceptions of the past.[94] In both cases, the interest is in the history of tradition, and, as such, the emphasis is on the commemorating communities. One is free to apply this method to commemorative activities that occur within the same generation of the event,[95] but in such cases the historian is obligated to fill out this picture by discussing personal testimonies (i.e., the memories of those contemporary to the event).[96] This measuring of commemorative aims against personal memories simply returns the discussion to "memory" as Halbwachs originally conceived it.[97]

Returning to two of the above examples, we saw that both Kessler's account of his encounter with Luther and the popular interpretations of Trumpeldor provide windows into the perceptions of these events within the same generation that they took place. In such cases, those contemporary to the historical events have a part in shaping how the memory is interpreted and thus distorted. I have highlighted these examples because the distortion has taken the form of typological interpretation and, in this way, anticipate the next chapter. My point at this stage, however, is a simple one: *in order for the historian properly to analyze such stories, commemoration analysis must be coupled with the analysis of personal memories.*

Within the first two generations of a historical event, it is nearly impossible to analyze the commemoration without also analyzing the initial perceptions, memories, and interpretations of that event. One cannot isolate a historical event from its impact and the trajectory of stories set in motion thereby.[98] At

---

[94] Schwartz.

[95] Cf. Zerubavel, "Legendary."

[96] J. Assmann suggests a span of forty years for "kommunikative Gedächtnis," or, more specifically, the period when the first generation begins to die. He juxtaposes this with "kulturelle Gedächtnis" (*Das kulturelle Gedächtnis: Schrift, Erinnerung und politische Identität in frühen Hochkulturen* [Munich: Beck, 1992], 11, 50–56). Elsewhere he speaks of communicative memory in terms of a three-generation framework (*Religion und kulturelle Gedächtnis: Zehn Studien* [Munich: Beck, 2000], 30). M. Bockmuehl has recently suggested a "living memory" that extends to the second generation (approx. 70–150 years) ("New Testament Wirkungsgeschichte and the Early Christian Appeal to Living Memory," in *Memory and Remembrance in the Bible and Antiquity* [ed. L. T. Stuckenbruck, S. C. Barton, B. G. Wold; Tübingen: Mohr Siebeck, 2007]).

[97] Again, I must point out the notable caveat that contemporary social memory theorists return to this discussion with historiographical interests. As discussed, this is a departure from Halbwachs' interests.

[98] Cf. M. Moxter, "Erzählung und Ereignis: Über den Spielraum historischer Repräsentation," in *Der historische Jesus: Tendenzen und Perspektiven der gegenwärtigen Forschung* (ed. J. Schröter and R. Brucher; BZNW 114; Berlin: De Gruyter, 2002), 78–87, who borrows from Ricoeur in his discussion of the relationship between event and story.

this point, I react against the tendency of previous schools of historiography that reduced historical episodes to simple sociotypical categories and "lawlike generalizations on human behaviour."[99] While conventionalization is a common form of memory distortion, it does not act as an all-encompassing umbrella that covers the unique features contributed by the historical agent which set the episode in motion.

As discussed above, narrativization is a kind of conventionalization. Stories tend to follow certain patterns. But what must be emphasized is that the individuals who first experience a historical event (or themselves act it out) follow such patterns. Upon reflection and retelling of these events, individuals will further conventionalize/narrativize their stories. Denton summarizes that narrative is not "an incidental means of writing up the findings of research, but a way of knowing and of describing experience that cannot be reduced to other terms (e.g. the generalizations of analysis)."[100] Thus, it is important to grant that such narrative distortions happen at the stage of personal memory long before these stories enter the realm of commemoration.

In this way, I also aim to temper the efforts of Hayden White to reduce all historical narrative to literary device. White's idea of "emplotment" is a valuable contribution to this discussion. Inevitably, historical memories must be emplotted in a way that makes sense of the important elements of "the plot." Part of this process involves the imposition of "importance" upon such elements.

When the historian selects events to be set within a narrative, a fundamentally distortive (and thus mnemonically valuable) effect happens simply by truncation.[101] By truncation I mean that stories require a beginning, middle, and end that are not present in the actuality of time. From the human perspective, time seemingly runs backward and forward *ad infinitum*. Sequenced events in time do not have beginnings and ends, merely previous causes and later effects. On the other hand, stories (including histories) always have beginnings and ends. Therefore, all histories must truncate time at both ends. When choosing to begin a story, a historian employs the first refractive tool: where to begin? For example, should the story of America begin with European exploration or with Native Americans? Should the story of Gandhi begin in Britain, India, or South Africa? Such discernment requires interpretation.

---

[99] D. L. Denton Jr., *Historiography and Hermeneutics in Jesus Studies: An Examination of the Work of John Dominic Crossan and Ben F. Myers* (JSNTSup 262; London: T&T Clark, 2004), 169; Denton does well to critique, in this respect, C. G. Hempel, "The Function of General Laws in History," *Journal of Philosophy* 39 (1942): 35–48.

[100] Denton, 169.

[101] What has been called *distanciation* above.

Another distortive feature of narrativization involving beginnings is what White calls the "inaugural motif." When a historical event is employed to introduce a story, it will inevitably take a different shape than if it is employed elsewhere in the story. According to White, the same is true when employing a "transitional motif" or a "terminating motif."[102] The narrativization of the historical event colors the interpretation of the event.

> It is sometimes said that the aim of the historian is to explain the past by "finding," "identifying," or "uncovering" the "stories" that lie buried in the chronicles; and that the difference between "history" and "fiction" resides in the fact that the historian "finds" his stories, whereas the fiction writer "invents" his. This conception of the historian's task, however, obscures the extent to which "invention" also plays a part in the historian's operations.[103]

White is correct to notice that this emplotment of history is much like the process of writing a fiction.[104] However, he underemphasizes the constraints imposed upon the historian (or, to use social memory terminology, commemorator) by those who previously narrativized the episode. Because the first memories of a historical event are narrativized at the start by the acting agents themselves, these remembering individuals impact how their stories will be retold. "Narrative does indeed create meaning, but it does so in the course of life, and not simply after the fact."[105] Moreover, this becomes an absolutely crucial point to underscore when the historical memories are being narrativized within the lifetime of those who experienced these events.

If a story becomes culturally significant enough to transcend its original application and is applied to a larger ideological framework, a distance is created between the story and the event. Even so, such distortion is held in check by the initial interpretations of that event. The further removed the commemoration is from the historical event, the less likely these spheres will interact. Memory theorists call this transition a "crisis of memory." But until

---

[102] H. White, *Metahistory* (Baltimore: Johns Hopkins University Press, 1973), 5ff.

[103] White, *Metahistory*, 7.

[104] Functionally, the term *narrativization* is not dissimilar to the term *fictionalization* referred to by Holmberg in "Questions of Method in James Dunn's *Jesus Remembered*," *JSNT* 26 (2004): 445–57. Here he borrows the idea from J. Schröter, "Die Frage nach dem historischen Jesus und der Charakter historischer Erkenntnis," in *The Sayings Source Q and the Historical Jesus* (ed. A. Lindemann; Leuven: Leuven University Press, 2001), 228–33. However, I prefer the term narrativization because the fictionalizing process does not render a memory story fiction, it merely renders the memory to look like fiction. That is to say, both memory stories and fictional stories are narratives. So I think the designation *narrativization* more aptly describes the process under discussion.

[105] Denton, 172; here he draws primarily from D. Carr, "Narrative and the Real World: An Argument for Continuity," *History and Theory* 25 (1986): 124–28.

this crisis has completely run its course, commemorative analysis must be coupled with memory analysis.

I contend that social memory's historiographical interest in commemoration should only be applied independently when there are no personal memories to be measured. To avoid discussion of personal memory when the commemoration has been shaped by living memories of the historical event is irresponsible. Indeed, to do so misleads the analysis. Evidence of early memory demands historiographical analysis appropriate to this phenomenon.[106] Dunn has observed that social memory has tended to place "emphasis on the creative, rather than the retentive function of memory."[107] In his view, an overemphasis on the interpretive reinforcement (i.e., distortion) of memory weights the analysis too heavily toward "the character of the communities which maintained the tradition."[108] Dunn's criticism suitably describes the tendencies of commemorative analysis.[109] As argued here, this tendency can and should be tempered when coupled with memory analysis.

Because the Gospels represent a marriage between memory and commemoration, neither social memory approach is independently sufficient for a mnemonic analysis of the Jesus tradition. But conversely, when social memory is applied in both respects to the Gospels, one can expect results that shed light both on how Jesus was initially remembered and how these memories contributed to his commemoration in early Christianity.

In the following chapter, I adapt some of the key concerns of social memory with this critique in mind. In doing so, I suggest a theoretical model that aims to manifest some of the strengths of the historiography discussed in this chapter and hopes to avoid some of the pitfalls.

---

[106] J. D. G. Dunn, "History, Memory and Eyewitnesses," *JSNT* 26, no. 4 (2004): 478–79.

[107] J. D. G. Dunn, "Social Memory and the Oral Jesus Tradition," in *Memory and Rememberance in the Bible and Antiquity* (ed. L. T. Stuckenbruck, S. C. Barton, and B. G. Wold; Tübingen: Mohr Siebeck, 2007), 179–94.

[108] Dunn, "Social Memory," 180.

[109] As he points out within this context, there is a certain affinity here with classic form criticism.

4

Memory and Typology

The present chapter relies heavily on the research presented in the previous chapter. In what follows, I offer my own adaptation of social memory theory which attempts to be sensitive to the concerns of historiography first discussed from Spinoza to Bultmann and which is sensitive to current historical Jesus research that has explored the relationship between history and memory. In this chapter, I offer the theory and method that constitute my primary thesis. I argue that the analysis of memory refraction provides the Jesus historian a means to locate and chart historical memories that betray typological interpretation.

To provide illustrations of my theory and method, I employ the example of John the Baptist. My aim in doing so is not to contribute something original to John the Baptist research, but to illustrate how my theoretical models might look when applied to a historical figure like Jesus.

Social Memory: An Adaptation

Social memory theory is not without its shortcomings. I am attracted to social memory because it attempts to take seriously several key hermeneutical concerns that have challenged contemporary historiography. While I do consider social memory to advance this ongoing discussion in a number of ways, the application of social memory to historical methodology must be done with caution. In the following section, I offer a critical adaptation of social memory, one that specifies my own assessment of the central issues and establishes a working model for how historical memory functions.

The Mnemonic Cycle

In the previous chapter, I introduced several suppositions and arguments that characterize social memory. Among these, I highlighted three conceptual elements that attempt to describe the mnemonic process: previously established mnemonic frames (here I call these "categories"), memory refraction, and localization. What might be evident from my survey of social memory theorists is that the emphasis on these concepts varies depending on the theorist. Social memory is a relatively young field that is still trying to clarify its methods, but all social memory theorists agree that the mnemonic process involves the interaction between these three mnemonic aspects. The purpose of attempting to describe this process is to supplant the "uncritical" model of memory as passive recall. The diagrams presented here represent my appraisal of this discussion and serve to illustrate the concepts previously discussed.

Figure 4.1
The Passive Recall Model

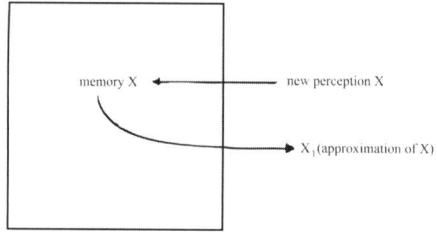

The Passive Recall Model (shown in Figure 4.1) illustrates the model of memory that social memory seeks to supplant. This model describes memories as simple approximations of perceptions (X). The intake of perception acts like a filing system that preserves this perception as a "memory." The notion that memory is a sort of storage unit or filing system is thought to be inadequate, and for good reason. Having already explored the rejection of this concept, I only reiterate here that this model does not appropriately describe the essential concepts that seem to be at work in the mnemonic process. Indeed, this model presupposes a relative lack of process; a new perception is simply stored and recalled in close approximation to what was initially perceived.

Figure 4.2
The Mnemonic Cycle

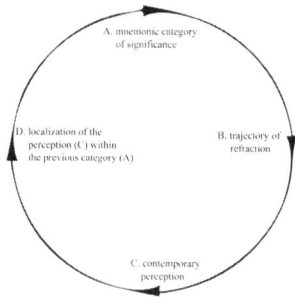

Figure 4.2 illustrates what I consider to be the essential aspects of the mnemonic process as introduced in the previous chapter. Although I have assigned particular letters (A–D) to this process, the circular (and therefore ongoing) nature of the process illustrates that memory does not have an absolute point of departure and ultimate telos. As such, movement A represents an entry point into the analysis of memory and not the starting point of memory. It is also important to see each aspect represented here as movements along an ongoing process rather than points along a linear progression.

Movement A represents a particular mnemonic category of significance. In Halbwachsian terms, this could be thought of as a "mental frame."[1] Or in the terminology of Hutton, this could be thought of as a mental context associated with the past.[2] The basic concept here is that of a previously established category (A) by which a person is able to associate new perceptions (C).

The reader might already notice some affinity between this model and my previous discussion of the hermeneutical circle. Because I did not initially conceive the present model in response to Schleiermacher, I do not attempt to force the two together. But because there is an affinity between this model and the hermeneutical circle, I briefly suggest here how the two might relate: Point A is not dissimilar to Schleiermacher's conception of "pre-understanding"[3] or Heidegger's descriptions of "fore-conception."[4] Or, to bring this discussion to contemporary thought, one might describe movement A in terms of "guess" and point C in terms of "validation."[5]

I have honed my own historiographical interests in dialogue with social memory because, in many ways, I think it improves upon these discussions. What the present model provides, which is not emphasized with enough clarity in discussions of the hermeneutical circle, is an analysis of the movement from A to C and vice versa. With this in mind, movements B and D provide the chief advances upon previous discussions.

As all memory is refracted memory, movement B could represent any number of previously discussed distortions (instrumentalization, distanciation, etc). Each new perception (C) that enters the mnemonic cycle must be recognized and interpreted to some extent. In order for C to be categorized within a meaningful frame, it must have been given meaning by a mind

---

[1] M. Halbwachs, *On Collective Memory* (trans. L. A. Coser; Chicago: University of Chicago Press, 1992), 37–46.
[2] P. Hutton, *History as an Art of Memory* (Hanover, N.H.: University Press of New England, 1993), 78.
[3] Cf. F. D. E. Schleiermacher, *Hermeneutik, Nach den Handschriften neu herausgegeben und eingeleitet von Heinz Kimmerle* (Heidelberg: Karl Winter Universitätverlag, 1959), 40.
[4] Cf. M. Heidegger, *Sein und Zeit* (Tübingen: Max Niemeyer, 1961), 150–51.
[5] P. Ricoeur, *Interpretation Theory: Discourse and the Surplus of Meaning* (Fort Worth: Tex. Christian University Press, 1976), 79.

composed of prior memories and therefore accustomed to certain patterns of refraction. Movement B thus represents the necessary refracting process that renders a new perception intelligible to a socially and culturally conditioned context.

Just as the movement from A to C serves to refract the new perception, this newly assimilated information serves to refract the previous frame of meaning (A).[6] If a new perception is to be classified as "new," it must vary from the familiar in some way. The memory of C is therefore added to what was previously understood about the categories to which C had been associated. Both A and C have been mnemonically reinforced in this synthesis. Movement D, then, represents the refracting effect that the novum has on the previous category. When two concepts are set together to reinforce one another, both are refracted.

In the process of localization, there is often a dominant mnemonic framework that facilitates the significance of other concepts. When a concept is reinforced within a larger framework, both the concept and the framework are refracted in the merger. Most often, the dominant and controlling mnemonic paradigm (the framework) is distorted to a lesser degree. Conversely, the concept is meaningful insofar as it conforms to the framework; thus, it is distorted to a greater extent.[7]

Take, for example, John the Baptist. Because he is a historical figure, we can assume that he was particularly memorable. Indeed, the Jesus of Q appeals to this memory:

> [Jesus] began to speak to the crowds about John, "What did you go out into the wilderness to see? A reed shaken by the wind? But what did you go out to see? A man dressed in soft clothing? Those who are splendidly clothed and live in luxury are found in royal palaces! But what did you go out to see? A prophet? Yes, I say to you, and one who is more than a prophet." (Luke 7:24-26; cf. Matt 11:7-9)

This saying provides a fascinating window to the relationship between Jesus and John and perhaps (implicitly) Herod. But for the purpose of my present discussion, it also aptly illustrates the mnemonic cycle. Jesus' series of rhetorical questions draws upon the concept of pre-categorization. One might paraphrase Jesus' question as follows: "Well, what did you think you would find

---

[6] This will manifest in varying degrees depending on the impact of C.

[7] This concept is further explored in my discussion of proof-texting vs. typological interpretation in chap. 5. But it should also be pointed out that not all mnemonic categories act dominantly. Some categories act less like frameworks (that provide structure for new perceptions) and more like less rigid categories (that might be more inclined to reshape according to the new perception).

out there?" Such a question presupposes that his audience had some prior notion of what sort of person lives and preaches in the Judean wilderness. The implied answer is that everyone who made the effort to go out to see John had already anticipated what they might find. Helpfully for those of us who do not share this historical context, Jesus then supplies the "obvious" answer: those who made the trek out to see John had already some understanding of where prophets reside, what they might wear, what their socioeconomic status might be, and so on. Such mental associations with the category "prophet" betray what I have described as movement A.

If it can be determined that the perceivers of John had certain prophetic expectations of him before they actually perceived him, such pre-categorization of John would have inevitably colored (refracted) their actual perceptions of him. The most obvious kind of distortion in this case would be that of conventionalization: the tendency for memories to conform to sociotypical experiences. Jesus and his audience seem to agree that prophets in the wilderness tend to behave and dress in certain ways. Going out to see a prophet presupposes a certain sociotypical experience within that historical context. This would include conforming to the sociotypical roles of speaker-audience. It also might include some symbolic reenactment of a previously known ritual. The list could continue, but the point has already been made: if you go out to see a man and expect a prophet, it will refract your perceptions and interpretations of him along these lines.

Another possible refraction would be narrativization: the tendency for memories to be conventionalized through the constraints of storytelling. In the mnemonic sphere under analysis (the sayings source: Q), Jesus follows the above quote by claiming that John "is the one about whom it is written, 'Behold, I send my messenger before your face, who will prepare your way before you'" (Luke 7:27 // Matt 11:10). In this way, Q (and perhaps Jesus) interpreted John's significance by associating him with a particular Scripture (Mal 3:1). Having already perceived John as a prophet, Jesus has further interpreted him through the association of prophecy. There is perhaps no clearer statement of narrativization: Jesus claims that John is Malachi 3:1. Thus, both by conventionalization and narrativization,[8] the memories of John were refracted, what I have here described as movement B.

That Jesus has presupposed that his audience has indeed perceived John is evident, and thus we move from C to D. The point that Jesus is making about John is that he is not only a prophet but "more than a prophet." Here

---

[8] A fuller treatment would also have to discuss instrumentalization: the tendency for memories to be reinterpreted to serve the present better. Surely Q (and perhaps Jesus) has distorted John's memory via the interpretation of Jesus' own ministry.

Jesus' interpretation illustrates the accommodation of the novum. John is a "prophet," which presupposes a familiar association for Jesus' audience. But John is also "more than a prophet," which argues that John's significance has the capacity to reinterpret the previous parameters of prophethood. In this case, Jesus' interpretation of John's significance suggests that one can be both a prophet and the fulfillment of a prophecy. Thus, the previous category of significance ("prophet") must be refracted to accommodate for the novum (the new perception of John).

Furthermore, if one takes Malachi 3:1 as a category of significance, Jesus' application of this passage to John demands that the passage itself be reinterpreted in light of John's significance. In Halbwachsian terms, we could say that John's significance has been "localized" within the framework of Malachi; conversely, the significance of Malachi has been "reinforced" within the new perception of John the Baptist. In both of these ways, the previous categories of significance have been mnemonically synthesized (refracted), what I have described as movement D.

Mnemonic Continuity and Trajectory

The present section brings to the fore a crucial aspect of my thesis as it is central to my understanding of historical memory. At this point, I move from synchronic to diachronic analysis. In doing so, I argue that the analysis of memory refraction allows a charting of memory trajectories that can be measured and triangulated. In this way my ultimate purpose is to postulate the plausible perception that gave rise to a particular memory (or memories). I further argue that the aim is not to postulate what an unrefracted memory probably looked like, but to postulate what an early refracted memory probably looked like.

In the previous section, I described what I have termed the mnemonic cycle. This model, in essence, is a rough guide for synchronic analysis of memory distortion. Using the example of Q's portrayal of John the Baptist via Jesus, I have demonstrated how the application of social memory theory can shed light on how a particular mnemonic sphere[9] can interpret (refract) memories according to the presuppositions and purposes therein. In describing movement D, I argued that the previous category of significance both refracts and is refracted by the mnemonic process of assimilating a new perception.

The reader who has followed the argument to this point will have recognized that movement A (the previous category of significance) cannot remain static. It must be continually refracted in order to accommodate for the novum (C). In this way, the mnemonic process is not, as Heidegger warned,

---

[9] Perhaps an author and/or community.

a vicious circle. It presupposes previous mnemonic cycles and propels subsequent mnemonic cycles. Therefore, synchronic analysis can only be completed in the move toward diachronic analysis. This assertion has led many to heed Heidegger's warning and to speak in terms of a hermeneutical "spiral."[10] Consider Figure 4.3.[11]

Figure 4.3
The Diachronic Continuity of Memory

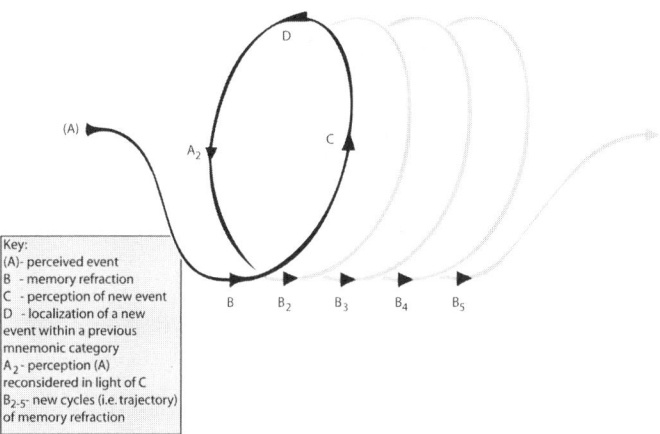

Figure 4.3 represents the logical move from the synchronic process of memory to diachronic continuity of memory. If it can be granted that new perceptions have a refractive effect upon previously established categories, movement A is reinterpreted along each memory cycle. With this in mind, A_2 represents this reinterpretation of that category. I have placed the initial category in parentheses to indicate that we are analyzing a mnemonic category and not the category as it existed independently of memory refraction.[12] Points B_2 through B_5 represent memory refraction as it evolves within each new memory cycle.

The "push" represented by movement D is the "impact"[13] of the novum (C). Indeed, if there was nothing essentially important, unique, or peculiar about the new perception, it would not be memorable. Depending on the

---

[10] E.g., A. C. Thiselton, *The Two Horizons: New Testament Hermeneutics and Philosophical Description with Special Reference to Heidegger, Bultmann, Gadamer, and Wittgerstein* (Exeter: Paternoster, 1980), 104; G. R. Osborne, *The Hermeneutical Spiral* (Downers Grove, Ill.: InterVarsity, 1991), 6ff.; W. Iser, *The Range of Interpretation* (New York: Columbia University Press, 2000), 80–83; cf. Ricoeur, *Interpretation*, 79ff.

[11] Again, it is necessary to point out that this diagram was initially conceptualized in dialogue with social memory theory and not primarily with general hermeneutical theory. Still, the conceptual affinity warrants mention and perhaps serves to ground this discussion within the larger and longer theoretical dialogue.

[12] This, after all, is an analysis of the nature of historical memory and not past actuality.

[13] I borrow this term from Dunn (I revisit this concept below).

extent of this impact, the momentum created by C can vary considerably. If something strikes you as mildly funny, it might be assimilated fairly easily into the previous category (A_2); if something forces a paradigm shift of your worldview (e.g., a religious experience), dramatic and forceful momentum can occur. Even so, most often, the mnemonic spiral serves to have a stabilizing effect upon new perceptions.

What is vital to this model is the concept of mnemonic continuity. In order for successive memory refractions to be thought of as a "trajectory," there is little room for dramatic refractions. Once a perception has been localized within a particular mnemonic category, the refractions thereafter will constitute only incremental modifications to that category. This, of course, is not an absolute. Certainly, human history is measured in terms of paradigm shifts. For example, the perception of celestial bodies underwent a dramatic shift in the post-Copernicus era. On a more personal level, a severe traumatic experience can have a similar effect. But even in such cases, societal constraints and the need for internal continuity tend to temper such paradigm shifts so that their effects are felt over a longer period of time. More commonly, memory progresses without dramatic shifts. To borrow again from Nora, memory remains in permanent evolution, ever upholding the completion of the present.[14]

In order for the importance of mnemonic continuity to be fully appreciated, I must reiterate and clarify my conception of memory refraction. As stated in the previous chapter, *memory distortion should not be immediately equated with "false" memory,* nor should it evoke notions of unreliability or uncertainty. For this reason I have chosen to coin the phrase "memory refraction" in lieu of what is more commonly phrased "memory distortion."

Memory refraction (à la distortion), in its most prevalent form, can be likened to the convex shape of a lens that receives and refracts light by the very parameters of its design. When performing its proper function, a telescope lens distorts an imaged object in order to magnify it. Depending on the quality of the lens, the viewer is able to perceive an approximate distortion of distant objects not visible to the naked eye. The fact that the lens does not "report" the object's image exactly how it was received is exactly its value. In the same way, memory refracts the past to render it intelligible to the present.

This analogy is perhaps idealized; some of our memories are more like kaleidoscopes, refracting uninteresting shapes into interesting abstractions. Yet most memories must lie somewhere between these two models. If these two models represent two extremes of a spectrum (telescopic on one end,

---

[14] P. Nora, "Between Memory and History: Les Lieux de mémoire," *Representations* 26 (1989): 9.

kaleidoscopic on the other), most memories are closer to the former, more objective[15] model of the telescope. This must be so because memory's primary function is to render the past (which is invisible to the naked eye) intelligible to the present. Such intelligibility demands an acceptable approximation of the past to maintain a certain level of diachronic continuity with the present.

Our memories demand a high degree of continuity in order to tie all of our shifting frames of meaning together. The integrity of this chain determines its reliability. I can account for where and who I am now (and why) by analyzing the continuity of this chain.

I contend that this continuity makes the charting of memory trajectories possible for the historian. Because memory refractions are most often spurred and constrained by previous and cognate refractions, it is possible to measure and relate refraction trajectories. Admittedly, once we expand this discussion from personal memory to commemorative traditions, the model of a simple spiral becomes inadequate by itself. When expanded, one could imagine a complex matrix of interconnected refractive spirals, each related to (and in some degree of tension with) other similar refractive spirals. The examination of cultural tradition is "complex, pluralistic and labyrinthine."[16] Thus we must avoid the concept of a single, all-encompassing macro-spiral akin to the concept of a single spiraling metanarrative.[17] Rather, the historian is provided with multiple trajectories that branch off in separate directions.

Still the essential continuity of tradition (commemoration) must be emphasized. It is because of these branching trajectories that the historian is able to comparatively analyze the development of thought and patterns of refraction. Each generation has a close relationship to the immediately previous generation, whether by affinity or reaction. No one commemorating community can be adequately discussed without explaining how this group might relate with the context that spurred and constrained their development.[18]

---

[15] Notice that I qualify this as a "more objective" model, rather than an "objective" model.

[16] Assmann, *Religion and Cultural Memory*, 29.

[17] As indicated in my discussion of narrativization, the role of metanarratives (plural) cannot be understated, but it is the diverse interpretations of culturally significant stories that propel the life of these stories forward. Cf. J. D. G. Dunn's critique of Wright in *Jesus Remembered* (Grand Rapids: Eerdmans, 2003), 331–32.

[18] W. Horbury has made a similar point in his discussion of the "continuity(ies)" of Jewish tradition from the second century BCE to rabbinic tradition. He points out the error in underemphasizing the continuous relationship between "pre-rabbinic" and post-Temple thought. Following Vermes, Flusser, and Sanders, he argues that the NT "belongs to a series of developments of Jewish interpretive tradition, running from the Septuagint and the [Dead Sea] Scrolls to the Targums and rabbinic literature" (*Herodian Judaism and the New Testament* [WUNT 193; Tübingen: Mohr Siebeck, 2006], 221–35, esp. 230f.). While he grants that the destruction of the Temple had an enormous impact upon Jewish thought in general, he avers against

Thus, in order adequately to account for the origin of a mnemonic trajectory, the historian must compare and contrast interpretive spheres (i.e., mnemonic cycles) that seem to be distorting a memory in opposite directions. Once these spheres are compared and contrasted, it is then necessary to postulate how these divergent traditions relate to one another.

With this in mind, the historian should not attempt to set aside traditional interpretations but to navigate through them.[19] This approach requires the historian to locate a synchronic interpretive sphere wherein a tradition has served a particular purpose, take inventory of the refractive tendencies of that sphere, and attempt to account for its relationship with other interpretive spheres. Once two or more mnemonic spheres are located and compared, the ensuing analysis moves from synchronic to diachronic analysis.[20] If it can be assumed that two or more spheres relate a cognate tradition, the comparison of this relationship will either suggest a common tradition that preceded both spheres or suggest dependence. In either case, it is now appropriate to speak in terms of memory trajectories that might be triangulated to postulate a common origin.[21] Fundamental to this analysis is the idea of continuity. If a tradition is to exist at all, it must have had some relationship to what came before it and an impact on what followed.[22]

This idea of continuity is not wholly incompatible with Sanders' description of "two contexts" discussed in chapter 1. He argued that

> the only way to proceed in the search for the historical Jesus is to offer hypotheses based on the evidence and to evaluate them in light of how satisfactorily they account for the material in the Gospels, while also making Jesus a believ-

---

the conclusion that this traumatic event broke the essential continuity of thought between the pre-Temple rabbis and post-Temple rabbinic literature. Indeed, it could be added (in light of the present discussion) that the fundamental importance of the post-Temple rabbis was to establish a cultural link between their own communities and the tradition that defined Jewish culture.

[19] Cf. G. Theissen and D. Winter, *The Quest for the Plausible Jesus: The Question of Criteria* (Louisville, Ky.: Westminster John Knox, 2002), 228–33.

[20] This approach is not dissimilar to Assmann's charting of the relationship between communicative memory and cultural memory: "cultural memory can be considered to be a special case of communicative memory. It has a different temporal structure. If we think of the typical three-generation cycle of communicative memory as a synchronic memory-space, then cultural memory, with its traditions reaching far back into the past, forms the diachronic axis" (Assmann, *Religion*, 8).

[21] This is further illustrated in the next section.

[22] This idea is at least as old as Leibniz, whose most celebrated contribution to historiography was his "law of continuity." See the reprint of his 1704 preface to his *New Essays on the Human Understanding* in G. H. R. Parkinson (ed. Leibniz: Philosophical Writings; London: J. M. Dent, 1973), 158: "Nature makes no leaps."

able figure in first-century Palestine and the founder of a movement which eventuated in the church.[23]

Sanders emphasized that Jesus must stand firmly within first-century Judaism(s); indeed, this is the chief contribution of his work and a highly influential one. Here he also emphasized that Jesus must stand in some relationship with the gospel material and the early church. I consider my present argument concerning the continuity of memory to fill out the gap created by Sanders' two contexts. I contend that the memory refraction evident within the Jesus tradition provides the historian with the data needed to establish the relationship between these two synchronic stages. Memory is in a constant process of refraction. Most of the time, this refracting process remains reliably stable and therefore historically chartable.

More recently, Schröter has made a similar point in discussing the relationship between historical event and historical story.[24] Schröter has argued that any interest in the historical Jesus must attempt to understand him in relationship to the effects that his life had on those who eventually told stories about him. If the historian is to take seriously the "history of effects" that stands between the initial memories of Jesus and the stories of Jesus, the two cannot be disjoined. To take this relationship seriously, he argues, means that the stories about Jesus cannot be simply set aside in search for the "real" Jesus; conversely, the historical Jesus cannot be simply ignored in favor of the stories. Schröter argues:

> If *every* historical construction represents the relationship between event and story (even those that are written within the rubric of the historical-critical consciousness) then a contemporary portrait of Jesus cannot simply set aside the narrative representations of the person of Jesus in the Gospels. On the contrary, this portrait has to be related to these representations and be reconstructed within the rubric of contemporary epistemology. The outcome is not the "real" Jesus behind the Gospels. The outcome is a historical construction which claims to be plausible within the rubric of contemporary epistemology.[25]

He concludes that "Mark's Gospel represents a historical story which is based on a relationship between event and story."[26] Schröter's argument

---

[23] E. P. Sanders, *Jesus and Judaism* (London: SCM Press, 1985), 166–67.
[24] J. Schröter, "Von der Historizität der Evangelien: Ein Beitrag zur gegenwärtigen Diskussion um den historischen Jesus," in *Der historische Jesus: Tendenzen und Perspektiven der gegenwärtigen Forschung* (ed. by J. Schröter and R. Brucher; BZNW 114; Berlin: De Gruyter, 2002),163–212; cf. M. Moxter, "Erzählung und Ereignis: Über den Spielraum historischer Repräsentation," in *Der historische Jesus*; ed. Schröter and Brucher, 78–87.
[25] Translated from Schröter, "Historizität," 205–6. Emphasis added.
[26] Translated from Schröter, "Historizität," 205.

is very close to my own in that I do not think that history is ever able to achieve a picture of the unremembered (unrefracted) past. *It is the effects of the past that are available for analysis and not the past itself.* This impossibility of obtaining "pastness" is what many scholars have in mind when they refer to the "real" Jesus. Indeed, those historians who think that history seeks to describe the "real" past will always lament, as Lessing did, that the task is ultimately futile.

So to offer my own qualification of Schröter's argument, I would add that what the postmodern mind has taught us is that we must always qualify what we mean by "real." What is real is that which has been perceived and interpreted and thus refracted. But once qualified it is no longer helpful to draw a distinction between the real Jesus and the remembered Jesus. For those disciples of the first generation, the real Jesus was the Jesus of their memory.

As argued to this point, memory refraction most often goes unnoticed by the rememberer. If Jesus was to have had any effect on what was remembered about him, we must assume that the refractions of Jesus' story as represented in the Gospels stand in relationship to the initial impact that Jesus had on the memories of his disciples. It is helpful at this point to recall Dunn's argument for the impact of historically memorable figures and events.[27] He argues that Jesus' impact can be readily seen in the divergent threads within the Jesus tradition. Dunn acknowledges his debt to Dahl's cross-section method as it attempts to locate shared characteristics in divergent traditions.[28] But my approach also attempts to locate *contrasting* memories; those which stand in tension to each other allow the historian to postulate the most plausible origin for such tensions. If one follows the theses of Dunn and Schröter, the next logical question is what to do with memories that are in sharp contrast to one another?

In this respect, I incorporate the thesis of Theissen and Winter who speak in terms of the plausibility of historical effects. In response to Lessing's resignation that historical assurance is impossible, the authors write that the "accidental truths of history are, however, the only possible basis of historical assurance."[29] It is not the historian's task to arrive at an absolute measure-

---

[27] J. D. G. Dunn ("History, Memory, and Eyewitnesses," *JSNT* 26, no. 4 [2004]: 478) writes, "What Jesus said (and did) changed the lives of these first disciples; it shaped them; it was truly bread of life for them; it became an integral part of their life-perspective." He emphasizes, "It is not 'ordinary' remembering that I have in mind, but the remembering of the transformative impact" (479); cf. Dunn, *Jesus Remembered*, 329, 882.

[28] N. A. Dahl, "The Problem of the Historical Jesus," in *Jesus the Christ: The Historical Origins of Christological Doctrine* (ed. D. Juel; Minneapolis: Fortress, 1962), esp. 95.

[29] Theissen and Winter, 234; In recognition of the accidentalness of historical data, the authors claim that not only can we not take the data at face value (this is not a new observation), but we can be assured of the inability of humans comprehensively to falsify historical

ment of the past. Instead, the historian must account for contrary accounts and interpretations by plausibly rendering a history of effects. "Incoherent elements that can be coherently interpreted are the best evidence that we are getting close to the historical truth."[30] I would echo this aspect of their thesis in full voice.

Because memory refraction is constant, it is chartable and therefore historically measurable.

Memory, Typology, and Trajectory

In my treatment of social memory in the previous chapter, I argued that memory often survives by being articulated into narrative form. In my discussion of distortion by narrativization, I gave three examples of typological localization. In Burke's accounts of Kessler and Bunyan, it became evident they conflated their own stories with religious metanarratives. In Zerubavel's account of Trumpeldor, it became evident that contemporary political histories can be conflated with historical archetypes. This demonstrates that typological conflation between personal narratives and social narratives can be conceived within the life of personal memory. In the first two cases, the narrative conflations were imagined by those who themselves experienced and interpreted these events. In the case of Trumpeldor, the typological connections between him and Bar Kokhba were clearly made within months of his historical acts.

In light of these examples, it can be argued that typological narrativization is often a means of remembering itself and not necessarily a literary device employed in a far-removed context. In the following section I argue that the typological process is very closely related to the mnemonic process.

Having already detailed the steps of the mnemonic process, Figure 4.4 on page 78 should be immediately familiar to the reader. As such, I unpack my argument here with further analysis of John the Baptist. In this way, I both illustrate the typological cycle in historical terms and provide a precedent for typology from the same context as Jesus. With Figure 4.4 in mind, consider this saying by the Matthean Jesus:

---

truth. They argue that the more convinced we are of the "accidental" character of the data, the more "intuitive certainty is generated within us" (234). It is for this reason that the historian is most benefited from the (1) taintedness of the data (231) and the (2) accidentalness of the data (234). Because the data will betray both of these characteristics, it will inevitably provide a somewhat incoherent amalgamation of information. According to the authors, the historian's task is to make sense of this incoherence in the way that seems most plausibly coherent to the larger contextual picture. This includes both the context of the event(s) and the later effects of these events.

[30] Theissen and Winter, 234.

Figure 4.4
The Typological Cycle

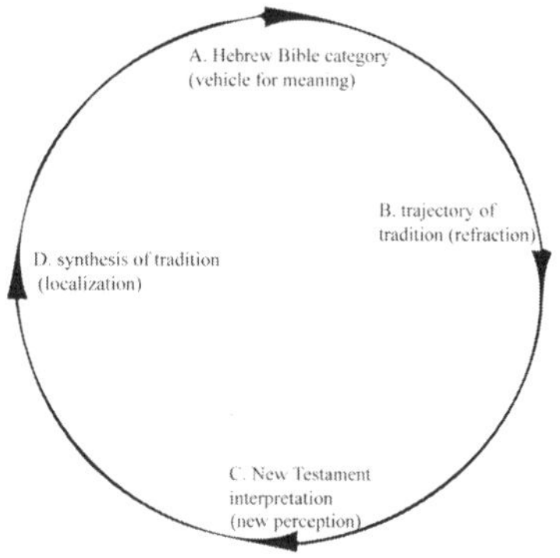

- A. Hebrew Bible category (vehicle for meaning)
- B. trajectory of tradition (refraction)
- C. New Testament interpretation (new perception)
- D. synthesis of tradition (localization)

> And from the days of John the Baptist until now the kingdom of heaven suffers violence, and violent men take it by force. For all the prophets and the Law prophesied until John. And if you care to accept it, he himself is Elijah, who was to come. He who has ears to hear, let him hear. (Matt 11:12-15)

This text clearly appeals to a particular category from the Hebrew Bible: Elijah. As such, Jesus' saying mnemonically evoked certain narratives from 1 and 2 Kings. Of particular interest is 2 Kings 2, where Elijah is taken up to heaven on YHWH's chariot. But in this context, the category seems to be eschatological and thus evokes memories of Malachi's appendix.[31] This could be thought of as movement A. Jesus' claim that John "is Elijah, who was to come" points to the possibility that John the Baptist was the fulfillment of this prophecy. Indeed, as seen above, Q contains a similar association between John and Malachi 3:1. Thus John, again, can be thought of as the new perception, or in literary terms, the New Testament category (C). This eschatological conflation between narrative category and contemporary figure is an excellent example of refraction via narrativization, what I have described as movement B. The fact that Malachi interprets Elijah in an eschatological way demonstrates that there was a refraction trajectory of Elijah tradition already in place. But at this point, we are chiefly concerned with how Matthew has commemorated these categories. Movement D represents the necessary interpretation of Elijah in light of John's significance. If Jesus' audience is able to accept this interpretation of John, they will be forced to read Malachi 4:5-6 differently than they formerly had. In this way, Matthew's commemoration

---

[31] "Behold, I am going to send you Elijah the prophet before the coming of the great and terrible day of YHWH. And he will restore the hearts of the fathers to their children, and the hearts of the children to their fathers, lest I come and smite the land with a curse" (Mal 4:5-6).

of Elijah was localized within perceptions of John, and John's significance was refracted by the previous category of Malachi 4:5-6.

So far, this analysis of typological memory has been chiefly synchronic. As is a matter of course, this analysis begs to be filled out by comparing this synchronic sphere to other similar manifestations of memory refraction. For example, the fact that John was remembered for baptizing calls to mind Elisha narratives (cf. 2 Kgs 5:10). Thus, the possibility emerges that memories of John were further refracted by such narrativization. In the simple addition of this detail, the present analysis has moved from the synchronic to the diachronic. Consider Figure 4.5.

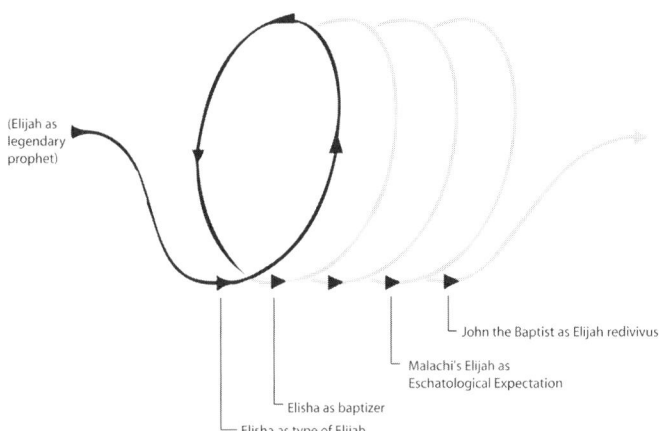

Figure 4.5
The Refraction Trajectory of Elijah Typology

As discussed in the previous section, a simple spiral cannot adequately model the complex matrix of commemoration(s) which constitute the life of a culturally significant tradition. What this model provides is a single trajectory of interpretation that extends from the traditional narrative to the contemporary figure.[32]

Again, I have placed the previous mnemonic category in brackets to indicate that it is the memory of Elijah's legend that interests us and not the actual Elijah. Also, it should be pointed out that this continuum has been significantly shortened to highlight only four shifts in distortion along the way. The first of these shifts is present, in the narrative of 2 Kings 2, in that Elisha is modeled as a type of Elijah. Standing by the Jordan River, Elisha witnesses Elijah's departure and receives both his "mantle" (2:13-14) and his "spirit" (2:15). As such, the first localization along this trajectory is a synthesis

---

[32] That is, this is only one possible trajectory among many; I have not yet attempted to compare and contrast this particular trajectory with others.

of the significance of Elijah and Elisha. Here emerges the possibility of a dual typology along later stages of this trajectory.[33] Part of Elisha's narrative included his prescription of baptism in the Jordan (2 Kgs 5:10). With these details in mind, we return to Jesus' typological interpretation of John the Baptist and notice remarkable similarities. Memories of John were dominated by his ministry as a baptizer in the Jordan near the very place where Elijah was taken to heaven.[34] Returning to our original context in Matthew, we see that Jesus' appeal to Elijah's significance was eschatologically filtered through Malachi.[35]

What I have demonstrated here is how a refraction trajectory can take on typological significance. To this point, this has been nothing more than a tradition-historical analysis. Indeed, this analysis has yet to make any claims concerning the historical John the Baptist. To do so will require a measuring of this trajectory against other trajectories in order to triangulate these and postulate a plausible historical perception that gave rise to such memories. With this in mind, the following section will move from mnemonic theory to historical method.

In sum, the present chapter has argued that (1) memory can adequately be described as a cyclical process that moves from previous category to new perception, (2) this process requires refraction in order to render the past intelligible to the present, (3) the mnemonic cycle moves diachronically to tie together an integral continuity, and (4) mnemonic analysis has the capacity to illuminate typological interpretation.

---

[33] C. A. Evans has argued that the Baptist's ministry evidences Elijah, Elisha, and Joshua typologies ("The Baptism of John in a Typological Context," in *Dimensions of Baptism* [ed. F. M. Cross and S. E. Porter; JSNTSup; Sheffield: Sheffield Academic Press, 2002], 44–70).

[34] J. A. Trumbower writes: "According to the [Fourth Gospel], John the Baptist began his baptizing career in Perea on the eastern side of the Jordan River (clearly in Jn 10.40 and also in 1.28, properly understood). According to 2 Kgs 2.8, Elijah was taken up to heaven from precisely this spot" ("The Role of Malachi in the Career of John the Baptist," in *The Gospels and the Scriptures of Israel* [ed. C. A. Evans and W. R. Stegner; JSNTSup; Sheffield: Sheffield Academic Press, 1994], 36–37). Cf. J. Murphy-O'Connor, "John the Baptist and Jesus: History and Hypotheses," *NTS* 36 (1990): 360n7.

[35] J. J. Collins has observed that 4Q521 f.2.3 reads, "fathers will turn to sons." This along with the fragmentary 4Q588 shows that some in the first century held a similar notion of Elijah's coming as that of Malachi (*The Scepter and the Star: The Messiahs of the Dead Sea Scrolls and Other Ancient Literature* [New York: Doubleday, 1995], 117–22). Also Sirach 48:10-11 reads: "Who is ready for the time? As it is written, 'To still the wrath before the fierce anger of God, to turn the hearts of the fathers back to the children and to restore the tribes of Israel. Blessed is he that sees you [Elijah] before he dies." Cf. J. E. Taylor, *The Immerser: John the Baptist within Second Temple Judaism* (Grand Rapids: Eerdmans, 1997), 146, 284.

Historical Method

My aim thus far has been to introduce a handful of theoretical concerns to historical Jesus research with the hope that the discussion of contemporary historiography might invite reassessment of historiography within that field. If I have done so successfully, the preceding discussion should be relatively unique among works on the historical Jesus. I highlight this now because, as I demonstrate my historiographical thesis, I take for granted several aspects common to many Jesus historians including redaction criticism, cultural exegesis, and so on. My application of memory theory undergirds this analysis and often surfaces in such discussions, but this is set alongside an exegetical analysis that will be familiar to most New Testament researchers. Although certain aspects of my method will be unfamiliar to historical Jesus research (e.g., the mnemonic value of typology and the process of triangulation), I believe that my "corrective" is (for the most part) compatible with the historical-critical exegesis already in place in historical Jesus research. Therefore, what is most unique about the present work will be felt most keenly in my critique and application of historiography and memory theory, but I advise the reader to keep my primary thesis in mind throughout the exegetical chapters.

Historical-Critical Exegesis

What the reader should look for in the exegetical chapters is not simply the mention of "mnemonic" and "refraction," but the overall argument of each chapter. In other words, my historiographical thesis is best demonstrated not in the exegetical details, but in the overarching exegetical telos.[36] I see this method as a natural outworking of my theory, which (out of necessity) involved big-picture historiographical concepts. What I provide in the exegetical chapters has in mind both the forest and the trees. Therefore, the reader should remain attentive to the larger themes developing throughout these chapters that will not come to fruition until the conclusion.

The remainder of this section serves to clarify my aim and method. A brief summary is offered, followed by explanation.

Each subsequent chapter demonstrates at least five steps in varying order:

1. I survey cultural traditions that look to be related to the New Testament passage of interest. I chart their interpretive trajectories previous to, parallel to, and following the New Testament text/subject of interest.

---

[36] No doubt both are important; thus my work with Son of David is considerably more detailed than my preliminary examples concerning John the Baptist.

2. I focus on two or more manifestations of the same episode (i.e., story/saying) within the Jesus tradition with specific attention to how this tradition functions mnemonically in its respective synchronic contexts. Moreover, I analyze this episode with an eye toward specific manifestations of memory refraction.
3. Once the synchronic function of the Jesus episode has been discussed, I analyze the episode's diachronic movement. I attempt to determine where each version of the episode stands in relation to the others and suggest one or more refraction trajectories of the Jesus tradition.
4. If it can be established that the synchronic context of this tradition represents a particular sphere along a diachronic refraction trajectory, due consideration is given to the possibility that the trajectory emerged prior to the tradition's literary form. At this point "authenticity criteria"[37] are employed to determine whether the tradition originated in memory or invention.
5. If it is possible to establish diverging redaction trajectories and the tradition seems to have been among the early and widespread memories of Jesus, I follow the trajectories and triangulate toward the most plausible historical scenario. At this stage, it is important that this historical context renders the episode intelligible to the cultural backdrop previously established in step 1.

1. Step 1 is, of course, a well-known step in historical Jesus research and historiography in general. Because the Jesus tradition emerged within the context of first-century Hellenistic Judaism, the examination of certain cultural traditions serves to anchor Jesus to this historical context. These include scriptural frameworks, ranging from metanarratives and archetypes to precedents and proof texts. These would also include popular ideologies, political climates, and so on. When dealing with the Hebrew Bible and Septuagint, I attempt to establish a tradition trajectory whereby a particular fountainhead (a text, or group of texts) has taken on special cultural significance over time. In this way, step 1 will follow Figure 4.3 to analyze the movement from [A] to and through B, to establish a trajectory of interpretation. It is important to emphasize that it is the movement from [A] to B that is available for analysis. The fountainhead has been set in parentheses to demonstrate that the uninterpreted/unrefracted past is ultimately unavailable to the historian.

For example, 2 Samuel 7 will prove important on several levels over the course of this book. In the following chapter I discuss the Davidic covenant as it is represented by (B) 2 Samuel 7, (B_2) Isaiah 11, (B_3) 1 Chronicles 17, and (B_4) *Psalm of Solomon* 17. Each point along this trajectory also represents a

[37] Discussed below.

synchronic rotation as represented by Figure 4.2. Thus, step 1 anticipates the full rotation of each synchronic circle (i.e., A, B, C, and D of Figure 4.2) but is primarily interested with movement B.[38] Each manifestation of the Davidic covenant will betray certain memory refractions according to the context, but in many ways the fountainhead engenders a certain degree of stability throughout this trajectory.[39]

2. Step 2 is a common step to redaction criticism. Students of the NT are taught to compare and contrast similar episodes in the Jesus tradition in order to determine the characteristics, agendas, and tendencies of each evangelist. The present study has described mnemonic distortion in similar fashion. As an episode of the Jesus tradition is adapted to the narrative world of an evangelist, it is distorted by that evangelist's authorial tendencies. Conversely, when that episode becomes a part of the evangelist's narrative, it contributes to the plot (and sometimes theme, characterization, and telos) of the story.[40] When (as is often the case) the evangelist's tendencies involve the application of scriptural categories to the Jesus tradition, one can expect the episode to be localized within such mnemonic frameworks. This corresponds to the movement from B to C in Figure 4.2. One can also expect that the NT category reinterprets the significance (however slightly) of the scriptural category. This corresponds to the movement from C to D in Figure 4.2. The synthesis (or mnemonic reinforcement/localization) of old and new categories promote the contemporary relevance of the scriptural category and thus propel the distortion trajectory of the fountainhead. This corresponds to the movement from D to A in Figure 4.2 and anticipates the movement from D to A_2 in Figure 4.4.

For example, in chapter 6, I demonstrate that the synchronic circle representing Matthew's commemoration of Jesus applies the title "Son of David" with more frequency than do the other evangelists. We are able to determine that Matthew is particularly interested in this title by comparing Matthew to Mark and others. In doing so, step 2 anticipates the diachronic concerns of step 3, where Matthew's use of previous tradition suggests a particular trajectory. Indeed, sometimes I set these steps together in the same section. But, and this is especially true of chapter 6, it is important to discuss thoroughly the world of Matthew's narrative; that is, my primary interest at this

---

[38] I should mention now that my use of diagrams and assigned letters (A, B, etc.) will be left behind in the exegetical chapters. While these were helpful in detailing my theoretical aims, they might prove cumbersome over the course of the exegetical chapters. Moreover, certain chapters require that I follow a different procession of steps depending upon the text and subject.

[39] See the discussion of continuity earlier in this chapter.

[40] At this point the present model conforms most easily to Schleiermacher's hermeneutical circle.

point is synchronic analysis. It will be demonstrated that Matthew's agenda to promote Jesus' significance via scriptural categories (e.g., Isaianic Messiah, Son of David, etc.) also projects new significance onto the Scriptures being employed.

3. Step 3 aims to establish particular interpretive tendencies that betray an episode's development over time. By comparing and contrasting different synchronic stages of the Jesus tradition (i.e., the Gospels), the discussion moves from the synchronic to the diachronic. This move is often made intuitively by New Testament scholars. By comparing Matthew to Mark, it is only natural for some speculation as to their literary relationship to come to the fore. Indeed, theories relating to the Synoptic Problem have been borne out of such discussions. What concerns the present step is the charting of commemorative development from Q to Mark, Mark to Matthew, Mark to Luke, and so on. This step is absolutely essential to my methodology as it hinges on my ability to establish two or more refractive tendencies that are suggestive of a particular interpretative trajectory. In some cases, the argument is strengthened if another independent and diverging distortion trajectory can be established that suggests a common point of departure.

For example, Jesus' entry into Jerusalem is examined in chapter 7. This examination demonstrates that Mark's account has been refracted by Matthew. It also suggests that Mark has reworked a previous tradition. Thus, these two evangelists propel this episode forward by adapting Jesus' entry to their respective refractive tendencies.

4. Step 4 speaks to the question of whether an episode of the Jesus tradition originated in memory or invention. This is discussed at length in the following section alongside a brief treatment of authenticity criteria.

5. Step 5 brings together the previous diachronic steps and postulates a historical portrait. If it can be established that an episode manifests itself in two or more points along an interpretive trajectory, that this episode represents an early and widespread memory, and that this episode is intelligible in the cultural context discussed in step 1, the trajectory(ies) can be charted toward a historical portrait. I refer to this effect as "triangulation."

I return here once more to the case of John the Baptist to exemplify step 5. I have already argued that John stood along a particular trajectory of interpretation that was spurred and contained by Elijah typology. This typology can be seen most clearly in the overt statement by the Matthean Jesus, "And if you care to accept it, he himself is Elijah, who was to come" (Matt 11:14). But so far, I have not established that this Elijah typology was a live interpretation during the historical ministry of John the Baptist. Indeed, this saying is singly attested by Matthew, which suggests the possibility that Matthew invented it. Perhaps typological interpretations of John's significance simply betray literary devices employed by the evangelists. In order to establish a historical portrait, it is necessary to measure the refraction trajectory represented by Matthew 11:12-15 against at least one other trajectory. Such is provided by the Fourth Gospel.

In the Fourth Gospel, the evangelist includes a dialogue between John and the Jewish authorities:

> And this is the witness of John, when the Jews sent to him priests and Levites from Jerusalem to ask him, "Who are you?" And he confessed, and did not deny, and he confessed, "I am not the Christ." And they asked him, "What then? Are you Elijah?" And he said, "I am not." "Are you the Prophet?" And he answered, "No." (John 1:19-21)

In this story, John is directly asked if he is Elijah, and he responds negatively. Here we have a direct contradiction with the Jesus saying in Matthew 11:12-15.

This is where, in my method, I employ triangulation. I have already established a refraction trajectory that is inclined to interpret John via narrativization. The first point along this trajectory is Q (Luke 7:24-26 // Matt 11:7-9) which localized John's significance within Malachi 3:1. The second point along this trajectory is Matthew 11:12-15, which localizes John's significance within Malachi 4:5. Thus, Matthew adopts Q's refraction and moves this trajectory forward with his own interpretation. In this way, these two points allow us to establish a distortion trajectory. We can call this trajectory X.

The story provided by the Fourth Gospel demonstrates a negative reaction to a similar typological interpretation. In this way, the Fourth Gospel does indeed show that some people were under the impression that John's ministry should be interpreted via Elijah typology. While the Fourth Gospel has attempted to downplay this typology, it still provides information regarding the possibility of John's typological significance. Furthermore, we have seen that the Fourth Gospel places John's ministry in the exact location where Elijah was taken to heaven (10:40, cf. 1:28). This detail was probably not invented by the evangelist, as it runs contrary to the Baptist's direct denial of this typology. Thus, the Fourth Gospel provides evidence of a separate refraction trajectory moving away from trajectory X. We can call this trajectory Y.

We have already established a refraction trajectory that moves from the Elijah/Elisha narrative into the first century's eschatological expectations (e.g. Mal 4:5). We can call this trajectory Z.

The historian's responsibility is to account for the relationship between these trajectories. With this in mind consider the following diagram, Figure 4.6.

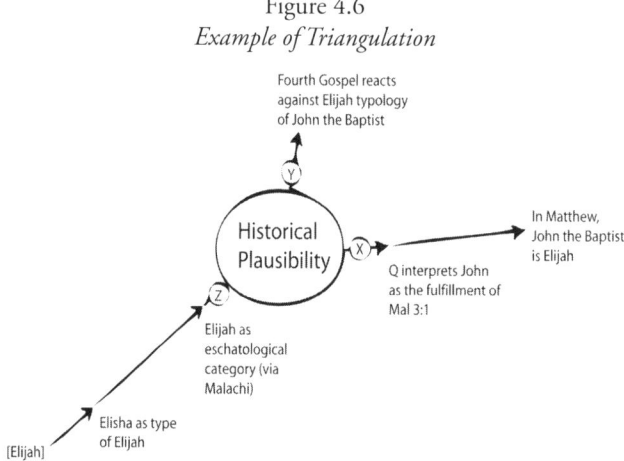

Figure 4.6
Example of Triangulation

I have here illustrated refraction trajectories in linear fashion. In doing so, I do not intend to negate the spiraling effect of memory refraction. Rather my intention is to highlight the continuity of refraction trajectories over time. As such, the reader should think of these trajectories in terms of Figures 4.3 and 4.5 provided above. The reader will notice that the arrows move in the direction of general chronological sequence.

As shown by the sphere in the center of these three trajectories, historical plausibility is given parameter by the extant literary trajectories. Triangulation does not pinpoint an exact historical reality; rather it describes the mnemonic sphere that best accounts for the mnemonic evidence.[41] The purpose of triangulation is to establish the most plausible intersection between the established trajectories.[42]

This, of course, assumes that there is reason to affirm the "historicity" of a perception (hence step 4). In order to establish this, it must be determined whether a narrative episode is best explained as the product of memory or the product of invention.

---

[41] Granted, I have not offered here a comprehensive treatment of the John the Baptist tradition; I have selected those details that serve to illustrate my models. Not every bit of mnemonic evidence can be treated in the same way. At times, the present study will need to grant that aspects of the Son of David tradition do not betray evidence of typology and thus have been refracted along different lines.

[42] Each of the two trajectories constitute a possible triangle when juxtaposed against a plausible point of intersection. Thus, only two established trajectories are required for a possible triangle. But the more trajectories that can be established, the more possible triangles can be applied.

The Question of Origin: Memory or Invention?

I have argued for a historical method that establishes trajectories of memory refraction. Building from my adaptation of social memory theory, this presupposes that all memory is refracted through the lens(es) of the mnemonic cycle. In this way, I have adapted Halbwachs' original idea of localization and subsequent studies of memory distortion.

Halbwachs was inclined to speak of memory in terms of imaginative reinforcement, which should not be confused with wholesale imagination. The acknowledgment that memory is a creative process should not be confused with wholesale creation. There is, after all, a difference between an invented story and a memory-story. While the two narratives might look similar, the initial act of telling a memory-story is different. First, if a storyteller narrates from personal memory, she thinks that she is transmitting a memory; she does not think that her story is being invented. Second, unless the teller intends to deceive her audience, the audience thinks that what they are hearing reflects a memory. If she does not intend to tell a memory-story, she will most often provide certain genre cues. While there is likely overlap in the diachronic processes, the crucial difference is this: Does the story have an origin in perception or invention? In most cases, the storyteller and the audience presuppose an answer to this question, and therefore the historian must attempt to answer it as well.

In answering, the historian attempts to establish early and widespread perceptions/interpretations/refractions of a memory. Traditionally, historical Jesus research has employed authenticity criteria to support arguments for historicity. With some qualification, the present study relies on some of these criteria.

The first qualification is that the connotations behind the words "authentic" and "historicity" must be reassessed according to the definition of the historical task discussed above. In asking the question of origin, the historian attempts to establish whether a story originated in the perceptions contemporary to the historical event. The aim is not to dig for an unrefracted memory; the historian's aim is to account for the earliest mnemonic refractions of a memory-story. As long as it is kept in mind that the historical goal is not to verify what "actually happened," I am comfortable with these terms.

Depending on which treatment one reads, there are anywhere from seven to twenty-five different authenticity criteria.[43] The present book exercises

---

[43] D. Polkow represents a larger division of criteria in "Method and Criteria for Historical Jesus Research," in *Society of Biblical Literature 1987 Seminar Papers* (ed. K. H. Richards; SBLSP; Atlanta: Scholars Press, 1987), 336–56. S. E. Porter prefers fewer divisions, which translates into fewer overall criteria, in *The Criteria for Authenticity in Historical Jesus Research* (JSNTSup 131; Sheffield: Sheffield Academic Press, 2000).

more caution than most in my application of these criteria. Criteria are always applied in plurality; I never appeal only to one criterion alone. In most cases, I do not argue for a story's (or saying's) origin in memory unless three or more criteria can be applied. Moreover, in my judgment, some criteria provide stronger results than others.[44] More often than not I avoid definitive argument for memory-origin unless one of the applicable criteria represents one of the stronger criteria. The present section briefly surveys the criteria that are employed over the course of this study. I list these in the order of relative strength.

Multiple Attestation: First suggested by Burkitt,[45] this criterion can be employed when two or more independent synchronic traditions convey a similar episode. Such multiple attested traditions suggest that the episode represents early and widespread material. Originally, Burkitt considered this criterion to be applicable for overlaps between Mark and Q.[46] More recently, this criterion has been applied to a wider spectrum of Jesus tradition.[47] It is important that this criterion is only employed when an episode in attested in independent traditions. As such, the application of this criterion presupposes the author's stance concerning the independence of John to the Synoptics and the existence of Q. I side with the scholarly majority in both cases and thus affirm both the (relative) independence of John[48] and the two-source

---

[44] Cf. J. P. Meier, *A Marginal Jew: Rethinking the Historical Jesus* (New York: Doubleday, 1991), 1:167–95; however, I do not follow Meier's assessment of which criteria are "primary" and which are "dubious."

[45] F. C. Burkitt, *The Gospel History and Its Transmission* (Edinburgh: T&T Clark, 1906), 147–68.

[46] Burkitt, 147.

[47] E.g., N. J. McEleney, "Authenicating Criteria and Mark 7:1-23," *CBQ* 34 (1972): 434; R. H. Stein, "The 'Criteria' for Authenticity," in *Gospel Perspectives: Studies of History and Tradition in the Four Gospels*, vol. 1 (ed. R. H. France and D. Wenham; Sheffield: JSOT Press, 1980).

[48] Pace F. Neirynck, J. Delobel, et al., *Jean et les synoptiques: examen critique de l'exégèse de M.-E. Boismard* (BETL 49; Louvain: University Press, 1979), and adherents. Because this hypothesis has compelled more dissent of late, I say a brief word here. There are basically three camps concerning John's relationship to the Synoptics. The majority still holds that John was largely ignorant of the Synoptic tradition (except perhaps in oral form). Yet Neirynck et al. have argued that John has closely followed Mark and adapted this tradition to his own framework (cf. M. E. Glasswell, "The Relationship between John and Mark," *JSNT* 23 [1985]: 99–115). The third camp takes a middle ground between these two by suggesting that John had limited knowledge of synoptic material but did not rely upon this material (e.g., D. A. Carson, *The Gospel according to John* [Grand Rapids: Eerdmans, 1991], 49–58). It should be said that the second camp represents (by far) the least popular hypothesis. If either the first or third camps are correct, one may judiciously apply the criteria of multiple attestation. But, as I remain unconvinced by either of the smaller camps, the present study presupposes John's (relative) independence and applies the criteria of multiple attestation accordingly.

hypothesis.[49] The present study applies the criteria of multiple attestation accordingly and considers this criterion to be among the stronger arguments when used in conjunction with any of the following.

Embarrassment. Following the lead of Meier,[50] I also consider this criterion to be among the stronger arguments. The supposition that the Gospels contain invented material is predicated upon the notion that early Christianity had motive to invent material as they commemorated Jesus' post-Easter significance. This commemoration tended to exalt Jesus in several ways and decrease or eliminate details that cast him in an embarrassing light. Because of this, episodes that do indeed contain such details are not easily explained as Christian invention. Moreover, the fact of their presence indicates that the episode was not removed from the tradition because it was well known among the memories of Jesus and carried some degree of authority.

Contrary tendency. This criterion is similar but not identical to the criteria of embarrassment.[51] This criterion presupposes the general findings of redaction criticism. If an episode contains details that promote an agenda that runs contrary to the evangelist's editorial tendencies, those details were not probably the product of his invention. One could put embarrassment under this heading in that embarrassing details run contrary to the tendency to venerate Jesus. However, not every detail that runs contrary to the tendencies of the evangelist is embarrassing in nature. Some have attempted to apply this criterion to the more general tendencies of early Christianity.[52] But Meier correctly argues that we should not suppose that every circle of early Christianity held common editorial tendencies.[53] However, unlike Meier, I do indeed think that this criterion can be confidently applied when the detail is measured against the particular (and well-accepted) tendencies of the individual evangelists.[54] For example, if one of Luke's key agendas is to extend Jesus' significance to Gentiles, any details within Luke that run contrary to this agenda are best explained as early memory. Finally, it should be noted that the goal is not to find data in Luke's tradition that is "uninterpreted" but to find interpretations that the evangelist has chosen not to develop.

Multiple forms. This criterion should not be confused with multiple attestation. Instead of appealing to a similar episode in independent traditions

---

[49] *Pace* W. R. Farmer, *The Synoptic Problem* (New York: Macmillan, 1964); M. Goulder, "On Putting Q to the Test," *NTS* 24 (1978): 218–34; and respective adherents; most recently M. S. Goodacre, *Goulder and the Gospels: An Examination of a New Paradigm* (JSNTSup 133; Sheffield: Sheffield Academic Press, 1996).
[50] Meier, *Marginal Jew*, 1:168.
[51] Porter, *Criteria*, 106–10, describes these two as a single criterion.
[52] E.g. Stein, "Criteria," 145–48.
[53] Meier, *Marginal Jew*, 1:182.
[54] C. A. Evans, *Jesus and His Contemporaries* (AGJU 25; Leiden: Brill, 1995), 18.

(à la multiple attestation), the criterion of multiple forms appeals to similar content that is featured in different kinds of genre. If similar content appears in a saying and also in a parable, or if similar content appears in the narration of Jesus' actions and also in dispute dialogue, this criterion is warranted. For example, Jesus' respect for John the Baptist appears both in logia and in the narration of his baptism. This, of course, does not speak to the historicity of the final form of these sayings/stories, it merely indicates that such respect was remembered of Jesus' historical life and ministry.

Coherence. I consider this criterion among the weaker arguments against invention. This criterion may be applied if a particular content coheres with core material that is little disputed among Jesus historians. The trouble with such application is twofold. First, it presupposes that certain characteristics of Jesus are of little dispute in historical Jesus research. Such characteristics are very few.[55] Second, it is possible that a characteristic well known to early memory may have bled into other episodes during narration. For these reasons, this criterion is employed only with caution and only in conjunction with two or more other criteria.

Semitisms and Semitic influence. These criteria represent two sides of the same coin. The appeal to Semitisms deals primarily with evidence of Semitic language, and the appeal to Semitic influence deals with evidence of larger cultural and geographical categories. Both should be applied with caution. The former presupposes that Jesus and his Jewish contemporaries most commonly spoke Aramaic and/or Hebrew. The latter presupposes that Jesus and his contemporaries thought in categories common to Jews living in first-century Semitic culture. Since the Gospels are written in Greek, such criteria argues that certain Greek grammatical structures, loan words, and translations betray an origin in Semitic memory.[56] As such, if one is able to identify a Semitism or Semitic influence with confidence, it might place the episode that manifests this feature closer to Jesus' historical context. There are several objections to the use of this criterion.

First, evidence for such features might simply betray the evangelist's spoken language.[57] Second, there are often alternative grammatical explanations

---

[55] C. E. Carlston has argued that this criterion is only warranted when an episode coheres with Jesus' eschatological call to repentance ("A Positive Criterion of Authenticity," *Biblical Research* 7 [1962]: 34). This aptly demonstrates that this criterion has a tendency to confirm the presuppositions of the scholar.

[56] E.g., M. Black, *An Aramaic Approach to the Gospels and Acts* (Oxford: Clarendon, 1967); J. A. Fitzmyer, *A Wandering Aramaean* (Grand Rapids: Eerdmans, 1997 [1979]), 1–27; M. Casey, *Aramaic Sources of Mark's Gospel* (SNTSMS 102; Cambridge: Cambridge University Press, 1998).

[57] This is perhaps to be considered in the case of Matthew's gospel.

for many so-called Semitisms.[58] Third, some Jesus historians have suggested that Jesus might have spoken Greek.[59] Indeed, such objections have shown the limitation of Matthew Black's once-standard work on the subject. Still, there are certain cases where a Semitism seems most probable. Such cases include the overt presence of Semitic vocabulary, cases where the saying presupposes a Semitic word play,[60] and cases where the use of a word or grammar has consistently defied easy explanation on the basis of Greek grammar. With these concerns in mind, I apply this criterion in such cases and in conjunction with other (stronger) criteria. The criterion of Semitic influence is similarly applied with caution in instances where a Semitic cultural category (beyond grammar/vocabulary) suggests an origin in Semitic memory.

Before moving forward, I state again here that the use of authenticity criteria is simply one stage of my historical method. I employ these criteria in an attempt to distinguish between memory and invention. I am not under the impression that the simple appeal to such "historicity" completes the historian's task. With this in mind, this section needs to be taken within the larger argument of chapters 1–4.

Conclusion

This chapter has attempted to clarify my historiographical theory and method. I have argued that the analysis of memory refraction and the mnemonic process in general are valuable resources for historical inquiry. Moreover, I have argued that historical typology exemplifies the relationship between memory and history. As discussed in the previous chapter, one of the virtues of typology is that it betrays narrativization more obviously than most forms of mnemonic refraction. Thus, typology provides the present study with a window into mnemonic distortion that can be readily applied to the Jesus tradition.

My method is an outworking of my theory. I have tried to demonstrate in this chapter how the Jesus historian can relate the separate synchronic commemorations of Jesus as represented by the Gospels to establish diachronic refraction trajectories that have been set in motion by early memories of the historical Jesus. I have employed the example of John the Baptist to illustrate how this might look when applied to the Gospels. From here forward, this book demonstrates my theory and method by looking at a particular group of texts concerning the title "Son of David."

---

[58] E.g., L. D. Hurst, "The Neglected Role of Semantics in the Search for the Aramaic Words of Jesus," *JSNT* 28 (1986): 63–80; Porter, *Criteria*, 126–80.

[59] E.g., S. E. Porter, "Did Jesus Ever Teach in Greek?" *TynBul* 44, no. 2 (1993): 199–235.

[60] E.g., Matt 3:9.

Over the course of my exegetical chapters I argue that certain typological interpretations were applied to early memories of Jesus and thus give a window into historical memory. Once such historical memories have been established, I can apply my historiographical theory to historical Jesus research. In doing so, I hope also to contribute to the ongoing discussion concerning the significance of the title "Son of David." With this in mind, I consider the following exegetical chapters to provide a worktable on which my historiographical theory and method might be displayed.

5

Son of David and Typology

As argued in the previous two chapters, typology can be thought of as a form of memory refraction in that it is a powerfully mnemonic tool and a highly influential interpretive cipher. I now apply my historiographical model to a specific typological characteristic of the Jesus tradition. The remainder of this book examines the title "Son of David" with an aim to (1) ascertain the title's entry point into the Jesus tradition, (2) analyze the ways that it was mnemonically refracted in the interpretation of Jesus' ministry (and vice versa[1]), and (3) discuss how this refracted the more developed (i.e., formalized) Jesus tradition in early Christianity.

I have chosen the title "Son of David"[2] for two reasons. First, while a form of Davidic messianism seems to have been significant in proto-Christian thought,[3] it did not maintain prominence in the writings of the New Testament. There are many NT texts that take Jesus' Davidic status for granted, but this concept has been all but eclipsed by other christological claims and titles. In some of these texts it is possible that "Son of David" was intentionally downplayed; in others it served as a backdrop for Christology but still relatively less prominent as compared with titles like "Son of Man," "Son of God," "Christ," and "Lord." Because the title has been relegated to obscurity in the Jesus tradition, the passages that betray its presence tend toward the less developed stages along christological trajectory(ies). This said, we will see that "Son of David" is not prominent in the earliest stages of the tradition either.

---

[1] Following the mnemonic cycle, we should expect that if the title was used in or about the career of Jesus, this application refracted both the significance of the title and the significance of Jesus' ministry.

[2] For the sake of brevity I henceforth use "Son of David" in place of the phrase "the title Son of David." At times I need to refer to a nontitular idea or figure using a form of this moniker; in such cases I simply refer to "David's son."

[3] By "proto-Christian" I mean the particular Jewish messianic circle that began to emerge around the ministry of Jesus that would eventually become a christological circle composed of both Jews and Gentiles.

In this way, the title stands at a bridge between the initial memories of Jesus and the Jesus tradition as it was commemorated by the authors of the NT. Moreover, it will be possible to chart the mnemonic sphere associated with "Son of David" from early perception refraction (memory) to later tradition refraction (commemoration).

The second reason for choosing "Son of David" as a test case is that there is need for an exploration of the possibility that this title is derivative of typological interpretation of both the Davidic and Solomonic traditions. Studies on this topic commonly take the title to stem from either Davidic messianism or Solomonic exorcistic activity. Yet in most cases these categories are treated as mutually exclusive options. I argue that these overlapping mnemonic spheres reinforced one another to mutually refract the memories of Jesus and provided a mnemonic framework for "Son of David." My overarching exegetical aim is to demonstrate that the mnemonic background of "Son of David" was both Davidic and Solomonic, that it was typological in nature, and—above all—that the charting of memory refraction will show how early memories of Jesus were initially shaped by typological interpretation. In these ways, my exegetical aim provides a work table for my primary theoretical and methodological arguments.

In this chapter, I suggest the possibility of a Solomon typology in Jesus' historical context. This chapter is weighted toward the analysis of literary trajectories of Solomonic tradition, because previous studies have tended toward a strictly Davidic reading of many texts that have close ties to Solomonic tradition. I do not intend to argue in favor of the latter at the expense of the former. But because texts like 2 Samuel 7, Isaiah 11 and *Psalm of Solomon* 17 have long attracted strictly Davidic interpretations, a Solomonic perspective helps to fill out the discussion and at points offers corrective exegesis. In these ways, I offer a fresh perspective on the mnemonic lenses evoked by Son of David typology.

My aim with this chapter is to provide a general backdrop by which specific acts and words of Jesus can be mnemonically measured. I proceed by discussing the uses of "Son of David" in the HB and in *Psalm of Solomon* 17. Given these aims, this chapter serves as an extended treatment of what I have called step 1 of my proposed exegetical process.[4]

"Son of David" in the Hebrew Bible

The most common starting point for Son of David studies is a discussion of how the phrase relates to royal messianism and when the phrase was first

---

[4] Because I do not examine any texts within the Jesus tradition in this chapter, my method is not displayed in full until the chapters that follow.

used as a messianic title. While these questions are important and need to be addressed in due course, very few studies begin by asking how the title was used in the HB. Remarkably, what should be seen a foundational element of the discussion has been relegated to footnotes and passing mentions.

Burger, whose work provided the most extensive treatment of "Son of David," was particularly deficient in this regard. His "Jewish background" devoted little more than a single paragraph to the HB before moving to first-century texts![5] Lohse incorrectly claimed, "The title Son of David occurs for the first time in Ps. Sol. (17:21), which belonged to the middle of the 1st cent. B.C."[6] The few studies that have devoted attention to the pre-messianic development of the phrase have tended to bracket these results when the discussion shifts to messianic texts.[7] This tendency has painted the title as a tradition-historical conundrum that emerged in the first century rootless and without precedent. Neugebauer's comment is very telling:

> [From 10 to 200 CE] "Son of David," besides "messiah," is the only common title for the coming salvation-bringer. Evidence for this exists only after 70. The reason for this is that before this period messianic statements were missing in general.[8]

Neugebauer assumed the premise on which many biblical scholars approach this topic: because the title is believed to be of messianic origin, the pre-messianic use of "Son of David" is largely ignored.[9] This premise misleads the discussion from the start and is in desperate need of reconsideration.

---

[5] C. Burger, *Jesus als Davidssohn: Eine traditionsgeschichtliche Untersuchung* (FRLANT 98; Göttingen: Vanderhoeck and Ruprecht, 1970), 16–24.

[6] E. Lohse, "υἱὸς Δαυίδ," in TDNT 8, 480. No doubt, Lohse intended to say that *Ps.Sol.* 17 contains the first messianic application of the title; still the oversight was and is a costly one and bespeaks a larger neglect with regard to Son of David scholarship. It may well be the case that Lohse's oversight has had an unfortunate impact upon a large segment of NT scholarship. W. L. Lane (*The Gospel of Mark: The English Text with Introduction, Exposition and Notes* [Grand Rapids: Eerdmans, 1974], 435) cited Lohse and mimicked his error. This error is repeated by R. H. Gundry in *Mark: A Commentary on His Apology for the Cross* (Grand Rapids: Eerdmans, 1992), 718; D. R. Bauer, "Son of David," in *Dictionary of Jesus and the Gospels* (ed. J. Green and S. McKnight; Downers Grove, Ill.: InterVarsity, 1992), 767; and B. Witherington, *The Gospel of Mark: A Socio-Rhetorical Commentary* (Grand Rapids: Eerdmans, 2001), 332.

[7] E.g., J. A. Fitzmyer, *The Semitic Background of the New Testament* (Grand Rapids: Eerdmans, 1997), 119; B. M. Nolan, *The Royal Son of God: The Christology of Matthew 1-2 in the Setting of the Gospel* (Orbis Biblicus et Orientalis 23; Fribourg: Biblical Institute of the University of Fribourg, 1979), 166.

[8] Translated from F. Neugebauer, "Die Davidssohnfrage (Mark xii 35-7 parr.) und der Menschensohn," *NTS* 21 (1974): 85.

[9] E.g., Burger, 17.

What these studies have understated is that messianism was a result of prophetic hopes and typological categories that predate the fully developed messianism(s) of the first century BCE. It is crucial to emphasize that "Son of David" has discernible roots in proto-messianic mnemonic categories that provide evidence of its development.[10] Previous studies have yielded unsatisfactory results because they have downplayed the first and dominant interpretive context of the title in the HB. They have proved unsatisfactory in a number of ways, including the tendencies to maintain an unhelpful dichotomy between Davidic and Solomonic categories, to misinterpret and misuse *Psalm of Solomon* 17, and to truncate the conceptual sphere from which early Christianity borrowed when the title was adapted to Jesus.

Recently, a modest but provocative advance has been made by Pablo Torijano in his monograph *Solomon the Esoteric King*.[11] Torijano's chapter on Son of David (chap. 6) builds from his sound and thorough analysis of Solomonic tradition beginning with 2 Samuel and its subsequent trajectory to and through Hellenistic Judaism. While this chapter is brief,[12] it convincingly demonstrates the need for further "research into the relationship between the wise king and this title to see whether the title was used as a substitute for the king's name or whether it embodied a particular characterization of the king that could be adapted to other situations."[13]

The present study aims to provide an analysis along these lines. Therefore, my contribution to Son of David research begins from the simple premise that "Son of David" virtually always refers to Solomon in the HB.[14] Therefore, when later texts apply this phrase as a title, the first and most obvious explanation is that it is Solomonic.[15] Unless there is good reason to

---

[10] J. Zimmermann rightly posits, "The foundations for the later messianic expectation of an anointed king are to be looked for not only in the overt mentions of משיח in the Old Testament but above all in the Davidic king-theology of the Old Testament which is found in texts of different genres from different times"; translated from *Messianische Texte aus Qumran: Königliche, priesterliche und prophetische Messiasvorstellungen in den Schriftfunden von Qumran* (WUNT 2.104; Tübingen: Mohr Siebeck, 1998), 47.

[11] P. A. Torijano, *Solomon the Esoteric King: From King to Magus, Development of a Tradition* (JSJSup 73; Leiden: Brill, 2002).

[12] His treatment of "Son of David" in the NT is a mere eight pages within the chapter, yet succinct and suggestive.

[13] Torijano, 106.

[14] Torijano, 25, 106; he argues that there is only one exception where "Son of David" is applied to someone other than Solomon (the title is applied to Absalom in 2 Sam 13:1). He has overlooked 2 Chronicles 11:18 where the phrase is applied to Jerimoth. Even so, his point is clear: exceptions aside, "Son of David" is a distinctly Solomonic designation. Cf. G. Schneider, "Zur Vorgeschichte des christologischen Prädikats 'Sohn Davids,'" *TTZ* 80 (1971): 247–53.

[15] It is noteworthy that the only use of the phrase "Son of David" in the Dead Sea Scrolls

suppose otherwise, the presence of this title in a passage in (or contemporary to) the NT ought to be first measured against this mnemonic category.

Son of David in the Monarchial Narratives

That "Son of David" refers to Solomon is most obvious in the monarchial narratives of 1 and 2 Chronicles. This feature does not appear in the books of Samuel or Kings. "Son of David" as a formal title for Solomon seems to be a product of the Persian period or shortly before. This said, the present discussion is aided by attention to Solomon's place in the larger biblical narrative, which requires preliminary attention to 2 Samuel.

It is well known that 2 Samuel 7's account of the Davidic covenant was an important text (if not the most important text) for establishing Israel's ideal political relationship with God, foreign nations, and the temple.[16] I include here Nathan's oracle as represented by 2 Samuel 7:8-17:[17]

> Now therefore, you shall say to my servant David: "Thus says YHWH of Hosts [יהוה צבאות], I took you from the pasture, from following the sheep, that you should be ruler over my people Israel. And I have been with you wherever you have gone and have cut off all your enemies from before you; and I will make you a great name, like the names of the great men who are on the earth. I will also appoint a place for my people Israel and will plant them [ונטעתיו], that they may live in their own place and not be disturbed again, nor will the wicked afflict them any more, as formerly, ever since the day that I commanded judges to be over my people Israel; and I will give you rest from all your enemies. YHWH also declares to you that YHWH will make a house [בית] for you. When your days are complete and you lie down with your fathers, I will raise up your seed [והקימתי את־זרעך] after you, who will come forth from you, and I will establish his kingdom. He shall build a house [בית] for my name, and I will establish the throne of his kingdom forever. I will be a father to him and he will be a son to me; when he commits sin, I will correct him with the rod of men and the strokes of the sons of men, but my love [וחסדי] shall not depart from him, as I took it away from Saul, whom I removed from before you. And your house and your kingdom shall endure before me forever; your throne will be established forever." In accordance with all these words and all this vision, so Nathan spoke to David.

(4Q398 f.11 13.1) attributes the title to "Solomon, Son of David." This text is revisited in chap. 6.

[16] A. Anderson, *2 Samuel* (WBC 11; Dallas: Word, 1989), 112: "2 Sam 7 is, without doubt, the theological highlight of the Books of Samuel if not of the Deuteronomistic History as a whole."

[17] While my inclusion of biblical quotes most often reflects my own translation, I have in many places cross-referenced my interpretation against the New American Standard's translation.

Because I need to interact with this text over the course of this book, the full importance of this text for my study is not realized until the conclusion. But I do intend for the present chapter to set a firm foundation for the rest of my exegetical chapters, so I discuss here what I anticipate to be principal concepts for later exegesis.

The scholarly majority considers at least parts of Nathan's oracle to represent the earliest form of the Davidic covenant;[18] and others argue that this text is based upon an earlier (nonextant) form.[19] While this passage is replete with Deuteronomist language, redactional cues, and theology, the title יהוה צבאות at least is indicative of the antiquity of the tradition.[20] All seem to acknowledge that 2 Samuel 7 is the proper place to begin any discussion of this covenant, regardless of origin.[21]

Mowinkel regarded this passage as an etiology meant to explain why Solomon, and not David, built the temple.[22] This view remains a valid reading,[23] if not the most probable. Attempts to argue otherwise have had to contend with the (possible) tension between 7:5-7 and 7:13.[24] The former verses seem to have a negative tone with regard to anyone building a temple; the latter verse anticipates Solomon's dedication of the temple. Weinfeld argued that 7:8-17 has affinity to Hittite and Assyrian "grant" treaties.[25] These options need not be mutually exclusive.

It is important to highlight that the essential features of this covenant involve the juxtaposition between the building of a בית (the Solomonic temple) and the establishing of a בית (the Davidic dynasty).[26] This wordplay

---

[18] L. Rost, *The Succession to the Throne of David* (Sheffield: Almond Press, 1982 [1926]), 35–37; F. M. Cross, *Canaanite Myth and Hebrew Epic: Essays in the History of the Religion of Israel* (Cambridge, Mass.: Harvard University Press, 1973), 254–57; G. H. Jones, *The Nathan Narratives* (JSOTSup 80; Sheffield: Sheffield Academic Press, 1990), 70–92; G. Gakuru, *An Inner-Biblical Exegetical Study of the Davidic Covenant and the Dyanastic Oracle* (Mellen Biblical Press Series 58; Lewiston, Maine: Edwin Mellen, 2000), 49–50.

[19] R. A. Carlson, *David, The Chosen King: A Traditio-Historical Approach to the Second Book of Samuel* (Uppsala: Almquist and Wicksell, 1964), 108–25; J. Van Seters, *In Search of History* (New Haven, Conn.: Yale University Press, 1983), 276–77; H. Kruse, "David's Covenant," *VT* 35 (1985): 140–41, 163.

[20] Rost, 36.

[21] Kruse, 141; See Gakuru (chap. 3) for a fuller treatment of tradition-critical issues.

[22] S. Mowinckel, "Israelite Historiography," *ASTI* 2 (1963): 10.

[23] Anderson, *2 Samuel*, 113.

[24] The attempt by Gakuru (50) to harmonize this tension is unconvincing.

[25] M. Weinfeld, "The Covenant of Grant in Israel and the Ancient Near East," *JAOS* 90 (1970): 184–203; M. Weinfeld, *Deuteronomy and the Deuteronomist School* (Oxford: Clarendon, 1972), 79ff. This theory has garnered considerable support, but for an objection to this view see Gakuru, 53–55, who argues that 7:1-17 is best seen alongside neo-Assyrian salvation oracles (56–71).

[26] See fuller discussion in H. W. Hertzberg, *I & II Samuel: A Commentary* (trans. J. Bowden; London: SCM Press, 1964 [1960]), 281–88.

thus sets "house" as referent alongside "house" as metaphor; YHWH will allow the former to be built for him (7:11), while YHWH himself will establish (or build) the latter (7:13).[27] That these concepts are connected is seen most clearly in the complementary parts of 7:13: "He shall build a house for my name, and I will establish the throne of his kingdom forever."

It is most common for scholars to take 13a as a later insertion, which served to narrow a more general promise of perpetual lineage to a specific promise concerning Solomon.[28] This point will prove important in what follows in that it demonstrates that later interpreters considered the Davidic covenant to be primarily referring to Solomon, the archetypal temple builder.[29] This might be further confirmed by the singular "seed" language,[30] which can be seen to carry the connotation of a singular figure.[31] Moreover, the prerequisite of "rest" from Israel's enemies (7:1, 11)[32] might be a conceptual prefiguring of Solomon's legacy of peaceful dominance.[33] More conclusively, 7:14-15 provides the best evidence that Nathan's oracle has been edited with

---

[27] In the LXX, this is further emphasized by the double use of the verb "οἰκοδομέω." In 7:11 YHWH "οἶκον οἰκοδομήσεις αὐτῷ," and in 7:13, the promised king "οἰκοδομήσει ... οἶκον." Cf. Ps 89:4.

[28] E.g., Hertzberg, 287; Anderson, 2 Samuel, 121–22; the phrase "a house for my name" is a Deuteronomic feature (cf. 1 Kgs 3:2; 5:3; 8:18).

[29] Cf. D. J. McCarthy, "II Samuel 7 and the Structure of the Deuteronomic History," *JBL* 84 (1965): 134, who argued that both Solomon's story and the fulfillment of the Davidic covenant are brought to a climax in 1 Kings 8 when Solomon dedicates the temple. This connection is revisited in chap. 8.

[30] The significance of vegetation language is dealt with elsewhere. At this point it should be mentioned that the use of זרע is striking considering the use of נטע in 7:10. D. Juel suggests that this concept serves to connect the Davidic covenant with Exod 15:17, which also uses נטע (*Messianic Exegesis: Christological Interpretation of the Old Testament in Early Christianity* [Philadelphia: Fortress, 1988], 65).

[31] T. Veijola, *Die Ewige Dynastie: David und die Enstehung seiner Dynastie nach der deuteronomistischen Darstellung* (Helsinki: Suolmalainen Tideakatemia, 1975), 69–70; Gakuru, 74; cf. Paul's argument concerning the Abrahamic covenant in Galatians 3:16.

[32] J. Laansma, *I Will Give You Rest* (WUNT 98; Tübingen: Mohr Siebeck, 1997), 26, has argued that the concept of rest both points backward to Deuteronomy 12; 31:1-6 and forward to 1 Kings 8. As such this passage serves to tie together Israel's connection to the land, their leader, and the cult. Laansma's argument might be further strengthened by the recognition of the use of the verb נטע in the description of Israel's rest within the land. This vegetation metaphor is perhaps conceptually linked to the metaphorical זרע of David. This dual imagery might serve to tie YHWH's previous promises concerning the land to the present promise of political dominance.

[33] Hertzberg, 287; cf. 1 Chr 22:7-10, which refers to 2 Sam 7:14 and contrasts Solomon's legacy to that of David: "Behold, a son will be born to you, who shall be a man of rest; and I will give him rest from all his enemies on every side; for his name shall be Solomon, and I will give peace and quiet to Israel in his days" (1 Chr 22:9). For a fuller discussion on the etymology of Solomon's name and how this relates to his legacy, see W. Johnstone, *1 and 2 Chronicles* (JSOTSup 253; Sheffield: Sheffield Academic Press, 1997), 241.

Solomon's legacy in mind, both the good and bad of it. YHWH promises to be a father to "him" and thus specifies a particular figure by using the third-person singular. While "he" is expected to commit sin, he will not be in danger of losing YHWH's favor; this is an unmistakable apology for Solomon's famous disobedience (cf. 1 Kgs 11:34-36).

More important for the present study than the oracle's original form is its influence on later commemorative narratives. Nathan's prophecy sets in motion a mnemonic trajectory that eventually finds its way to multiple forms of messianic eschatology in later Judaism and Christianity. Burger rightly observed that, in later messianic texts, the language of 2 Samuel 7 is routinely used to describe the Davidic messiah. "The comparison [between the expected Son of David and his precedents] demonstrates an almost stereotypical terminology which can be traced back to a narrow, limited canon of Old Testament places."[34] This is our first indication that typological comparison is at work. When language is routinely exported from a cultural archetype and employed in the description of a new category, we must entertain the possibility of typology. The ensuing analysis proceeds by asking: has the latter end of the mnemonic trajectory (i.e., the later interpreter) attempted to emphasize specific characteristics of a new category (e.g., a contemporary figure or event) that cohere with the mnemonic legacy of an archetype or metanarrative? But before I am in a position to ask and answer this question, it is necessary to establish certain characteristics that have taken on archetypical significance in the mnemonic trajectories of Israel's tradition.

It has become commonplace in NT scholarship to point to 2 Samuel 7 as the fountainhead of later Davidic categories. But what has been often overlooked is the fact that the language does not point to David's legacy alone but also to Solomon's. Many previous analyses have made this mistake. Lohse hit painfully close to the mark but ultimately missed:

> In the messianic expectation of the synagogue, the name of the sprout of David is always named but actually there's never another word added about his person. It is enough to have pointed out the *pre-image* of King of David in order to mark the path and mission of the messianic ruler sufficiently.[35]

Lohse overstates the scarcity of the data but his point is well taken. The pre-image of monarchy (he points only to David), in many cases, provided a suitcase loaded with meaning and able to be easily imported into royal eschatology by mere evocation. No doubt, David mnemonically anchored Israel's

---

[34] Translated from Burger, 18.

[35] Translated from E. Lohse, "Der König aus Davids Geschlecht. Bemerkungen zur messianischen Erwartung der Synagoge," in *Abraham unser Vater. Festschrift für Otto Michel* (Leiden: Brill, 1963), 343 (emphasis added).

commemoration of the once-great monarchy and thus served as a royal archetype. But appealing to David alone misleads the discussion. It must be emphasized that YHWH's promise was first fulfilled in the person and reign of Solomon. Because the aim of 2 Samuel 7 was to describe Solomon, many "Davidic" attributes ascribed to later royal figures were prefigured in the person and reign of Solomon. In many cases, Davidic hopes and figures are described with attributes that were first embodied in Solomon's legacy.

As is examined in more detail over the course of this book, later eschatological texts tended to attract certain key attributes that help to identify the eschatological Davidic figure: he is related to David, he is uniquely endorsed by God, he is endowed with YHWH's spirit, he reigns over the foreign nations, he is a wise judge, he builds the temple, and so on.[36] These mnemonic categories manifest themselves in several different combinations depending upon the agenda of the community and the other scriptural precedents and paradigms employed in the description.[37] But almost all of these later texts seem to be influenced and held in check by their mnemonic fountainhead: 2 Samuel 7.

This is not to say that every eschatological interpretation of 2 Samuel 7 was working with a Solomon typology. While attention to Solomon's legacy will prove extremely helpful in my discussion of Davidic categories, it must also be acknowledged that the most important aspect of Solomon's legacy is that he was David's son. In this way, Solomon was an archetype in conjunction with his father; many of his archetypal characteristics were an extension of characteristics that David embodied. Certainly not all of Solomon's characteristics were prefigured in David (e.g., Solomon as temple builder), but enough to view Solomon's legacy as an extension of David's. As such, the evocative language of 2 Samuel 7 does not stem from a single archetype (as it might for someone like Adam or Abraham). Instead it calls to mind the divinely promised relationship between the two archetypes; the Davidic covenant was given *to* David *through* Solomon.

I suspect that this is why later interpreters (like the Chronicler) employed the title "Son of David": because this title mnemonically evokes an archetypal relationship rather than a single archetypal figure. It is to be expected that some typological comparisons tended toward one archetype at the expense of the other. But, in varying degrees, 2 Samuel 7 held such refractions in check.

---

[36] For a somewhat dated but still useful discussion of messianic criteria, see G. L. Davenport, "The Anointed of the Lord in *Psalms of Solomon* 17," in *Ideal Figures in Ancient Judaism: Profiles and Paradigms* (ed. J. J. Collins and G. W. E. Nickelsburg; Chico, Calif.: Scholars Press, 1980); he focuses mainly on the first three of the above categories.

[37] For example, it was common for later interpreters to localize the Davidic covenant within the framework of Isaiah 11, as discussed in detail below.

With this in mind, I presently explore the nature of this father-son relationship and how it was commemorated in the monarchial narratives.

Solomon's introduction to the narrative is described in 2 Samuel 12:24, where David comforts Bathsheba after the death of their son. In this context, the physical conception of Solomon is described: David "went in to her and lay down with her,[38] and she gave birth to a son, and he named him Solomon. And YHWH loved him." The coital act is here doubly described[39] to emphasize the fulfillment of YHWH's promise of David's seed [זרע (or semen)] who would eventually build the temple, have eternal reign, and enjoy a father-son relationship with YHWH (2 Sam 7:12-14).

The birth of Solomon was the fulfillment of 2 Samuel 7. This is confirmed by the extremely rare statement of YHWH's affection for the child: "and YHWH loved him [ויהוה אהבו]" (12:24). There is only one other time in the HB that YHWH is said to "love" someone (Mal 1:2). Moreover, Solomon is the only individual[40] ever said to be so loved (cf. Neh 13:26). This statement of affection recalls 2 Samuel 7:15, where YHWH promises, "My love [חסד] shall not depart from him."

It is, however, interesting to note 2 Samuel 7's use of חסד as opposed to 2 Samuel 12's use of אהב. One possibility is that the former connotes YHWH's covenantal commitment to David's son[41] while the latter connotes YHWH's emotional commitment to him. Perhaps, then, אהב represents a heightening of YHWH's relational bond to Solomon. Von Rad has called this "the quite irrational love of God for this child" that should be seen as "a paradoxical act of election on the part of God."[42] It is therefore likely that this statement of love is an outworking of YHWH's promise, "I will be a father to him and he will be a son to me" (2 Sam 7:14). For even though Solomon would "commit iniquity" (7:14), YHWH would continue to love him unconditionally,[43] like a son (7:15).[44] In this way, Solomon's father-son relationship

---

[38] ויבא אליה וישכב עמה.

[39] This is the only place in Scripture where coitus is doubly described. Elsewhere the verb בוא is used alone (cf. Gen 16:4; 30:4; 38:2; Judg 16:1; 2 Sam 16:22; Ezek 23:44).

[40] In Malachi, Jacob represents a collective.

[41] Cf. 1 Kings 8:23 where Solomon states "Oh YHWH, the God of Israel, there is no God like you in heaven above or on earth beneath, keeping covenant [ברית] and love [חסד] to your servants."

[42] G. von Rad, "The Beginnings of Historical Writing in Ancient Israel," in *The Problem of the Hexateuch and Other Essays* (New York: McGraw-Hill, 1966), 199. Here von Rad attempted to account for YHWH's unwavering commitment to Solomon despite his eventual disobedience.

[43] P. Saachi, *Jewish Apocalyptic and Its History* (trans. W. J. Short; Sheffield: Sheffield Academic Press, 1990), 76; K. E. Pomykala, *The Davidic Dynasty Tradition in Early Judaism: Its History and Significance for Messianism* (Society of Biblical Literature Early Judaism and Its Literature 7; Atlanta: Scholars Press, 1995), 13.

[44] 2 Samuel 7:15 demonstrates that YHWH's love for Solomon should be seen in opposi-

to both David and YHWH are confirmed as Solomon is introduced to the narrative in 2 Samuel 12:24. Thus, Solomon's character is introduced in two ways: (1) he is the fulfillment of the "seed/semen" promised to David and, (2) he is uniquely loved as a son by YHWH. This background will prove important as this discussion moves forward to Chronicles. It suggests that Solomon's designation as Son of David was not a mere reminder of physical relationship; it was meant to recall the Davidic covenant.

Chronicles extrapolates from what is largely implicit in 2 Samuel 7 and 12 to give a detailed account of how the covenant played out in the relationship between David and Solomon. This is most vividly seen in David's provision for, advice to, and commissioning of Solomon as temple builder (1 Chr 10–29; esp. 17:11-14; 22:1-19).[45] The Solomon of Chronicles is portrayed not merely as David's progeny nor his immediate heir, but as the fulfillment of the Davidic covenant and thus the extension of David's legacy.[46] At this point we turn our attention to the overt manifestations of the title. Torijano has shown that in the postexilic texts the monikers "Solomon" and "Son of David" were invariably linked.[47] While he takes for granted that the phrase is titular, more could and should be said in confirmation of this probability. Compare the following texts from 2 Chronicles (emphasis added):

> 2 Chr 11:18: And Rehoboam took for himself a wife, Mahalath, the daughter of *Jerimoth, the son of David* [בן־דויד], and of Abihail, the daughter of Eliab, the son of Jesse.
>
> 2 Chr 30:26: So there was great joy in Jerusalem; for since the time of *Solomon, the Son of David* [בן־דויד], *King of Israel*, there were none like him in Jerusalem.
>
> 2 Chr 35:3: And he said to the Levites that taught all Israel, who were holy to YHWH, "Put the holy Ark in the house which *Solomon, the Son of David* [בן־דויד], *King of Israel* did build. . . ."

The first of these examples is the sole text in 2 Chronicles where the phrase בן־דויד does not refer to Solomon. Notice that, in this example, the context is that of simple familial relations. For each primary character, their father and grandfather are mentioned. There is no reason to think that "Son of

---

tion to YHWH's very conditional commitment to Saul. This further suggests that Solomon's relationship to YHWH was particularly determinative of his love-covenant.

[45] On the commissioning of Solomon, see R. L. Braun, "Solomon, the Chosen Temple Builder: The Significance of 1 Chronicles 22, 28 and 29 for the Theology of Chronicles," *JBL* 95 (1976): 58–90.

[46] W. Brueggemann, *Solomon: Israel's Ironic Icon of Human Achievement* (Columbia: University of South Carolina Press, 2005), 162–65.

[47] Torijano, 24–25, 106.

David" is applied as a title in this case. The Chronicler has simply used lineage to specify how these obscure characters relate to previously mentioned characters. While it may be suggested that the phrase functions likewise in the case of Solomon, the latter two examples demonstrate otherwise. In these cases, "Son of David" is couched between Solomon's name and the obvious title, "King of Israel." Thus, given the context, "Son of David" seems to be one of two titles designating Solomon's rank. Notice also that "Son of David" is primary and "King of Israel" is secondary.

The Chronicler's agenda to paint Solomon as the ideal king is seen most directly in his redaction of Nathan's prophecy (emphasis added):

2 Samuel 7:12-16	1 Chronicles 17:11-14
When your days are complete and you lie down with your fathers, I will raise up your seed after you, who will come forth from you, and I will establish his kingdom. He shall build a house for my name, and I will establish the throne of his kingdom forever. I will be a father to him and he will be a son to me; when he commits sin, I will correct him with the rod of men and the strokes of the sons of men, but my love shall not depart from him, as I took it away from Saul, whom I removed from before you. And your house and your kingdom shall endure before me forever; your throne shall be established forever.	And it shall come about when your days are fulfilled that you must go to be with your fathers, that I will establish your seed after you, *who shall be of your sons* [מבניך יהיה]; and I will establish his kingdom. He shall build for me a house [בית], and I will establish his throne forever. I will be his father, and he shall be my son; and I will not take my love away from him, as I took it from him who was before you. But I will settle him in *my house* [ביתי] and in *my kingdom* [מלכותי] forever, and *his throne* [כסאו] shall be established forever.

The only significant changes to this tradition serve to emphasize Solomon's fulfillment of this prophecy.[48] The first redaction is the additional phrase "shall be of your sons" (1 Chr 17:11). The emphasis of the idea of sonship may point to Solomon's sonship to David, but in and of itself does not convince of a Solomonic emphasis. However, the second redaction is the absence of the phrase "when he commits sin, I will correct him with the rod of men" (2 Sam 7:14). This confirms the Chronicler's agenda to portray Solomon as the ideal king.[49] Solomon's sins are forgotten all together in Chronicles, and

---

[48] For a treatment of the minor variances, see R. L. Braun, *1 Chronicles* (WBC 14; Waco, Tex.: Word, 1986), 196–98.

[49] J. A. Fitzmyer, "The Son of David Tradition and Mt. 22.41-46 and Parallels," in *Essays on the Semitic Background of the Old Testament* (London: Geoffery Chapman, 1971), 118.

this passage coheres with that agenda. The third redaction involves the shift from the second-person singular "your house" (i.e., David's lineage) to the first-person singular "my house" (i.e., the temple).[50] Also, it is his (Solomon's) throne that will be established and not David's. In this way, Solomon's relationship to the temple is further emphasized under the authority of YHWH's ultimate ownership of both temple and kingdom. In these ways, the Davidic covenant in 1 Chronicles 17 places a greater emphasis on Solomon in comparison with 2 Samuel 7.[51]

In general, the Chronicler's portrait of Solomon conforms to the commemorative interests of Israel as a primarily cultic community.[52] In the Persian period, Israel had little political autonomy except for a firm center of gravity in their (modestly) rebuilt temple.[53] Within this social framework, Israel's kings are "presented primarily as patrons and leaders of the temple cult."[54] Brueggemann continues:

> In the environment of the Persian period, the maintenance of a distinctive Jewish identity would seem to be a primarily rhetorical-interpretive concern. This agenda, in the horizon of the Chronicler, is taken to be the maintenance of Jewish identity through participation in the temple cult. This means, in turn, that the temple cult in Jerusalem is imagined in this literature not in terms of its actual modesty but in terms of the remembered and imagined first temple that is the gift of Solomon. Thus the Solomon imagined here is a glorious figure without blemish or flaw.[55]

In stark contrast to the ironic and paradoxical portrait of Solomon in 1 and 2 Kings, "Solomon, the Son of David" was the image of the ideal king of Israel's golden age. The importance of this nuance must be underscored.

As mentioned, "Son of David" is used as a title (among the monarchial narratives) only by the Chronicler. The depiction of Solomon in Chronicles is that of the ideal king, cultic leader, economic genius, and so on.[56] Thus,

---

[50] Pomykala, 89; Johnstone, 206; E. von Nordheim, "König und Tempel: Der Hintergrund des Tempelbauverbotes in 2 Samuel vii," *VT* 27 (1977): 452, argued that "my house" (17:14) refers to the people of Israel, rather than the temple. This is improbable considering that בית is used as a temple referent in 17:12 and given the general emphasis on the temple cult in Chronicles; cf. P. Dirksen, *1 Chronicles* (Leuven: Peeters, 2005), 235.

[51] Braun, *1 Chronicles*, 198–99.

[52] D. N. Freedman, "The Chroniclers Purpose," *CBQ* 23 (1961): 440f.; Dirksen (232, 235) has argued that the Chronicler's version of the Davidic covenant deemphasizes the dynastic promise and emphasizes instead Solomon the temple builder.

[53] J. K. Berquist, *Judaism in Persia's Shadow: A Social and Historical Approach* (Minneapolis: Fortress, 1995), 24ff.

[54] Brueggemann, *Solomon*, 161.

[55] Brueggemann, *Solomon*, 161.

[56] Cf. R. L. Braun, "Solomonic Apologetic in Chronicles," *JBL* 92 (1973): 503–16.

Son of David was a mnemonic category[57] that evoked Solomon as he was commemorated by Chronicles: practically perfect in every conceivable way. With this in mind, the introductory line of 2 Chronicles summarizes the aim and content of the book (emphasis added):

> Now *Solomon, the Son of David* was strengthened in his kingdom, and YHWH his God was with him, and magnified him exceedingly. (2 Chr 1:1)

Brueggemann pithily describes the Chronicler's portrayal as "Solomon Glorious, One-Dimensional, Minus Irony."[58] It is this commemorative revision of Solomon's life that "Son of David" was meant to label. One could think of this in terms of intentional distanciation: Solomon's sins were forgotten in order to create the memory of an ideal monarchy and temple cult. In sum, "Son of David" finds its entry point into the Davidic interpretative trajectory with an overt refraction of Solomon's character.

Son of David as Archetypal Sapiential Author

The other major employment of "Son of David" is found in wisdom literature, where it is used as an appeal to pseudepigraphal authority. Compare the above text (2 Chr 1:1) to the following (emphasis added):

Proverbs 1:1:   The proverbs of *Solomon, the Son of David, King of Israel*.

Qoheleth 1:1:   The words of the *Preacher, the Son of David, King in Jerusalem*.

I specifically highlight these introductory verses because they seem to have been influenced by a well-known form of the title, which is also attested in 2 Chronicles 30:26 and 2 Chronicles 35:3. In the case of Proverbs, the form of the title mirrors that which is later found in the narrative of Chronicles:

Proverbs 1:1:   שלמה בן־דוד מלך ישראל

2 Chronicles 30:26:   שלמה בן־דויד מלך ישראל

Save only the form of David's name (note the addition of the yod), the two are identical. Since the phrase seems to have titular significance for the Chronicler, there is good reason to believe that the sapiential occurrence of the same form is used in a titular way.[59] Proverbs follows the more primitive form of David

---

[57] Cf. E. Lohmeyer, *Gottesknecht und Davidsohn* (FRLANT 61; Göttingen: Vandenhoeck and Ruprecht, 1953), 68, who described the title as an information package which carried a particular paradigm of meaning.

[58] Brueggemann, *Solomon*; the title of his ninth chapter.

[59] Contra D. C. Duling, "Solomon, Exorcism and the Son of David," *HTR* 68 (1975): 237.

(דוד) that is common to classical biblical Hebrew, while 2 Chronicles 30:26 (et al.) predictably follows the form common to late biblical Hebrew (דויד).[60] Qoheleth 1:1 unexpectedly follows the primitive form: "Qoheleth, Son of David, King in Jerusalem [קהלת בן־דוד מלך בירושלם]."[61] This might suggest that the title was well known prior to Chronicles and that its form remained intact over a long period. We cannot, however, rule out the possibility that all of the above were prefixed to the tradition by later editors.[62]

That Solomon's name was an attractive pseudonym is well known.[63] In most cases the aim was to appeal to Solomon's divinely bestowed wisdom (cf. 1 Kgs 3:11; 3:28; 5:9) and the fact that he was reputed to be sapiential author (1 Kgs 4:29-34; 5:12).[64] The overarching portrayal of Solomon in 1 Kings 3–5 is that of the archetypal wise king. Much like 2 Samuel 7, which served as a catalyst for messianism, 1 Kings 4:32 was a fountainhead for subsequent wisdom trajectories.

Solomon's reputation grows in quality and quantity in the Septuagint (LXX). In the Masoretic Text (MT) of 1 Kings 4:32, Solomon is said to have "spoken [וַיְדַבֵּר]" 3,000 "proverbs [מָשָׁל]" and 1,005 "songs [שִׁיר]." The number of parables increased in the LXX to 6,000 and the number of songs increased to 5,000.[65] Moreover, in the LXX, the book of Proverbs is attributed solely to Solomon; all other supposed authors are eclipsed.[66] In the MT, Proverbs is conveyed as a composition of Solomon's sayings alongside those which he has compiled from other wisdom teachers. But in the LXX, these other wisdom teachers, such as "the wise" (22:17), "Agur" (30:1), and

---

[60] Qumran exclusively uses דויד (sans CD 7:16); R. E. Brown, *The Birth of the Messiah: A Commentary on the Infancy Narratives in Matthew and Luke* (Garden City, N.Y.: Doubleday, 1979), 81–82.

[61] It is generally agreed that Qoheleth was authored ca. 250 BCE. However D. C. Fredericks, *Qoheleth's Language: Re-evaluating Its Nature and Date* (Lewiston, Me.: Mellen, 1988), 266–78, has argued that Qoheleth's language is in accord with preexilic Hebrew and has thus suggested that an earlier date must be reconsidered.

[62] See discussion in P. W. Shekan, "A Single Author for the Whole Book of Proverbs," in *Studies in Israelite Poetry and Wisdom* (Washington, D.C.: Catholic Biblical Association, 1971), 15–26.

[63] E.g., *Odes of Solomon*, *Wisdom of Solomon*, Songs of Solomon, *Testament of Solomon*; on Solomon as sapiential pseudonym, see A. Alt, "Solomonic Wisdom," in *Studies in Ancient Israelite Wisdom* (ed. J. L. Crenshaw; New York: Ktav, 1976), 102–17; D. Dimant, "Pseudonymity in the Wisdom of Solomon," in *La Septuaginta en la investigacion contemporanea* (Madrid: Instituto Arias Montano, 1985), 243–55; R. E. Clements, "Solomon and the Origins of Wisdom in Israel," *Perspectives in Religious Studies* 15, no. 4 (1988): 23–36.

[64] Brueggemann, *Solomon*, 181.

[65] This aspect of Solomon's reputation played into Solomon's legendary authority over the demonic realm (see chap. 6).

[66] M. V. Fox, *Proverbs 1–9* (AB 18A; New York: Doubleday, 2000), 56–57.

"Lemuel" (31:1), were downplayed so to purport Solomon as the one and only sapiential author.

Concerning Qoheleth 1:1, Torijano argues that while there is no direct mention of Solomon, the combination of the titles "son of David" and "king in Jerusalem" together with the sapiential content of the text support the argument for a specific pseudepigraphical attribution.[67] He reasons that because in most cases these titles are set together, Solomon's name was probably implied. Therefore he insists that "the royal title and the 'Son of David' formula, which seem to have been naturally linked with Solomon, would be viewed then as referring to *the* king and *the* Son of David *par excellence*."[68] If one is convinced by Torijano's assessment of Qoheleth, it would also follow that the title's referent was so exclusively applied that even without explicitly naming Solomon, it was understood as a Solomonic referent.

But Torijano's argument does not answer the most obvious question: if the author meant to appeal to Solomon pseudepigraphically, what has been gained by the omission of his name? The argument could be made that the *raison d'être* of the pseudonym is that a name is employed. This is exactly what Qoheleth avoids! Perhaps a better solution is that "the Preacher" has cast himself as a type of Solomon. By all accounts, Solomon was considered to be the archetypal wise king.[69] With this in view, Qoheleth might have fancied himself as a Solomonic antitype. He has given himself "Solomon-like traits to make him a suitable figure for the examination of wealth and wisdom that the book reports."[70] As such, the Preacher is not meant to be Solomon in a pseudepigraphal sense; rather he is Solomonic in a typological sense. It is not necessary to see a hard and fast dichotomy between these two categories.[71] In this case, however, the Preacher seems to have chosen a literary device that looks more like typology than pseudonymity.

Finally, some comments are warranted on Psalm 72. While the title בן־דוד is not used in this psalm, it provides an interesting parallel in the first line: בן־מלך. The MT heading attributes this psalm לִשְׁלֹמֹה. Likewise, the Septuagint attributes this psalm εἰς Σαλωμων (LXX 71:1), but this heading is absent in the earliest manuscripts. Mowinckel concluded that the heading

---

[67] Torijano, 24.

[68] Torijano, 23 (emphasis in original).

[69] Or as J. Blenkinsopp puts it, Solomon was the "undisputed patron" of the sapiential tradition (*Sage, Priest, Prophet: Religious and Intellectual Leadership in Ancient Israel* [Louisville, Ky.: Westminster John Knox, 1995], 85).

[70] Fox, 56.

[71] Moreover, it is not clear that pseudepigraphy in the way that we know it through apocalyptic literature was well established at the time of Qoheleth. Thus it is not advisable to draw too hard a distinction between the two. My thanks to Loren Stuckenbruck for this point.

"is sure to belong to the latest additions to the psalm texts."[72] The editor has no doubt recognized the several points of reference to Solomon tradition in this psalm and assigned it to Solomon accordingly.[73] Not the least of these is the original first line's reference "to the son of the king [לבן־מלך]." This further confirms that later interpreters considered Solomon to be the son of the king and not just one among many. Among the many points of reference to Solomonic tradition are the gift of gold from Sheba in 72:10 and 15 (cf. 1 Kgs 10:10) and from Tarshish in 72:16 (cf. 1 Kgs 10:22).

That this psalm evidences the development of Solomon tradition is obvious. This is important to the present study in that Psalm 72 was likely not intended to be sung to a specific king, but repeated from king to king and "intended for an ideal type of king and appointed to be used continually."[74] In this way, Solomon tradition was used to honor subsequent kings of Israel as a way to embody their kingship with Solomonic traits.[75] We see here that the ideal king is one who typologically mimics Solomon's legacy. Gunkel said it best when he commented that this psalm does "not portray a particular king as such. Rather, the singers carry the ideal ruler in their heart which they place upon the rulers of their time like a wonderful majestic coat."[76] Seen in this way, this psalm was not so much an homage to Solomon as it was a passing on of Solomon's mantle. This is a key function of typology.

Fortuitously, the final verses of this psalm (72:18-19) seem to be a later addition that marks the conclusion of the section of "Psalms (Prayers [תפלה]) of David, son of Jesse." But this divisional note must have preceded the division of the Psalter into five books and is thus a very early notation.[77] We see again that Solomon tradition was understood to be an extension of David tradition. Indeed, the original opening line refers to both the king and his son: "Give the king your judgments, Oh God, and your righteousness to the son of the king." This line uses parallel imagery where "judgments" is associated with "righteousness" and "the king" is another way to say "son of the king." This parallel serves to cast the new king in the model of the established legacy.

Thus we witness in the redaction of Psalm 72 three steps along a Solomonic trajectory parallel to that of the Son of David tradition.

---

[72] S. Mowinckel, *The Psalms in Israel's Worship* (Grand Rapids: Eerdmans, 2004 [1962]), 102–3.
[73] J. L. Mays, *Psalms* (Louisville, Ky.: Westminster John Knox, 1994), 238.
[74] A. Weiser, *The Psalms: A Commentary* (trans. H. Hartwell; London: SCM Press, 1962 [1959]), 502.
[75] Contrast this with the simple appeal to the lineage of David in Ps 132:11-12.
[76] H. Gunkel, *An Introduction to the Psalms: The Genres of the Religious Lyric of Israel* (trans. J. Nogalksi; Macon, Ga.: Mercer University Press, 1998 [1933]), 112.
[77] Weiser, 504.

1. In the earliest form of the psalm, Solomon's legacy was used typologically to model the ideal kingship and, in this way, to honor new Solomon antitypes.
2. The postscript demonstrates that Solomon's legacy was understood to be an extension of David's legacy.
3. The heading shows that Solomon was ultimately known as the archetypal royal "son."[78]

Psalm 72 will be important in what follows as this tradition was refracted through the lenses of Isaiah 11 and *Psalm of Solomon* 17. To this we now turn.

Isaiah 11:1-9

I here break from my chronological analysis of the Son of David tradition and backtrack to Isaiah. Isaiah 11 is included at this point because this "Davidic" text proves especially pertinent to my discussion of *Psalm of Solomon* 17 in the following section. As such, the significance of this passage for the present study will not be fully appreciated until then. The passage reads:

> Then a shoot will spring from the stump of Jesse, and a branch from his roots will bear fruit [ויצא חטר מגזע ישי ונצר משרשיו יפרה]. And the Spirit of YHWH will rest on him, the spirit of wisdom and understanding, the spirit of counsel and strength, the spirit of knowledge and the fear of YHWH. And he will delight in the fear of YHWH. And he will not judge by what his eyes see, nor make a decision by what his ears hear; but with righteousness he will judge on behalf of the poor, and decide with fairness for the afflicted of the earth. And he will strike the earth with the rod of his mouth, and with the breath of his lips he will slay the wicked. Also righteousness will be the belt about his waist, and faithfulness the belt about his waist. Then the wolf will dwell with the lamb, and the leopard will lie down with the kid, and the calf and the young lion and the fatling together, and a little boy will lead them. Also the cow and the bear will graze; their young will lie down together, and the lion will eat straw like the ox. And the nursing child will play by the hole of the cobra, and the weaned child will put his hand on the viper's den. They will not hurt or destroy in all my Holy Mount, for the earth will be full of the knowledge of YHWH as the waters cover the sea. (Isa 11:1-9)

Isaiah 11 begins with a barrage of vegetation imagery. This should be seen as a continuation of the forest imagery in Isaiah 10.[79] Isaiah 10 ends with the

---

[78] It is also interesting to note that the targum of Psalm 72 attributes the psalm not to Solomon but to the Messiah. Cf. the "messianic" interpretation of the Davidic covenant in 2 Chr 6:42 where Solomon is likely in view, so Fitzmyer, "Son of David Tradition," 119.

[79] W. A. M. Beuken, *Jesaja 1-12* (Herders Theologischer Kommentar zum Alten Testament; Freiburg: Herder, 2002), 304.

image of a forest being clear-cut, representing YHWH's destruction.[80] Thus, amid this divine judgment, 11:1 portrays the remnant of righteous Israel (cf. 10:21) from which a divinely endorsed king will emerge. In addition, this vegetation metaphor might recall 2 Samuel 7 where (as seen above) David's "seed [זרע]" is promised.[81] This is one possible royal allusion among many in this passage.

The prophet reinforces the royal imagery by claiming that this figure will have divinely bestowed wisdom (11:2). Previously in 10:13, YHWH boasts of his victory over Assyria "by my wisdom" and "understanding." In 11:2 these attributes are transferred to the king by means of YHWH's spirit of wisdom and understanding.[82] Considering the affinity between the royal "seed" language of the Davidic covenant and this passage, it is not surprising to see a possible allusion to Solomon's divinely bestowed wisdom (1 Kgs 3:11; 3:28; 5:9). Wildberger commented that the spirit resting upon the king is a common notion (1 Sam 10:6, 10; 11:6; 16:13, 14; 19:9; 20:23), but this spirit is specifically called a "spirit of wisdom." He pointed to Solomon's request and divine endowment of wisdom as the "prime example" of divine wisdom granted so that the king is equipped to act as judge [שפט] over his people.[83] Solomon's wisdom is granted in relation to his installment as king over Israel.[84] Wildberger also observed that 1 Kings 3:9 provides the correct sense evoked by שפט in Isaiah 11:2, 4.[85]

Brueggemann comments that the king's duty to judge righteously on behalf of the poor (11:4) echoes the "crucial programmatic royal statement of Ps 72:1-2, 4."[86] The fact that Isaiah 11 describes the king in terms of "righteousness" (11:4, 5) is owed to Psalm 72:1-3 where righteousness is mentioned three times:

---

[80] Commentators are divided as to whether the forest represents the Assyrian army (e.g., B. S. Childs, *Isaiah* [Louisville, Ky.: Westminster John Knox, 2001], 97) or corrupt Israel (e.g., J. D. W. Watts, *Isaiah 1–33* [WBC 24; Waco, Tex.: Word, 1985], 163–64). What will prove important in what follows is that YHWH is understood as the "Divine Forester" (Watts' term). On this point there is no disagreement.

[81] This allusion is likely an explication of Isa 6:13, which equates the "stump [מצבה]" of righteous Israel with the "holy seed [זרע קדש]."

[82] "ונחה עליו רוח יהוה רוח חכמה ובינה."

[83] H. Wildberger, *Isaiah 1–12* (Minneapolis: Fortress, 1991 [1972]), 471–72; cf. Childs, *Isaiah*, 103.

[84] W. Hildebrandt, *An Old Testament Theology of the Spirit of God* (Peabody, Mass.: Hendrickson, 1995), 128–29.

[85] Wildberger, 472.

[86] W. Brueggemann, *Isaiah 1–39* (Louisville, Ky.: Westminster John Knox, 1998), 100; cf. Wildberger, 474.

> *A Psalm of Solomon.* Give the king your judgments, Oh God; and your righteousness to the king's son. May he judge your people with righteousness, and your afflicted with justice. Let the mountains bring peace to the people, and the hills in righteousness.

Isaiah's divine declaration, "They will not hurt or destroy in all my Holy Mount" (11:9) is likely borrowed from Psalm 72:3, "Let the mountains bring peace to the people."[87] Furthermore, the image presented in Isaiah 11:9, "for the earth will be full of the knowledge of YHWH as the waters cover the sea" echoes Psalm 72:8, "May he also rule from sea to sea." This might further support the Solomonic character of Isaiah 11 because Psalm 72, in both name and content, is a psalm "Of Solomon."[88]

It has been suggested that the combination of attributes assigned to this figure demonstrates that Isaiah expects a specific type of king[89] and is not simply describing the common expectation for all kings of Israel.[90] If this is so, Isaiah 11 has developed Solomonic tradition and applied it to a subsequent king. Much like Psalm 72, this passage has endowed its king with distinctly recognizable Solomonic characteristics. The prophet has here described his hope for a king to fulfill what was promised in 2 Samuel 7, who would model attributes first assigned to Solomon.

Isaiah 11:4 is perhaps the verse that most interests the present study as later tradition will allude to it in conjunction with Son of David: "And he will strike the earth with the rod of his mouth,[91] and with the breath of his lips[92] he will slay the wicked." This metaphor should be seen as an outworking of the previous endowment of wisdom.[93] The wise king is able to exert

---

[87] This has clearly been developed toward a cultic ideology (perhaps by a later redactor).

[88] We must also entertain the possibility that the psalmist borrowed from Isaiah 11. Perhaps the safest of all positions is to say that both texts have drawn from similar mnemonic spheres.

[89] M. Tate, "King and Messiah in Isaiah of Jerusalem," *RevExp* 65, no. 4 (1968): 409–21.

[90] J. N. Oswalt, *The Book of Isaiah: Chapters 1–39* (Grand Rapids: Eerdmans, 1986), 281.

[91] The LXX reads, "τῷ λόγῳ τοῦ στόματος." The insertion of "word" instead of "rod" perhaps demonstrates a trajectory of this tradition that has associated political power with the ability to speak forth the wisdom of God; cf. W. Horbury, *Jewish Messianism and the Cult of Christ* (London: SCM Press, 1998), 91. This is revisited below.

[92] Cf. Ps 33:6; 147:18; Jth 16:5; *2 Bar* 21:6.

[93] A brief word is warranted on the use of metaphors. The employment of violent metaphors does not necessarily suggest that the subject matter is violent. Consider the following statements: Gandhi fought British imperialism. Wilberforce *led the charge against* the slave trade. Knox *sparred with* Queen Mary. In each of these examples, the language of violence has been used to refer to a nonviolent historical event. Or, to place this discussion closer to our topic, consider the following statement: "No one can tame the tongue; it is a restless evil and full of deadly poison" (Jas 3:8). Here James develops a longstanding metaphor of Hebrew wisdom tradition which thought the tongue to be "deadly." Cf. "By forbearance a ruler may be persuaded, and a soft tongue breaks the bone" (Prov 25:15). This is a textbook example of a "metaphor by juxtaposition" (N. Frye, *The Great Code: The Bible and Literature* [New

power merely by the wisdom of his words.[94] The phrase "the breath [רוּחַ] of his lips" (11:4) demonstrates that his divinely given "spirit [רוּחַ] of wisdom" (11:2) is what will make him dominant. As such, the dual metaphor in 11:4 represents the application of the king's divinely given wisdom.[95] Compare also the imagery of Isaiah 9 where Israel will break "the rod of their oppressor" (9:4) due to the birth of a child who "will sit on the throne of David" (9:7). In this context, YHWH is angry with his enemies because "every mouth is speaking foolishness" (9:17). Isaiah 11's wise king is therefore set in antithesis to YHWH's foolish enemies described in Isaiah 9.[96] The power of wisdom is thus the central attribute of this king.[97] This is brought to a climax at the end of the oracle where the "the Earth will be full of the knowledge of YHWH" which brings about uncontested worship in the temple (11:9).

Commenting on Isaiah 11:4, Kaiser wrote that the attributes of understanding and wisdom "have in mind the judicial capacity of a king, which determines his activity in internal and foreign policy."[98] Kaiser points to 1 Kings 3:16-28 as a particularly memorable example of judicial wisdom: Solomon's most legendary judgment. Directly after YHWH endows Solomon with wisdom (1 Kgs 3:5-15), the author of 1 Kings demonstrates the outworking of this gift with a story about a dispute between two harlots over a baby. Each woman claiming that the child is her own, Solomon calls for a sword and commands that the baby be divided between the two. The true

---

York: Harcourt Brace Jovanovich Pardes Ilana, 1982], 57). Wisdom tradition believed the spoken word to hold real power, much like a weapon. Shrewd speech was a powerful weapon in diplomacy; it could "break bones." Truly, "death and life are in the power of the tongue" (Prov 18:21). Isa 11:4 should be seen along the lines of these metaphors. G. B. Gray (*The Book of Isaiah* [ICC; Edinburgh: T&T Clark, 1969], 217), wrote of Isaiah 11, "There is certainly no hint that the king will be a warrior: he reigns after war has been abolished" (cf. 9:4f). Wildberger, 478, similarly writes, "It is possible that for Isaiah the power-laden word of the Messiah is simply his administration of justice, which does not destroy the evildoer directly" . . . and more directly, "The Messiah is no battlefield hero. . . . The Messiah is a prince of peace" (483).

[94] Cf. Beuken, 312.

[95] P. D. Wegner, *An Examination of Kingship and Messianic Expectation in Isaiah 1–35* (Lewiston, Me.: Mellen Biblical Press, 1992), 255, observes that "strike with the rod of his mouth" is a phrase normally descriptive of YHWH (cf. 2 Sam 22:9; Ps 18:8; Mal 4:6).

[96] Beuken, 304.

[97] In the HB, there are examples of both priests and prophets who "slay by the words of my [YHWH's] mouth" (Hos 6:5; cf. Jer 18:18; Isa 49:2). But "similar expressions about the typical king are, of course, very difficult to discover. . . . The OT does not say [elsewhere] that the king strikes with his words" (Wildberger, 477). Therefore, while this metaphor is well-known to the wisdom and prophetic tradition, it cannot be assumed that it has been well worn as a common royal attribute. The fact that this metaphor has been applied to a royal figure further suggests that Isa 11 is describing a king who will be especially known for his wisdom.

[98] O. Kaiser, *Isaiah 1-12: A Commentary* (Philadelphia: Westminster, 1972), 158.

mother (the one who is prepared to relinquish the baby in order to spare its life) cries out for mercy upon hearing Solomon's command. Solomon then spares the child and discerns correctly which woman has told the truth.[99] Thus, the power of Solomon's words negated the need for his sword.

Isaiah 11 tells of a Davidic king who is given special wisdom by YHWH so that he can impart justice for the poor of Israel. Rather than wielding a literal weapon, this king imparts justice using only the words of his mouth. Isaiah 11:2-4 may well allude to this ironic juxtaposition between word and weapon. Indeed, according to 1 Kings 3:28, this story of judgment is what made Solomon renowned for divine wisdom.[100] In sum, the divinely given wisdom is used by the king to judge for his domestic poor, maintain dominant peace in foreign relations, and establish a secure context for the temple. Each of these traits echoes Solomon's legacy.

It is not crucial to my study to convince that Isaiah was specifically referring to Solomon. Given the quantity of echoes, this may well be the case, but it is enough simply to recognize that the king of Isaiah 11 has Solomonic traits. We must keep in mind the possibility that both Isaiah 11 and 1 Kings took initial shape around the seventh century BCE. It is possible that the monarchial narratives were influenced by similar ideals and characterized Solomon accordingly.

Psalm of Solomon 17

Written in the first century BCE, *Psalm of Solomon* 17 is an important text, as it develops longstanding Hebrew concepts along messianic lines within a Hellenistic context.[101] The following passage employs Son of David language against this backdrop:

From their ruler to the smallest of the people they [were] with every kind of sin: the king with the transgression of the law, and the judge with disobedience, and the people with sin. See, Lord, and raise up for them their king, the son of David [τὸν βασιλέα αὐτῶν υἱὸν Δαυιδ], to rule over Israel, your servant, in the time which you chose, O God, Undergird him with the strength to destroy the unrighteous rulers, to cleanse Jerusalem from gentiles who trample her to destruction; to drive out in wisdom and in righteousness the sinners from the inheritance [ἐν σοφίᾳ δικαιοσύνης ἐξῶσαι ἁμαρτωλοὺς ἀπὸ κληρονομίας]; to crash the arrogance of sinners like a potter's jar [ἐκτρῖψαι

---

[99] Psalm 72:4 reads: "May he vindicate the afflicted of the people, save the children of the needy, and crush the oppressor. Instead of "crush the oppressor [דכא עושק]" the LXX reads "humiliate the false accuser [ταπεινώσει συκοφάντην]." This in itself may be an allusion to Solomon's "saving" of the harlot's child.

[100] "When all Israel heard of the judgment which the king had handed down, they feared the king, for they saw that the wisdom of God was in him to administer justice" (3:28).

[101] I follow here the Greek version and numeration.

ὑπερηφανίαν ἁμαρτωλοῦ ὡς σκεύη κεραμέως]; to smash all their confidence with an iron rod [ἐν ῥάβδῳ διφηρᾷ συντρῖψαι πᾶσαν ὑπόστασιν αὐτῶν]; to destroy the lawless nations with the word of his mouth [ὀλεθεῦσαι ἔθνη παράνομα ἐν λόγῳ στόματος αὐτοῦ]. (17:20-24)

Psalm of Solomon 17 is specifically important to the present study in two ways. The first and most obvious is that it is the only occurrence of "Son of David" as a pre-Christian, messianic title. Together with chapter 18, it is widely considered the *locus classicus* for Davidic messianism of this period.[102]

The second is that this psalm provides an excellent example of how historical events near the turn of the Common Era were seen through mnemonic lenses and how they were interpreted and refracted thereby.

While it is often controversial to presume the historical value of Jesus' deeds, no scholar disputes the basic history of the relationship between the Hasmoneans, the Pharisees, and Pompey (or, if one prefers, Herod the Great[103]). As discussed in chapter 1, it is too often assumed that evidence of scriptural allusions and typologies in the portrayal of Jesus betray the interests of literary invention. For this reason, it serves my thesis to analyze a scripturally influenced text that reflects undisputed historical events.

Having already discussed the precedents for Son of David in the HB, it is clear that the titular form was always employed to evoke Solomonic tradition. Yet there are at least two distinct fountainheads (and therefore at

---

[102] E.g., A. S. van der Woude, *Die Messianischen Vorstellungen der Gemeinde von Qumrân* (Assen: Gorcum, 1957), 114. Most studies approach this text by surveying the text-critical issues related to the use of "messiah" (see discussion in M. de Jonge, "The Expectation of the Future in the *Psalms of Solomon*," in *Jewish Eschatology, Early Christian Christology and the Testaments of the Twelve Patriarchs: Collected Essays of Marinus de Jonge* [NTSup 63; Leiden: Brill, 1991]). I sidestep this discussion here as I am more concerned with the way "Son of David" has been employed. Suffice it to say that whether there are four mentions of messiah or less (there are omissions in the Syriac), there is enough evidence for one to assume that "Son of David" has been applied in terms of messianism in *Ps.Sol.* 17. Also, while it is interesting to note that the hand of a Christian scribe might have changed the original genitive to a nominative (i.e., "[the] Lord's Anointed" vs. "Lord Christ" in 17:32), this discussion is not ultimately crucial to my study. Both sides of the argument grant that the original was employed as a messianic category.

[103] Recently K. Atkinson, "On the Herodian Origin of Militant Davidic Messianism at Qumran: New Light from *Psalm of Solomon 17*," *JBL* 3 (1999): 435–60, has revived the argument that "the man not of our race" was Herod rather than Pompey. Even so, this thesis does not negate the likelihood that the Hasmoneans are the previously mentioned non-Davidic rulers under indictment. For earlier versions of this thesis, see O. Eissfelt, *The Old Testament: An Introduction* (trans. P. R. Ackroyd; Oxford: Blackwell, 1965), 612; A. Schalit, *König Herodes: Der Mann und sein Werk* (Studia Judaica 4; Berlin: de Gruyter, 1969), 463–64, 471; and Nolan, 155. Those who are somewhat sympathetic to a Herodian date include M. Aberbach, "The Historical Allusions of Chapters IV, XI, and XIII of the *Psalms of Solomon*," *JQR* 41 (1959): 379; M. Hengel, *Die Zeloten: Untersuchungen zur Jüdischen Freiheitsbewegung in der Zeit von Herodes I. bis 70 N. Chr.* (Leiden: Brill, 1961), 328.

least two sometimes overlapping mnemonic trajectories) from which this traditional trajectory flows: 2 Samuel 7 and 1 Kings 3–5. The author of *Psalm of Solomon* 17 has recognized both of these trajectories as they have been developed by Isaiah 11. The psalmist has localized contemporary historical events within this Isaianic framework and as a result has endowed contemporary religious/political figures with typological significance by following the lead of Isaiah.[104] I presently argue that this context best explains *Psalm of Solomon* 17's employment of Solomon's title: Son of David.

Psalm of Solomon 17 and Isaiah 11

The fact that this psalm has utilized Isaiah 11 is widely recognized. *Psalm of Solomon* 17:24 contains an unmistakable allusion to Isaiah 11 where the wise king defeats the wicked using only the "rod of his mouth" and the "breath of his lips" (cf. Isa 11:4). Scholarship has been quick to discuss the relationship between these texts in this regard, but what has received very little attention is the relationship between the nontitular vegetation metaphor in Isaiah 11:1 ("shoot/branch" [נצר/חטר]) and "Son of David" as it has been employed in *Psalm of Solomon* 17:24. The connection between the two is obviously Davidic, but because the psalmist has changed the vegetation metaphor of Isaiah 11 into a title formerly used only of Solomon, more analysis is required. I suggest here the possibility that the psalmist, having the benefit of hindsight, has recognized the Solomon-like traits of Isaiah 11 and has thus applied "Son of David" to this tradition.

Torijano has rightly described *Psalm of Solomon* 17–18 as an application of Solomonic tradition to first-century messianism. He argues:

> The future "Son of David" described in the Psalm is depicted according to the principal positive traits that characterized Solomon in 1 Kings. Besides, it echoes the canonical Psalm 72 (which is also entitled "Psalm of Solomon"), which may provide further support for an early ascription of the *Psalms of Solomon* to the wise king.[105]

Torijano correctly notices the Solomonic traits of this messiah, but his observation warrants more attention than he was able to dedicate due to the broad scope of his study. Torijano moves from this argument to explain the psalmist's interpretation of historical events via a rubric of Solomonic tradition. While his analysis is helpful, he has arrived at his position prematurely. Perhaps the facts that (1) Son of David is previously only a Solomonic title and (2) the

---

[104] That this is also an eschatological framework needs to be taken for granted at this point. This unique social framework (and how it factors into the mnemonic equation) is discussed below.

[105] Torijano, 107.

title appears in a collection titled the *Psalms of Solomon* are enough to convince that *Psalm of Solomon* 17 is a development of Solomonic tradition. But since this connection has escaped the eyes of the vast majority of *Psalms of Solomon* scholarship, more support is necessary. Moreover, Torijano neglects to demonstrate how the psalmist's interest in Isaiah applies to his treatment.

The following chart (p. 118) lists the conceptual parallels between Isaiah 11 (and context) and *Psalm of Solomon* 17–18. I have ordered these parallels in order of strength rather than textual sequence.

As demonstrated in this chart, the psalmist's interest in Isaiah 11 extends well beyond the most commonly pointed-out allusion (B).[106] The first three parallels (A, B, Γ) seem to have taken on concepts directly from Isaiah. Parallels Δ through Θ might not be convincing if considered in isolation, but the quality of the first three parallels alongside the quantity of the others leaves little doubt that all of the above are owed to the influence of Isaiah 11 and context.[107]

The A parallel represents so many conceptual commonalities (I have pointed out five) that one could almost consider it a paraphrase. Indeed the single point of dissimilarity is the mention of "righteousness" in 17:37, but even here can be seen thematic overlap (Γ). As shown by H, *Psalm of Solomon* 18:7 has recognized that the "breath of his lips" is a manifestation of the "spirit of wisdom" mentioned in Isaiah 11:2. Thus the psalmist has juxtaposed the "rod" with the "spirit of wisdom." Parallel Γ further demonstrates that the psalmist is acutely interested in wisdom. As he paraphrases Isaiah 11:4, he speaks of "the wisdom of his righteousness" rather than just "righteousness."

Several commentators recognize the echo of Psalm 72:2 in Γ. It is possible that the psalmist has drawn directly from Psalm 72.[108] It is also possible that Psalm 72 has been recognized via Isaiah 11 and thus incorporated into *Psalm of Solomon* 17:29. We saw previously that Isaiah 11 owes its interest in royal and judicial righteousness to Psalm 72:1-3 (or perhaps these traditions were mutually interpretive). In similar fashion, *Psalm of Solomon* 17 may owe its interest to righteousness to both texts. But given the several allusions and echoes of Isaiah, Isaiah 11 seems to be the controlling mnemonic paradigm. Moreover, the conceptual progression in *Psalm of Solomon* 17 more or less follows the causal relationships in Isaiah:

---

[106] Cf. J. Theisohn, *Der auserwählte Richter: Untersuchungen zum traditionsgeschichtlichtem Ort der Menschensohngestalt der Bilderreden des Äthiopischen Henoch* (SUNT; Göttingen: Vandenhoeck and Ruprecht, 1975), 232.

[107] It is therefore incorrect to suggest that the psalmist's use of Scripture was a product of casual association, contra S. Holm-Nielsen, *Die Psalmen Salomos* (JSHRZ 4.2; Gütersloh: Gütersloher Verlagshaus, 1977), 101.

[108] So M. De Jonge, "χρίω," *TDNT* IX (ed. G. Kittel; Grand Rapids: Eerdmans, 1965), 514; Holm-Nielsen, 100–10; Torijano, 107.

	Isaiah 11 and Context	***Psalm of Solomon* 17–18**
A	"And the Spirit[A] of YHWH will rest on him, the spirit of wisdom[B] and understanding,[C] the spirit of counsel[D] and strength,[E] the spirit of knowledge and the fear of YHWH." (11:2)	"God made him powerful in the Holy Spirit[A] and wise[B] in the counsel[D] of understanding,[C] with strength[E] and righteousness." (17:37)
B	With "the spirit of wisdom . . . he will strike the earth with the rod of his mouth." (11:2, 4)	He will "drive out in wisdom . . . with an iron rod to destroy the lawless nations with the word of his mouth" (17:23-24). Cf. "the rod of discipline of the Messiah of YHWH, in the fear of his God, in wisdom of spirit." (18:7)
Γ	"with righteousness he will judge on behalf of the poor." (11:4)	"He will judge peoples and nations in the wisdom of his righteousness." (17:29)
Δ	A child is born who will sit on "the throne of David" (9:7) and usher in an era of peace. (9:7; 11:6-10)	The usurpers of "the throne of David" (17:6) achieve it by violent means (17:5), but the Son of David will not rely on horse, rider, bow or army nor will finance war. (17:33)
E	The expected figure will be a royal "branch/shoot of Jesse." (11:1)	The expected messiah will be "the Son of David." (17:21)
Z	Nations will be vacated (11:13) or remain in subservience. (11:14)	The foreign nations will be disallowed in land (17:28) or remain in subservience. (17:30)
H	"Righteousness" is a common theme. (9:7; 10:22; 11:4, 5)	Righteousness is a common theme. (17:19, 23, 26, 29, 32, 37, 40; 18:7, 8)
Θ	There will be a return from exile. (11:11-16)	Although they presently "wander in the wilderness" as "exiles" (17:17-18), the children will be brought home by the nations as offerings (17:31); the tribes will be assembled. (17:44)

1. God acts decisively to end the conflict between Israel and her enemies (Isa 10:33-34 // *Ps.Sol.* 17:7-9, 12, 34).
2. The Davidic covenant is reestablished (Isa 11:1, 10 // *Ps.Sol.* 17:4, 10, 21).
3. The king's attributes are described (Isa 11:2-5 // *Ps.Sol.* 17:22-25, 36-43).
4. His reign will usher in an era of peace (Isa 9:7; 11:6-8 // *Ps.Sol.* 17:33-35).
5. Israel's enemies will be cast from the land or allowed to stay in subservience and worship (Isa 11:13-14 // *Ps.Sol.* 17:28, 30).
6. There will be a return from exile (Isa 11:10-12, 15-16 // *Ps.Sol.* 17:31, 44).
7. All of the above will establish a context for cultic purity (Isa 11:9 // *Ps.Sol.* 17:30-31, 43, 45).[109]

Isaiah 11's oracle devotes most of its attention to the attributes of the king (3; cf. A, B, Γ, H above) and the depiction of the peaceable kingdom (4; cf. Δ above). Predictably, the psalmist devotes considerable attention to developing these characteristics. For the psalmist, however, the peaceable kingdom is described mainly in terms of Israel's relationship with foreigners (point 5; cf. Z). This is discussed further below when I address the psalmist's concept of militancy.

There are, of course, many other passages in Isaiah that resemble the themes and motifs addressed here. Both Watts and Pao have argued extensively that Isaiah's "new exodus" paradigm was highly influential in first-century thought.[110] With this in mind, it is likely that the psalmist was familiar with this paradigm and has naturally depicted his eschatological cause-effect accordingly. In other words, from an Isaianic paradigm, it would be natural for a well-known Isaianic theme to evoke (call to memory) the teleological emphasis of Isaiah: YHWH as warrior, leads to new exodus, leads to proper foreign relations, and so on.

---

[109] Several commentators have argued that the Son of David in this psalm is expected to be responsible for cultic purity alongside his royal office. This topic is addressed in my discussion of Mark 12:35-37 in chap. 7.

[110] R. E. Watts, *Isaiah's New Exodus in Mark* (Grand Rapids: Baker Academic, 2000 [1997]); D. W. Pao, *Acts and the Isaianic New Exodus* (Grand Rapids: Baker Academic, 2002 [2000]); cf. the earlier work of M. J. Suggs, "Wisdom of Solomon 2:10–5: A Homily Based on the Fourth Servant Song," *JBL* (1957): 26–33. Closer to the present concerns, G. S. Oegema, *The Anointed and His People: Messianic Expectations from the Maccabees to Bar Kochba* (JSPSup; Sheffield: Sheffield Academic Press, 1998), 83–85 has argued for a similar use of Isaiah 11 in *SibOr* 3:767–808; Zimmermann, 71, has argued that 4Q161 shows an eschatological timeline that follows Isaiah 10:22–11:5.

I do not think that the psalmist was rigidly and systematically guided by the conceptual sequence of Isaiah 11. Rather, he has most likely consciously employed language from Isaiah 11, which, in turn, called to mind (consciously or subconsciously) the mnemonic lens associated with this language.

Observe that *Psalm of Solomon* 17's conscious allusions to Isaiah 11 focused primarily on his description of the Solomonic king (Α, Β, Γ, Δ). The psalmist's primary interest in Isaiah was for this description. Secondarily (perhaps subconsciously) the language from Isaiah 11 served as a mnemonic force of gravity that pulled the Isaianic framework into place. Once in place, the inclusion of other concepts and texts in *Psalm of Solomon* 17 must ultimately cohere with the Isaianic framework.

This will be seen more clearly in the psalmist's refraction of Psalm 2:9 and Deuteronomy 17:16-17 below. At this point, it is more important to observe that *Psalm of Solomon* 17 has localized Psalm 72 within an Isaianic framework and portrayed the coming royal figure in this light. The presence of Psalm 72 in the psalmist's memory is highly likely. There are multiple echoes (and at least one allusion) of Psalm 72 in *Psalm of Solomon* 17, but none with the pervasive strength of those concerning Isaiah 11. In this way, Isaiah provided the dominant mnemonic paradigm that evoked associations with other like passages.

This mnemonic lens is further confirmed by the fact that the psalmist introduces the Davidic covenant with the phrase "the throne of David." This phrase is used in relation to the Davidic covenant in 1 Kings 2:45, "But King Solomon shall be blessed, and the *throne of David* shall be established before YHWH forever" (emphasis added). This is seen through the mnemonic lens of Isaiah 9:6-7 as this text describes the royal son, the prince of *shalom* (emphasis added):

> For a child will be born to us, a son will be given to us. And the government will rest on his shoulders, and his name will be called wonderful counselor, mighty god, eternal father, prince of peace. There will be no end to the increase of his government or of peace. *On the throne of David* and over his kingdom, to establish it and to uphold it with justice and righteousness thereafter and forevermore.

That Isaiah 11:6-10 is a further development of this picture has already been established above. That this king will be known for his legacy of peace is central to Isaiah 11's portrait. We are now in the proper position to gauge the function of "Son of David" as it has been employed by *Psalm of Solomon* 17.

If it can be granted that *Psalm of Solomon* 17 was heavily influenced by Isaiah in both language and concept (and perhaps overarching theme), why has the psalmist not used the royal moniker supplied by Isaiah 11? If he was intent to recall the Davidic covenant in 17:4 and 10, why has the title "Son of

David" been substituted for the more common and contextually appropriate vegetation language?

The answer to this question builds from Torijano's recognition of Solomonic categories. First, Isaiah 11 has described the royal figure using distinctly Solomonic language; the prophet has alluded to or echoed 2 Samuel 7, 1 Kings 3 and/or Psalm 72 to depict his king in terms of Solomon's legacy. Second, *Psalm of Solomon* 17's royal figure has followed Isaiah 11 most closely where the royal characteristics are the most recognizably Solomonic. Third, *Psalm of Solomon* 17 seems to have followed Isaiah's lead thematically and within this framework has similarly borrowed from Psalm 72 and 1 Kings 2:45. Thus *Psalm of Solomon* 17 has made explicit what was implicit in Isaiah 11: Solomon typology.

The psalmist has recognized from Isaiah 11 affinities to Solomon tradition and applied the title "Son of David" to this royal figure, a phrase that is only used in a titular way of Solomon. Moreover, the application of the title is not that of mere precedent or generic Davidic hope. It is specifically typological because the psalmist hopes for a "Davidic" figure that embodies both the characteristics and legacy of Solomon. We may now add to this foundation Torijano's original observations that Son of David is specifically a title for Solomon in the HB and that it has been employed here in the climactic chapter of a text titled *Psalms of Solomon*. Torijano also argues that the psalmist has in mind an idealized Solomon who is "free from sin" (17:36). In other words, this Solomonic figure will possess all of Solomon's admirable qualities and none of his faults.[111] Therefore, much like the Chronicler, "Son of David" connotes a mnemonically refracted version of Solomon's legacy.

In sum, there are six reasons to believe that *Psalm of Solomon* 17:21 bears evidence of Solomon typology:

1. Elsewhere, the phrase is used as a title only when applied to Solomon.
2. The title is found in a text attributed to Solomon.
3. Isaiah 11 is likely Solomonic and has heavily influenced this psalm's characterization of the king.
4. Both Isaiah 11 and *Psalm of Solomon* 17 echo Psalm 72, which is Solomonic and is also called a psalm "Of Solomon."
5. The psalmist's appeal to the Davidic covenant uses language from 1 Kings 2:45.

---

[111] Torijano, 106–8. I argue below that the sinless state of the Son of David should be read in contrast with the sins of the non-Davidic rulers and the foreign oppressors previously mentioned in the psalm (17:5, 8, 23). But this interpretation is not necessarily mutually exclusive from Torijano's reading.

6. The Son of David in this psalm is portrayed primarily as a peaceful king, which recalls Solomon's legacy. Point 6 is addressed presently.

The Role of Militancy in Psalm of Solomon 17

It is often supposed that Jesus was misunderstood by his contemporaries because the idea of a nonmilitaristic messiah was unfamiliar to Jewish thought.[112] Collins has concluded that the expectation for a militant messiah was so prevalent in the thought-world of Jesus' contemporaries that the nonmilitaristic application of this title was confusing for them. His rationale is that since Jesus seems to have been nonviolent, "The idea that he was the messiah, son of David, must have seemed extremely paradoxical to most Jews of the time."[113] If we follow Collins on this point, we would be led to believe that "most Jews" were only familiar with militaristic royal messianism, yet Hurtado does well to qualify this notion since "it is not so clear how widely embraced such a hope was."[114] Indeed, while there is no doubt that many Jews did expect an eschatological warrior figure, evidence suggests the presence of alternative mnemonic categories closer to those employed around the career of Jesus.

De Jonge suggests that while the figure in *Psalm of Solomon* 17 is characterized in terms of militancy, the "awaited prince does not fight only with military and political weapons . . . *Ps.Sol.* 17:32-34 stresses the spiritual aspects of the reign of this king by God's grace."[115] De Jonge is right not to overemphasize the violent metaphors used by the psalmist. Similarly, the present

---

[112] E.g., D. R. Bauer, 767.

[113] J. J. Collins, *The Apocalyptic Imagination: An Introduction to the Jewish Matrix of Christianity* (New York: Crossroad, 1984), 278.

[114] L. W. Hurtado, "Christ," in *Dictionary of Jesus and the Gospels* (ed. J. Green and S. McKnight; Downers Grove, Ill.: InterVarsity, 1992), 107; cf. J. H. Charlesworth, "The Son of David: Solomon and Jesus (Mark 10.47)," in *The New Testament and Hellenistic Judaism* (Oxford: Arden, 1995), 73–74.

[115] "χρίω," 514n109. Others who support a nonmilitaristic reading of *Ps.Sol.* 17 include M. Hengel, *Victory over Violence: Jesus and the Revolutionists* (trans. D. Green; Philadelphia: Fortress, 1973 [1971]), 42–43; U. B. Müller, *Messias und Menschensohn in jüdischen Apokalypsen und in der Offenbarung des Johannes* (Studien zum Neuen Testament Band 6; Gütersloh: Gütersloher Verlagshaus, 1972), 119–20; J. H. Charlesworth, "The Concept of the Messiah in the Pseudepigrapha," *ANRW* 2.19.1 (1979): 198–99; L. T. Stuckenbruck, "Messianic Ideas in the Related Literature of Early Judaism: An Assessment and Prospects for Further Study," in *The Christ and Christs in the Old and New Testaments* (ed. S. E. Porter; Grand Rapids: Eerdmans, 2007). Both de Jonge and Stuckenbruck suggest this reading with some caution or qualification. Atkinson, "Herodian Origin," 444, misrepresents Charlesworth's position. Atkinson claims that Charlesworth argues for a nonviolent reading of both *Ps.Sol.* 17 and Tg. Ps.J. Gen 49:11. On the contrary, Charlesworth contrasts these two texts granting that the latter is indeed "bloody."

section aims to demonstrate that *Psalm of Solomon* 17 does not describe an eschatological warrior figure. Rather the Son of David described in this psalm achieves his rule over the Gentile nations through YHWH's violent intervention on his behalf. I do not intend to argue that the Son of David in this passage is a pacifist messiah. Rather, this figure is the beneficiary of YHWH's deliverance and placed in power to keep the peace on Israel's behalf. As will be seen in what follows, such "peace-keeping" is not the same as pacifism, but requires the defense of Israel and the temple. I argue that the psalmist has been heavily influenced by Isaiah 11 (and context) in this regard.

Crucial to my argument is the difference between typological exegesis and other kinds of eschatological interpretation. In what follows, I distinguish such interpretation by providing examples of how Isaiah 11 was utilized in the different texts circa first century.

Recently Atkinson argued that *Psalm of Solomon* 17 describes the expectation for a violent and militant Davidic messiah who will lead Israel in war against their foreign oppressors.[116] In support of his argument, Atkinson appeals to several texts in the Dead Sea Scrolls that seem to portray a militaristic Davidic figure. He claims that the depiction of a militaristic messiah figure "is not completely new since it builds upon the violent messianic descriptions found in Psalm 110, Isaiah 11 and other biblical texts."[117] This point is crucial to Atkinson's thesis because several of these texts allude to Isaiah 11.[118] Moreover, these allusions tend to center on Isaiah 11:4, which (as seen previously) describes a weapon emerging from the mouth of the Davidic figure. Atkinson surveys several texts (4Q161, 4Q285 f7, 4Q252, 4Q174, 1QM 1.5, 4Q246, and 1QSb 5), all of which, according to him, portray a militaristic Davidic figure. While Atkinson often mistakes political dominance for implicit military action, there are at least two explicit examples of eschatological militancy (1QSb 5 and 4Q285). Thus, his analysis is helpful with regard to these texts.[119] However, his study omits any treatment of *4 Ezra* 13:8-13, a text that also alludes to Isaiah 11:4's oral weaponry,[120] but does so in antithesis to the use of literal weaponry.

---

[116] K. Atkinson, *I Cried to the Lord: A Study of the Psalms of Solomon's Historical Background and Social Setting* (JSJSup 84; Leiden: Brill, 2004), 129–79; Atkinson, "Herodian Origin."

[117] Atkinson, *I Cried*, 151.

[118] That the Dead Sea Scrolls ever alludes to Psalm 110 is doubtful (contra J. Marcus, *The Way of the Lord: Christological Exegesis in the Gospel of Mark* [Louisville, Ky.: John Knox, 1992], 133). Even so, it should be said that Psalm 110 was interpreted in rabbinic thought as evidence that YHWH fights on behalf of the messiah while the messiah passively sits. Midr Ps 110 states, "The Holy One, blessed be He, declared, 'he will sit, and I will make war'" (parasha 4). Thus Psalm 110 need not be interpreted in terms of militant messianism.

[119] These are addressed in due course.

[120] Juel, *Messianic Exegesis*, 162.

> After this I looked, and behold, all who had gathered together against him [i.e., the "man"], to wage war with him, were much afraid, yet dared to fight. And behold, when he saw the onrush of the approaching multitude, he neither lifted his hand nor held a spear or any weapon of war; but I saw only how he sent forth from his mouth as it were a stream of fire, and from his lips a flaming breath, and from his tongue he shot forth a storm of sparks. All these were mingled together, the stream of fire and the flaming breath and the great storm, and fell on the onrushing multitude which was prepared to fight, and burned them all up, so that suddenly nothing was seen of the innumerable multitude but only the dust of ashes and the smell of smoke. When I saw it, I was amazed. After this I saw the same man come down from the mountain and call to him another multitude which was peaceable. Then many people came to him, some of whom were joyful and some sorrowful; some of them were bound, and some were bringing others as offerings.

While *4 Ezra* evidences several interesting characteristics of early messianism,[121] I focus here only on the use of Isaiah 11:4. From this context, the violent weaponry emerging from the mouth of this figure (in this case, "flames") are clearly not to be associated with literal weapons of war. The author explicitly states that the man will not lift a hand for warfare. In this way, the author has followed the significance of Isaiah's metaphor.

Stone has done well to compare this text with others where the words of YHWH have the power to kill. Texts like Wisdom 18:15 and Hosea 6:5 demonstrate this imagery. And closer to our present text, the messianic lion of *4 Ezra* 11:38–12:3 kills the Gentile eagle by way of his speech.[122] The metaphor of oral fire thus represents the concept of divine utterance, which is important in that it shows that the strength of this messiah is to be equated with his ability to speak the words of God.[123]

But given that we are explicitly told that this man wields a non-warlike power, what are we to do with the fact that he then uses this power to burn alive an onrushing army? It cannot mean that the man destroys the nations in conquest because the "other multitude" is a peaceable group composed

---

[121] See discussion in Stuckenbruck. I leave open the question of whether or not the "man" in this passage is actually a messianic figure. What is more important to this discussion is how the metaphor from Isa 11:4 has been understood by the author.

[122] M. E. Stone, *Fourth Ezra* (Hermeneia; Minneapolis: Fortress, 1990), 386–87.

[123] This particular text is complicated further by the possibility that this messiah is in some sense divine (so Müller), or at least bearing "angelic and superhuman traits" (so Horbury, *Jewish Messianism*, 86). But Horbury is careful to qualify this description by emphasizing that Israel's king was sometimes described as "the angel of God" (e.g., 2 Sam 14:17, 20). Noteworthy for my present concerns, David is called "angel of God" in connection with his ability to speak the wisdom of God.

of both Jews and Gentiles.[124] The difference between the onrushing multitude and the peaceable multitude is that the former is aggressively attacking. Therefore, while not a man of war, this figure will indeed destroy invading armies to protect Israel.[125] In other words, he is not a man of conquest, but a defender. Indeed, there is no need for conquest because all foreign nations who do not attack Israel will come of their own volition, submissive and bringing with them the exiled children of Israel. The author of *4 Ezra* 13 has followed Isaiah's depiction of a messiah who uses words rather than weapons to maintain political dominance. But *4 Ezra* emphasizes the caveat that this messiah will defend Israel against nations intent on the conquest of Israel.[126]

We witness a similar tension in *Psalm of Solomon* 17. While the psalmist clearly states that the Son of David will not rely on horse, bow, or army, there is a clear allusion to Psalm 2:9, "You shall break them with an iron rod; you shall shatter them like pottery." *Psalm of Solomon* 17:23-24 expects the Son of David to "rub out the arrogance [ὑπερηφανίαν] of sinners like a potter's jar; to shatter all their confidence [ὑπόστασιν[127]] with an iron rod." Yet the psalmist is even more reluctant to use militaristic language than was the author of *4 Ezra*. Instead of rubbing out the sinners, the Son of David rubs out the "arrogance" of the sinners. Instead of shattering the people, the Son of David shatters their "confidence." In this way, the psalmist's use of Psalm 2:9 should be seen as an extension of Isaiah 11:4. While both metaphors are violent images, the nonviolent significance of Isaiah's metaphor trumps that of Psalm 2:9. The psalmist is committed to an Isaianic paradigm in which the coming king is portrayed as a person of wisdom and peaceful domination. Psalm 2:9 has been seen through the lens of Isaiah 11 and has been refracted accordingly. Isaiah 11 is therefore the dominant mnemonic lens which has focused upon similar concepts but refracted them within its own telos.

In order to demonstrate this more clearly, it will be necessary to compare *Psalm of Solomon* 17's use of Isaiah 11 with another text that alludes to Isaiah

---

[124] That "some were bringing others as offerings" is a metaphor used by Isaiah to portray Gentiles carrying home the children of Israel to return them from exile (Isa 66:20). Cf. Müller, 117.

[125] In *4 Ezra* 12:32-33, the Davidic messiah (in the form of a lion) is depicted as a defender of Israel against Rome (obviously a nation that has invaded the borders of Israel). Cf. M. E. Stone, "The Concept of the Messiah in IV Ezra," in *Studies in the History of Religions* 14 (Leiden: Brill, 1968), 302.

[126] Müller (120) also points out that this figure possesses many theophanic characteristics that do not seem to stem from Isaiah 11; cf. Wegner, 255.

[127] Many translators incorrectly translate ὑπόστασις as "substance" in this context. In rare cases, the word does denote "being" as such (cf. Heb 1:3), but it is used most commonly to convey confidence, steadiness, or assurance. Given that the word is being paralleled with ὑπερηφανίαν, there is no reason to appeal to the lesser-used definition.

11 but is not controlled by its framework. 1QSb provides an excellent contrast as it appeals to Isaiah 11:4 but in a much different way. 1QSb 5:24–29 describes the "Prince of the Community [נשיא העדה]" (5:20),[128] borrowing the metaphor of verbal weaponry. The relevant portion of this text reads:[129]

וה]ייתה [...] בעז [פי]כה בשבטה תחריב ארץ וברות שפתיכה
תמית רשע יתן [לכה רשת עצ]ה ונגבורת עולם רות דאת ויראת אל והיה
צדק אזור [מותניכה ואמונ]ה אזור תלציכה [ו]ישם קרניכה ברזל
ופרסותיכה נתושה

תנכה כפ[ר ... ותרמוס עמ]ים כטיט תוצות כיא אל הקימכה לשבט
למושלים לפ]ניכה ... כול לא]ומים יעובדוכה ובשם קודשו יגברכה
והייתה כא[ריה ... חרב[130]]כה טרף ואין משי[ב] ופרשו [ק]ליכה על ...

May you be r[ighteous] by the strength of your [mouth,] lay waste the earth with your rod! With the breath of your lips may you kill the wicked![131] May He give [you a spirit of coun]sel and eternal might [rest upon you], the spirit of knowledge and the fear of God.[132] May righteousness be the belt [around your waist, and faithful]ness the belt around your loins.[133] May He make your horns iron and your hoofs bronze![134] May you gore like a bu[ll. May you trample the nati]ons like mud in the streets! For God has established you as the scepter[135] over the rulers; bef[ore you peoples shall bow down, and all nat]ions shall serve you. He shall make you mighty by His holy name, so that you shall be as a li[on among the beasts of the forest;] your [sword will devour] prey, with none to resc[ue.] Your [sw]ift steeds shall spread out upon [the earth].

---

[128] The idea that "Prince of the Community" was a Davidic title at Qumran seems to have won scholarly consensus, so Woude, 114–15; J. J. Collins, *The Scepter and the Star: The Messiahs of the Dead Sea Scrolls and Other Ancient Literature* (New York: Doubleday, 1995), 60–63; Oegema, 92–93; Zimmermann, 68, 94, and esp. 125.

[129] Unless otherwise noted, I follow the reconstruction of D. Parry and E. Tov, *The Dead Sea Scrolls Reader* (2 vols.; Leiden: Brill, 2004).

[130] The reconstruction of חרב is by no means certain. I here follow the reconstruction offered by both Parry and Tov and Michael Wise et al., *The Dead Sea Scrolls: A New Translation* (San Francisco: HarperSanFrancisco, 1996), 150, although it is not crucial to the present argument that this reconstruction is followed.

[131] Isa 11:4.

[132] Isa 11:2.

[133] Isa 11:5.

[134] Mic 4:13.

[135] שבט is here translated "scepter," but it should be noted that it is the same noun used for "rod" in 5.25; cf. Num 24:27; Gen 49:10.

At first glance, Isaiah 11 seems to be the controlling mnemonic paradigm that has also attracted other scriptural allusions. In this way, Atkinson has correctly recognized conceptual parallels between the texts.[136] However, his treatment confuses the concepts presented in both cases. At several points in his study, he claims that "Isaiah's verbal weaponry has been replaced with a literal instrument of execution."[137] On the contrary, the imagery in this text is no less metaphorical than the language of Isaiah. Just like Isaiah 11:4, the author of 1QSb 5:25 associates the weapon with "the strength of your [mouth]." This is confirmed by how the author follows the next metaphor for wisdom used by Isaiah: "With the breath of your lips may you kill the wicked." While the imagery is violent, the referent of the metaphor, like Isaiah, is still "the spirit of knowledge and the fear of God" (1QSb 5:25). The author of 1QSb has kept the violent metaphor (oral weaponry) and has even maintained the same referent (wisdom), but has changed the significance of the referent.

Isaiah's appeal to wisdom demonstrated that the king had no need for literal weaponry; the power of his words alone demanded deference. In contrast, the author of 1QSb appeals to wisdom as the ultimate strength behind his military prowess. Thus, Atkinson is correct in claiming that 1QSb depicts a militant messiah.[138] This is seen more vividly in 1QSb's distortion of Isaiah's other metaphors (like bulls goring and lions preying), which do indeed refer to violent content (i.e., warfare). 1QSb 5:27-29 records the violent metaphors of Isaiah 11:4 in an almost unaltered way while he subverts the peaceful metaphors of Isaiah 11:6-7:

---

[136] Cf. Zimmermann, 50, 58, 71, 94.

[137] Atkinson, *I Cried*, 142, 169–70, 173. He claims this of all the texts that employ Isaiah 11:4 including *Ps.Sol.* 17. Cf. J. J. Collins, "'He Shall Not Judge By What His Eyes See': Messianic Authority in the Dead Sea Scrolls," *DSD* 2 (1995): 154.

[138] I have presently challenged Atkinson's reasoning and not his conclusion with regard to 1QSb. This will become important in his treatment of *Ps.Sol.* 17 where Atkinson's (similar) reasoning has led to an incorrect conclusion.

	Isaiah 11	**1QSb**
A	righteousness will be the belt about his waist, And faithfulness the belt about his waist. (Isa 11:5)	May righteousness be the belt [around your waist, and faithful]ness the belt around your waist. (1QSb 5:26)
Ω	And the wolf will dwell with the lamb, and the leopard will lie down with the young goat, and the calf and the young lion and the fatling together; and a little boy will lead them. Also the cow and the bear will graze, their young will lie down together, and the lion will eat straw like the ox. (Isa 11:6-7)	May he (i.e., YHWH) make your horns iron and your hoofs bronze! May you gore like a bu[ll. May you trample the nati]ons like mud in the streets! . . . He shall make you mighty by His holy name, so that you shall be as a li[on among the beasts of the forest;] your [sword will devour] prey, with none to resc[ue.] Your [sw]ift steeds shall spread out upon [the earth]. (1QSb 5:27-29)

Up until the end of 1QSb 5:26, the author seems to have more or less followed the lead of Isaiah. I have emphasized this by showing in A that the author of 1QSb directly quotes Isaiah 11:5. However in Ω, 1QSb has transformed the Isaianic beast metaphor and has moved in the exact opposite direction from the telos provided by Isaiah. Instead of peaceful beasts, we see violent beasts. In Isaiah, the cow and the lion graze; in 1QSb, the bull gores[139] and the lion preys. Commenting on 1QSb 5, Wildberger writes,

> It is apparent that Isaiah's terminology has been used; however, in his imagery of the king, Isaiah has placed emphasis upon one who establishes righteousness (and along with that peace); in the above cited passage that emphasis is [. . .] abandoned in favor of concepts such as those found in Psalm 2 and other passages.[140]

The author of 1QSb seems to have utilized Isaiah 11 to support concepts to which he is previously committed. In this way, Isaiah 11 is not the dominant mnemonic lens; the author of 1QSb has seen Isaiah through the lens of militancy. Rather than following the lead of Isaiah 11, the author refracts the text to support his conception of a militant figure. This text seems to be along the

---

[139] It is difficult not to see here affinity with the bull of the animal apocalypse which was identified with the Davidic messiah by earlier generations of scholarship; so R. H. Charles, *The Book of Enoch or 1 Enoch* (Oxford: Clarendon, 1912), 215–16. This, however, has been recently challenged, e.g., in G. W. E. Nickelsburg, *George W. E. Nickelsburg in Perspective: An Ongoing Dialogue of Learning*, vol. 1 (Leiden: Brill, 2003), 69–70.

[140] Wildberger, 484.

same trajectory as 4Q285 f7,[141] which most likely portrays a violent "Branch of David" piercing his enemy to death.[142]

After refracting the metaphors of Isaiah, the author of 1QSb extols the size and efficiency of the figure's cavalry: "Your [sw]ift steeds shall spread out upon [the earth]" (5:29). Contrast this with *Psalm of Solomon* 17:33: "For he will not trust in horse and rider and bow, nor will he multiply his gold and silver for war. Nor will he gather hope in a multitude for a day of war." In this way, the psalmist appeals to the restrictions of the king's power in Deuteronomy 17:16-17. *Psalm of Solomom* 17:33 adds that the king should not collect horses "for war [εἰς πόλεμον]." The mention of war is an addition to Deuteronomy 17:16.[143] So, seen through this Isaianic lens, the quote of Deuteronomy 17:16-17 has been refracted toward the interpretation of a dominant but peaceful king and kingdom. Atkinson neglects to discuss how this passage might fit into his reading of *Psalm of Solomon* 17.

The ideal king hoped for by the psalmist is specifically not a warrior king. Instead, he is expected to rely on YHWH alone for his strength.

> The Lord himself is his king, the hope of the strong. Through the hope in God he will even show mercy to all the nations who stand before him in fear. For he will strike the earth with the word of his mouth forever; he will bless the Lord's people with wisdom and joy. (17:34-35)

Here, for a second time, Isaiah 11:4 is paraphrased; from this context, it is clear that Isaiah's metaphorical oral weaponry has been interpreted in contrast to literal weaponry. In other words, the power of the king's wisdom negates the need for literal weapons. Müller rightly understood the lack of earthly weapons to be a negation of the need for military might. Instead the figure relies upon divine intervention. According to Müller the lack of earthly weaponry demonstrates the messiah's faith, which relies on his "confidence in the power of God, God is his strength. The power which is based on weapons for

---

[141] Zimmermann, *Messianische Texte*, 68.

[142] I read the controversial verb והמיתו as a hiphil third-person singular verb with a third-person masculine singular suffix as argued by G. Vermes, "The Oxford Forum for Qumran Research Seminar on the War Rule from Cave 4 (4Q285)," *JJS* 43 (1992): 85–94. In support of Vermes, see, e.g., Zimmermann, 84–86; Pomykala, 207–9; For a fuller discussion of this topic see M. Bockmuehl, "A 'Slain Messiah' in 4Q Serekh Milhamah (4Q245)?" *TynBul* 43 (1992): 155–69.

[143] It is possible that the psalmist is not responsible for this addition. Cf. a similar addition in the Temple Scroll 56:15-18; D. Rosen and A. Salvesen, "A Note on the Qumran Temple Scroll 56:15-18 and *Psalm of Solomon* 17:33," *JJS* 38 (1987): 99–101. Even so, it is clear that the psalmist has utilized the Deuteronomy passage to depict the Son of David as a nonmilitaristic figure as he omits the other prohibitions between Deuteronomy 17:16a and 17c that are not relevant to the issues of warfare.

war is substituted by the power which consists of the fact that God strengthens the messiah."[144] Müller concludes that the victory over foreign powers will come not from military might or strategy but from the hand of God.[145]

Isaiah is helpful to the notion of a militant messiah insofar as it depicts a Davidic figure ruling over the foreign nations who have submitted out of fear of the Lord and his Anointed.[146] It is important to realize that, in general, the expectations of the messianic age included liberation from oppression of the enemies of God. Within this broad expectation were varieties of portraits of how this liberation would come about. Some portraits portrayed a messianic figure as the central liberator. In these cases, the language of messianic militancy is more common. In other cases, God himself is Israel's liberator, and the messianic figure takes on the role of peacetime governor or purifier. Isaiah 11 better fits this second portrait. *Psalm of Solomon* 17 has followed in similar fashion.

But this is where the author of 1QSb and the psalmist part ways: the two authors have chosen to reinforce the Isaiah paradigm with similar metaphors but with opposite conceptual aims. The psalmist has followed the lead of Isaiah in depicting a dominant but peaceful king who relies on God's intervention in matters of warfare. The author of 1QSb expects that this royal figure will be YHWH's agent for militancy. It is therefore incorrect to claim that 1QSb and *Psalm of Solomon* 17 have interpreted Isaiah 11 toward a common end.[147]

The difference between *Psalm of Solomon* 17 and 1QSb provides an excellent example of how mnemonic lenses function and have the capacity to refract. As is common to eschatologically minded texts of this period, the authors have drawn from a variety of different scriptural passages to support their portrait of YHWH's unfolding plan. However, it is crucially important to recognize that not every allusion to Scripture functions in the same way. In some cases, a passage can function as the controlling mnemonic paradigm by which other concepts are localized and given meaning within a particular framework. In other cases, a passage can be localized within an already existing framework and thus receives its significance insofar as it coheres to the dominant paradigm. As discussed in the previous chapter, both the dominant framework and the new concept are altered in this process, but the domi-

---

[144] Translated from Müller, 119–20.

[145] Müller, 170.

[146] There can be no dispute that YHWH's eschatological war does not include the universal extermination of the Gentiles. Those who do fear God will coexist with Israel in submission to the king. Zimmermann, 58, has rightly pointed to Genesis 27:29 (alluded to by 1QSb) and Isa 60:12 as the conceptual background for this.

[147] Contra Atkinson, *I Cried*, 129–79, and Zimmermann, 58.

nant mnemonic paradigm tends to remain more stable while the concepts imported into it tend to be altered to a greater extent. More often than not, when two Scriptures are set together, one will have the dominant influence.

In keeping with our central metaphor, dominant texts serve as lenses, and recessive texts refract within the convex of such lenses. Now, because the mnemonic process is circular, "recessive" texts also have refractive influence, but to a lesser extent. For the author of 1QSb, Isaiah was recessive, malleable, an object to be refracted. For the psalmist, Isaiah 11 was the dominant lens, instructive and refractive.

In *Psalm of Solomon* 17, Isaiah seems to function as the dominant and controlling paradigm: Isaiah's figure ushers in an era of peaceful postwar coexistence with God-fearing Gentiles, so the psalmist's eschatological community should expect a similar type of redemption. In contrast, 1QSb has imported Isaiah 11 into a paradigm to which he is previously committed: as learned from other Scriptures, God's plan requires a militant redeemer figure. So Isaiah must contribute to this notion. Therefore the psalmist has tended to refract his eschatological concepts to fit the mold of Isaiah, while 1QSb has conformed Isaiah to fit the mold of his eschatology.[148] In the former text, the hope for a Son of David is seen through the mnemonic lens provided by Isaiah 11. In the latter, Isaiah 11 has been seen through the lens of eschatological hope for a militant Davidic figure. In sum, Isaiah 11 looks to be the controlling mnemonic paradigm of *Psalm of Solomon* 17 but only a contributing concept for the author of 1QSb.

From this vantage point, it is possible to suggest a distinction between typological exegesis and the eschatological exegesis employed by the author of 1QSb. Typological exegesis tends to cast eschatological categories into larger scriptural frameworks; archetypal figures of the past are transposed along with their ancient contexts (and significance) onto events of the present and near future. On the other hand, the author of 1QSb tended to reinterpret passages from Scripture according to the needs of eschatology. Of course, one would be ill advised to draw this distinction too firmly,[149] but we can say that typological exegesis is interested in the relation of the similarity of paradigms past and present[150] rather than the "free association of biblical texts."[151]

The psalmist's appeal to the Son of David does not simply recall a single aspect of the archetypal royal figure, he appeals to the entire mnemonic

---

[148] Cf. Woude, 123.

[149] C. A. Evans, "Typology and First-Century Exegesis," in *Dictionary of Jesus and the Gospels* (ed. J. Green and S. McKnight; Downers Grove, Ill.: InterVarsity, 1992), 862.

[150] L. Goppelt, *Typos: The Typological Interpretation of the Old Testament in the New* (trans. D. H. Madvig; Grand Rapids: Eerdmans, 1982 [1964]), 199–202.

[151] Translated from Müller, 110.

framework of the figure as provided by Isaiah 11. Since this figure was portrayed as David's heir, with divinely bestowed wisdom, as a wise judge, as a bringer of *shalom*, the psalmist imprints these characteristics upon his eschatological hope. That all of these characteristics recall Solomon's legacy is not lost on the psalmist, and he therefore favors the title applied only to Solomon: Son of David.

History and Typology in Psalm of Solomon 17

I have intentionally avoided discussion of the historical context of *Psalm of Solomon* 17 until this point. In order to demonstrate how a religious-political text can project a typological interpretation upon contemporary historical events, I have first attempted to set the literary and ideological mnemonic lenses in place. Having done so, I hope to demonstrate that this psalmist has interpreted historical events and relationships by seeing them through the lens of Isaianic eschatology.

De Jonge has insightfully commented that the *Psalms of Solomon* "do not describe historical events, but reflect them."[152] Indeed, one could make a similar argument for all works of history, even those that aim to be more descriptive. His point is well taken, however. The author of *Psalm of Solomon* 17 intends to stand along the tradition of the Psalter (even if he has broadened this genre to a certain extent). As such, the interpretation of historical events in *Psalm of Solomon* 17 "reflects" history through the distorted mirror of scriptural paradigms and eschatological worldview.

Our historical backdrop begins with the Hasmoneans and their claim to Israel's monarchy.[153] After his twenty-seven-year reign, Alexander Jannaeus left the throne to his wife Salome Alexandra. In contrast to her husband, Salome took a great interest in the proper execution of Jewish law and, by doing so, endeared herself to the people. Josephus described Jannaeus as a bloodthirsty ruler who mistreated and killed his own people (cf. Sota 47a).[154] Salome, wanting to distance herself from her husband's reputation, showed great interest in the "proper" interpretation of Jewish law. Guided by her interest in piety, she elevated the Pharisees to the role of religious and political counselors. According to Josephus, the Pharisees enjoyed enormous political influence during this time (cf. *b. Ta'an* 23a).[155] Salome gave them authority to administrate public affairs and to jail, banish, or execute whomever they

---

[152] *Outside the Old Testament* (Cambridge: Cambridge University Press, 1985), 160.

[153] Rather than recounting the history from Judas to Simon, we pick up the story from *JW* 1.5-9.

[154] F. F. Bruce, *New Testament History* (Garden City, N.Y.: Doubleday, 1971 [1969]), 76.

[155] E. Schürer, *The History of the Jewish People in the Age of Jesus Christ* (175 B.C.–A.D. 135), 3 vols. (ed. G. Vermes et al.; Edinburgh: T&T Clark, 1973–1987), 1:231–32.

pleased. She was content to allow the Pharisees to handle domestic government while she handled foreign concerns. Ultimately, while her reign was remembered as a time of prosperity in Israel, she became less and less autonomous. Josephus says that "while she ruled others, the Pharisees ruled her."[156]

She established her son Hyrcanus II as high priest and had intended for him also to take the throne in her wake, but this never happened. Her death in 67 BCE spurred a power struggle between Hyrcanus II, Salome's younger son Aristobulus II, and Herod Antipater. Pompey entered the picture in 63 BCE and, by taking advantage of this instability, took over Jerusalem. Hyrcanus II eventually returned as high priest under Roman rule via Herod Antipater. Meanwhile, the Pharisees fell from influence and never enjoyed so much power again. We learn from *Psalm of Solomon* 17 that they were violently removed (17:4-6) and chased from the city (17:16-19). The first of these passages is very telling of the overall concerns of the psalmist and reflects the key problems of his historical context:

> Lord, you chose David as the king over Israel, and you swore to him regarding his descendants forever so that his kingdom would not fail before you. But because of our sins [ἁμαρτίαις], sinners [ἁμαρτωλοί] rose up against us, they attacked us [ἀπέθεντο ἡμῖν] and expelled us [ἔξωσαν ἡμᾶς]. Those to whom you did not promise robbed us by force [βίας ἀφείλαντο] and did not glorify your glorious name. With glory they set up a monarchy for the sake of their haughtiness; they made desolate [ἠρήμωσαν] the throne of David as a price of arrogance.

Psalm of Solomon 17:4 sets the stage from an eschatological perspective, recalling the Davidic covenant and projecting this forward to the resolution of Israel's plight (cf. 17:21f.).

In what follows, the psalmist explains the reason that the eschatological kingdom has been delayed; it was "due to our sins." The wordplay between ἁμαρτίαις and ἁμαρτολοί is important in that it speaks to the type of sin being described. The sinners are those who "rise up and attack" and "expel," who "rob by force" and make "desolate." Thus, Schüpphaus rightly equated the sin mentioned in 17:5 with the violent sins of the Romans.[157]

This violent description of the "sinners" is due to the similar sins of domestic Israel. It is an apt interpretation of the historical context described above: the domestic battles between Hyrcanus II and Aristobulus II left the outward defenses considerably weaker than they were under Salome. As a direct result,

---

[156] *JW* 1.110.
[157] J. Schüpphaus, *Die Psalmen Salomos: Ein Zeugnis Jerusalemer Theologie und Frömmigkeit in der Mitte des vorchristlichen Jahrhunderts* (Leiden: Brill, 1977), 140.

Pompey was given opportunity to move in and besiege Jerusalem.[158] Violence from within invited violence from the outside.

The psalmist's interpretation of YHWH's hand in these events is due to his dominant mnemonic lens: basic to the worldview of ancient Israel was the notion that nationally committed sin invited divine retribution on a national level. Isaiah's voice on this subject (as discussed previously) was no small factor. From this mnemonic lens the psalmist naturally associated Pompey's violent removal of Israel's corrupt leadership with the way that YHWH typically works (cf. Isa. 10:33-34).

YHWH would eventually act as "Savior" (*Ps.Sol.* 17:3), but this is always accomplished by divine intervention. Within an Isaianic framework, Israel is never saved by rising up against her oppressors; YHWH always acts as divine warrior on Israel's behalf. Violent uprising on the part of Israel was not an option because foreign oppressors always represented YHWH's punishment until they were removed from power (either by another foreign power or by YHWH himself[159]). The psalmist thus interprets Pompey's actions as YHWH's divine punishment of the civil war between Salome's two sons. This lens also colored the psalmist's interpretation of Pompey's ultimate demise in *Psalm of Solomon* 2:26-27.

> And I did not wait long until God showed me his arrogance pierced on the mountains of Egypt, more set at naught than the smallest thing on earth and sea. His body was carried about on the waves in much disgrace and there was no one to bury it, for God had disdained him with contempt.[160]

Pompey, who had arrogantly entered the Holy of Holies fifteen years prior, fled to Egypt only to be assassinated upon his arrival. Here the psalmist interprets his death as divine retribution. Clearly, the psalmist did not think that the messianic Son of David played a part in this vindication. As always, from an Isaianic perspective, YHWH himself exacted his own vengeance. Pompey was simply a tool used by YHWH to correct Israel. After the tool had been used, YHWH discarded it. In this case, it was through the instrument of another Gentile power. This is another repeated feature in Isaiah.

Once YHWH had acted as divine warrior, his king would rise up from the remnant of Israel to protect the peace and act as domestic judge. This is the

---

[158] Müller, 76; Pomykala, 159–60; G. W. E. Nickelsburg, *Jewish Literature between the Bible and the Mishnah: A Historical and Literary Introduction* (Philadelphia: Fortress, 1981), 203–4; C. Bennema, "The Sword of the Messiah and the Concept of Liberation in the Fourth Gospel," *Biblica* 86 (2005): 38.

[159] These categories are given to overlap (cf. Isa 13:4, 17).

[160] Jonge, *Outside*, 160–61.

mnemonic frame provided by Isaiah 11. Childs' comments on Isaiah 11:2 are especially pertinent:

> Solomon, as a type of the wise king (1 Kings 3:9), is given wisdom in order to govern rightly, distinguishing good from evil. Counsel is the capacity needed for sagacious diplomacy among the peoples, and is joined with the required power needed to achieve a goal. In contrast to Assyria's ruthless exercise of brute force, this counsel controls [the use of power] for establishing order and welfare of those governed.[161]

This, the central conveyed historical interest of Isaiah 11, provided a standard by which the Pharisees could measure their own historical context. The overt appeal to Isaiah 11:4 in *Psalm of Solomon* 17:23-24 shows that the true king will govern with wisdom rather than militancy.[162]

> For he will strike the earth with the word of his mouth forever; he will bless the Lord's people with wisdom and joy. And he himself will be free from sin [ἁμαρτίας], in order to rule a great people, to put to shame officials and to win sinners [ἁμαρτωλοὺς] by the strength of the word. (17:35-36)

Instead of mirroring the violent sins of the sinners (like Salome's sons), the Solomonic king is contrasted with the sinners. His only weapon is the wisdom of his word; thus, he is without sin. He will not rely on horse, bow, or army because YHWH will be warrior on his behalf (*Ps.Sol.* 17:33-34). Unlike the civil war between Salome's sons and the ensuing siege by Pompey, the Solomonic king was expected to usher in an era of *shalom* (Isa 11:6-8).

From this perspective one wonders whether the Pharisees, as political advisors, publicly promoted the image of Alexandra as a Solomon antitype. This might explain her official title and legacy: "Salome, the Peace of Zion."[163]

What can be said with some certainty is that the Pharisees had for nine years with Salome (from their perspective) the ideal interim state until YHWH's messiah came.[164] They were able to decisively enact domestic justice and purity for Israel as they saw fit. And, in the meanwhile, they lived like

---

[161] B. S. Childs, 103.

[162] Wildberger, 461, observed that the MT's rendering of Isaiah 11:4, "strike the earth [אֶרֶץ] with the rod of his mouth," seems to interrupt the flow of thought. He argued, "The almost universally accepted emendation עָרִ(י)ץ 'violent ones,' very likely reflects the correct reading." While this reconstruction would be advantageous to the present study, it is unlikely. First, the present translation of *Ps.Sol.* follows the LXX of Isaiah: γῆν. Second, 1QSb, quoting Isaiah 11:4, supports the Hebrew: אֶרֶץ.

[163] See discussion in Bruce, *New Testament History*, 6, 76–77.

[164] The Hasmoneans obtained their leadership on a "temporary" basis; that is to say, "until a true prophet should arise" (1 Macc 14:41).

royalty. When they were ousted by Salome's sons (probably Aristobulus[165]), they viewed it as an Isaianic-type exile. They were the righteous remnant waiting for YHWH to cut down Israel's corrupt leadership and finally establish an era of *shalom*, such as they had under Salome. But when the time came, the true Solomonic antitype would establish an eternal golden age of *shalom*, secure the temple from invaders, and govern the people with wisdom. In this way, the Messiah would be the antithesis to the present political-religious leadership in Israel.

As the present book moves forward to discuss the mnemonic lenses and typological interpretations of the historical Jesus, it will be beneficial to keep in mind that the Pharisees were close ideological cousins with Jesus' first followers and among Jesus' first perceivers. As such, the initial perceptions and memories of Jesus would be closely related to the mnemonic lenses betrayed by this psalmist.[166]

In my discussion on *Psalm of Solomon* 17, I have aimed to demonstrate that one should expect among Jesus' contemporaries that the application of scriptural paradigms and typologies was an integral aspect of historical interpretation. These worked as mnemonic lenses that were commonly employed on the subconscious level of worldview. Because of this, overt and intentional (i.e., conscious) appeals to scriptural and archetypal categories seemed intuitive and, indeed, necessary to interpret properly the significance of historical memories. History is often seen through the lens of typology. The history of Jesus is no exception.

---

[165] Josephus writes that the enemies of the Pharisees sought protection from Aristobulus during Salome's reign (*JW* 1.114).

[166] Also, it is no coincidence that Matthew is the lone evangelist with special interest in Son of David typology, while at the same time intent on antagonizing the Pharisees. This is discussed in more detail in chaps. 7 and 8.

6

The Therapeutic Son of David

In 1963 Ferdinand Hahn began his chapter on the title "Son of David" by observing, "There is no comprehensive recent study of the 'Son of David' tradition." This comment was still relevant in 1969 when the English translation of Hahn's work was published.[1] Christoph Burger attempted to fill this lacuna in 1970. Burger's *Jesus als Davidssohn* [*Jesus as Son of David*] represented the most comprehensive study to date on the title "Son of David."[2] Burger's work touched a wide range of relevant biblical and extracanonical texts and discussed the christological as well as the historical implications of his analysis. This book was never translated into English, making Hahn's statement relevant even today for the English-speaking world. This fact weighed heavily upon my decision to make Son of David a test case for my historiographical thesis.

Burger's book might have become the standard treatment of this topic had it not been for a blind spot in his research. It was unfortunate that Burger's study was unaware of a short essay by Loren Fisher.[3] What must have seemed a small oversight in 1970 rendered Burger's work all but outmoded only a decade later.

Fisher's essay very modestly suggested that Son of David might have been initially applied to Jesus in response to his reputation as a Solomon-type exorcist.[4] Burger's treatment was oblivious to this possibility and, as a result,

---

[1] *The Titles of Jesus in Christology: Their History in Early Christianity* (trans. H. Knight and G. Ogg; London: Lutterworth, 1969 [1963]), 240.

[2] C. Burger, *Jesus als Davidssohn: Eine traditionsgeschichtliche Untersuch* (FRLANT 98; Göttingen: Vanderhoeck and Ruprecht, 1970).

[3] L. R. Fisher, "Can This Be the Son of David?" in *Jesus and the Historian, Ernest Cadman Colwell Festschrift* (Philadelphia: Westminster, 1968), 82–97.

[4] While ultimately influential, Fisher's work was limited in two ways: (1) Fisher's treatment utilized Montgomery's publication of the Aramaic texts and Yamauchi's incantation bowl inscriptions that appealed to the authority of "King Solomon, Son of David [מלכא דויד בר דשלמוה / דשלימון]" (J. A. Montgomery, *Aramaic Incantation Texts from Nippur* (Philadelphia: University of Pennsylvania Museum Publications, 1913]; E. M. Yamauchi,

was unable to anticipate subsequent research about the ways that demonology, exorcism, and healing had been incorporated into the Jewish thought-world.[5] Burger was under the impression that healing and exorcism were

---

"Aramaic Magic Bowls," *JAOS* 85, no. 4 [1965]: 551–23. While important as corroborating evidence for later scholarship, his seminal study cautiously pointed to evidence that postdated the NT by five hundred years (Fisher, 84–85); as such, his results remained tentative. (2) He did not recognize the likelihood that "Son of David," as it was applied to exorcism in Matt 12:33, was a product of Matthean redaction (92–93). Even so, Fisher sufficiently demonstrated that exorcistic activity was well at home in certain segments of Judaism and was linked to Solomonic tradition. His unique insight set the stage for the more detailed work of D. C. Duling, "The Promises to David and Their Entrance into Christianity—Nailing Down a Likely Hypothesis," *NTS* 20 (1974): 55–77; E. Lövestam, "Jésus Fils de David chez les Synoptiques," *Studia Theologica* 28 (1974 [1972]): 97–109; and K. Berger, "Die Königlichen Messiastraditionen des Neuen Testaments," *NTS* 20 (1984): 1–44.

[5] E.g., V. K. Robbins, "The Healing of Blind Bartimaeus (10:46-52) in the Marcan Theology," *JBL* 92 (1973): 224–43; D. C. Duling, "The Therapeutic Son of David: An Element in Matthew's Christological Apologetic," *NTS* 24 (1977–1978): 392–410; D. C. Duling, "The Eleazar Miracle and Solomon's Magical Wisdom in Flavius Josephus' *Antiquitates Judaicae* 8.42-49," *HTR* 78 (1985): 1–25; D.C. Duling, "Matthew's Plurisignificant 'Son of David' in Social Science Perspective: Kinship, Kingship, Magic and Miracle," *BTB* 22 (1992): 99–116; E. R. Dodds, *The Ancient Concept of Progress and Other Essays in Greek Literature and Belief* (Oxford: Clarendon, 1973), 156–210; K. Grayston, "Exorcism in the NT," *Epworth Review* 2 (1975): 90–94; B. D. Chilton, "Exorcism and History: Mark 1:21-28," in *Gospel Perspectives* 6 (Sheffield: JSOT, 1976), 253–71; M. Smith, *Jesus the Magician: Charlatan or Son of God?* (San Francisco: Harper and Row, 1978); D. E. Aune, "Magic in Early Christianity," *ANRW* 2.23.2 (1980): 1507–57; W. R. G. Loader, "Son of David, Blindness, Possession, and Duality in Matthew," *CBQ* 44 (1982): 570–85; E. M. Yamauchi, "Magic or Miracle? Diseases, Demons and Exorcisms," in *Gospel Perspectives 6: The Miracles of Jesus* (ed. D. Wenham and C. Blomberg; Sheffield: JSOT, 1986); E. M. Schuller, *Non-Canonical Psalms from Qumran: A Pseudepigraphic Collection* (Atlanta: Scholars Press, 1987); P. Hollenbach, "Jesus, Demoniacs, and Public Authorities: A Socio-Historical Study," *JAAR* 49 (1988): 567–88; S. R. Garrett, *The Demise of the Devil: Magic and the Demoniac in Luke's Writings* (Minneapolis: Fortress, 1989); P. Saachi, *Jewish Apocalyptic and Its History* (trans. W. J. Short; Sheffield: Sheffield Academic Press, 1990), chap. 12; M. J. Davidson, *Angels at Qumran: A Comparative Study of 1 Enoch 1-36, 72-108 and Sectarian Writings from Qumran* (Sheffield: Sheffield Academic Press, 1992); C. L. Hogan, *Healing in the Second Temple Period* (NTOA 21; Göttingen: Vandenhoeck and Ruprecht, 1992); G. H. Twelftree, *Jesus the Exorcist: A Contribution to the Study of the Historical Jesus* (Peabody, Mass.: Hendrickson, 1993); G. H. Twelftree, *Jesus the Miracle Worker: A Historical and Theological Study* (Downers Grove, Ill.: InterVarsity, 1999); G. Stanton, "Jesus of Nazareth: A Magician and False Prophet Who Deceived God's People?" in *Jesus of Nazareth Lord and Christ: Essays on the Historical Jesus* (ed. J. Green and M. Turner; Grand Rapids: Eerdmans, 1994), 164–80; A. Jeffers, *Magic and Divination in Ancient Palestine and Syria* (Leiden: Brill, 1996); J. Frey, "Different Patterns of Dualistic Thought in the Qumran Library: Reflections of Their Background and History," in *Legal Texts and Legal Issues: Proceedings of the Second Meeting of the International Organization for Qumran Studies, Cambridge 1995, Published in Honour of Joseph M. Baumgarten* (ed. M. Bernstein, et al.; STDJ 23; Leiden: Brill, 1997), 275–336; A. Lange, "The Essene Position on Magic and Divination," in *Legal Texts and Legal Issues: Proceedings of the Second Meeting of the International Organization for Qumran Studies, Cambridge 1995, Published in Honour of Joseph M. Baumgarten* (STDJ 23; Leiden:

not compatible with the expectations of the Son of David. He argued that the Jewish concept of Son of David stood in direct tension with the more Hellenistic notion of ("Divine-man") therapeutic activity.[6] He was convinced that the latter concept influenced Mark's portrayal of Jesus and subsequently concluded, "The idea of Jesus doing miracles as the Son of David does not come from contemporary Judaism but from Mark."[7] According to Burger, Matthew's therapeutic emphasis on the title could not have arisen from the Jewish thought-world.[8]

Contemporary historians are keenly aware of just how deeply embedded demonology was in the worldview of Jesus' contemporaries. It is now common among NT scholars to suggest (among other possibilities) a conceptual connection between the "Son of David" title and Solomon's legendary prowess as an exorcist.[9] But the questions of Jesus' relationship with this tradition and how it might have influenced the evangelists (especially Matthew) have divided scholarship. All now agree that Matthew's use of "Son of David" takes on therapeutic significance, but not all are convinced that this points to Solomonic typology. In sum, Burger's thesis that Matthew's application of the title is in some way linked with therapeutic activity has won the day, but his argument that this betrays a Gentile understanding of Son of David has been largely rejected. This has left many who are not persuaded by the Solomonic exorcism paradigm to voice uncertainty. France admits that "it

---

Brill, 1997); L. Novakovic, *Messiah, the Healer of the Sick: A Study of Jesus as the Son of David in the Gospel of Matthew* (WUNT 170; Tübingen: Mohr Siebeck, 2003); C. Wahlen, *Jesus and the Impurity of Spirits in the Synoptic Gospels* (WUNT 2.185; Tübingen: Mohr Siebeck, 2004).

[6] Burger, 42–71, esp. 43–44.

[7] Translated from Burger, 79.

[8] Burger argued that Matthew's portrayal of Son of David as a healer betrays "his lack of knowledge concerning the Jewish background of the title Son of David" (translated, 169–70). Meier speaks for many contemporary scholars in saying that Burger's treatment "betrays a surprising ignorance of . . . Solomon as exorcist and miracle worker" (J. P. Meier, "From Elijah-like Prophet to Royal Davidic Messiah," in *Jesus: A Colloquium in the Holy Land* [ed. D. Donnelly; London: Continuum, 2001], 76). But to his credit, Burger was among the first to emphasize that it was in a therapeutic sense that Matthew applied the title to Jesus (170); cf. Lövestam, 99; B. M. Nolan, *The Royal Son of God: The Christology of Matthew 1-2 in the Setting of the Gospel* (Orbis Biblicus et Orientalis 23; Fribourg, Switzerland: Biblical Institute of the University of Fribourg, 1979), 158–215.

[9] E.g., W. D. Davies and D. C. Allison Jr., *The Gospel According to Saint Matthew* (3 vols.; ICC; Edinburgh: T&T Clark, 1997 [1988]), 1:157; B. D. Chilton, "Jesus ben David: Reflections on the Davidssohnfrage," in *The Historical Jesus: A Sheffield Reader* (ed. C. A. Evans and S. E. Porter; Sheffield: Sheffield Academic Press, 1995), 207; J. H. Charlesworth, "The Son of David: Solomon and Jesus (Mark 10.47)," in *The New Testament and Hellenistic Judaism* (Oxford: Arden, 1995); J. H. Charlesworth, "Solomon and Jesus: The Son of David in Ante-Markan Traditions (Mk 10:47)," in *Biblical and Humane: A Festschrift for John F. Priest* (ed. L. B. Elder, D. L. Barr, and E. S. Malbon; Atlanta: Scholars Press, 1996), 125–51; Meier, "Elijah-like Prophet," 57, 66; Novakovic, 96–109.

is not immediately clear why Matthew has chosen to link healing so specifically with the 'Son of David' motif."[10] Stanton lamented that the connection "remains something of an enigma."[11]

The present chapter is guided then by three questions/topics: (1) If the Solomonic exorcism paradigm did indeed influence Jesus or the early Christians, how so? (2) Given that Matthew has developed Son of David more than any NT author, what mnemonic lens has he assumed and how has this interpretive trajectory been further refracted by Matthew? After addressing these concerns, I (3) discuss where the historical Jesus likely stood in relation to these mnemonic trajectories.

The Background(s) for Jesus' Therapeutic Activity

There are multiple precedents for healing in the HB (e.g., Gen 20:12, 17-18; 2 Kgs 5; Isa 35:5-6; 53:4) so there is no disagreement that YHWH's intervention sometimes included relief from illness.[12] Exorcism, on the other hand, has proved a very difficult mnemonic category to trace. It is all but absent from the HB,[13] only to be picked up with fervor in the NT. Moreover the Synoptics and Acts give the impression that demon possession was a common occurrence and that exorcism was a well-known practice. It seems that demonology and measures taken in response to it represent a very slowly moving mnemonic trajectory that suddenly exploded in several directions shortly before the turn of the first century BCE. Before the Persian period, there were mnemonic lenses in place in which demonology would eventually find a home (i.e., mythological, apocalyptic, and eschatological worldviews[14]), but certainly not of the ilk that we find in the NT. Therefore, before any observations can be made of the trajectory of Jewish thought on this subject, a brief word is warranted on Persia's influence on the Greco-Roman world.

In the sixth century BCE, the Median tribe (known as a tribe of priests) was reputed to have uncanny insight into the occult.[15] Although they were

[10] R. T. France, *Matthew: Evangelist and Teacher* (London: Akademie, 1989), 285; he continued by saying that healing and exorcism "are not the 'deeds of the Messiah' which would have been the natural connotations of 'Son of David' in many Jewish minds."

[11] G. Stanton, "The Origin and Purpose of Matthew's Gospel: Matthean Scholarship from 1945 to 1980," in *ANRW* (ed. H. Temporini and W. Haase; Berlin: de Gruyter, 1985), 1923–1924.

[12] See the fuller treatment of healing in the HB in H.C. Kee, *Medicine, Miracle and Magic in the New Testament Times* (SNTS 55; Cambridge: Cambridge University Press, 1986), 9–26.

[13] 1 Samuel 16:14-23 is discussed in detail below.

[14] E. Sorensen, *Possession and Exorcism in the New Testament and Early Christianity* (WUNT 157; Tübingen: Mohr Siebeck, 2002), 129; Garrett, 46.

[15] A. D. Nock, "Paul and the Magus," in *The Beginnings of Christianity. Part 1: The Acts of the Apostles* (ed. F. Jackson and K. Lake; London: Macmillan, 1920–33), 164–65.

revered for this, they were also feared[16] and the object of polemic. *Magos* is a Persian loan word and was often used as a polemical designation.[17] Greco-Roman culture included several different occult sciences, such as divination, astrology, alchemy, and exorcism.[18] But the category "magic" is more difficult to define. The use of this term varies widely and often includes association with these other categories. Indeed, many now think that the term is of such little help that it should be avoided altogether as a descriptive designation. But the term is most often associated with suspicion; it most often becomes a label for questionable activity. Thus I briefly address this usage.

For the most part, practices associated with "magic" were prohibited in the Greco-Roman world. Practitioners of "magic" were ostracized or executed. MacMullen summarized that there was "no period in the history of the empire in which the magician was not considered an enemy of society."[19] But even though many looked suspiciously on magic and in general considered it evil, it was widely popular.[20] By the turn of the Common Era, the practices listed above were so widely used that that they were incorporated into religious life in many different sects, including Judaism and Christianity,[21] and garnered interest across socioeconomic lines.[22] As such, "magic" became less taboo in some circles. But Judaism, mirroring Greco-Roman culture, needed to keep a firm distinction between legitimate and illegitimate magic.[23] Exorcism seems to have been eventually accepted as a legitimate practice in Greco-Roman culture, which included certain Jewish circles. One could safely say that, once a group had legitimized a kind of "magic" it ceased to be referred to (polemically) as magic.[24]

---

[16] Cf. Isaiah 13, where YHWH's heavenly host is riding to war against Israel. The army consists of heavenly beings (13:4-5) but also is said to include the Medes (13:17). Perhaps then, this tribe was known for its association with heavenly beings.

[17] Garrett, 12.

[18] Cf. Garrett, 12–13.

[19] R. MacMullen, *Enemies of the Roman Order: Treason, Unrest and Alienation in the Empire* (Cambridge, Mass.: Harvard University Press, 1966), 125–26.

[20] On this point see the very helpful discussion of magic and religious life in Aune; however, for an alternative view which emphasizes that many were skeptical of the supernatural, see F. G. Downing, "Magic and Skepticism in and around the First Christian Century," in *Magic in the Biblical Word: From the Rod of Aaron to the Ring of Solomon* (ed. T. E. Klutz; London: T&T Clark, 2003), 86–99. Downing is able to argue to this end by distinguishing healing from magic (87). I am less confident that these two (very amorphous) categories can be so neatly separated.

[21] Aune, 1516.

[22] G. Theissen, *Miracle Stories of the Early Christian Tradition* (Edinburgh: T&T Clark, 1983), 271.

[23] Philo, *Spec.Laws* 3.110–11.

[24] Cf. the discussion of Essene "magic" in Lange, 377ff. But keep in mind that, for many

It seems that Jewish concepts of cosmic dualism and evil agency underwent dramatic reinterpretation leading up to the first century. This change led texts like Philo, *Jubilees*, and *1 Enoch* to refract Israel's patriarchal history.[25] 1QapGen 20.16-21, 28-29 portrays Abraham as an exorcist. 4Q242 references an anonymous Jewish exorcist (perhaps Daniel[26]). 11Q5 27.10 mentions psalms that David prescribed for singing over the possessed. 11Q11 records four psalms fitting this description (plus Psalm 91, which may function similarly).[27] The possibility that David's legacy was interpreted demonologically is dealt with here in due course. Of present interest is how this ideology might have contributed to Davidic messianism.

Isaianic Therapy in 4Q521

Novakovic has recently concluded that Jewish messianism and Jewish therapeutic ideology were altogether separate categories in first-century Judaism. Novakovic bases her conclusions "on the assumption that the link between the Davidic messiah and healing cannot be found as such in the extant early Jewish literature."[28] This assumption is confirmed in her analysis of 4Q521. She argues that this early Jewish text (which possibly links the expectation of healing to the messianic age) is too fragmentary to allow us to come to any definite conclusion with regard to the subject performing the healing acts mentioned. Questions remain about how the first part of this text relates to the latter portion.[29]

The first line explicitly claims that "[the hea]vens and earth will listen to his messiah [למשיחו]." The text goes onto apply the promises of Isaiah 61:1-2 eschatologically. These include, "freeing prisoners, opening eyes of the blind [פוקח עורים], raising up those who are bow [. . .] (line 8)" and thus eschatological therapeutic activity is explicitly described. However, it is possible that these two portions of the text were not intended as a continuous commentary and perhaps should not be read as mutually interpretive. Thus, whether this messiah is the doer of these Isaianic deeds in line 8 is unclear. Novakovic correctly suggests that YHWH might be the logical subject of these acts.[30]

Jews, the authority behind the practice was more important than the type of practice (cf. Mark 3:22); contra M. Smith, 68–80.

[25] For a recent study on the reinterpretation of Genesis 6:1-4 in light of later demonology, see A. T. Wright, *Origin of Evil Spirits: The Reception of Genesis 6:1-4 in Early Jewish Literature* (WUNT 198; Tübingen: Mohr Siebeck, 2005).

[26] Hogan, 154.

[27] Novakovic, 99.

[28] Novakovic, 185.

[29] There seems to be a sense break in line 3 and the text becomes garbled in lines 9 and 10. See plate II in É. Puech, *Qumrân Grotte 4.XVIII* (DJD 25; Oxford: Clarendon, 1998).

[30] Novakovic, 174–75.

She also reiterates that it is unclear whether line 1 refers to a single figure, "to his messiah [למשיחו cf. לִמְשִׁיחוֹ]," or plural, "to his messiahs [cf. the defective pl. לִמְשִׁיחָו]."[31] It is also unclear whether this text refers to a uniquely prophetic messiah over and against a priestly or royal messiah,[32] or perhaps a fusion of all three offices.[33] Because of these ambiguities Novakovic concludes that 4Q521 cannot be numbered among the later Jewish texts which attribute the act of healing to the Davidic messiah. Novakovic is unconvinced that 4Q521 is royal in character and thus argues that this text should not be used to describe first-century Davidic messianism. She writes:

> We must thus conclude that interpretations which aim to clearly define the role and character of God's Messiah in line 1 by seeing him as God's agent in bringing about the end-time blessings remain highly speculative. The text neither clarifies the relationship between God and Anointed nor gives any specific information about his identity.[34]

I find Novakovic's reading of this text to be excessively cautious and ultimately unsatisfying. While it would be unwise to conclude too much about the royal messiah's eschatological activity on the basis of the text, two suggestions are warranted.

First and foremost, line 7 promises that YHWH will place his "devout [חסידים] on a throne of an everlasting kingdom [על כסא מלכות עד]."[35]

---

[31] É. Puech, "Une Apocalypse Messianique (4Q521)," *RevQ* 15 (1992) 475–519; Novakovic, 171; J. Zimmermann, *Messianische Texte aus Qumran: Königliche, priesterliche und prophetische Messiasvorstellungen in den Schriftfunden von Qumran* (WUNT 2.104; Tübingen: Mohr Siebeck, 1998), 386.

[32] J. J. Collins, "The Works of the Messiah," *DSD* 1 (1994): 98–112; "A Herald of Good Tidings: Isaiah 61:1-3 and Its Actualization in the Dead Sea Scrolls," in *The Quest for Context and Meaning: Studies in Biblical Intertextuality* (ed. C. A. Evans and S. Talmon; BIS 28; Leiden: Brill, 1997).

[33] Zimmermann, 382–85, tends toward Collins' argument that 4Q521 has primarily a prophetic messiah in mind, but nuances Collins' distinction between these offices.

[34] Novakovic, 176.

[35] The use of the plural, both here and in line 5, might support the thesis that multiple messiahs are in view (M. Becker, "4Q521 und die Gesalbten," *RevQ* 18 [1997]: 78). But it could also refer to the collective of "devout" Israel who will share in the final victory of the Messiah. It has been pointed out to me that Revelation 3:19-21 might be an apt conceptual parallel. If so, perhaps those who occupy this "throne" are not royal figures. However, it should be pointed out also that Revelation 3:21 presupposes that Jesus (as messianic conqueror) is first seated on his Father's throne before the people of God are welcomed to be seated. Indeed, this royal "throne" imagery is continued through chaps. 4 and 5 where Jesus is called the "Root of David" (Rev 5:5). It seems that the most natural reading of Revelation 3–5 is that where "throne" imagery is employed, a royal figure is primarily in view, and then only by extension the devout of God's people are welcomed to be seated. If 4Q521 does have a collective enthronement in mind, one might expect a similar eschatology. But the application of Revelation's throne imagery to 4Q521 will have to remain speculative.

That "kingdom" and "throne" are indicators of royal imagery should go without saying. But the fact that these concepts are coupled with the idea of an "everlasting" tenure suggests that line 7 alludes to 2 Samuel 7:13 where YHWH promises to "establish the throne of his kingdom forever." This imagery, coupled with the explicit reference to "his messiah(s)" in line 1, suggests that the two parts of this text are meant to be mutually interpretive.[36] As such, we must remain open to the possibility that, in the first century, Isaianic promises for therapeutic activity (e.g., healing the blind) were expected of the royal messiah.[37]

Secondly, Q (Matt 11:2-5 // Luke 7:19-22) contains a conceptual parallel to 4Q521 in its eschatological application of Isaiah 61:1-3 (cf. Isa 35:5-6).[38] In this text, Jesus sends word to the imprisoned John the Baptist by quoting Isaiah 61. I sidestep here the question of historicity at this point and merely point out that both Matthew and Luke presuppose that Jesus is, in some sense, the Messiah.[39] Thus, when the Baptist questions whether Jesus is "he who is to come" (Matt 11:2), Jesus' messianic identity is clearly being clarified for the reader. In this context, Jesus presumes that the fulfillment of such Isaianic promises (including therapeutic activity) will serve to answer the Baptist's question.

> "Go and tell John what you hear and see: the blind receive their sight and the lame walk, lepers are cleansed and the deaf hear, and the dead are raised up, and the poor have good news preached to them." (Matt 11:4-5)

Most often, 4Q521 has been used to shed light on this Q saying, and rightly so. My point, in this case, is that the reverse is also true. By appealing to the apparent fulfillment of Isaiah 61:1-3, Jesus clarifies his identity to the Baptist as the "one who is to come"—the one who John previously predicted would come (Matt 3:11-12 // Luke 3:15-17[40]). When 4Q521 is read in this light, the possibility is strengthened that the therapeutic promises of Isaiah 61 were applied as manifestations of the messianic age.[41] Furthermore, both the Q

---

[36] So J. A. Fitzmyer, *The Dead Sea Scrolls and Christian Origins* (Grand Rapids: Eerdmans, 2000), 36–38.

[37] I extend my gratitude to James Charlesworth for his lively critique on this point. I remain respectfully unconvinced of his argument to the contrary.

[38] C. A. Evans, "Jesus and the Dead Sea Scrolls from Qumran Cave 4," in *Eschatology, Messianism and the Dead Sea Scrolls* (ed. C. A. Evans and P. W. Flint; Grand Rapids: Eerdmans, 1997), 96–97; Fitzmyer, *Dead Sea Scrolls*, 37–38.

[39] This is discussed more thoroughly over the course of the present and subsequent chapters.

[40] The Lukan version of the Baptist's prediction places the expectation of this eschatological figure after a question concerning the identity of "the Christ" (Luke 3:15).

[41] One might also appeal to 11Q13, which describes the eschatological judgment by

saying and 4Q521 add an element that is absent from the text of Isaiah: resurrection (4Q521 f.4 2.12; Matt 3:5 // Luke 3:17). With this in mind, it seems prudent to suggest that these interpretations of Isaiah 61 represent parallel mnemonic trajectories of this passage, both seen through eschatological and messianic lenses.

Novakovic's claim that this text does not give any specific information about the messianic figure referred to in 4Q521 is misleading. While the possibility that 4Q521 links royal messianism to Isaianic therapy should not be overstated, there is also a danger in understating this possibility.

In her excessive caution, she draws an overly rigid distinction between YHWH's activity in the messianic age and the explicit statements of messianic agency. Collins has argued convincingly that, with regard to Isaiah 61, YHWH's promised actions in the eschaton find particular extension through the agency of his Anointed.[42] On the other hand, Novakovic's strict distinction between Davidic, therapeutic, and messianic categories does not seem to represent the mnemonic categories of the first-century texts discussed in this section; such dichotomies mislead the discussion.

I am not suggesting that such distinctions are always unhelpful. My point is that, in many cases, these categories are not mutually exclusive and often share the same conceptual framework and proof-texts. In the case of 4Q521, it is possible that the language of royal messianism has been mnemonically localized within the interpretation of Isaiah 61. In light of Matthew 11:4-5, 4Q521 might provide an early link between eschatological therapeutic activity and royal messianism as well as evidence that messianic categories can be conceptually reinforced without regard to rigid exegetical categories.

In sum, first-century Judaism was influenced by a wide range of ideologies, foreign and domestic. The influence of Gentile magic (including exorcistic practice) must be underscored. This seems to have created a cultural tension, not only for Israel but also for the wider Greco-Roman culture. Yet certain forms of therapeutic activity were domesticated by some circles and thus legitimized. As 4Q521 might suggest, Isaianic promises for therapeutic activity were utilized as a mnemonic cipher by which contemporary notions of therapy could be interpreted and related to first-century messianism. We cannot say with any confidence that therapeutic activity was a prominent feature among the messianic expectations of the first century. But we can

---

Melchizedek as heralded by a messenger who is "[an]ointed of the Spir[it]" (2.18). 11Q13 2.4-25 quotes, paraphrases, or alludes to Isaiah 61 no fewer than four times (2.4, 9, 14, 19). But since this text is not quite as overtly "messianic," I merely suggest the possibility. What is perhaps even more intriguing is that Melchizedek, both an eschatological and royal figure, is linked with such Isaianic promises.

[42] Collins, "Herald," 235–36.

conclude that any messianic ideology that took seriously the promises of Isaiah would have been open to the concept of messianic therapy. This might explain why the Qumran library commemorates David both as the father of the messiah and as the prescriber of therapeutic exorcisms.

The Testament of Solomon

Solomon's legacy included many archetypal features, but it was not until this period that he was commemorated as the exorcist par excellence. In this way, Solomon's legacy presents a fascinating case of commemorative refraction. Since the fountainhead and trajectory for Solomon the exorcist tradition is difficult to fix with certainty, it will behoove the present study to begin with the fully developed commemorative narrative and work backward.

The *Testament of Solomon* is by far the most developed frame along our trajectory. All other references to this tradition are implicit, fragmentary, or take the form of parenthetical comment. In contrast, the author of *Testament of Solomon* tells an elaborate story about Solomon's authority over the demonic realm, the source of his authority, the means by which he subdues demons, and what he does with them once they have been subdued. It even goes so far as to purport that Solomon forced his demon slaves to help him construct the temple (1.7; 2.8; 6.12; 12.5).[43]

The text was important for Lövestam as he dated the text earlier than most. He suggested that the earliest form of the tradition might precede Christianity.[44] Berger was more cautious with the date but relied even more heavily upon the text in his treatment of Son of David.[45] The text is commonly placed between the first and fourth centuries CE. Charlesworth has suggested that the tradition likely extends to the earlier end of this spectrum.[46] What can be said with certainty is that *Testament of Solomon* was subject to Christian (and other) interpolation[47] and should be used with caution.[48] What *Testament of Solomon* provides for the present study is an extreme end to a mnemonic trajectory. With this in mind, it is not surprising

---

[43] One is left to wonder whether this author had any concern or knowledge of Jewish cultic purity!

[44] Lövestam, 101.

[45] Berger, 6–8.

[46] Charlesworth, "Son of David," 82.

[47] See the (still useful) discussion in C. C. McCown, *The Testament of Solomon* (Leipzig: J. C. Hinrich, 1922); More recently, McCown's textual analysis has been challenged by T. E. Klutz, "The Archer and the Cross," in *Magic in the Biblical Word: From the Rod of Aaron to the Ring of Solomon* (ed. Klutz; London: T&T Clark, 2003), 219–44. He has argued that Q should be given more textual priority and be seen on par with D. Based on this reconstruction, Klutz argues for a revised literary arrangement.

[48] D. C. Duling, "Solomon, Exorcism and the Son of David," *HTR* 68 (1975): 242.

to see that at least some segments of Christianity took interest in this story and localized the Jesus tradition within it.[49] So, here at the end of the trajectory, the tradition attracted Christian interest.[50]

Both Lövestam and Berger emphasized the fact that Solomon is titled "Son of David" in the context of exorcism (*TSol* 1:7; 20:1[51]). While it is possible that one or both of these is independent of NT influence, this cannot be assumed with any confidence.[52] Berger argued that 20:1's phrase: "King Solomon, Son of David [βασιλεῦ Σολομῶν υἱὸς Δαυείδ]"[53] is a formula unparalleled in the Synoptic tradition[54] and is most likely free from Synoptic influence.[55] But given the other Christian redactional activity of this text (cf. also *TSol* 12:3), Berger's argument is difficult to defend.[56]

What is more important for the present study is the recognition that "Son of David" was considered Solomonic at the earliest frame of the Solomonic mnemonic trajectory (see chap. 5) and here at the most fully developed frame. Moreover, these occurrences of "Son of David" demonstrate that later Christians had no problem with the application of this title to Solomon instead of Jesus.

Charlesworth has helpfully emphasized a decidedly pre-Christian element of *Testament of Solomon* concerning the relationship of exorcism to illness.[57] He has pointed out a common motif[58] throughout the text in which Solomon demands to know the demon's abilities.[59] His study catalogues several cases

---

[49] I here follow the translation and numeration of F. C. Conybeare, "The Testament of Solomon," *JQR* 11 (1898): paragraph 122: "And I (Solomon) said to him: 'By what angel art thou frustrated?' And he (the demon) answered: 'By the only-ruling God, that hath authority over me even to be heard. He that is to be born of a virgin and crucified by the Jews on a cross. Whom the angels and archangels worship. He doth frustrate me, and enfeeble me of my great strength, which has been given me by my father the devil'" (cf. N 15:10-12).

[50] That this tradition was also present in later Jewish thought has been demonstrated by J. Bowman, "Solomon and Jesus," *Abr-Nahrain* 23 (1984–1985): 1–13; he surveyed a wide range of rabbinic texts which, among other things, commemorate Solomon as an exorcist. He also points to Solomon's similar reputation in early Islamic texts.

[51] Cf. also the Greek heading (1:1).

[52] Duling, "Solomon," 243–44. The occurrence in 1:17 was thought by McCown to be in the earliest form of the text; that which he associated most closely with D. Moreover, Duling points out that this occurrence is attested in H, I, L, V, W, P, and Q.

[53] This formulation is found in H.

[54] Cf. Mark 10:47.

[55] Berger, 7–8.

[56] Duling, "Solomon," 249; Novakovic, 101–2.

[57] Charlesworth, "Son of David," 81.

[58] Twelftree correctly observes that the general pattern of exorcism in *T.Sol.* does not seem to be modeled after the NT (*Jesus the Exorcist*, 36).

[59] The other elements of this pattern of exorcism includes Solomon demanding (1) the demon's name, (2) the name of the angel that is able to thwart the demon, (3) what the demon

where the demon admits to causing physical infirmity or illness. I select only a few here: one demon causes boys to grow thin (2:2); another attacks ten-day-old infants, inflames the limbs and feet, and causes festering sores (9.6); another prevents people from recovering from disease (11:2); another blinds children [τυφλῶ τὰ παιδία] in the womb (12:4-5); still another causes eye injuries (13:7).

This sampling from Charlesworth's list demonstrates that the demonological belief system represented by *Testament of Solomon* extended to a wide variety of infirmities. The last two in particular are important to the present study in that they show that blindness, both from birth and as caused by injury, are the result of demonic influence.[60] From the perspective of *Testament of Solomon*, demons influence fetal defects, illness in young children, and "accidental" illness later in life. Charlesworth rightly suggests the possibility that Solomon was considered a healer[61] as well as an exorcist.[62] Taking his suggestion further, one could say that Solomon was a healer by way of exorcism. He rooted out the causes of many illnesses: demons.

Antiquities 8.42f., LAB[63] *60, 11Q11, and Wisdom of Solomon 7*

Josephus' *Antiquities* 8.42ff. has been called the locus classicus for the tradition of Solomon as exorcist. I here offer an abbreviated version:

> Now the sagacity and wisdom which God had bestowed on Solomon was so great, that he exceeded the ancients (8.42). [. . .] He also composed 1005

---

can do, and (4) either the submission of the demon or some sort of negotiation on the part of the demon in Solomon's favor.

Sorensen (119–20) suggests that power over the demonic realm is linked with wisdom. The first step in exerting authority over a demon is determining its name. In his study on ancient Mesopotamia, A. L. Oppenheim associates wisdom with the knowledge of names. The ability to name the objects of one's environment was indicative of knowledge of the nature and purposes of those objects. The knowledge of "names and their individual features and behavior was considered the privilege of the sage" ("Man and Nature in Mesopotamian Civilization" [vol. 15, Sup. 1 of *Dictionary of Scientific Biography*; ed. C. C. Gillespie; New York: Scribners, 1978], 1:634). Sorensen builds from this in his examination of exorcism in early Hellenistic culture. "The importance of the name even in early Greece, however, is demonstrable as a method of 'diagnosis' to determine the agent of affliction" (Sorensen, 120n4).

[60] This is shown in my discussion of Matthew's emphasis on the healing of blindness.

[61] Similarly, Origen tells that Jewish Christianity commemorated Solomon as a healer in the form of a shrine (*PG* 13). J. M. Hull suggests that this might have been located at the probatic pool (*Hellenistic Magic and the Gospel Tradition* [London: SCM Press, 1974], 33–34). Cf. G. Vermes, *Jesus the Jew: A Historian's Reading of the Gospels* (Minneapolis: Fortress, 1981), 61–69.

[62] Charlesworth, "Son of David," 82. With this in mind, U. Luz misleads this discussion by arguing that Solomon was reputed as an exorcist but never as a healer (*Matthew 8–20: A Commentary* [Minneapolis: Augsburg Fortress, 2001], 42).

[63] Pseudo-Philo's *Liber antiquitatum biblicarum*.

books of odes and songs, of parables and similitudes 3000; for he spoke a parable upon every sort of tree (44) [. . .] and in like manner also about beasts, about all sorts of living creatures, whether upon the earth, or in the seas, or in the air; for he was not unacquainted with any of their natures, nor omitted inquiries about them, but described them all like a philosopher, and demonstrated his exquisite knowledge of their several properties. God also gave him knowledge of the art used against demons for the benefit and healing of humans. He also composed incantations by which fevers are relieved, and left behind forms of exorcisms with which those possessed by demons drive them out, never to return and this method of cure is of great force until this day.[64]

Josephus first refers to Solomon's divine bestowal of wisdom (1 Kgs 3) and claims that he was the wisest and most learned person in history (most of this section has been excluded in my abbreviation). He then goes on to tell of Solomon's legacy as a sapiential author. He follows the Hebrew account of 1 Kings 4:29-34 rather than the LXX's expansion.[65] Solomon's encyclopedic knowledge of the natural world is then recounted. He is purported as having knowledge concerning the natures and properties of every creature and plant. From this context, Josephus introduces Solomon's skill in exorcism.

Josephus continues (beyond the portion here provided) to tell of Solomon's method for exorcism, which was practiced by one of Josephus' contemporaries, an exorcist named Eliezar. This included the use of a ring (for abstracting the demon) and a bowl of water (to prove that the demon had left the victim). The mention of this ring is reminiscent of *Testament of Solomon* wherein Solomon uses a signet ring (*T.Sol.* 1.5).[66] Elsewhere, Josephus' description of demonological healing included the use of Baaras root (*JW* 7.185).[67] This would seem to cohere with the preface of this section, which recounts Solomon's knowledge of plants. The connection between Solomonic authority and the bowl of water has some affinity with the inscriptions mentioned previously in my discussion of Fisher.[68] Therefore, moving backward from *Testament of Solomon* and the later archaeological evidence, the commonalities in Josephus (1) demonstrate a mnemonic sphere in which Solomon tradition was localized and (2) point back to 1 Kings 3–4 as the fountainhead of this trajectory.

[64] Translation from W. Whiston, *The Works of Josephus* (Peabody, Mass.: Hendrickson, 1987).
[65] "and his songs were 1,005" (4:32); cf. "and his songs were 5000" (4:32 LXX).
[66] The use of the ring varies from text to text: Josephus' Eliezer places the ring in the possessed person's nose, while *T.Sol.* portrays Solomon as wearing the ring engraved with a pentagram (cf. *b. git.* 68a, where the ring is engraved with the tetragrammaton).
[67] It is noteworthy that Josephus calls this a procedure for healing the effects of illness caused by demons. This point is revisited below.
[68] For a more recent treatment, see Charlesworth, "Son of David," 79–80; for the original text see Montgomery, *Texts from Nippur*, 231.

There is some dispute as to whether Wisdom of Solomon 7:17-21 should be placed along this trajectory. If it does belong, it would provide an earlier and less developed point of reference for the Solomon-as-exorcist tradition.[69] Wisdom of Solomon 7:20 is of immediate interest (I have set this verse in italics):

> For he has given me certain knowledge of the things that exist, namely, to know how the world was made, and the operation of the elements; The beginning, ending, and duration of the times; The alterations of the turning of the sun, and the change of seasons; The cycles of years, and the positions of stars; *The natures of living creatures, and the furies of wild beasts: the violence of spirits* [πνευμάτων βίας], *and the reasonings of men; The species of plants* [διαφόρας φυτῶν] *and the powers of roots* [δυνάμεισ ῥιζῶν]; And all such things as are either secret or manifest, I know them.

Solomon, the supposed speaker, here recounts the origin and extent of his knowledge. In this context, knowledge is best understood as a synonym for wisdom. Gilbert argued that this passage occupies a central place in Pseudo-Solomon's "concentric pattern." Among the several features of this pattern, Pseudo-Solomon refers to his gift of divine wisdom, which precedes a description of his wisdom, its nature, origin, and function.[70] Both features can be seen in this passage. Dimant has argued that the entire book should be seen in relation to its pseudonymic framework which guides the author's patterns and themes.[71] Chief among these is the theme of divine wisdom. When seen in this light, Wisdom of Solomon 7:17 is an unquestionable allusion to 1 Kings 3, where God bestows wisdom on Solomon. The author proceeds in boasting of Solomon's encyclopedic knowledge of the created order[72] and thus shows close affinity to *Antiquities* 8.42ff. Both Josephus and Pseudo-Solomon begin by appealing to 1 Kings 3 and follow by explaining the extent of Solomon's wisdom.

The central point of contention among scholarship has to do with whether "πνευμάτων βίας" refers to "violent (evil/unclean) spirits" in a demonological

---

[69] A wide range of dates have been suggested for this composition (third century BCE to second century CE), but the more extreme suggestions have been largely rejected (L. L. Grabbe, *Wisdom of Solomon* [Sheffield: Sheffield Academic Press, 1997], 89–90). The range that garners the most support spans from 31 BCE to 41 CE. See discussions in C. Larcher, *Le Livre de la Sagesse ou la Sagesse de Salomon* (3 vols.; nouvelle série 1; Paris: Gabalda, 1983), 1:148–61; and D. Winston, *Wisdom of Solomon* (AB 43; Garden City, N.Y.: Doubleday, 1979), 20–25. Larcher argues for a date between 31 and 10 BCE. Winston suggests 37–41 CE.

[70] M. Gilbert, "Wisdom Literature," in *Jewish Writings of the Second Temple Period* (ed. M. E. Stone; Philadelphia: Fortress, 1984), 302–3.

[71] D. Dimant, "Pseudonymity in the Wisdom of Solomon," in *La Septuaginta en la investigacion contemporanea* (Madrid: Instituto Arias Montano, 1985): 243–55.

[72] On the function of "Listenwissenschaft" in the ancient Near East, see Grabbe, 64–66.

sense, or whether it might simply betray a sort of animism where "winds/breaths" are endowed with malicious intentions (cf. John 8:24).[73] Novakovic has recently argued for the latter and concludes that this passage is not to be placed along the Solomon-as-exorcist trajectory. Her reasoning is that this particular sequence recounts Solomon's "knowledge of healing arts,"[74] which includes the therapeutic natures of "roots [ῥιζῶν]" and "plants [φυτῶν]." She argues that exorcism should be categorized separately from healing; thus, "spirits" should not be taken as demons in this context. While Novakovic is correct to see the therapeutic connection between roots and plants, she draws an unhelpful dichotomy between exorcism and healing.[75] Novakovic appeals to Josephus' connection between roots and healing properties in *Jewish War* 2.136,[76] but fails to connect this concept with *Jewish War* 7.185, which explicitly states that the Baaras root was used for illness caused by demonic possession.[77] A more natural solution is to see the last three categories as references to the natures of sickness (as caused by spirits) and remedy. Moreover, Hübner argued that a reference to "winds" in this context seems out of place:

> But after previously talking about wild (i.e., dangerous) beasts, it is a reasonable suggestion that the author talks about another thing, that being the influence of evil spirits on the thoughts and desires of humans.[78]

Hübner then suggests that this progression of ideas leads to the healing properties of plants seen at the end of the list. In this way, the list refers to dangerous beings and culminates with the most dangerous of these: violent spirits. This association then invites the inclusion of Solomon's knowledge of how to handle such dangers.

Given the context (especially the immediately following context), it is best to affirm McCown's early assessment[79] that Wisdom of Solomon 7:16-20

---

[73] Hogan, 52.
[74] Novakovic, 98.
[75] Novakovic, 99.
[76] "[T]hey inquire after such roots and medicinal stones as may cure their fevers" (2.136).
[77] "[Baaras root] is only valuable for one of its virtues: if it is only brought to sick persons, it quickly drives away those called demons, which are no other than the spirits of the wicked, that enter into men that are alive and kill them, unless they can obtain some help against them" (7.185). Cf. also *1 Enoch* 8:3 where the leader of the fallen angels teaches humanity the uses of roots in magic. *Jubilee* 10ff. explains that Noah was taught how to use herbs to cure illness caused by demons. M. Hengel observed: "As sicknesses were of demonic magical origin, they could only be effectively combated by a kind of 'white magic' taught by the good angels" (*Judaism and Hellenism* [trans. J. Bowden; Minneapolis: Fortress, 1974], 241).
[78] Translated from H. Hübner, "Die Weisheit Salomons" (ed. O. Kaiser and L. Perlitt; *Das Alte Testament Deutsch: Apokryphen*; Göttingen: Vandenhoeck and Ruprecht, 1999), 100–110.
[79] McCown, 91.

does indeed provide a background for Solomon's power over the supernatural causes of sickness,[80] what later mnemonic categories referred to as demons.[81] In sum, three features of this text suggest that it provides an earlier and less developed precedent for *Antiquities* 8.42ff. and *Testament of Solomon*: (1) the implied backdrop of 1 Kings 3, (2) the detailed list of Solomon's knowledge of the natural and supernatural world, alongside (3) the likelihood that this knowledge included demonological illness and healing.

The most common move in previous studies has been to fill out the portrait provided by Josephus and *Testament of Solomon* with corroborating texts like *LAB* 60:3 and 11Q11. But this line of reasoning fails to recognize the distinctive characteristics of these texts suggestive of a parallel mnemonic trajectory concerning Solomon and exorcism. *LAB* 60 records an elaboration of 1 Samuel 16:14-23. I offer here an abbreviated version.[82]

> And at that time the spirit of the Lord was taken away from Saul, and an evil spirit was terrifying him. Saul sent and brought David, and he played a song on his lyre by night. This is the song he played for Saul so that the evil spirit would depart from him, "[. . .][83] do you not remember that your brood was created from an echo in the abyss? But the new womb, from which I was born, will rebuke you, from which in time one will be born from my loins and will rule over you."[84] And when David sang praises, the spirit spared Saul. (*LAB* 60:1-3)[85]

Berger suggested that the promised descendant of David represents an expectation for a royal messiah.[86] Charlesworth and Novakovic follow the lead of McCown in arguing that *LAB* 60.3 refers to Solomon.[87] The lat-

---

[80] Duling, "Solomon," 239.

[81] Cf. Lövestam, 99.

[82] Translation from H. Jacobson, *A Commentary on Pseudo-Philo's Liber Antiquitatum Biblicarum* (2 vols.; Leiden: Brill, 1996), 1:187–88.

[83] The song sung by David is a fascinating window into the origin of evil spirits that may or may not cohere with the myth of the watchers. It recounts the order of creation and reminds the demon that evil spirits were "second born." It is on this basis that the demon must submit to David's authority. The appeal to a Davidic descendant seems to be a further appeal to authority, perhaps a spiritual trump card.

[84] *Arguet autem te metra nova unde natus sum, de qua nascetur post tempus de lateribus meis qui vos domabit.*

[85] It is possible that Pseudo-Philo considers this punishment for the fact that "Saul has not driven the wizards [*malefici*] from the land." It is interesting that Saul, commemorated for his association with the evil spirit, also carried the reputation of having consulted with the occult at Endor. "Behold he will go to those whom he has scattered, to obtain divination [*divinatio*] from them, because he has no prophets" (*LAB* 64:1). On the relationship between the function of diviners and prophets see Garrett, 14–15.

[86] Berger, 6.

[87] McCown, 91; Charlesworth, "Son of David," 141; Novakovic, 100–110.

ter interpretation is to be preferred, although the royal imagery cannot be denied. The language used is similar to that of 2 Samuel 7:12 (LXX).[88] But there is no need to see these two options as mutually exclusive. Duling rightly observed that "royal language does not *exclude* Solomon!"[89]

What is striking about this passage is that a clearly demonological mnemonic sphere has been projected upon a story other than 1 Kings 3. There is no mention of divinely bestowed wisdom in reference to David's descendant. Furthermore, there is no evidence that the mnemonic trajectory anchored by 1 Kings 3 had direct influence on this text. There is no mention of rings, bowls, roots, or information gathering on the part of David. Furthermore, the title "Son of David" is not present in this text.[90] As such, *LAB* 60:3 seems to represent a parallel but separate mnemonic trajectory.

This is confirmed by the Dead Sea Scroll's interpretation of Psalm 91. As mentioned, 11Q5 27 refers to four prayers prescribed by David for praying over "the stricken [הפגועים]." 11Q11 records four psalms to be used to combat evil spirits (cols. 1–5) and includes a form of Psalm 91 that has been reformatted demonologically (col. 6).[91] Puech concluded that this grouping represents a ritual that predates the Qumran community.[92] This ritual seems to mirror biblical psalms such as Psalm 6,[93] rather than contemporary magical procedures.[94] The procedure consists of singing psalms and thus parallels *LAB* 60; it bears little affinity to the procedure described in *Antiquities* 8.42ff. Notice the use of Solomon's name in association to this ritual: 11Q11 2.2-4 reads:[95]

[...]ה שלומה[...]ויקר[א
[...] הרו[ח]ות[96] [...]והשדים
[...] אל[ה [הש]דים זמ[ר המשט]מה

---

[88] 2 Sam 7:12 LXX: "ἔσται ἐκ τῆς κοιλίας σου."

[89] Duling, "Solomon," 240 (emphasis in original).

[90] Novakovic, 103.

[91] It remains inconclusive as to whether the author of 11Q5 had particular knowledge of the tradition represented by 11Q11. While a possibility, it is presently only necessary to notice how David was doubly commemorated as such in the Dead Sea Scrolls.

[92] É. Puech, "11QPsAp(a): Un ritual d'exorcismes. Essai de reconstruction," *RevQ* 14 (1990): 401–2, 408.

[93] A. T. Wright, "Prayer and Incantation in the Dead Sea Scrolls," in *Studies in Jewish Prayer* (ed. R. Hayward and B. Embry; Oxford: Oxford University Press, 2005).

[94] B. Nitzan argues that the invocation of the divine name (5.6-10) distinguishes this incantation not only from Gentile magic but also from other Jewish magical texts (*Qumran Prayer and Religious Poetry* [trans. J. Chipman; Leiden: Brill, 1994], 235).

[95] Reconstruction followed from Puech, "Ritual." He suggested that the name of Solomon gave greater authority to the ritual (408).

[96] Does the feminine ending denote liliths? Cf. the Babylonian Talmud (b. git. 68a; cf. Pesiq. Rab. 15) which renders Qoh 2:8b "male and female singers [שָׁרִים וְשָׁרוֹת]" as "male and female demons [שֵׁדָה וְשֵׁדוֹת]."

154   The Historiographical Jesus

> [. . .] Solomon, [. . .] and he shall invo[ke
> [. . . the spi]rits, [. . .] and the demons,
> [. . .] These are [the de]mons. And the p[rince of enmi]ty

When the four psalms are taken together, it seems that the story of David's singing over Saul alongside his reputation as a psalmist provides the mnemonic backdrop for this tradition. Because the reference to Solomon is so fragmentary, little more can be said of Solomon's role in this procedure. But before moving on, two observations are necessary: (1) the Solomon-as-exorcist tradition was a live cultural category prior to Jesus' historical context. (2) There is a definite association between Solomon and David's legacy as an author of psalms for the purpose of exorcism. Therefore, while previous studies have taken for granted that a demonological interpretation of 1 Kings 3 provided the fountainhead for the Solomon-as-exorcist tradition, *LAB* 60 and 11Q11 point us in the direction of 1 Samuel 16 as an alternative possibility. With this in mind, a closer look at this text is warranted.

A Demonological Reading of 1 Samuel 16

As discussed, we do not find the sort of demonology in ancient Israel that we find near the turn of the Common Era. Sorensen suggests that the practice of exorcism was likely classified alongside necromancy and conjuring and thus condemned by earlier generations (cf. Exod 22:18; Lev 19:26, 31; 20:6, 27; Deut 18:10-11).[97] However, the idea that humanity was the battleground for spiritual beings seems to have manifested itself in other beliefs before a fully developed Jewish demonology evolved. Indeed the plight of Job seems to have been thought of (at least by later redactors) in terms of spirits contending (cf. Job 1–2). Perhaps the closest cousin of a possession-exorcism story in the HB is that of Saul and the evil spirit from YHWH:

> Now the Spirit of YHWH departed from Saul and an evil spirit from YHWH [רוח־רעה מאת יהוה רוח־רעה מאת יהוה] terrorized him. Saul's servants then said to him, "Look now, an evil spirit from God [אלהים רעה רוח] is terrorizing you. Let our lord now command your servants who are before you. Let them seek a man who is a skillful player on the harp; and it shall come about when the evil spirit from God is on you, that he shall play with his hand, and you will be well. (1 Sam 16:14-16)

The story concludes, "So it came about that whenever the spirit from God [רוח־אלהים] came to Saul, David would take the harp and play with his hand; and Saul would be refreshed and be well, and the evil spirit [רוח הרעה] would depart from him" (16:23).

---

[97] Sorensen, 47–48.

As has been shown in the above discussion of 11Q11, this story was likely seen through the lens of possession and exorcism by later psalmists.[98] This story seems to betray the belief (common to other texts in Mesopotamia[99]) that a good spirit could depart from a person and thus open the door to misfortune.[100] In this case, the misfortune is directly caused by an "evil spirit." Due to the limits of this study, the question of YHWH's relationship with this evil spirit will be bracketed.[101] Presently important is Saul's relationship with the spirit.

In this story, the departure of YHWH's spirit symbolizes the "withdrawal of favour from Saul."[102] It demonstrates that YHWH's spirit now rests upon David[103] and foreshadows the transfer of the kingship to David.[104] Interesting to our discussion of demonology is the fact that the departure of YHWH's spirit is directly linked to the employment of the evil spirit; YHWH's removal of one spirit made way for the entry of another kind.[105] Saul was rendered powerless to help himself. David, on the other hand, has power in this regard. We are told in this context that "YHWH is with him" (16:18). Keep this context in mind as Saul is alluded to in the giving of the Davidic covenant.

The present study has previously discussed the Davidic covenant (see chap. 5). What has been left untouched until now has been the allusion to Saul in the Davidic covenant. Through Nathan, YHWH tells David, "My love [חסד] shall not depart from him, as I took it away from Saul, whom I removed from before you" (2 Sam 7:15). That this alludes to the symbolic removal of YHWH's spirit is possible. But what can be said with confidence is that the mention of Saul in 2 Samuel 7:15 presupposes the narrative

---

[98] In the original story, the spirit "terrorizes," "startles," or "falls upon" [בעת] Saul. An interesting parallel might be seen in the concept of YHWH's spirit "resting upon [נוח]" human figures. One is left to wonder whether possession in the sense of indwelling is an appropriate description; contra R. W. Klein, "2 Samuel," in *WBC* 10 (Dallas: Word, 1983): 164. On נוח, see discussion in W. Hildebrandt, *An Old Testament Theology of the Spirit of God* (Peabody, Mass.: Hendrickson, 1995), 101–3, 128.

[99] Sorensen, 18–32.

[100] Cf. the misfortune of Samson due to the departure of YHWH's spirit (Judg 16:19-20).

[101] The story certainly betrays some level of cosmic duality; the nature and extent of this duality will have to be the subject of another study. For an excellent treatment of the categories of demonology and duality in later Judaism, see Wright, "Origin," chap. 6.

[102] P. R. Ackroyd, *The Second Book of Samuel* (Cambridge: Cambridge University Press, 1977), 78.

[103] Klein, "2 Samuel," 159.

[104] D. A. Gunn called 1 Samuel 16:14-23 the "microcosm" of the rest of Saul's story (*The Fate of King Saul* [JSOTSup 14; Sheffield: JSOT Press, 1980], 78).

[105] T. W. Cartledge, *1 & 2 Samuel* (SHBC 7; Macon, Ga.: Smyth and Helwys, 2001), 210, relates this idea to Jesus' parable of the exiting and returning spirits (Matt 12:43f. // Luke 11:24f.).

context of YHWH's rejection of Saul in favor of David. As Gunn et al. have observed, 2 Samuel 16 is the quintessential presentation of this shift in YHWH's favor. This said, it should also be observed that no direct mention of the role of YHWH's spirit appears in the Davidic covenant. It is possible to associate חסד conceptually with YHWH's spirit, but it is at best only implied.[106] Even so, the role of the spirit in the fulfillment of the Davidic covenant becomes paramount for other interpretations such as Isaiah 11 (and especially later messianic interpretations).[107] It is precisely this perspective that interests this study.[108]

YHWH promised that his relationship with Solomon would stand in direct contrast to that of Saul.[109] It is possible that the promise of YHWH never to remove his covenantal love (= favor/commitment) from David's son invited later speculation from a demonological perspective. Unlike Saul, David's son would always have the benefit of the spirit of YHWH and thus be invulnerable to evil spirits. Just as David was able to perform an "exorcism" because YHWH was with him, Solomon would always have the spirit of YHWH and thus authority over evil spirits.

The suggestion of this alternative fountainhead is admittedly dependent on how 2 Samuel 7 was possibly interpreted in conjunction with 1 Samuel 16 rather than on hard evidence. But this alternative must be taken seriously for two reasons. (1) *LAB* 60 has localized 1 Samuel 16 within a demonological framework and used this text as a springboard to associate the story with David's progeny. As shown, this reference seems to depend upon language from the LXX of 2 Samuel 7:12. (2) Neither *LAB* 60 nor 11Q11 appeal to 1 Kings 3.

In this way, it is appropriate to observe that later interpreters associated David's possession of the divine Spirit to be an effective combatant of evil spirits. As the contrast of Saul is mentioned in 2 Samuel 7, Solomon too might enjoy such abilities. All considered, it is best to remain open but cautious of this possibility.

Matthew's Portrayal of the Son of David

While it is true that Matthew employs "Son of David" more than any other NT author, it should be made clear that he uses this title only a handful

---

[106] P. Kalluweettil, *Declaration and Covenant* (AnBib 88; Rome: Biblical Institute Press, 1982), 48.

[107] See the previous discussion on Isaiah 11 and *Ps.Sol.* 17 in chap. 5.

[108] I should emphasize that I am primarily interested in the possible conflation of these concepts in later interpretations and not what is to be drawn out of 1 Samuel 16 and 2 Samuel 7 as they related prior to a demonological perspective.

[109] A. Anderson, *2 Samuel* (WBC 11; Dallas: Word, 1989), 122.

of times and in various contexts. Matthew uses the title twice to emphasize Jesus' royal lineage (1:1, 20), twice in the context of (only) blindness (9:27; 20:30-31), once in the context of healing the lame and blind (21:15), twice in the context of therapeutic exorcisms (12:33; 15:22) and twice to highlight Jesus' relationship to Jerusalem/Temple (21:9, 15). (I have not included here Matthew's account of the question concerning the Messiah's identity in Matthew 22:41-46. As discussed later, Matthew avoids using the title in his account.[110]) It is important to recognize this general diversity in that there is a danger in drawing too much significance from any one of these contexts.

In this section, I focus primarily upon those instances where Matthew's redaction is most evident, which guides the present study to discuss the title's employment in contexts of therapy. But it must be kept in mind that Matthew was comfortable with the title's plurisignificance[111] in that he was generally happy to include the Son of David tradition that was not localized within a therapeutic agenda. From this premise, two questions arise: How did Matthew alter the tradition that he received? And what did Matthew contribute to this overall portrait of Son of David?

The Jericho Healing and Parallels

Burger rightly concluded that Matthew's interest in Son of David was sparked by the Markan words of Bartimaeus. That Matthew significantly expanded this context(s) and reapplied the title throughout his gospel is evidence that his understanding of the title went well beyond that of Mark.[112] Because of this, my analysis of Matthew will begin with a comparison of Mark 10:46-52 and Matthew 20:29-34 // 9:27-31. It will be necessary to look closely at the Greek vocabulary of these texts. Before doing so, the New American Standard reads:

> Mark 10:46-52: Then they came to Jericho. And as He was leaving Jericho with His disciples and a large crowd, a blind beggar *named* Bartimaeus, the son of Timaeus, was sitting by the road. When he heard that it was Jesus the Nazarene, he began to cry out and say, "Jesus, Son of David, have mercy on me!" Many were sternly telling him to be quiet, but he kept crying out all the more, "Son of David, have mercy on me!" And Jesus stopped and said, "Call him *here*." So they called the blind man, saying to him, "Take courage, stand

---

[110] This might suggest the limits of Matthew's diversity and at the same time speak to the extent of his inclusion of tradition. Because Mark 12:35-37 can be read in a way that disassociates Jesus from "Son of David," Matthew disassociates the title from the question concerning David's son. Yet the account is not altogether excluded.

[111] Cf. Duling, "Plurisignificant," 116.

[112] Cf. Loader, 579–80; contra Burger, 79.

up! He is calling for you." Throwing aside his cloak, he jumped up and came to Jesus. And answering him, Jesus said, "What do you want Me to do for you?" And the blind man said to Him, "Rabboni, I *want* to regain my sight!" And Jesus said to him, "Go; your faith has made you well." Immediately he regained his sight and began following Him on the road.

Matthew 20:29-34: As they were leaving Jericho, a large crowd followed Him. And two blind men sitting by the road, hearing that Jesus was passing by, cried out, "Lord, have mercy on us, Son of David!" The crowd sternly told them to be quiet, but they cried out all the more, "Lord, Son of David, have mercy on us!" And Jesus stopped and called them, and said, "What do you want Me to do for you?" They said to Him, "Lord, *we want* our eyes to be opened." Moved with compassion, Jesus touched their eyes; and immediately they regained their sight and followed Him.

Matthew 9:27-31: As Jesus went on from there, two blind men followed Him, crying out, "Have mercy on us, Son of David!" When He entered the house, the blind men came up to Him, and Jesus said to them, "Do you believe that I am able to do this?" They said to Him, "Yes, Lord." Then He touched their eyes, saying, "It shall be done to you according to your faith." And their eyes were opened. And Jesus sternly warned them: "See that no one knows *about this*!" But they went out and spread the news about Him throughout all that land. (emphasis added)

These stories share several similarities, which has led many to think that Matthew has modeled both of his stories after Mark's Jericho healing. But when these stories are seen in parallel, another possibility emerges:

	Mark 10:46-52	Matthew 20:29-34	Matthew 9:27-31
A	Καὶ ἔρχονται εἰς Ἰεριχώ. Καὶ ἐκπορευομένου αὐτοῦ ἀπὸ Ἰεριχὼ καὶ τῶν μαθητῶν αὐτοῦ καὶ ὄχλου ἱκανοῦ ὁ υἱὸς Τιμαίου Βαρτιμαῖος, τυφλὸς προσαίτης, ἐκάθητο παρὰ τὴν ὁδόν. Καὶ ἀκούσας ὅτι Ἰησοῦς ὁ Ναζαρηνός ἐστιν ἤρξατο κράζειν καὶ λέγειν· υἱὲ Δαυὶδ Ἰησοῦ, ἐλέησόν με.	Καὶ ἐκπορευομένων αὐτῶν ἀπὸ Ἰεριχὼ ἠκολούθησεν αὐτῷ ὄχλος πολύς. Καὶ ἰδοὺ δύο τυφλοὶ καθήμενοι παρὰ τὴν ὁδόν ἀκούσαντες ὅτι Ἰησοῦς παράγει, ἔκραξαν λέγοντες· ἐλέησον ἡμᾶς, κύριε, υἱὸς Δαυίδ.	Καὶ παράγοντι ἐκεῖθεν τῷ Ἰησοῦ ἠκολούθησαν αὐτῷ δύο τυφλοὶ κράζοντες καὶ λέγοντες· ἐλέησον ἡμᾶς, υἱὸς Δαυίδ.

The Therapeutic Son of David 159

	Mark 10:46-52	Matthew 20:29-34	Matthew 9:27-31
B	Καὶ ἐπετίμων αὐτῷ πολλοὶ ἵνα σιωπήσῃ· ὁ δὲ πολλῷ μᾶλλον ἔκραζεν· υἱὲ Δαυίδ, ἐλέησόν με.	Ὁ δὲ ὄχλος ἐπετίμησεν αὐτοῖς ἵνα σιωπήσωσιν· οἱ δὲ μεῖζον ἔκραξαν λέγοντες· ἐλέησον ἡμᾶς, κύριε, υἱὸς Δαυίδ	
C	Καὶ στὰς ὁ Ἰησοῦς εἶπεν· φωνήσατε αὐτόν. Καὶ φωνοῦσιν τὸν τυφλὸν λέγοντες αὐτῷ· θάρσει, ἔγειρε, φωνεῖ σε. Ὁ δὲ ἀποβαλὼν τὸ ἱμάτιον αὐτοῦ ἀναπηδήσας ἦλθεν πρὸς τὸν Ἰησοῦν. Καὶ ἀποκριθεὶς αὐτῷ ὁ Ἰησοῦς εἶπεν· τί σοι θέλεις ποιήσω;	Καὶ στὰς ὁ Ἰησοῦς ἐφώνησεν αὐτοὺς καὶ εἶπεν· τί θέλετε ποιήσω ὑμῖν;	Ἐλθόντι δὲ εἰς τὴν οἰκίαν προσῆλθον αὐτῷ οἱ τυφλοί, καὶ λέγει αὐτοῖς ὁ Ἰησοῦς· πιστεύετε ὅτι δύναμαι τοῦτο ποιῆσαι;
D	Ὁ δὲ τυφλὸς εἶπεν αὐτῷ· ραββουνί, ἵνα ἀναβλέψω.	Λέγουσιν αὐτῷ· κύριε, ἵνα ἀνοιγῶσιν οἱ ὀφθαλμοὶ ἡμῶν.	Λέγουσιν αὐτῷ· ναὶ κύριε.
E	Καὶ ὁ Ἰησοῦς εἶπεν αὐτῷ· ὕπαγε, ἡ πίστις σου σέσωκέν σε. Καὶ εὐθὺς ἀνέβλεψεν καὶ ἠκολούθει αὐτῷ ἐν τῇ ὁδῷ.	Σπλαγχνισθεὶς δὲ ὁ Ἰησοῦς ἥψατο τῶν ὀμμάτων αὐτῶν, καὶ εὐθέως ἀνέβλεψαν καὶ ἠκολούθησαν αὐτῷ.	Τότε ἥψατο τῶν ὀφθαλμῶν αὐτῶν λέγων· κατὰ τὴν πίστιν ὑμῶν γενηθήτω ὑμῖν. Καὶ ἠνεῴχθησαν αὐτῶν οἱ ὀφθαλμοί.
F			καὶ ἐνεβριμήθη αὐτοῖς ὁ Ἰησοῦς λέγων· ὁρᾶτε μηδεὶς γινωσκέτω. Οἱ δὲ ἐξελθόντες διεφήμισαν αὐτὸν ἐν ὅλῃ τῇ γῇ ἐκείνῃ.

As seen in the first two columns, Matthew's Jericho healing follows the overall structure of Mark's. (A) The setting of Jericho is specified and the blind person(s), who are sitting by the side of the road, call out to Jesus saying "Son of David, have mercy . . . !" (B) The blind person(s) is rebuked by the crowd but cries out again for the Son of David. (C) Jesus replies and asks, "What do you want me to do for you?" (D) The blind person(s) requests to "see again." (E) Jesus heals and the person(s) follows Jesus.

Aside from Mark's characterization of Bartimaeus, this is essentially the same story. Matthew follows Mark's setting, sequence, and telos. While Matthew's language is not identical to Mark's in this account, many of the variations can be explained by the shift from singular to the plural: For example, the singular ἀκούσας is changed to the plural ἀκούσαντες (A). The singular ἐλέησόν με is changed to the ἐλέησον ἡμᾶς (B). The singular καὶ εὐθὺς ἀνέβλεψεν is changed to the plural καὶ εὐθέως ἀνέβλεψαν (E).[113] Thus, much of the vocabulary is the same, only inflected differently according to person. Furthermore, Mark's introduction to this character (A) and his detail concerning his cloak (C) have been understandably omitted. In sum the shift in characterization accounts for most of the variants. Aside from the character difference, Matthew's Jesus is moved with compassion and heals by touch rather than mere words (E).[114]

When Matthew 20:29-34 is compared with Matthew 9:27-31, the reverse is true: the characterization is of the same mold but the stories differ in setting, sequence, and telos. There are two figures instead of one.[115] The figures are nameless.[116] They are blind.[117] At points the language is identical. For example:

A: λέγονες· ἐλέησον ἡμᾶς [. . .] υἱὸς Δαυίδ. = λέγοντες· ἐλέησον ἡμᾶς, υἱὸς Δαυίδ.
D: Λέγουσιν αὐτῷ· κύριε = Λέγουσιν αὐτῷ [. . .] κύριε.

Notice that, in the first of these (A), Matthew has placed the title at the end of the sentence in the emphatic position. The evangelist has done this every time that he has employed the title throughout his gospel.[118] In sum, the similarities between Matthew 9:27-31 and 20:29-34 simply manifest what is common to Matthean redaction throughout the First Gospel. On the other hand, the differences in content are manifold and lead us to the heart of this discussion.

It seems that the sequence and telos of Matthew 9:27-31 have been determined by what Luz refers to as a quilting effect. He observes that this story

---

[113] This last example is interesting because ἀναβλέπω is not common in Matthew. We return to his anomaly below.
[114] A closer look at the grammatical anomalies in Mark's story is dealt with below.
[115] Cf. Matt 4:18, 21; 8:28; 18:19-20; 20:30; 21:1, 7; 22:40; 26:60; 27:21, 38.
[116] Cf. Matt 8:28; 9:18; 20:30; 21:1; 26:60; 27:38.
[117] Matt 11:5; 12:22; 15:14; 15:30-31; 20:30; 21:14; 23:16-26.
[118] Loader, 572.

"appears almost like a quilt made of patches from earlier stories."[119] Matthew has made use of Mark 1:43, which had been previously omitted. In this way, the story's telos is that of the messianic secret motif (F), which is not present in either version of the Jericho healing. The belief motif determines the dialogue between Jesus and the men (C, D). Instead of Jesus asking what the men want of him, he asks if they believe he is "able to do this" (9:28). The referent of the demonstrative is simply implied by the context. Their reply to this question is strikingly similar to Matthew 13:51.[120] The contribution of πίστις in Matthew 9:28 might have been taken from Mark 10:52, which Matthew has omitted from his own Jericho account. This is one of the very few similarities that are shared between Mark 10 and Matthew 9.[121]

It can be concluded from this analysis that Matthew's account of the Jericho healing has been taken from Markan tradition and modified according to the tendencies of Matthew. Moreover, Matthew has taken a title that Mark only associates with Jesus' presence in Jerusalem[122] and applies it in like contexts in other places in his narrative.[123] The present study has not surveyed enough texts to see a theme developing, but this is made clear in due course. At this point it suffices to say that Matthew has understood the Jericho healing to be a story of great significance and has thus applied "Son of David" with more emphasis than did Mark.

This approach explains the application of the title in Matthew 9:27-31, but the overall story is not easily explained as a duplicate of the Jericho healing. The most common suggestion is that Matthew has modeled both of his accounts after Mark 10:46-52,[124] but equally common to this discussion is an acknowledgment of uncertainty. After extensive analysis, Fuchs concluded that Matthew was privy to a different version of Mark.[125] My analysis has shown that aside from the use of the cry, "Son of David, have mercy . . . ," Matthew 9:27-31 has very little in common with Mark 10:46-52.

---

[119] Luz, 46; he also points out that Matt 9:27-31 is rich with Matthean vocabulary.
[120] Matt 13:51: Συνήκατε ταῦτα πάντα; λέγουσιν αὐτῷ· ναί.
[121] See also the form of the plea: "ἐλέησον!" This is common to all three stories; so J. M. Gibbs, "Purpose and Pattern in Matthew's Use of the Title 'Son of David,'" *NTS* 10 (1963–1964): 449.
[122] Burger, 58–59; J. Gnilka, *Das Evangelium nach Markus* (2 vols.; Zürich: Benzinger, 1978), 2:171.
[123] Burger (170) wrote: "Erscheint ferner bei Markus Jesu Auftreten als Davidide noch mit Jerusalem verknüpft, ist bei Matthäus dieser Zusammenhang gelöst . . . und die Vorstellung vom heilenden Davidssohn durchzieht sein ganzes Evangelium."
[124] Of the many commentators that hold this position, see e.g. Duling, "Therapeutic," 399; Loader, 572; D. A. Hagner, *Matthew 1–13* (WBC 33A; Dallas: Word, 1993), 252; Luz, 46.
[125] A. Fuchs, *Sprachliche Untersuchungen zu Matthäus und Lukas: Ein Beitrag zur Quellenkritik* (Rome: Biblical Institute Press, 1971), 168–70.

The fact that there are several affinities between Matthew's revision of the Jericho healing (20:29-34) and this account does not ultimately convince that this story is a duplicate. As I have pointed out, these affinities are easily explained as typical Matthean features. A better solution emerges when Mark 8:22-26 is considered in tandem with the above analysis.

> And they came to Bethsaida. And they brought a blind man to Jesus and implored him to touch him. Taking the blind man by the hand, he brought him out of the village; and after spitting on his eyes and laying his hands on him, he asked him, "Do you see anything?" And he looked up and said, "I see men, for I see them like trees, walking around." Then again he laid his hands on his eyes; and he looked intently and was restored, and began to see everything clearly. And he sent him to his home, saying, "Do not even enter the village."

This healing story is commonly thought to be one of the few omissions of Mark's narrative in Matthew. Given the difficulty of relating Matthew 9:27-31 to Mark 10:46-52, we might take seriously the possibility that the evangelist has not wholly omitted this episode. Rather he has received the tradition (likely orally) that stands behind Mark 10:46-52[126] and has heavily reworked this story to echo typical Matthean motifs and language. Consider the following parallels: (1) In both passages Jesus heals the blind. (2) In both passages Jesus heals by touching the eyes. (3) Both passages end with a form of the messianic secret motif. (4) Add to this the possibility that both healings were done in private. Perhaps Matthew has used the general framework of the story and filled it out with details that better suit his portrayal of Jesus.

There are several reasons for doing so, including the embarrassment of the partial failure of Jesus' first attempt.[127] Also Matthew seems to prefer such characters to lack individual characteristics so that it "is easier to identify with them."[128] Also, Jesus is not generally portrayed as having made use of physical media in healing. The evangelists (Matthew included) generally prefer to display Jesus' power via the spoken word or simple touch. But most important to this chapter is the possibility that Matthew has intentionally excluded details that call to mind foreign "magical" practice, à la Caesar worship.

---

[126] H. J. Held, "Matthew as Interpreter of the Miracle Stories," in *Tradition and Interpretation in Matthew* (ed. G. Bornkamm, G. Barth, and H. J. Held; London: SCM Press, 1963 [1960]), esp. 219–25.

[127] Cf. Matthew's elimination of the similar "second try" (Mark 5:8-10) in the story of the Gadarene demoniacs (Matt 8:28-34). In Matthew's portrayal, the exorcism takes much less effort on the part of Jesus.

[128] Luz, 47.

Jesus' act of spitting in the Mark 8 account resembles a story told of Vespasian.[129] Matthew similarly omits Jesus' use of saliva as detailed by Mark 7:31-37 (Matt 15:29-31).[130] By distancing Jesus' healing from that of Gentile therapy (i.e., that which might be polemicized as magic), Matthew has painted Jesus' therapeutic activity in a particularly Jewish light. Thus, the title "Son of David" has the effect of associating Jesus' therapeutic activity within a Jewish mnemonic frame rather than otherwise. This agenda is made clearer in my analysis of the Beelzebul controversy below. Before doing so, a final observation is necessary with regard to Matthew's use of the Jericho healing.

Matthew's portrayal of Jesus' therapeutic activity should be read in connection with his interpretation of Isaiah 35:5-6 and Isaiah 61:1-2. Isaiah 61:1 LXX promises "sight to the blind [τυφλοῖς ἀνάβλεψιν]." As demonstrated above, ἀναβλέπω is not common in Matthew. He borrows this word from Mark infrequently, only twice.[131] In response to the Baptist's question, Jesus alludes to Isaiah 35:5-6 // Isaiah 61:1-2. Jesus instructs John's disciples to tell him that the "blind see again [τυφλοὶ ἀναβλέπουσιν]" (Matt 11:5). Matthew's rare use of this word in the Jericho healing (Matt 20:34) serves to connect this activity to Isaiah by way of Matt 11:5.[132] A similar use of Isaianic (LXX) language is seen in Matt 9:30 where it says that "their eyes were opened [ἠνεῴχθησαν αὐτῶν οἱ ὀφθαλμοί]." Matthew has likely intended an evocation of Isaiah 35:5: "τότε ἀνοιχθήσονται ὀφθαλμοὶ τυφλῶν."[133] The plural of "the blind" in this context might explain why Matthew prefers to have his healings done in multiples.[134]

Matthew's interest in Isaiah 35:5 may have influenced how he has arranged his sequence of pericopes in 9:27-34. In the first pericope the blind are healed (9:27-31); in the second the deaf hear (9:32-34). This corresponds to Isaiah 35:5: "Then the eyes of the blind will be opened, and the ears of the deaf will be unstopped." Lastly, Gibbs has noticed a common formula used in

---

[129] Suetonius wrote: "A man of the people, who was blind, and another who was lame, together came to [Vespasian] as he sat on the tribunal, begging for help for their disorders which Serapis had promised in a dream; for the god declared that Vespasian would restore the eyes, if he would spit upon them, and give strength to the leg, if he would deign to touch with his heel. Though he had hardly any faith that that could possibly succeed, and therefore shrank even from making the attempt, he was at last prevailed upon by his friends and tried both things in public before a large crowd; and with success" (*Vesp.* 7.2–3). NB: Serapis was known as a healing god (Theissen, *Miracle Stories*, 269).

[130] Cf. John 9:1-12.

[131] Matthew 14:19 is the other occurrence, and it is used in a context other than healing the blind.

[132] Davies and Allison, 2:140.

[133] Luz (46) points out that ἀνοίγω is used in conjunction with ὀφθαλμοὶ no fewer than fifteen times in the LXX.

[134] Cf. my discussion of the two animals in Matthew 21:7 (see chap. 7).

Matthew 9:27-28; 15:22, 25; 17:15; 20:30-33 involving "have mercy" and the titles "Son of David" and "Lord."[135] In Matthew 11:2-6 the works of the "coming one" consist of having mercy and healing.[136] Matthew's portrayal of the therapeutic "Son of David" demonstrates that Israel's hopes of restoration have been realized in Jesus. The Son of David is specifically associated with Jesus' Jewishness and disassociates him from Gentile therapy.

Therapeutic Exorcisms in Matthew

Theissen observed that Mark tends to dichotomize the categories of healing and exorcism (Mark 1:32-33; 3:10-11; 6:13).[137] In contrast, Matthew occasionally changes Mark's exorcism stories [ἐκβάλλω] and describes them in terms of "therapy" [θεραπεύω or ἰάομαι]. What is not immediately clear is if this shift represents an implied distinction between healing and exorcism on the part of Matthew.

Novakovic and Duling have argued that Matthew has intentionally downplayed Son of David as exorcist in favor of a portrayal of Son of David as healer.[138] But this dichotomy is unwarranted for three reasons. The first is that Matthew is not averse to referring to exorcism as "ἐκβάλλω"; in fact he does so frequently, often to describe Jesus' therapeutic ministry.[139] The second is that even though Matthew prefers θεραπεύω in Son of David contexts, he occasionally employs ἐκβάλλω in conjunction with θεραπεύω (Matt 8:16; 10:1; 10:8). In these cases θεραπεύω is meant to qualify ἐκβάλλω, not replace it. Lastly, as Charlesworth has shown with the *Testament of Solomon*, sickness was often understood demonologically.[140] This has been confirmed in my own analysis of Josephus.

That Mark tends toward this dichotomy[141] suggests that varying interpretations of this relationship existed in the first century. But this only confirms that Matthew's interpretation was more in line with Josephus and the author of *Testament of Solomon* as the evangelist has chosen to blur the distinction set in place by Mark. It should be pointed out that not every illness was thought to have been caused by demons. Exorcism seems to be under the larger therapeutic umbrella but not identical with it.[142] Matthew was intent to por-

---

[135] Gibbs, 449–50.

[136] France, 285; Berger, 13.

[137] Theissen, *Miracle Stories*, 85; he admits that this dichotomy should not be taken too far in that the two are obviously related and thus associated with one another.

[138] Duling, "Therapeutic," 398; Novakovic, 105–9; cf. Luz, 48.

[139] Matt 7:22; 8:16, 31; 9:33, 34; 10:8; 12:24, 26, 27, 28; 17:19.

[140] Charlesworth, "Son of David," 82.

[141] Sorensen (135) demonstrates that Mark consistently uses separate verbs for exorcism, which suggests that he classified these as separate therapeutic categories.

[142] Theissen, *Miracle Stories*, 85.

tray Jesus as the healing Messiah and has included Mark's exorcism stories because he understands exorcism to be a form of healing. This is important for Matthew, who wants Jesus to be understood as the divinely authorized messianic healer rather than associated with foreign therapy. "Son of David" features prominently in this agenda, as shown in the following analysis of Matthew 12:22-28 and 15:21-28.

The Beelzebul controversy has attracted an enormous amount of scholarly interest. It is often viewed as a window into (the historical) Jesus' personal interpretation of his ministry of exorcism[143] and its relationship to the kingdom of God.[144] My present interests are more concerned with how Matthew has seen this story through the lens of his own agenda. Matthew 12:22-28 reads:

> Then a demon-possessed man, blind and mute, was brought to Jesus and he healed [ἐθεράπευσεν] him, so that the mute man spoke and saw. All the crowds were amazed, and were saying, "This man cannot be the Son of David, can he?" But when the Pharisees heard, they said, "This man casts [ἐκβάλλει] out demons only by Beelzebul, the ruler of the demons!" And knowing their thoughts Jesus said to them, "Any kingdom divided against itself is laid waste; and any city or house divided against itself will not stand. If Satan casts out [ἐκβάλλει] Satan, he is divided against himself; how then will his kingdom stand? If I by Beelzebul cast out demons [ἐκβάλλω τὰ δαιμόνια], by whom do your sons cast out? [οἱ υἱοὶ ὑμῶν ἐν τίνι ἐκβάλλουσιν;] For this reason they will be your judges. But if I cast out demons [ἐκβάλλω τὰ δαιμόνια], by the Spirit of God, then the kingdom of God has come upon you.

The Markan arrangement of this tradition (in all likelihood, independent from Q) does not narrate an exorcism story. Mark's version takes the form of an independent accusation from the "scribes." For the most part, Matthew has followed Q. Luke 11:14 reflects Q's introduction, "Now he was casting out a demon . . . [Καὶ ἦν ἐκβάλλων δαιμόνιον . . .]." Novakovic is correct to observe that Matthew has intentionally omitted the term "exorcism [ἐκβάλλω]" from this introduction.[145] But it cannot be doubted that Matthew intends this

---

[143] E.g., J. D. G. Dunn, *Jesus and the Spirit* (Grand Rapids: Eerdmans, 1975), 44–49; N. T. Wright, *Jesus and the Victory of God* (Minneapolis: Fortress, 1996), 195, 438; M. Bockmuehl, *This Jesus* (Downers Grove, Ill.: InterVarsity, 1994), 56.

[144] Lövestam summarizes the relationship between demons, illness, and kingdom nicely: "In the NT, demons are an emanation, the representatives of a single power hostile to God. In the Synoptics their action is manifested in their sickness, physical, or psychological, or both at the same time" (99 [author's translation]). Thus, in both his therapeutic and exorcistic ministry, Jesus was battling a unified power hostile to God.

[145] Novakovic, 104; cf. a similar redactional pattern in Matt 4:23, 24; 9:35; 15:30; 21:14. Novakovic also notes that "even though Matthew 4:24 mentions demoniacs (δαιμονιζόμενοι), they belong to a more general category (those afflicted with various diseases and pains) whom Jesus healed (ἐθεράπευσεν)."

story to be associated with exorcism. Indeed, ἐκβάλλω is used five times in the following sequence of sayings. It is clear from this context that Matthew was comfortable classifying Jesus' exorcism under the umbrella of therapy. Sorensen speaks to Matthew's agenda in this respect:

> By classifying exorcism as a form of healing [Matthew gains] the practical advantage of connecting Jesus' activity to the biblical prophetic tradition about the works that identify the true messiah which otherwise did not mention exorcism among Jesus' messianic acts, even though it was not prescribed by prophecy.[146]

This is an extremely important point that must be underscored. Matthew understood Jesus' therapeutic ministry in light of the promises of Isaiah. It is important to recognize that Matthew has placed this controversy directly after a fulfillment formula that quotes Isaiah 42.[147] The verse immediately preceding our passage specifies that the messiah's task involves blessings for Gentiles (Matt 12:21 // Isa 42:4). Matthew is careful to follow this quotation with a story that emphasizes Jesus' Jewishness. Sorensen is thus correct that this played into Matthew's decision to classify this exorcism as an act of Isaianic therapy.[148]

This agenda is further clarified as Matthew aimed to disassociate Jesus' ministry from foreign therapy. Jesus is accused of acting on the authority of a foreign deity. By accusing Jesus of being in league with Beelzebul (the ancient God of Ekron[149]) the Pharisees associated Jesus with foreign therapy. If so, Jesus would have been understood as an outsider and an enemy of YHWH and his people. Matthew has used this dialogue as an opportunity to demonstrate that Jesus acts on behalf of YHWH and Israel by the power of the spirit of God.[150] While the Pharisees tried to paint Jesus as an outsider, Matthew's

---

[146] Sorensen, 135–36.

[147] "Behold, my servant whom I have chosen; my beloved in whom my soul is well-pleased; I will put my Spirit upon him and he shall proclaim justice to the Gentiles. He will not quarrel, nor cry out; nor will anyone hear his voice in the streets. A battered reed, he will not break off, and a smoldering wick, he will not put out, until he leads justice to victory. And in his name the Gentiles will hope" (Matt 12:18-21; cf. Isa 42:1-4).

[148] It is also notable that Isaiah 42 heavily concentrates on blindness (42:7, 16, 18 and three times in v. 19). The verse closest to the Matthew quotation promises "to open blind eyes" (Isa 42:7). It is then no coincidence that Matthew has followed his fulfillment formula with the healing of a blind man.

[149] Ekron was originally associated with Canaanite territory (Josh 13:3). See W. E. M. Aitkins, "Beelzebul," *JBL* (1912): 34–53; Beelzebul is featured prominently in *T.Sol.* (2:8–3:6; 6:1-11) as "the ruler of the demons," but it is difficult to determine how much this reflects NT influence.

[150] Notice that Matthew has not attached the circumlocution "τῶν οὐρανῶν" as is his tendency. Davies and Allison (2:339–40) argue that Matthew has intentionally maintained this

Jesus refutes this accusation by appealing to other precedents for Jewish exorcism. The logic here is that if Jesus is acting on the authority of Satan, the other "sons" of Israel must do so as well. Thus, the key issue in the Beelzebul controversy is whether Jesus is a practitioner of foreign therapy[151] or if he ought to be counted among the "sons" of Israel.

I have so far left unmentioned Matthew's application of "Son of David" to this context. This has been necessary to determine the central issue(s) in Matthew's received tradition. We are now in a position to determine what it was that attracted the title to this context. Because the crux of Jesus' argument was his appeal to the precedent of other Jewish exorcists, Matthew has attempted to associate Jesus, not with foreign deities, but with a true "son" of Israel: the Son of David.

At the same time, Matthew has associated Jesus with the most well-known (indeed the archetypal) precedent for exorcism: Solomon, the Son of David. Matthew's portrayal of Jesus is that of an exorcist so talented and successful that he struck awe into his supposed onlookers and invited the possibility that he was Solomon *redivivus*. Jesus does not act on the authority of foreign deities; he is among the *sons* of Israel, and, moreover, he is *the Son* of David. On this basis he has authority to cast out demons therapeutically.

I am not persuaded by the argument that Matthew has in mind only Isaianic fulfillment of messianic healing.[152] There can be no doubt that this framework was crucially important to Matthew; it has led him to classify Jesus' exorcism as a therapeutic act. But the fact that he specifically associated this passage with "Son of David"[153] (a title not taken from Isaiah) shows that Matthew had a broader notion of how to interpret Jesus' therapeutic ministry.

---

language to call attention to the contrast between the kingdom of Satan and the kingdom of God. This concept of the duality of spiritual kingdoms is reminiscent of the belief manifested at Qumran that Belial's kingdom stood in direct opposition to the people of the community (4Q286 f7 2.1-6). Cf. also the role that the Spirit plays in establishing YHWH's true community in 1QS 3.6 and the duality of spirits referred to in 1QS 3.18-19. For an assessment of duality (both cosmic and ethical) in the latter test see Frey, 294.

[151] On the perception of Jesus as a magician, see Aune, 1523–29; Stanton, "Jesus of Nazareth," esp. 171–75; N. T. Wright, *Victory of God*, 440; pace M. Smith, *Jesus the Magician*, 94–139.

[152] Novakovic argues that Matthew emphasizes Jesus as the healing messiah and deemphasizes Jesus the exorcist. Central to her conclusion is a dichotomy between the Solomon-the-exorcist tradition and Davidic messianism. Novakovic argues that the title "Son of David" should be understood exclusively in terms of healing and rejects the notion that Matthew has inherited a tradition which has fused these two categories. She concludes that Matthew "neither presupposes nor accomplishes the converging of the traditions about Solomon as exorcist and the Davidic Messiah. . . . Jesus' healing miracles function as the messianic deeds and not as the acts of the miracle worker after the order of Solomon" (107).

[153] Charlesworth, "Son of David," 84.

Because exorcism was such a large part of his received tradition and because it (at least in this case) carried the negative connotation of foreign exorcistic practice, Matthew had need of a category that was in line with both royal messianism and Jewish exorcism.[154] Solomon typology served to bridge these two mnemonic spheres for Matthew.

Matthew's account of the Canaanite woman and her daughter sheds further light upon Matthew's Son of David agenda (Matt 15:22-28):

> And behold, a Canaanite woman came out from that region, and began to cry out, saying, "Have mercy on me, O Lord, Son of David; my daughter is cruelly demon-possessed." But he did not answer her a word. And His disciples came and kept asking him, saying, "Send her away, for she is shouting out after us." But he answered and said, "I was sent only to the lost sheep of the house of Israel." But she came and began to bow down before him, saying, "Lord, help me!" And He answered and said, "It is not good to take the children's bread and throw it to the dogs." But she said, "Yes, Lord; but even the dogs feed on the crumbs which fall from their masters' table." Then Jesus answered and said to her, "O woman, your faith is great; be it done for you as you wish." And her daughter was healed at once.

This is a fascinating story that is not treated in full presently. However, several brief observations are warranted to confirm my previous analysis. (1) Jesus is hailed as Son of David in conjunction with a request for exorcism. (2) Matthew has emphasized that the "demon-possessed [δαιμονίζομαι]" has been "healed [ἰάομαι]."[155] (3) The issue of Jesus' relationship to foreigners is at center stage as the woman is a Canaanite.[156] (4) Matthew has made three significant conceptual alterations to this story that warrant further detail and comment: (4A) Matthew has added to this dialogue Jesus' words: "I was sent only to the lost sheep of the house of Israel" (Matt 15:24). (4B) Matthew has omitted from this dialogue Jesus' words: "Let the children be fed first . . ." (Mark 7:27a). (4C) Matthew has added to this dialogue the woman's words: "Son of David" (Matt 15:22).

In this passage we see a similar network of interlocking concerns as were present in Matthew 12:22-28. Matthew is chiefly interested in showing that

---

[154] Cf. Berger, 13; he concluded that Son of David was a Solomonic category and, at the same time, in complete coherence with Matthew's Deutero-Isaianic program.

[155] This story demonstrates that exorcism and healing are overlapping mnemonic frames. D. Trunk has argued that Matthew has downplayed exorcism but admits that he is unsure whether this story fits the form of a healing story either (*Der messianische Heiler: eine redaktions- und religionsgeschichtliche Studie zu den Exorzismen im Matthäusevanglium* [Freiburg: Herder, 1994], 142); Davies and Allison, 2:544, have called this story a "mixed-form."

[156] Cf. the previous association with Ekron (a territory historically associated with Canaan) in Matthew 10:25; 12:24.

Jesus' therapeutic activity confirms his Jewishness and is in no way to be associated with foreigners. The Matthean Jesus emphasizes this by saying that his ministry is only aimed at Israel (4A). Mark's story hints in the direction of a hierarchical sequence: *first* Israel, *then* the Gentiles. By Matthew's account, Jesus has no intention of ever coming to the aid of Canaan (4B)! Matthew has taken every effort to portray Jesus' therapeutic ministry as a distinctly Israelite blessing (4C). Within this context the application of "Son of David" serves to align Jesus' ministry of exorcism with the distinctly Jewish archetype, Solomon. Matthew's Jesus, as Son of David, cannot be accused of having any sympathy for the therapy of Gentiles.

The woman eventually receives the benefits of the Son of David's therapeutic ministry because she assumes the posture that is theopolitically correct: she kneels.[157] She comes to Jesus in complete deference and submission[158] and thus receives the superfluous blessings from the table of YHWH's chosen people.[159] Even then, Jesus heals by distance rather than entering the house of a Gentile.

In summary, this section has argued that Matthew subsumed exorcism under the heading of therapy, not because he has chosen to downplay exorcism, but because he understands Jesus' exorcisms to be in line with Isaiah's promised healing. By associating Jesus' therapeutic ministry with Isaiah, Matthew has distanced Jesus from any accusation of foreign therapy or Gentile sympathy. The Solomonic title "Son of David" aptly serves this agenda in that it provides a Jewish precedent for exorcism. Jesus as Son of David is fashioned after the archetypal royal exorcist: Solomon.

Son of David, Authority, and Metaphorical Blindness

Kingsbury argued that, because "Son of David" is most common in the context of Jesus healing the blind, it represents a literary symbol on the part of Matthew to contrast the metaphorical blindness of Israel (represented by the Pharisees) with the opening of the eyes of true Israel (represented by Jesus' followers).[160] I am largely sympathetic to this thesis and would also

---

[157] Theissen, *Miracle Stories*, 53.

[158] Trunk (149–50) argues that Mark's aorist προσέπεσεν (Mark 7:25) has been changed by Matthew to the imperfect προσεκύναει in order to show even more humility on the part of the woman (Matt 15:25). Berger (22) very helpfully extended this theme to Matthew's infancy narrative (Matt 2). Here the foreign Magi come in proper deference and submission to the true king of Israel.

[159] C. E. B. Cranfield, *The Gospel according to St. Mark* (CTGC; Cambridge: Cambridge University Press, 1963), 249.

[160] J. D. Kingsbury, "The Title 'Son of David' in Matthew's Gospel," *JBL* 95 (1976): 601–2; T. Y. Mullins calls this Matthew's "three-motif constellation" ("Jesus, the 'Son of David,'" *AUSS* 29 [1991]: 123).

add an observation based on my previous examination of *Psalm of Solomon* 17. Because *Psalm of Solomon* 17 is commonly attributed to the Pharisees, one might consider the possibility that one of Matthew's arguments with the Pharisees concerned the proper understanding of the title "Son of David."[161]

With this in mind, there is a repeated motif in Matthew's gospel where the title is applied to Jesus by a lesser member of society, which sparks a negative comment on the part of the Jewish leadership (12:23-24; 21:15). Considering Matthew's indictment of the Pharisees and scribes in Matthew 23:16-26 (where they are insultingly called "blind" no fewer than five times),[162] this is no doubt part of Matthew's agenda. Although it must be said that this idea manifests itself in an overarching theme more than it does in a frequently repeated motif. As mentioned, there are only two occurrences where "Son of David" is localized within a leadership dispute. The first instance, the Beelzebul controversy, has already been discussed. I also briefly touch upon the second instance, Jesus' healing in the temple, in the following chapter. With this in mind, I circumvent redundancy as much as possible and focus on Matthew's larger thematic picture. After all, one must try to avoid "the folly of interpreting the individual pericopae of the gospel in isolation from each other." In the end, the "many pieces of Matthew hang together and were intended to shed light upon one another. Meaning resides not just in the parts but in the whole."[163]

As seen in my analysis of the Beelzebul controversy, Matthew has taken a dispute concerning the authority behind his exorcisms and has turned it into a platform for his Son of David agenda. Kingsbury pointed out that part of this agenda included a polemical portrayal of Israel's leadership. Matthew's account is essentially a demonological "healing" followed by three responses. Matthew has couched the first response (the crowd's Son of David association) between Jesus' healing exorcism and the second response (the Pharisees' accusation). The third response is reserved for Jesus, who has the final word. More accurately, Jesus has several final words as Matthew (following Q) launches into a series of rebukes aimed at the Pharisees. In this way, Matthew's crowd is open to the possibility of Jesus as the Son of David because he has restored sight and speech to a blind and mute person. In contrast, Israel's leadership is "blind" to this possibility, and they are silenced by Jesus' rebuke.

---

[161] J. W. Bowker, *Jesus and the Pharisees* (Cambridge: Cambridge University Press, 1973), 38–52, argued that Jesus was condemned as a false elder who had led Israel astray. The point is worth repeating, however, that the Pharisees probably represent the first-century group most ideologically similar to that of Jesus' movement (and perhaps Matthew's community).

[162] Cf. the similar but more modest accusation in 15:14.

[163] Davies and Allison, 2:141.

This thesis has been picked up by Trunk. He correctly observes that the dispute concerning the authority of Jesus' exorcisms "gains a paradigmatic meaning for the dispute about the Messiah of Israel, the Son of David."[164] Matthew's climactic healing in the temple[165] should be seen from this vantage point.

As discussed in the next chapter, the Matthean Jesus enters Jerusalem amid acclamations that publicly declare him the Son of David. Upon entering the temple, Jesus "drove out [ἐξέβαλεν]" the merchants (21:12).[166] Immediately after his demonstration,

> The blind and the lame came to him and he healed them. But when the chief priests and the scribes saw the wonderful things that he had done, and the children who were shouting in the temple, "Hosanna to the Son of David!" they became indignant and said to him, "Do you hear what these are saying?" (21:14-16)

In accordance with the motif, Jesus has the final word and the dialogue ends. So again we have a healing followed by three responses in the exact order of the Beelzebul controversy: (1) The amazed onlookers apply "Son of David" to Jesus; (2) Israel's leadership attempts to correct this interpretation of Jesus' healing; (3) Jesus rebukes Israel's leadership.

But more important than the motif (which is rare in Matthew[167]) is the theme that stands behind it: Jesus as Son of David has divine authority to subdue the enemies of God's people, whether they are demons or false leaders. Jesus' authority within the temple precincts further demonstrates his condemnation of Israel's leadership. As the Son of David, Jesus heals the blind

---

[164] Translated from Trunk, 92.

[165] D. Senior, *The Gospel of Matthew* (Nashville: Abingdon, 1997), 153.

[166] Pertinent to this usage is Twelftree's survey of how ἐκβάλλω generally functions in the LXX [*Jesus the Exorcist*, 110]: It is primarily used when Yahweh's enemies are about to be cast out of the land. "Most occurrences of ἐκβάλλω in the LXX are in contexts where an enemy, frustrating or standing in the way of God fulfilling his purpose for his chosen people of Israel, is cast out (ἐκβάλλω) *so that God's purpose can be fulfilled*. This purpose is most often the possession of the promised land." Cf. LXX Exod 23:20; Deut 33:27-28.

[167] Given that this motif is only used twice by Matthew, the possibility emerges that these accounts are metaphorically related. The healing exorcism of Matthew 12:22ff. was used by the evangelist as a springboard for sayings related to exorcism. In this context ἐκβάλλω is used four times (12:24, 26, 27, 28). This is the highest concentration of such vocabulary in Matthew. It is possible that when Jesus "drove out [ἐξέβαλεν]" the merchants, he performed a metaphorical exorcism of the temple. Furthermore Jesus' reference to the "house [οἰκία]" of the strong man (12:29) might anticipate "my house will be called a house of prayer [οἶκός μου οἶκος προσευχῆς κληθήσεται]" (Matt 21:13; cf. Isa 56:7; Jer 7:11). From this possibility, we might reconsider the possibility that Beelzebul was appealed to for the etymology of the name "Lord of the House (= Temple?)" that was first suggested by L. Gaston, "Beelzebul," *TZ* 18 (1962): 253–54.

and lame in the temple and continues to condemn the temple establishment through sayings, disputes, and parables until his ultimate indictment of the Pharisees as "blind guides" in Matthew 23.

Thus far I have followed Kingsbury in arguing that Matthew's juxtaposition of literal blindness and metaphorical blindness is directly related to Jesus' status as Son of David. It is now necessary to offer a possible reason that Matthew has associated "Son of David" with this theme. Building upon earlier suggestions,[168] Paffenroth has argued that Jesus' temple healings as the Son of David should be read in light of a particular episode from the life of the historic David.[169] I offer here an abbreviated version of 2 Samuel 5:3-10 (emphasis indicative of pertinence).

> So all the elders [. . .] anointed David king over Israel. David was thirty years old when he became king [. . .] Now the king and his men went to Jerusalem against the Jebusites, the inhabitants of the land, and they said to David, "You shall not come in here, but the blind and lame will turn you away"; thinking, "David cannot enter here." Nevertheless, David captured the stronghold of Zion, that is the city of David. David said on that day, "Whoever would strike the Jebusites, let him reach *the lame and the blind*, who are hated by David's soul, through the water tunnel." Therefore they say, "*The blind or the lame shall not come into the house.*" So David lived in the stronghold and called it the city of David. [. . .] David became greater and greater, for YHWH, God of hosts, was with him.

Paffenroth argues that Jesus as Son of David has been "contrasted, not compared, with his father David: David was a powerful warrior" while "Jesus is a powerful healer." She argues that the central parallel is that David excluded the blind and lame from the city (and temple by way of the saying associated with the story), while Jesus cured the blind and lame in the temple. Mullins suggests that Matthew inherited the three-motif constellation and did not himself see a connection with 2 Samuel 5.[170] Trunk observes that there must be some connection but gives no suggestion of how these stories might relate.[171] The problem commonly felt in this discussion is that the

---

[168] J. C. Fenton, *Saint Matthew* (Baltimore: Pelican, 1963), 334; E. Schweizer, *The Good News according to Matthew* (Philadelphia: Westminster, 1975), 408; R. H. Gundry, *Matthew: A Commentary on His Literary and Theological Art* (Grand Rapids: Eerdmans, 1982), 413; Mullins; Davies and Allison, 3:140; D. J. Harrington, *The Gospel of Matthew* (Sacra Pagina 1; Collegeville, Minn.: Liturgical Press, 1991), 294.

[169] K. Paffenroth, "Jesus as Anointed and Healing Son of David in the Gospel of Matthew," *Biblica* 80 (1999): 547–54.

[170] Mullins (122–25) argues, "The First Gospel probably did not see a special importance in the references to blindness in conjunction with the Son-of-David."

[171] Trunk, 61–63.

title "Son of David" serves to associate Jesus (in some sense) with the historic David, but Jesus seems to be opposite to David with respect to his healing of the blind and lame.

A better solution to this problem is seen when one takes seriously Matthew's interest in metaphorical blindness. In my estimation, Jesus as the healing Son of David is typologically similar to David in this respect.[172] Therefore Paffenroth's argument for contrast is misplaced.[173] Matthew has typologically called to mind David's hatred for the blind and his refusal of their presence in Jerusalem/temple. But for Matthew, the question is *who is really blind?* According to the evangelist, it is not the literally blind that the Son of David hates; in fact, Jesus restores sight to these marginalized members of society. In such contexts, the Matthean Jesus is reputed for his compassion (Matt 9:36; 14:14; 15:32; 20:34). Rather, the worst kind of blindness is metaphorical: Israel's leaders, especially the Pharisees, represent spiritual blindness and thus are condemned from a pulpit of temple authority. This is the context that best explains Matthew's use of Isaiah 56:7 on the lips of Jesus. Isaiah 56:7-10 reads (emphasis added):

> Even those I will bring to my Holy Mount and make them joyful in my house of prayer. Their burnt offerings and their sacrifices will be acceptable on my altar. For my house will be called a house of prayer for all the peoples. YHWH God, who gathers the dispersed of Israel, declares, yet I will gather to them, to those gathered. All you beasts of the field, all you beasts in the forest, come to eat. *His watchmen are blind; all of them know nothing.* . . .

As seen previously, Matthew's blindness theme was taken in large part from Isaiah 35:5 and 61:1-2. It is evident from the context of Isaiah 56 (from which Jesus quoted during his temple demonstration) that Matthew's interest in metaphorical blindness has also been informed by Isaiah. This climactic quotation of Isaiah also brings to fruition Matthew's Jewishness-versus-foreigner theme. Jesus is here portrayed as an advocate for foreign worship in the temple. Matthew's quote demonstrates that this concept does not stem from Jesus' foreign sympathies but from Isaianic theology: if the nations come in deference and submission to YHWH and his chosen people, their sacrifices will be acceptable on the altar.

---

[172] Cf. D. Patte, *The Gospel according to Matthew: A Structural Commentary on Matthew's Faith* (Philadelphia: Fortress, 1987), 288–90.

[173] Paffenroth (553) argues that because David was unable to save his child from death (2 Sam 12:16ff.) he was understood to have been a poor healer; in contrast, Jesus is an excellent healer. This connection seems vague and is contrary to David's reputation as discussed earlier in this chapter.

To this theme, the evangelist again has appended Son of David typology in order to lend authority to Jesus. "Son of David" connects Jesus to Solomon in that Jesus is portrayed in terms of therapy and in terms of temple authority. The title also connects him with David, who was also known for therapeutic activity and, most importantly, his rejection of the blind from Jerusalem.[174] As should be expected from this mnemonic sphere, "Son of David" evokes a dual typology.[175] There seems to be no tension in Matthew's program between a healing Davidic messiah and an exorcizing Solomon *redivivus*. Both support Matthew's thesis that Jesus is the Son of David.

Matthew's gospel betrays a tension between Jesus' association with foreign sympathies and his own belief that Jesus was the Jewish Messiah. Matthew's application of Isaiah serves to locate Jesus within a distinctly Jewish agenda. His application of "Son of David" serves to disassociate him from foreign sympathies and clarify his appeal to Isaiah. The evangelist has reinforced both mnemonic categories in his presentation as a response to non-Christian Jews who associate the Jesus movement with Gentile sympathies and non-Jewish ideology.

Jesus as Solomonic Exorcist

Generally speaking, NT scholarship is divided into three (sometimes overlapping) theories about Jesus' ministry of exorcism. The first is that Jesus' exorcisms betray an apocalyptic and eschatological worldview.[176] This group argues that the historical Jesus (and/or the evangelists[177]) understood his exorcisms as the initial binding of Satan in preparation for the eschaton.[178] The second group argues that Jesus' exorcistic ministry was ultimately about ritual purity.

---

[174] It should also be noted that the by-product of Jesus healing the blind in the temple is that these "impure" people were no longer blind! Thus, issues of purity are satisfied and Jesus' association with David is intact; that is, Jesus, like David, does not suffer the presence of blind people in the temple; he remedies this impurity by healing them.

An interesting observation has been made by Davidson, 185–86; he points out that at Qumran, the blind (among others) are excluded from the congregation because of the presence of angels (CD 15.15b-17a par. 4QDa 8 1.6-7 and 1QSa 2.4b-9). Perhaps the rationale here is that demons are associated with physical defect and angels are associated with temple worship, and the two are opposed to one another. Cf. also the exclusion of the ritually impure due to the presence of angels in 1QM 7.1-7.

[175] Cf. my example in chap. 4 of John the Baptist's affinity to both Elijah and Elisha typology.

[176] E.g., Sorensen, 129; Garrett, 46.

[177] Garrett (59) argues that every exorcism in Luke serves the purpose of demonstrating Satan's cosmic defeat (cf. Luke 10:17-20).

[178] Twelftree, *Jesus the Exorcist*, 173, 224. Most studies from this perspective see the sayings associated with the Beelzebul controversy as the hermeneutical key by which one can unlock Jesus' intentions.

Kee has argued that the purpose of Jesus' ministry was to restore the covenantal relationship between the community and its marginalized "impure" members. He thus extends Jesus' association with sinners and the physically afflicted to Jesus' ministry of exorcism.[179] The third group understands Jesus' exorcistic activity as a metaphor for liberation from Roman imperialism.[180] Others have postulated a combination of the above.[181] I am inclined to agree that the best explanation must include a combination of facets from all three perspectives. However, I presently bracket the question of Jesus' intentions and attempt to address how Jesus was perceived by his contemporaries.

The present chapter has thus far focused on the possible backgrounds for first-century exorcist/therapeutic ideology and Matthew's redactional agenda with regard to "Son of David" and therapy. In the first section, my interest was primarily diachronic. This discussion showed that the subject of "magic" brought with it great cultural tension. While many facets of magical practice were considered evil, certain therapeutic facets such as exorcism were legitimatized and incorporated into religious life, including the localization of Israel's archetypal figures within demonological categories. My largely synchronic analysis of Matthew demonstrated that many of these concerns and interpretive moves were reflected in his presentation of Jesus as Son of David. As I now turn to discuss the historical Jesus, it is necessary to locate his exorcistic and therapeutic activity somewhere along the mnemonic trajectory and in some relationship to the mnemonic sphere.

Evidence of Memory

That Jesus was perceived as an exorcist by his contemporaries is one of the few positions that enjoys virtual scholarly consensus. In his seminal examination of Jesus' miracles, Strauss concluded that Jesus' exorcisms were among those that had a high claim to historicity.[182] Every generation of scholarship

---

[179] Kee, 78–79; cf. H. Hübner, "Clean and Unclean (NT)" (vol. 6 of Anchor Bible Dictionary; ed. D. N. Freedman; Garden City, N.Y.: Doubleday, 1992), 6:742.

[180] E.g., R. A. Horsley, *Jesus and the Spiral of Violence: Popular Jewish Resistance in Roman Palestine* (San Francisco: Harper and Row, 1987), 184–90; J. D. Crossan, *The Historical Jesus: The Life of a Mediterranean Jewish Peasant* (San Francisco: HarperSanFrancisco, 1992), 313–18; C. Myers, *Binding the Strong Man: A Political Reading of Mark's Story of Jesus* (Maryknoll, N.Y.: Orbis, 1988), esp. 190–94. Most studies from this perspective utilize Mark's story of the Gerasene demoniac as the hermeneutical key by which one can unlock the other stories of exorcism. Sorensen (130) disagrees with this theory, arguing that there is insufficient evidence that there was hostility toward Roman occupation or that this is a theme in Mark. I find Sorensen's objection unconvincing.

[181] E.g., J. Marcus, *The Way of the Lord: Christological Exegesis in the Gospel of Mark* (Louisville, Ky.: Westminster John Knox, 1992), 144–45; N. T. Wright, *Jesus*, 195, 438.

[182] D. F. Strauss, *The Life of Jesus Critically Examined* (London: SCM Press, 1946 [1892]), 92–93.

since has confirmed this assessment with the majority.[183] It then becomes less a question of whether Jesus' contemporaries perceived events that they interpreted as exorcisms, but which accounts within the synoptic tradition are best explained as memory rather than invention. I argue that four of the passages surveyed in this chapter are the product of early memory.

Mark 8:22-26: (1) As briefly discussed above, Mark 8:22-26 seems to have embarrassed Matthew. Luke has likely omitted this story altogether for similar reasons. I have previously referred to this account as Jesus' "second-try" healing. In his first attempt, the blind man only sees blurrily; people look like moving trees. In contrast, Matthew's Jesus always heals effectively on the first try and with little effort. (2) Jesus spits on the man's eyes in this process. Not only does this act describe more effort than Matthew was willing to afford, it (3) calls to mind foreign therapy where saliva was thought to have healing properties (à la Caesar worship).[184] Thus, the criterion of embarrassment can be applied in three ways in this case. Furthermore, Jesus uses physical media to heal and therefore strays from the formula of healing via the spoken word or simple touch. The criterion of contrary tendency thus applies. For these reasons, Mark 8:22-26 looks to represent an account of early memory rather than invention.

Matthew 15:21-28 // Mark 7:24-30: (1) The account of the Canaanite/Syrophoenician woman's daughter is a story that was likely embarrassing on several levels. For Matthew, the fact that this woman is a Gentile requires a heightening of Jesus' unsympathetic demeanor. As discussed, Matthew's minor refractions to this tradition probably betray his apologetic debate with non-Christian Jews. (2) From a Gentile perspective, the fact that Jesus refers to the woman as a dog would have been highly embarrassing. The observation that κυνάριον refers to a domesticated dog rather than a stray dog[185] does not assuage the tension created by the assumed theopolitical hierarchy on Jesus' lips. It is not surprising that Luke has altogether omitted this account. (3) This woman refuses to be deterred by Jesus and ultimately wins the argument. This occurrence is extremely rare in the Gospels and runs contrary to the editorial tendencies of Mark and Matthew. (4) It is possible, although not conclusive, that Matthew's account represents a source independent from Mark.[186] There can be no doubt that Matthew had knowledge of Mark's ver-

---

[183] E.g. Bultmann, *Jesus* (Berlin: Deutsche Bibliothek, 1926), 124; J. M. Robinson, *A New Quest of the Historical Jesus* (London: SCM Press, 1959), 121; Crossan, *Historical Jesus*, 313–14.

[184] Matthew and Luke similarly omit Mark's account of Jesus' healing of the deaf man wherein Jesus uses his saliva (Mark 7:31-37; cf. Matt 15:29-31).

[185] Trunk, 144.

[186] Matt 15:22-28 and Mark 7:26-30 show very little evidence of literary dependence. Of

sion, but it seems as though he chose not to use it in preference for his own source. If this is so, the criterion of multiple attestation might be cautiously applied. (5) The phrase "ἧς εἶχεν τὸ θυγάτριον αὐτῆς πνεῦμα ἀκάθαρτον" might betray Semitic influence as well as a grammatical Semitism. The first is that "unclean spirit" is a particularly Jewish designation that has connotation of purity.[187] Second, "ἧς ... αὐτῆς [whose ... her]" seems redundant in Greek but not in Aramaic or Hebrew. A Semitic formulation would include the indeclinable relative pronoun ד (Aramaic) or אשר (Hebrew).[188] All considered, this story is one of the most difficult in the NT to attribute to invention. It therefore is very likely that this story has origins in memory.

Matthew 12:22-28 // Mark 3:21-27 // Luke 11:14-22: (1) The variations between the Markan and Q versions of the Beelzebul controversy suggest independence. As such the story is multiply attested. (2) Furthermore Mark's account does not take the form of an exorcism story; rather, it is an independent saying. The saying form of this controversy in Matthew 10:25 confirms that the criterion of multiple forms is warranted. (3) In the Markan version, the context is that of a dispute between Jesus and his family. In addition, Jesus has here been accused of being both insane and in league with a foreign deity. These details were obviously embarrassing to Matthew in particular and potentially embarrassing to those who held James and Mary in high regard. This story is best explained as having derived from early memory.

Matthew 20:29-34 // Mark 10:46-52: (1) It is worth reiterating that Mark's gospel was not particularly motivated by a Son of David agenda. Anderson suggests, "Mark may have seen a connexion between the designation Son of David here and the messianic fervour of the people on the entry into Jerusalem in 11:9-11."[189] If he did, he has not spelled it out for his reader. As discussed in chapter 7, Mark does not make use of the title in the account of Jesus' entry into Jerusalem, and then provides a very ambiguous use of the title in Mark 12:35-37 (see chapter 8). It seems clear that the title was relatively unimportant for Mark and that he has probably not invented it in this context. (2) In addition, the phrasing of "[Jesus, Son of David] υἱὲ Δαυὶδ Ἰησοῦ" (10:47)

---

the 140 words in Matthew and the 130 words in Mark, the two stories share fewer than 40 words in common (so, Davies and Allison, 2:542); J. D. G. Dunn, "Jesus in Oral Memory," in *Jesus: A Colloquium in the Holy Land* (ed. D. Donnelly; London: Continuum, 2001), 101–2, has offered a comparison of these stories as a case for his thesis of synoptic orality and done so compellingly. These stories seem to betray "spontaneously different variations (retellings) on a theme (the identifiable theme and core)."

[187] R. H. Gundry, *Mark: A Commentary on His Apology for the Cross* (Grand Rapids: Eerdmans, 1992), 373.

[188] E. C. Maloney, *Semitic Interference in Marcan Syntax* (SBLDS 51; Missoula, Mont.: Scholars Press, 1980), 116–18.

[189] H. Anderson, *The Gospel of Mark* (London: Oliphants, 1976), 259.

and "[the Jesus] τὸν Ἰησοῦν" (10:50) are anomalous formulations in Mark. The second of these is particularly difficult to explain.[190] These titles run contrary to the editorial tendencies of Mark in both form and function. (3) The phrase "ὁ υἱὸς Τιμαίου Βαρτιμαῖος" (Mark 10:46) contains the obviously Aramaic בַּר preceded by the explanation of this designation in Greek.[191] (4) The title "ῥαββουνί" (10:51) reflects a heightening of רַב: רַבָּן or רִבּוֹן with the suffix נִי. Hence רִבּוֹנִי or רִבּוֹנִי רִבּוֹנִי.[192] These Aramaisms suggest that the original story was not told in Greek, and this story is very difficult to explain grammatically at times. For these reasons this story was likely based on memory rather than invention.

In sum, the stories that seem most likely to have originated from memory are Mark's "second-try" healing, the exorcism of the Syrophoenician daughter, and the Beelzebul controversy. In each of these cases, Jesus has been remembered for his relationship to Gentiles or Gentile magical practice. In the latter two stories, "Son of David" has been attached to the tradition by Matthew. The one case where "Son of David" has been remembered in the career of Jesus is in the Bartimaeus healing. This is the only case where "Son of David" does not seem to have been employed as a part of a christological program, since Mark does not seem interested in relating the title to any christological claim.

Evaluation of the Evidence

Having discussed the mnemonic trajectories, spheres, and frameworks associated with Jesus' historical context, the present chapter is now in a position to ask the crucial question: How does the title "Son of David" relate to Jesus' historical career as an exorcist and healer? Based on my treatment of the evidence in this chapter, the entry point of "Son of David" into the Jesus tradition seems to have been Bartimaeus' cry for healing. That Jesus was known for his therapeutic activity seems certain. We cannot say with certainty that this took place in Jericho or that it occurred in Jesus' final week. It is not clear whether

---

[190] Charlesworth ("Son of David," 78) suggests that "the Jesus" perhaps demonstrates that there was something in the name that was titular and connotative of healing, like Joshua Ben Parahyah, who was reputed as healer in Aramaic incantation texts; cf. Montgomery, no. 17, line 14.

[191] Gundry, *Mark*, 599, supports the argument that the Aramaic טְמֵא reflects the conceptual connection of impurity "be unclean [טָמֵא]," which would have made the Greek meaning of "Timaeus [honored one]" misleading to Mark's audience. Gundry also observes that Mark usually introduces the translation of a Semitism by including "ὅ ἐστιν," i.e., "ὅ ἐστιν (μεθερμηνευόμενον)"; cf. Mark 3:17; 5:41; 7:11, 34; 12:42; 15:16, 22, 34, 42. He has not done so in this case.

[192] W. Bauer, *A Greek-English Lexicon of the New Testament and Other Early Christian Literature* (trans. W. F. Arndt and F. W. Gingrich; Chicago: University of Chicago Press, 1979 [1958]), 733.

"Son of David" was a central part of Jesus' reputation or whether it was applied only in this case. As the title is employed in Mark, it remains relatively underdeveloped and isolated. As will be seen, we are not ultimately helped by its application in Mark 12:35-37, and so our only recourse is to measure the title's significance against the mnemonic trajectories leading up to and through the first century and the mnemonic spheres available to this period.

I have demonstrated previously that (1) as a title, "Son of David" carried Solomonic significance from its earliest manifestations in the HB, (2) it maintained this significance until the first century BCE, (3) it is only extant in the Dead Sea Scrolls when used of Solomon, and (4) it continued to be applied to Solomon's legacy as it took on demonological significance in the *Testament of Solomon*. Given this trajectory, I would agree with Charlesworth "that the most probable explanation of Bartimaeus' 'οἰὲ Δαυίδ' is some Solomonic denotation."[193]

Having made this point, the red thread that has run throughout this chapter is Jesus' relationship to foreign ideas, his possible sympathy to these, and Matthew's legitimizing apologetic. What has been most clear from the texts surveyed and the redactional agenda(s) of Matthew is that Jesus' therapeutic career was marked with suspicion and conflict. Such suspicions and disputes are evident in the earliest tradition and continue throughout Jesus' legacy. The characters in Matthew's gospel reflect well the multicultural tensions discussed in the first part of this chapter. Indeed, Matthew's stance on the significance of Jesus' therapeutic ministry seems a natural reaction to accusations like the one leveled by Celsus:

> Jesus, on account of his poverty, was hired out to go to Egypt. While there he acquired certain (magical) powers which Egyptians pride themselves on possessing. He returned home highly elated at possessing these powers, and on the strength of them gave himself out to be a god. (Origen, *Cels.*, 1.28)

Celsus' quote (solidly placed in the second century) offers an alternative interpretation of Jesus' healing career. This trajectory is also evident in the much later Talmudic literature: In *b.Sanh.* 107b, Jesus is accused of being a false teacher, "and the master said: Yeshu practiced magic [כשׁיף] and deceived and led Israel astray." Similarly *b.Sanh.* 43a recounts an execution where Yeshu [ישׁו] "is going to be stoned for practicing magic [כשׁיף] and leading Israel astray." These latter quotes are problematic in several respects, including the problem of determining if Yeshu refers to Jesus of Nazareth. If so, we must also take seriously the possibility that this tradition has reacted to a much later and formalized version of the Jesus tradition. However, it is

---

[193] Charlesworth, "Son of David," 87.

interesting to note that the claim of execution by stoning does not seem to reflect gospel tradition.

Perhaps a less tenuous manifestation of this trajectory can be found in Josephus' famous "Jesus" passage. It has been widely suggested that once the "Christian interpolations" have been removed, an original core might be established. Meier's reconstruction reads:

> At this time there appeared Jesus, a wise man. For he was a doer of startling deeds, a teacher of people who receive the truth with pleasure. And he gained a following among many Jews and among many of Gentile origin.[194]

However, considering what has been suggested by the non-Christian witnesses thus far, Stanton's reconstruction might be closer to the original:

> Jesus was a doer of strange deeds, and a deluder of the simple-minded. He led astray many Jews and Greeks.[195]

While possible, such reconstructions will have to remain speculation. However, for my present purposes, the affinity between the Beelzebul controversy and the Celsus quote is enough to establish a contrary mnemonic trajectory. Jesus' opponents in the controversy accuse him of acting on the authority of a foreign deity. Celsus, who is otherwise skeptical concerning the supernatural,[196] accuses Jesus of practicing magic that he learned in Egypt.

Thus we have two separate interpretive trajectories. One (represented by Mark, Q, and Matthew) explains Jesus' healings and exorcisms as divinely authoritative. The other (betrayed by Mark and Q, and stated forthrightly by Celsus) explains Jesus as a foreign-trained magician and deceiver.

Evidence of this latter trajectory was picked up by Morton Smith.[197] He argued that Jesus' career as an exorcist (combined with certain accusations present in the sayings tradition and his eventual alienation from the Jewish religious establishment) is best explained in terms of magic. Especially pertinent to the present chapter is the observation that Mark's introduction to the Beelzebul controversy includes an accusation of insanity. Smith comments:

> From this [accusation] it seems that Jesus' exorcisms were accompanied by abnormal behaviour on his part. Magicians who want to make demons obey often scream their spells, gesticulate, and match the mad in fury.[198]

---

[194] J. P. Meier, *A Marginal Jew: Rethinking the Historical Jesus* (4 vols.; New York: Doubleday, 1991), 1:64.

[195] Stanton, "Jesus of Nazareth," 169–71.

[196] Downing, 88–91.

[197] M. Smith, 76–77.

[198] M. Smith, 43.

By appealing to a larger network of historical evidence from this period, Sanders argued that Jesus does not seem to fit the picture of a magician. He pointed out that Smith placed too much weight on the Greek magical papyri, and even if such literature were to be used judiciously, what we know of Jesus does not quite cohere with this context. Sanders contended that the fuller picture of Jesus' cultural milieu(x) measured against core gospel material makes Smith's magician portrait unlikely.[199] Sanders' objection is well taken and garners much of my sympathy. But two possible historical questions might be asked in this case. The first is, *Was Jesus a magician?* The second is, *Was Jesus perceived by many to be a magician?*

I would argue that the latter question is most helpful in this case. This is so because (as discussed above) being labeled as a magician was most often a polemical designation.[200] Much like being labeled a troublemaker, one did not choose this label in first-century Judaism; it was forced upon an individual by his (adversarial) contemporaries. One may ask the question, *Was Jesus a troublemaker?* But the historically responsible reply will have to qualify the answer by specifying who might have perceived Jesus as such. Jesus' actions may well have invited such suspicion. With this in mind, we might think of the label "magician" in the same way that we think of the perception of sedition. Jesus was thought to be seditious by those who felt threatened by his movement. In the same way, we might say that Jesus was perceived as "magician" by those who felt threatened by his career as an exorcist.

The evidence suggests that Jesus did attempt to heal people with various methods and various degrees of success. The Beelzebul controversy probably reflects the real concerns of Jesus' family and of the local religious leaders that Jesus' ministry incorporated foreign practice or sympathy. I think that this was how the historical stage was set when the title "Son of David" first entered the scene. Jesus or his disciples had need of an effective answer to these accusations. The Solomonic title "Son of David" served as a domestic precedent by which Jesus could be "properly" interpreted: *No, Jesus is not practicing foreign "magic." He is like Solomon, the Son of David. He is therefore acting on the authority of YHWH on behalf of Israel.* Such arguments most likely found support and set in place the mnemonic framework of typology.

Matthew's agenda to localize Jesus' significance within the therapeutic promises of Isaiah and interpret Jesus' personality via Solomon typology reflects the apologetic of an insider, and in this way is probably closer to how Jesus would have wanted to be perceived. Although the statement might seem counterintuitive, Matthew's refraction of the tradition might provide a better historical portrait of Jesus than the memories against which this refraction reacted.

---

[199] Sanders, *Judaism*, 165–73.
[200] Garrett, 12.

It is not advisable to take this rationale to an extreme; the reader must first be reminded of how I have used the word "refraction" in the present study. Matthew's distinctly Jewish apologetic has aimed to localize Jesus within the worldview that Jesus once inhabited. From the evangelist's perspective, those who had labeled Jesus a magician and consorter with foreign deities had misunderstood Jesus and the significance of his therapy. Jesus' rebuttal to this interpretation in the Beelzebul controversy (which I have argued to be the product of early memory) confirms that Jesus felt that he had been misunderstood. In this way, Matthew's redactional agenda has followed the mnemonic trajectory set in motion by the historical Jesus. I am convinced that Matthew did not see his alterations of Mark and Q in terms of "distortion" or "refraction"; his story was to him simply a better interpretation of the events and their significance.

Finally, a helpful parallel to this study can be seen in another work of apologetic by Flavius Philostratus.[201] Philostratus is a hagiographer who commemorated the life of Apollonius of Tyana. In contrast to Lucian, who accused him of being a charlatan,[202] Philostratus portrays Apollonius as a learned doer of miraculous deeds including healing.[203] Interestingly, the wonderworker also travels to the East to learn from magi:

> With respect to the Magi, Apollonius has said all there is to be said, how he associated with them and learned some things from them, and taught them others before he went away. [. . . One of his students] says that he once asked his master: "What of the Magi?" and the latter answered: "They are wise men, but not in all respects." (1.26)[204]

Thus we see a similar tension at work. Apollonius had obviously gained a reputation of having learned magic from foreign teachers. Many, like Lucian, were suspicious of him. This passage demonstrates Philostratus' attempt to distinguish Apollonius from foreign-taught magic. While he did learn from the magi, his wisdom was ultimately his own. One hundred years after the

---

[201] Translation from F. C. Conybeare, *Philostratus: Life of Apollonius of Tyana* (LCL 16, 17; London: Macmillan, 1912).

[202] H.-J. Klauck, *The Religious Context of Early Christianity* (ed. J. M. G. Barclay, J. Marcus, and J. Riches; Studies of the New Testament and Its World; Edinburgh: T&T Clark, 2000 [1995–1996]), 169.

[203] Trunk (328–51) gives a detailed treatment of the parallels between Apollonius and Jesus in his treatment of Jesus and the Canaanite woman. Philostratus recounts a story where Apollonius exorcises a demon from a distance. The woman is told by the demon that he will kill her child if she takes him before the exorcist, so the exorcist writes down an incantation for the mother so that he does not have to be present.

[204] Much of this account involves Apollonius traveling from country to country, learning and debating with other wise men.

life of Apollonius, Philostratus (much like Matthew) writes as an apologist against what he believed to be undue slander of the great man.

The author also, on occasion, attempts to rationalize the miraculous deeds of Apollonius. In one instance, the healer raises a girl from the dead. But Philostratus' commentary is especially indicative of his own dispositions:

> Now whether he detected some spark of life in her, which those who were nursing her had not noticed (for it is said that although it was raining at the time, a vapor went up from her face) or whether her life was really extinct, and he restored it by the warmth of his touch, is a mysterious problem which neither I myself nor those who were present could decide. (4.45)

Here Philostratus refracts the tradition he has received by suggesting the possibility that there was still a "spark of life" within the girl. It is important to recognize that the author is not simply attempting to make this story more palatable for his audience; he is sincerely attempting to make sense of the story for himself. Moreover, Klauck rightly observes, "Ironically, Philostratus' rationalistic tendency may mean that he has achieved a more accurate picture of what actually happened than the popular narrative version of the oral tradition."[205]

I would argue that Matthew's apologetic is very similar in this respect. Certainly Matthew is not at pains to rationalize or downplay Jesus' therapeutic career, but he does refract the Jesus tradition in a way that makes it "more authentic."[206] By refracting the Jesus tradition in order to make it more intelligible to a Jewish mnemonic sphere (i.e., what makes sense to Matthew), the evangelist returns Jesus to the approximate context in which he was originally interpreted. In this way, the mnemonic circle of Matthew's interpretation synthesizes the evangelist's perception of Jesus with familiar Jewish categories like Isaianic therapy and Son of David.

---

[205] Klauck, 174; I sidestep here any discussion of Klauck's own rationalizing tendency and concern for "what actually happened."

[206] Also, one must keep in mind the possibility that a later remembrancer (in this case, Matthew) has been influenced by an earlier tradition that was unknown to more immediate sources. My thanks to Loren Stuckenbruck for emphasizing this point in personal correspondence.

Excursus

THE PRESUPPOSITION OF DAVIDIC DESCENT

In a recent and very intriguing article, Levin explores the relationship between adoption and legal inheritance as it pertains to Jesus as both Son of David and Son of God.[1] Perhaps the most important contribution of this article is that it throws serious doubt upon the notion that Jesus' adoption by Joseph (as professed by the genealogies and infancy narratives) would have served to legitimate his claim as Davidic heir. Levin points out just how common this notion is within NT scholarship, often with little to no justification.[2] He argues that the evidence occasionally used to justify Jesus' inherited lineage[3] does not speak to the legal implications of inheritance and lineage. Levin concludes that "there is nothing in Jewish law, in either the Hebrew Bible or in later *Halakhah*, which can be seen as the model by which Jesus, Son of God, could have been considered the legal, but not genetic, heir to the Davidic throne."[4] Rather, this concept has been taken from the Roman law

---

[1] Y. Levin, "Jesus, 'Son of God' and 'Son of David,'" *JSNT* 28, no. 4 (2006): 424–42; cf. the observation by M. Gold ("Adoption: A New Problem for Jewish Law," *Judaism* 36 [1987]: 443) that the adopted son of Priest could not inherit the lineage necessary to serve as a priest.

[2] Levin gives a long bibliography of scholars who assume that legal adoption into paternal lineage (such as we see in both Matthew and Luke) was a well-known Jewish custom. This bibliography includes J. D. Kingsbury, "The Title 'Son of David' in Matthew's Gospel," *JBL* 95 (1976): 548; R. E. Brown, *The Birth of the Messiah: A Commentary on the Infancy Narratives in Matthew and Luke* (Garden City, N.Y.: Doubleday, 1979), 139, 288; W. D. Davies and D. C. Allison Jr., *The Gospel according to St. Matthew* (3 vols.; ICC; Edinburgh: T&T Clark, 1997 [1988]), 1:219–20; and J. P. Meier, *A Marginal Jew: Rethinking the Historical Jesus* (4 vols.; New York: Doubleday, 1991), 217.

[3] E.g., *b. Sanh.* 19b: "Whoever brings up an orphan in his home is considered by Scripture as though the child had been born to him." Cf. *b. B. Bat.* 8.6.

[4] Levin, 425; cf. the similar conclusion arrived in the consideration of Paul's adoption metaphor by F. Lydall, *Slaves, Citizens, Sons: Legal Metaphors in the Epistles* (Grand Rapids: Academie, 1984), 80–81. The following comment by A. Anderson, *2 Samuel* (WBC 11; Dallas: Word, 1989), 122, is also appropriate, "Extra-family adoption does not seem to be attested in the OT."

and practice that were employed in the succession of Caesars.[5] From this conclusion, Levin suggests that Matthew was not a Jew writing for a Jewish-Christian audience. Instead, Matthew is better understood from the standpoint of Greco-Roman culture.

While Levin provides a much-needed corrective to the common misconstrual of Jewish adoption and inheritance, his final suggestion concerning Matthew's identity is unwarranted. Moreover, I find this a curious move on Levin's part considering that he regards the infancy narratives of Matthew and Luke (the texts that most emphasize Jesus' Davidic descent) to have originated from a common oral tradition. With this in mind, there is no reason to project the inherent literary assumptions of Matthew's genealogy onto the gospel as a whole. If Levin is correct in this regard,[6] a less severe suggestion would be that Matthew has included a lineage tradition into his gospel that originated from Gentile Christianity. Indeed this solution fits well with what else we know of Davidic descent tradition in the NT. I will briefly sketch this progression in three stages.

The first stage is given voice by Romans 1:3-4 (cf. 2 Tim 2:8), which is generally considered to be a pre-Pauline creed taken from primitive Christianity.[7] From this text we learn that Jesus "came from David's seed according to the flesh; who was established the Son of God with power by the resurrection from the dead." In all likelihood, this creed originated as an early post-Easter reflection on Jesus' "messianic" status among his first Jewish followers. In other words, Jesus was perceived within a messianic lens before his execution, and this perception had to be refracted and made intelligible through a post-Easter lens.[8] One could think of this as the most dramatic occurrence of memory refraction in the memories of Jesus.[9] As this creed found its way

---

[5] Levin, 425–28.

[6] I think that he is correct for reasons that I explore shortly.

[7] J. D. G. Dunn (*Romans* [WBC 38A; Dallas: Word, 1988: 3–26]) gives seven reasons that support this thesis. I list here the five which I find most persuading: (1) two relative clauses in antithetic parallelism, (2) with parallel verbs as aorist participles, (3) with two sets of parallel phrases attached, (4) atypical Pauline language: ὁρίζω, and (5) the Semitism "spirit of holiness." Furthermore, Irenaeus (*Haer.* 1.10.1) considered Paul to have quoted an earlier creed; see O. Cullman, *The Earliest Christian Confessions* (trans. J. Reid; London: Lutterworth, 1949 [1943]), 55. Others who consider a form of Romans 1:3-4 to be a pre-Pauline creed include R. Bultmann, *Theology of the New Testament* (trans. K. Grobel; New York: Scribners, 1951–1955), 50–51; O. Cullman, *The Christology of the New Testament* (trans. S. Guthrie and C. Hall; London: SCM Press, 1963 [1957]), 291–92; Meier, "From Elijah-like Prophet to Royal Davidic Messiah," in *Jesus: A Colloquium in the Holy Land* (ed. D. Donnelly; London: Continuum, 2001), 50–52.

[8] The fact that this creed is antithetically juxtaposed perhaps betrays the resolution (i.e., synthesis) to the early tension caused by Jesus' "failure" as messianic claimant.

[9] As has been argued elsewhere in this book, life-changing religious experience or severe

into Gentile Christianity, it was looked upon through the lens(es) of Greco-Roman culture.[10]

This leads to the second stage of Davidic descent tradition: the genealogies. As Levin has helpfully pointed out, the idea of legal adoption into royal lineage was more at home in Greco-Roman culture than it was in Jewish culture. From this perspective, the claim that Jesus "came from David's seed" was likely reconsidered in terms of a Roman-like adoption into David's genealogy.[11] This is perhaps the best backdrop by which to measure the significance of Matthew's and Luke's genealogies.[12] In this new context, the belief represented by Romans 1:3-4 might have invited an etiological explanation of how Jesus could be descended from David and also be the Son of God.[13] As Levin

---

trauma has the capacity to significantly alter one's worldview and cause a person to reevaluate the significance of previous memories.

[10] It is necessary to keep in mind, however, that this segment of Gentile Christianity was composed of people who were keenly interested in Jewish concepts and Scripture. Therefore, we should expect a certain degree of respect for the original mnemonic framework.

[11] Brown (*Birth*, 75–82) argued that Matthew received the genealogy tradition rather than authoring it himself. Moreover, there is reason to believe that the tradition was Greek in origin. He argued that Matthew's genealogy is historically incomplete but intended to be orthographically uniform in that fourteen generations supposedly separate crucial generations of Israel's history. Brown pointed out that there are actually only thirteen generations from the exile to Jesus but Matthew 1:17 explicitly states that the number fourteen is intended to be emphasized. Among the many possible significances of the number fourteen, it orthographically represents the Hebrew name דוד (note that form דויד would have more correctly represented the Hebrew of this period). This in addition to the fact that David is placed at the crux of the first section (his is the 14th generation listed) and the fact that he is mentioned prominently in Matthew 1:1 and 1:17 support the idea that this genealogy represents a Davidic emphasis.

Brown was inclined toward the possibility that the omissions in Matthew's genealogy were not the work of the evangelist. Rather Brown thought it likely that he received this tradition already lacking certain names. His reasoning is that he thinks it "strange for [Matthew] deliberately to have omitted generations in order to create the pattern and then to have called the reader's attention to it as something marvelous and (implicitly) providential" (75). Moreover, Brown argued that the omission of kings Ahaziah, Jehoash, and Amaziah was the result of an accident due to the similarity of the names Uzziah (Azariah) and Ahaziah. Thus, what should have read "Joram was the father of Ahaziah" was "rendered Joram was the father of Uzziah." The possible confusion between these names is most plausible in the Greek where Ochozias (Greek for Ahaziah) looks similar to Ozias (Greek for Uzziah). If this is correct, then Matthew received this tradition in Greek and it was incomplete upon reception.

[12] Levin (417n7), writes, "Assuming the validity of the commonly held 'two source' or 'Markan priority' theory of the composition of the Synoptic gospels on one hand, and considering the vast literary differences between the annunciation, birth and infancy accounts in Matthew and Luke on the other, I would posit that both drew their stories from a common oral tradition, independent of Mark, Q or each other, which each transformed into writing in his own way, in accordance to his own purposes and style."

[13] For a discussion of the pre-Matthean sources of the larger infancy narrative, see Davies and Allison, *Matthew*, 1:190–95.

astutely points out, these two ideas are naturally linked in Jewish royal tradition,[14] so there would have been no need to explain how Jesus could be both without contradiction.[15] Matthew adapted this non-Jewish tradition into his gospel because, in his view, Jesus' attachment to David's family tree did not contradict his own conception of Jesus as Son of David; it only reinforced this concept from a different angle. Of course, where Matthew's redaction is most evident concerning Son of David is in the connection between the title and Jesus' therapeutic activity.

This leads to the third stage of Davidic descent tradition: Matthew's portrayal of Jesus' therapeutic ministry. As the Son of David, Jesus heals the blind and lame and casts out demons. In Matthew, the social outcasts (e.g., the blind) recognize Jesus as Son of David while the leadership of Israel attributes his work to Satan. Ironically the leadership is blind (23:16-26) and the blind see correctly.[16] Matthew's primary objective with regard to "Son of David" was therapeutic, not genealogical. While the Davidic descent tradition did not contradict his therapy agenda (thus he was happy to include it), it was not his chief concern.[17] Rather, Matthew's use of "Son of David" was guided by his interpretation of blind Bartimaeus' cry, "Son of David, have mercy on me!" (Mark 10:47-48). What in Mark is a singular story[18] becomes a repeated motif in Matthew. This is discussed more later in this volume, but it will suffice my present sketch to posit that Matthew's portrayal has something to do with Jesus performing the healings expected of the messianic age (cf. Isa 35:5-6; 4Q521).[19] In sum, Jesus' association with the Davidic

---

[14] In 2 Samuel 7 (to which Rom 1:3-4 alludes), Solomon is said to be both David's seed and YHWH's son. Cf. Ps 2:7. With these texts in mind, it would be much more natural for the Jewish mind to think in terms of a divine adoption of a human son, rather than the other way around.

[15] Levin, 419.

[16] J. M. Gibbs, "Purpose and Pattern in Matthew's Use of the Title 'Son of David,'" *NTS* 10 (1963–1964): 446–64; Kingsbury, "Son of David"; W. R. G. Loader, "Son of David, Blindness, Possession, and Duality in Matthew," *CBQ* 44 (1982): 570–85.

[17] Moreover, even though Matthew's genealogy emphasizes Davidic descent (see previous discussion from Brown above), the evangelist is much more intent on portraying Jesus as the Son of God. Brown (*Birth*, 142–43) ultimately concluded that the larger purpose of Matt 1 is to show that Jesus was of divine origin and not merely of Davidic origin. Cf. J. D. Kingsbury, *Matthew: Structure, Christology, Kingdom* (Philadelphia: Fortress, 1975), 42–53; J. D. G. Dunn, *Christology in the Making: A New Testament Inquiry into the Origins of the Doctrine of the Incarnation* (Grand Rapids: Eerdmans, 1989 [1980]), 49–50.

[18] Indeed the application of "Son of David" on the lips of the blind man is atypical for Mark; the evangelist does not develop this connection elsewhere.

[19] Contra M. Karrer, *Der Gesalbte: Die Grundlagen des Christustitels* (Göttingen: Vandenhoeck and Ruprecht, 1991), 284–87, 293–94 and G. S. Oegema, *The Anointed and His People: Messianic Expectations from the Maccabees to Bar Kochba* (JSPSup Sheffield: Sheffield Academic Press, 1998), 161. Karrer argues that, in the NT, "Son of David" should

covenant seems to have been (1) presupposed by the earliest Christians, (2) reformulated in terms of adoption from a Greco-Roman perspective, and (3) returned by Matthew to a more Jewish interpretation whereby the Son of David demonstrates his messianic status by performing the healings expected of the messianic age.[20]

---

be understood only as an appeal to Jesus' lineage and not to his status as the Messiah. Oegema similarly argues, "For the whole of the New Testament . . . the question of Jesus being the son of David is not used to designate him as Messiah, but to connect his origin to the house of David." Both are at odds with a large contingent of Matthean scholarship on this point.

[20] Other studies that address the larger developmental issues around this topic include W. Michaelis, "Die Davidssohnschaft Jesu als historisches und kerygmatisches Problem: Beiträge zum Christusverständnis in Forschung und Verkündigung," in *Der historische Jesus und der kerygmatische Christus* (ed. H. Ristow and K. Matthiae; Berlin: Evangelische Verlag, 1962), 317–30; Duling, "Promises"; Meier, "Elijah-like Prophet."

7

Jesus' Temple Procession

Jesus' entry into Jerusalem and procession toward the temple[1] is pertinent to the present study for several reasons. The most obvious is that Mark's account refers to the "Kingdom of our father David." Matthew reinforces this imagery by appending the title "Son of David" to the tradition (21:9). What is less obvious, but more important for our concerns, is the extent to which Psalm 118, Zechariah 9:9, and 1 Kings 1:34ff. have influenced this event and how it was remembered in the Jesus tradition.

This chapter is divided into four sections. First I assess Mark's presentation of the procession and argue that its core is a product of memory rather than invention. Then I aim to pinpoint the conceptual categories (e.g., scriptural precedents) at work in the tradition. It will then be necessary to discuss the trajectory that these scriptural types had previously taken in the HB. The third section discusses references to Davidic "offspring" language in the Dead Sea Scrolls to establish a parallel trajectory. Fourth, I discuss the shape that this tradition took in the wake of a narrativized Jesus tradition. This section continues to trace the previous trajectory(ies) as manifested in the literary categories employed by Matthew. I then postulate the most plausible sphere of historical memory.

In this way, my discussion continues to trace Son of David tradition from its seminal concepts in the HB to its fruition in the post-Easter Jesus tradition (and beyond[2]). By doing so alongside a discussion of parallel trajectories, this discussion attempts to establish where the historical Jesus' procession into Jerusalem stood along this trajectory.

---

[1] Henceforth: procession.
[2] In certain cases, it will be helpful to compare the Jesus tradition with rabbinic and targumic traditions.

Memory versus Invention

What is initially striking about Mark 11:1-11 is how legendary it seems. Jesus' prediction of the colt's location gives an impression of Jesus' foreknowledge (perhaps a divine attribute).[3] Also the story might be read as a legend intended to venerate Jesus as Christ. At first glance, Bultmann's assessment that the story is legendary (perhaps only containing a grain of reminiscence) is very attractive.[4] Yet it is difficult to dispute the logic of Taylor's rebuttal that no "legend would have broken off the account with the anticlimax [of 11:11] and it is only as a reminiscence that this statement is natural."[5] Evans continues this line of thought, "Had the early church invented the story of the entrance . . . we should have expected a more pronounced christological element and surely a more impressive conclusion."[6] In addition, the problem of the word "Hosanna" (Mark 11:9, 10) has proved to be a troublesome Semitism that seems uncomfortably rendered in the Greek.[7] One is hard-pressed to explain these features as literary invention.

If Bultmann's suggestion that this story originated from a "grain of reminiscence" is correct, this grain would likely be some common denominator between Mark and John (see chart on p. 193). Both record Jesus riding an equid into Jerusalem.[8] Both mention the use of foliage[9] to welcome Jesus. Both record the shout, "Hosanna [Ὡσαννα]," which quotes Psalm 118:25-26,[10] and both follow this with a mention of royalty. John thus confirms four out of five of Mark's narrative elements.[11] Therefore the criterion of multiple

---

[3] B. Kinman examines the importance of "special animals" in royal processions (*Jesus' Entry into Jerusalem: In the Context of Lukan Theology and the Politics of His Day* [AGJU 28; Leiden: Brill, 1995], 50–52). The mystery surrounding this animal serves to make it especially unique.

[4] R. Bultmann, *History of the Synoptic Tradition* (trans. J. Marsh; New York: Harper, 1963), 122.

[5] V. Taylor, *Formation of Gospel Tradition* (London: Macmillan, 1953), 151.

[6] C. A. Evans, *Mark 8:27–16:20* (WBC 34B; Nashville: Thomas Nelson, 2001), 138.

[7] This is discussed in more detail below.

[8] Mark uses πῶλον while John refers to the colt of a donkey, ὀνάριον. For a discussion on the ambiguity of the species of the beast, see F. F. Bruce, "The Book of Zechariah and the Passion Narrative," *BJRL* 43 (1960–1961): 339n1.

[9] The phrase "στιβάδας κόψαντες ἐκ τῶν ἀγρῶν" (Mark 11:8) could refer to stalks of grain or reeds of some sort. Evans (*Mark*, 144) prefers "tall grass," which corresponds better with the geography and available resources. According to John, palm branches (τὰ βαΐα τῶν φοινίκων) are waved (John 12:13). Also noteworthy is that Simon was hailed with palm fronds during his procession before rededicating the temple in 1 Macc 13:51 (cf. 2 Macc 10:1-7).

[10] Mark and John are identical in the phrasing at this point. This further supports the notion of a pre-Greek memory of the event.

[11] The fifth, which John has omitted, is Jesus' entry into the temple.

Mark 11:7-11	John 12:12-15
They brought the colt to Jesus and put their coats on it, and He sat on it. And many spread their coats in the road, and others spread leafy branches which they had cut from the fields. Those who went in front and those who followed were shouting: "Hosanna! Blessed is he who comes in the name of the Lord! Blessed is the coming kingdom of our father David! Hosanna in the highest!" Jesus entered Jerusalem into the temple; and after looking around at everything, He left for Bethany with the twelve, since it was already late.	On the next day the large crowd who had come to the feast, when they heard that Jesus was coming to Jerusalem, took the branches of the palm trees and went out to meet him, and to shout, "Hosanna! Blessed is he who comes in the name of the Lord, even the King of Israel!" Jesus, finding a young donkey, sat on it; as it is written, Fear not, daughter of Zion! Behold, your king is coming, seated on a donkey."
Καὶ φέρουσιν τὸν πῶλον πρὸς τὸν Ἰησοῦν καὶ ἐπιβάλλουσιν αὐτῷ τὰ ἱμάτια αὐτῶν, καὶ ἐκάθισεν ἐπ' αὐτόν. Καὶ πολλοὶ τὰ ἱμάτια αὐτῶν ἔστρωσαν εἰς τὴν ὁδόν, ἄλλοι δὲ στιβάδας κόψαντες ἐκ τῶν ἀγρῶν. Καὶ οἱ προάγοντες καὶ οἱ ἀκολουθοῦντες ἔκραζον· Ὡσαννά· εὐλογημένος ὁ ἐρχόμενος ἐν ὀνόματι κυρίου· Εὐλογημένη ἡ ἐρχομένη βασιλεία τοῦ πατρὸς ἡμῶν Δαυίδ· ὡσαννὰ ἐν τοῖς ὑψίστοις. Καὶ εἰσῆλθεν εἰς Ἱεροσόλυμα εἰς τὸ ἱερὸν καὶ περιβλεψάμενος πάντα, ὀψίας ἤδη οὔσης τῆς ὥρας, ἐξῆλθεν εἰς Βηθανίαν μετὰ τῶν δώδεκα.	Τῇ ἐπαύριον ὁ ὄχλος πολὺς ὁ ἐλθὼν εἰς τὴν ἑορτήν, ἀκούσαντες ὅτι ἔρχεται ὁ Ἰησοῦς εἰς Ἱεροσόλυμα ἔλαβον τὰ βαΐα τῶν φοινίκων καὶ ἐξῆλθον εἰς ὑπάντησιν αὐτῷ καὶ ἐκραύγαζον· Ὡσαννά· Εὐλογημένος ὁ ἐρχόμενος ἐν ὀνόματι κυρίου, [καὶ] ὁ βασιλεὺς τοῦ Ἰσραήλ. εὑρὼν δὲ ὁ Ἰησοῦς ὀνάριον ἐκάθισεν ἐπ' αὐτό, καθώς ἐστιν γεγραμμένον· Μὴ φοβοῦ, θυγάτηρ Σιών· ἰδοὺ ὁ βασιλεύς σου ἔρχεται, καθήμενος ἐπὶ πῶλον ὄνου.

attestation is warranted as one might expect from a public spectacle.[12] Still, this does not speak to the historicity of the first unit concerning the acquisition of the colt (Mark 11:1-6).

[12] J. P. Meier, "From Elijah-like Prophet to Royal Davidic Messiah," in *Jesus: A Colloquium in the Holy Land* (ed. D. Donnelly; London: Continuum, 2001), 67, suggests that the procession was a historical event, but suggests that it was not as grand as some might imagine. He opines that a smaller group of disciples might have engineered the pomp. Even so, it seems that the event had enough of an audience to have been remembered in independent circles.

Catchpole examines twelve examples of royal processions, six from 1 and 2 Maccabees and six from Josephus,[13] and determines certain common elements that form a pattern.[14] These elements include (a) a previously established status of the individual in question, (b) the previous defeat of an enemy, and (c) entry into the temple (if the city has one) followed by cultic activity.[15] Catchpole compares Jesus' procession to these formal processions and argues that Jesus' procession fits the form of a king's procession after a final defeat of his enemies. Catchpole considers Zechariah 9 an example of such a pattern and concludes that the story of Jesus' procession has been invented on the basis of this passage.

Witherington objects both to Catchpole's reading of Zechariah and to his assessment of Mark 11. With regard to the first, Witherington points out that Zechariah 9 does not speak of a royal procession following a victorious battle. Rather, it seems to speak of a king who proceeds into a city still occupied by the enemy.[16] This being so, the liberator of Zechariah 9:9 is welcomed for his anticipated (but yet to be realized) victory.[17] Witherington argues that Zechariah 9 does not fit Catchpole's model. If this is so, Catchpole has mistaken two competing models for a single model.

Building upon Witherington's objection, it should also be pointed out that Zechariah 9:9's purpose in the larger context of Zechariah is to affirm Zerubbabel's claim to the Davidic throne by mimicking the procession of Solomon (1 Kgs 1:32-40).[18] Solomon's prototypical procession served to solidify his claim as David's successor. In this way, the royal processions of 1 Kings and Zechariah 9 served the purpose of legitimizing the identity of a figure who has not yet achieved the status of king. This, the central purpose of the act, grates against the second element of Catchpole's pattern.

---

[13] 1 Macc 4:19-25; 5:45-54; 10:86; 13:43-48; 13:49-51; 2 Macc 4:21-22; *Ant* 11.325-39; 12.312; 12.348-49; 13.304-6; 16.12-15; 17.194-239; *JW* 1.194-239.

[14] D. R. Catchpole, "The 'Triumphal' Entry," in *Jesus and the Politics of His Day* (ed. E. Bammel and C. F. D. Moule; Cambridge: Cambridge University Press, 1984), 319–35.

[15] Catchpole, "Entry," 321. Catchpole's heading "cultic activity" includes (1) the offering of a sacrifice, or (2) the expulsion of objectionable people, and/or (3) purification of uncleanness. Given the broadness of this last heading, one must question the validity of a single pattern.

[16] B. Witherington III, *The Christology of Jesus* (Minneapolis: Fortress, 1990), 104–5.

[17] Witherington (*Christology*, 105) points to Zechariah 9:10 as evidence that before the king can be victorious "the war horses must be first cut off from Jerusalem." With this aim the king's purpose in this passage is to encamp around the city to guard against the passage of the army of the enemy. This is indicated in 9:8.

[18] Evans, *Mark*, 143. In further support of the Solomonic character of Zechariah 9:9, the following verse claims that this figure "will speak peace to the nations, and his dominion will be from sea to sea, and from the river to the ends of the earth" (9:10). Besides the echo of Solomon's name [שלם], this is a direct quote from Psalm 72:8 which is a "Psalm of Solomon"; cf. M. Fishbane, *Biblical Interpretation in Ancient Israel* (Oxford: Oxford University Press, 1985), 502.

Witherington's second objection to Catchpole's thesis parallels one of the central concerns of the present study.

> Catchpole appears to be guilty of a common fallacy when pursuing a [form-historical] approach to narrative: He assumes that because the narrative seems to fit a particular formal pattern, one can therefore draw conclusions about the historical authenticity of the narrative's essential content.[19]

In the case of Jesus' procession, it is the formal pattern that evokes the intended symbolism. It is possible that Jesus' actions did not actualize all of these elements. But even if eyewitnesses remembered a few elements, the refraction of conventionalization would invite social memory to fill in the remaining elements. In other words, if the memory of an event includes several elements of a pattern, it would be natural for a conventionalized memory to import other elements that typify that pattern.

More recently, Kinman has offered a material advance on Catchpole's study by surveying a wide variety of royal processions in antiquity and late antiquity.[20] Kinman sees less affinity between Jesus' procession and these precedents, which were generally accompanied with much more acclamation and the official welcome of the social elite. Kinman concludes:

> Clearly, nothing like this sort of welcome occurred at Jesus' Procession. No great battle had been waged and won, no slaves set free, no military opponents captured, paraded and prepared for slaughter, no great booty taken and no great company of victorious soldiers were there to accompany Jesus. Seen in this light, Jesus' Procession would, if anything, have stood as a modest embarrassment to those who might have hoped to see it in triumphalist colours.[21]

I would also add that in order to properly follow Jewish royal precedents, the high priest should have been present at the ceremony to endorse Jesus as the Messiah. While contemporary readers often refer to this as Jesus' "triumphal entry," the historical backdrop suggests otherwise. Jesus' procession served to highlight his rejection by Jerusalem's leadership and foreshadow his opposition to the temple establishment. We might then cautiously apply the criterion of embarrassment alongside Semitisms and multiple attestation.

If it is safe to assume that the latter half of Mark's account has roots in memory, it may then be asked: Was this act perceived as a typological mimic of Zechariah 9:9 or 1 Kings 1:32-40? Or was this act typologically modeled after these traditions as the account was passed down? I argue here that the

---

[19] Witherington, *Christology*, 104.
[20] Kinman, *Entry*, 25–64.
[21] Kinman, *Entry*, 122.

answer to both questions is yes. The point is addressed by tracing the refraction trajectories of this tradition and measuring these tendencies against the mnemonic lenses and frameworks common to Jesus' historical context.

Mark 11 and Scripture

Mark intends to show that Jesus choreographed this procession and that it was indeed symbolic.[22] In Mark 11:2, Jesus knows of and sends for the colt. We are told that the animal had never been ridden, not so subtly hinting that the animal was purposed for this particular occasion. As far as Mark is concerned, the colt is the key to understanding Jesus' symbolism and is essential to the meaning of this event.

The welcoming shout, "Blessed is the coming kingdom of our father David," makes it obvious that the symbolic significance of the colt is royal in nature. Mark's intention to demonstrate the royal nature of Jesus' procession is also seen in his mention of the disciples throwing their garments on the colt (11:7). This detail might allude to a tradition of honoring YHWH's anointed[23] (cf. 2 Kgs 9:13[24]). In addition to these considerations is the possibility of an appeal to Zechariah 9:9, where the prophet describes a similar procession. But because the evangelist does not make an overt appeal to Zechariah in this context, better light can be shed on Mark's intentions by first discussing the scriptural category that he directly employs: Psalm 118.

Psalm 118

Lohmeyer argued that the phrase "Kingdom of our father David [βασιλεία τοῦ πατρός ἡμῶν Δαυίδ]" should be seen as a later, non-Jewish interpretation of "Kingdom of God."[25] Schmithals, likewise, argued that the reference to David as "father" betrays a non-Jewish understanding of Israel's patriarchs.[26] He appealed to *b.Ber.* 16b, which reads, "The term fathers is only applied to three." The implied three are Abraham, Isaac, and Jacob. However, both Pesch and Evans rightly point out that *b.Mo'ed Qat.* 16b claims that "God

---

[22] J. D. Crossan, "Redaction and Citation in Mark 11:9-10 and 11:17," *BR* 17 (1972): 33–50.

[23] J. Gnilka. *Das Evangelium nach Markus* (2 vols.; Zürich: Berjinger, 1978), 2:117; cf. *Yal. Exod* 168; *b. Qetub.* 66b.

[24] In 2 Kings 9, Jehu is anointed as king and immediately his subjects cover his path with their garments. It is worth noting, however, that this story does not describe a royal procession where Jehu rides into the city seated on an animal.

[25] E. Lohmeyer, *Das Evangelium des Markus* (2 vols.; Göttingen: Vandenhoeck and Ruprecht, 1951), 231–32.

[26] W. Schmithals, *Das Evangelium nach Markus* (2 vols.; OTNT 1–2; Gütersloh: Mohn, 1979), 2:485.

will make [David] chief next to the three fathers." This inclusion is also seen in Sirach 45:25 (cf. also Sir 47:1-11).[27] Ernst suggested that the phrase is of Jewish origin but betrays Christian interpolation, which has identified Psalm 118's "one coming in the name of the Lord" with David's son.[28] He thus attempts to account for a Jewish tradition that has taken on a Christian trajectory. While this seems to take a middle ground, Evans demonstrates that the conflation of Psalm 118 and Davidic interpretation can be seen along a later Jewish trajectory as well. The targum of Psalm 118:22-29 considers this passage to have been written of David who is "worthy to be ruler and King."[29]

Psalm 118:25 was a prayer originally directed to YHWH. As such, it is important to determine whether the crowd's shout is here directed at YHWH or Jesus. Torrey suggested that rather than "God save us!" the cry is meant to mean "God save him!"[30] In this way, the supplication was something akin to "God save the Queen!" Coggan and Gundry have argued that "hosanna" should be understood in light of its etymological kinship to the name "Joshua (= Jesus)."[31] In this scenario, the crowd is perhaps reminding Jesus to be like his namesake and "save" them by leading them in conquest. But there is reason to believe that the use of Psalm 118:25 in this context is something other than a cry for help. The Greek transliteration ὡσαννα has eluded conclusive etymology. C. Burger took the odd form to be evidence of an author ignorant of Jewish customs.

> The entire exclamation shows so little Jewish form. Especially the formulation "hosanna in the highest" shows such little Judaic form it that cannot be historical and we must assume that the author wasn't at home with the language, the customs and the messianic expectations of Palestinian Judaism.[32]

Burger's logic is faulty. If this story has been invented by a Greek-speaking Gentile, what purpose is served by employing a Semitism unintelligible to him?[33] Moreover, one is hard-pressed to explain the Semitism's inclusion if

---

[27] Evans, *Mark*, 146; R. Pesch, *Das Markusevangeliem* (2 vols.; HTKNT; Freiburg: Herder, 1991), 2:185.
[28] J. Ernst, *Das Evangelium nach Markus* (Regensburg: Pustet, 1981), 322.
[29] Evans, *Mark*, 140.
[30] C. C. Torrey, *Our Translated Gospels* (London: Hodder and Stoughton, 1936), 21; cf. Taylor, *Formation*, 456.
[31] F. D. Coggan, "Note on the Word hosanna," *ExpTim* 52 (1940–1941): 76–77; R. H. Gundry, *Mark: A Commentary on His Apology for the Cross* (Grand Rapids: Eerdmans, 1992), 630.
[32] Translated from C. Burger, *Jesus als Davidssohn: Eine traditions geschicht lick Unter suchung* (FRLANT 98; Göttingen: Vandenhoeck and Ruprecht, 1970), 167.
[33] Luke's account (19:38) likely omits Hosanna for this reason.

the custom it represented was wholly unknown to the narrator. It is much more likely that this Greek-speaking storyteller is relaying a story that has origins in memory. The fact that the narrator is unfamiliar with the Semitism is evidence that (at least part of) this story has not been invented in Greek. The criterion of Semitic influence (already mentioned) is therefore warranted, but what is presently more important is that Burger's explanation of Gentile ignorance does little ultimately to solve the etymological problem.

One solution has highlighted the resemblance of "hosanna" to the short form of the imperative הוֹשִׁיאָה, which is rendered הוֹשַׁע (cf. Ps 86:2)[34] and conjectures a coupling with the precative particle נָא. This solution is supported by the unique presence of both words in Psalm 118:25: אָנָּא יהוה הוֹשִׁיעָה נָּא אָנָּא יהוה הַצְלִיחָה נָּא.[35] According to this solution, ὡσαννα reflects the transitive הוֹשִׁיעָה נָא. But as Fitzmyer has pointed out, this solution fails to explain the supposed shorter form of the phrase הוֹשַׁע נָא.[36] This hypothetical coupling never occurs in biblical Hebrew. Following Kautzsch,[37] Fitzmyer defends a competing solution that understands the term ὡσαννα to reflect the Aramaic הוֹשַׁע נָא rather than the Hebrew הוֹשִׁיעָה נָא.[38] This solution acknowledges that Psalm 118:25, in part, is responsible for the supplication, but concludes that this verse alone cannot explain the etymology of ὡσαννα. It is possible that there was Aramaic interference on the Hebrew verse at some point during its transmission. Perhaps the resemblance of the Hebrew phraseology to the Aramaic prayer invited such conflation.[39] In either case, the oddity of "hosanna" lies in the fact that the LXX, as a rule, translates הוֹשִׁיעָה as σῶσον and never uses a Semitic transliteration as is found in Mark 11:9-10. This fact suggests that, in this case, there was a certain phonetic value to the word that would have been lost if it had been rendered in Greek. The fact that the evangelist does not provide an explanation suggests that the meaning (or purpose) of this word has been taken for granted.[40] In this way, Mark's transliteration probably reflects a popularized proclamation that was familiar to his audience. Perhaps then the function of the cry "hosanna" is not in its etymology but in

---

[34] The longer form is far more common (cf. Ps 12:2; 20:10; 28:9; 60:7; 86:16; 108:7).

[35] Ps 117:25 LXX: ὦ κύριε σῶσον δή ὦ κύριε εὐόδωσον δή.

[36] J. A. Fitzmyer, *The Dead Sea Scrolls and Christian Origins* (Grand Rapids: Eerdmans, 2000), 123–24.

[37] E. Kautzsch, *Grammatik des Biblisch-aramäichen mit einer kritischen Erörterung der aramäichen Wörter im Neuen Testament* (Leipzig: F. C. W. Vogel, 1884), 173.

[38] Fitzmyer, *Dead Sea Scrolls*, 119–29.

[39] If this is so, Kautzsch (173) overstated the case by claiming that ὡσαννα cannot be identified with הוֹשִׁיעָה נָא. Surely there is some connection, seeing that Psalm 118:25 is the only instance in biblical Hebrew where הוֹשִׁיעָה and the particle נָא are so juxtaposed.

[40] Indeed it is Mark's tendency to provide such an explanation (cf. Mark 10:46).

its connotative value. In other words, the meaning of "hosanna" was not in the word's derivation but in its popular use.

Perhaps this word was akin to the use of "hallelujah" by modern English speakers. In popular English-speaking culture, "hallelujah" most commonly represents a proclamation of joy and does not necessarily connote praise to YHWH as the etymology denotes.[41] Similarly, it is possible that "hosanna" did not connote a supplication to God for salvation (as the etymology implies) but rather a stereotypical greeting of pilgrims common to Jerusalem festivals.

Similarly, later rabbinic commentary associates Psalm 118:25-26 with the Feast of Tabernacles and Hanukkah.[42] This seems to be the sense later given to the phrase in *Didache* 10:6[43] which mirrors the dative of Matthew's ὡσαννὰ τῷ υἱῷ Δαυίδ (21:9). Fitzmyer concludes:

> The best explanation of the dative τῷ υἱῷ Δαυίδ remains that הושע נא had lost its original meaning of a cry for help and had become a cry of greeting to pilgrims coming to Jerusalem for feasts. If this be correct, then the other cry, Ὡσαννὰ ἐν τοῖς ὑψίστοις is equally explicable: Let the greeting being given to the Son of David extend even to the heights of heaven (where God Himself dwells)![44]

So in Fitzmyer's view, the greeting is directed to both Jesus as Messiah and, by extension, God. Given Mark's "Son of God" Christology, the evangelist was probably comfortable with the ambiguity, but this ambiguity also calls attention to Mark's apparent lack of redaction in 11:9-10. Given the agenda delineated in Mark 1:1, one would expect at least the title "Christ" if not "Son of God." For this reason, it is probable that Mark has chosen not to alter substantially the actual words of the shout present in the tradition passed to him. Mark's motivation was not passive, however. There is good reason to believe that Mark has left the crowd's shout relatively unaltered in order to localize his procession narrative within a Psalm 118 framework.[45] As such,

---

[41] Cf. T. R. Hatina, *In Search of a Context: The Function of Scripture in Mark's Narrative* (JSNTSup 232; Sheffield: Sheffield Academic Press, 2002), 294.

[42] J. A. Sanders, "A New Testament Hermeneutic Fabric: Psalm 118 in the Entrance Narrative," in *Early Jewish and Christian Exegesis* (ed. C. A. Evans and W. F. Stinespring; Atlanta: Scholars Press, 1987), 179; See *b. Sukk* 45a; *b. 'Arak* 10a; *m. Pesah* 5:5; 10:6; *b. Pesah* 117a; 118a; 119a. This has led some, justifiably so, to question Mark's (and John's) dating of the event, e.g., T. W. Manson, "The Cleansing of the Temple," *BJRL* 33 (1950/1): 271–82.

[43] "Let generosity come, and let this universe pass away. Hosanna to David's son [ὡσαννὰ τῷ υἱῷ Δαυίδ]!"

[44] Fitzmyer, *Dead Sea Scrolls*, 128.

[45] Cf. E. Lohse, "Hosianna," *NovT* 6 (1963): 113–19; J. A. Sanders, 181.

it seems that Mark 11 represents a refraction redirected through the lens of Psalm 118.

Evans follows Cranfield[46] by calling attention to the similar immediate contexts of Mark 11 and Psalm 118:25.[47] According to the psalm, the blessing is shouted "from the House of YHWH" (v. 26). This "blessing" is an outworking of the homogeny between the "house of Aaron" and the rest of Israel already demonstrated at the start of this psalm.[48] It is then no coincidence that Jesus' procession *toward the temple* invites a quotation of this psalm. Mark's utilization of Psalm 118 was likely intended to put Jesus' relationship to the temple at center stage. Marcus posits, "Mark links the Davidic thrust of the crowd's acclamation (11:9-10) with Jerusalem and the Temple by juxtaposing the acclamation with the redactional verse 11:11."[49] Given this juxtaposition, the lack of acknowledgment by the temple establishment was tantamount to an overt rejection of Jesus' messianic agenda.[50] Mark takes this a step further in his juxtaposition of Psalm 118's homogenous relationship between the "house of Aaron" and "he who comes in the name of YHWH" against the apparent lack of homogeny between Jesus and the temple establishment. The anticlimax of Jesus' uneventful arrival to the temple grounds and quick departure thereafter may simply be the exclamation point punctuating this very loud silence on the part of the priesthood.[51]

Zechariah 9:9 and 1 Kings 1:32-40

Many commentators see Jesus' procession as an allusion to Zechariah 9:9:[52]

---

[46] C. E. B. Cranfield, *The Gospel according to St. Mark* (CTGC; Cambridge: Cambridge University Press, 1963), 351.

[47] Evans, *Mark*, 145.

[48] "Let Israel now say that his mercy endures forever! Let the house of Aaron now say that his mercy endures forever!" (Ps 118:2-3).

[49] J. Marcus, *The Way of the Lord: Christological Exegesis in the Gospel of Mark* (Louisville, Ky.: Westminster John Knox, 1992), 138.

[50] Sanders, 188.

[51] There is no doubt that Mark's anticlimax is in part a result of his literary motif where one story is couched between the bookends of a symbolically related story. For the most comprehensive treatment of Mark's use of the withered fig tree in connection to Jesus' temple demonstration, see W. R. Telford, *The Barren Temple and the Withered Tree* (JSNTSup 1; Sheffield: JSOT Press, 1980), 39–68. It should be noted, however, that Jesus does indeed enter the temple briefly upon his arrival and with no welcome. Thus, Mark's anticlimax highlights Jesus' nonrelationship with the temple establishment and foreshadows Jesus' temple demonstration. This coheres well with Telford's treatment of Mark's agenda.

[52] E.g., J. M. Creed, *The Gospel according to St. Luke* (London: Macmillan, 1942), 240; Bruce, "Book of Zechariah," 339; V. H. Patsch, "Der Einzug Jesu in Jerusalem: ein historischer Versuch," *ZTK* 68 (1971): 6; Catchpole, "Entry"; M. Hooker, *The Gospel according to Mark* (Peabody, Mass.: Hendrickson, 1991), 257; Marcus, 157; B. Witherington III, *The Gospel of Mark: A Socio-Rhetorical Commentary* (Grand Rapids: Eerdmans, 2001), 308. Those who

> Rejoice greatly, O daughter of Zion! Shout, O daughter of Jerusalem! Behold, your king is coming to you; He is righteous and endowed with salvation, humble, and mounted on a donkey [חמור],[53] even on a colt [עיר],[54] the foal of a donkey [בן־אתנות].[55]

This prophecy was originally intended to legitimate Zerubbabel, a descendant of David, as king in a time when there had been an absence of this office in Israel. In this way, Zechariah 9:9 became a particularly popular text for later messianic circles.[56] But before the significance of Zechariah can be fully appreciated, it must be pointed out that this passage is itself an allusion to 1 Kings 1:32-40.

> Then King David said, "Call to me Zadok the priest, Nathan the prophet, and Benaiah the son of Jehoiada." And they came into the king's presence. And the king said to them, "Take with you the servants of your lord, and have my son Solomon ride on my own mule [פרדה],[57] and bring him down to Gihon. "And let Zadok the priest and Nathan the prophet anoint him there as king over Israel, and blow the trumpet and say, 'Long live King Solomon!' "Then you shall come up after him, and he shall come and sit on my throne and be king in my place; for I have appointed him to be ruler over Israel and Judah." And Benaiah the son of Jehoiada answered the king and said, "Amen! Thus may YHWH, the God of my lord the king, say. As YHWH has been with my lord the king, so may He be with Solomon, and make his throne greater than the throne of my lord King David!" So Zadok the priest, Nathan the prophet, Benaiah the son of Jehoiada, the Cherethites, and the Pelethites went down and had Solomon ride on King David's mule, and brought him to Gihon. Zadok the priest then took the horn of oil from the tent and anointed Solomon. Then they blew the trumpet, and all the people said, "Long live King Solomon!" And all the people went up after him, and the people were playing on flutes and rejoicing with great joy, so that the earth shook at their noise.

For the purposes of the present study, it is crucial to point out that David never mounts an animal in this manner to legitimate his claim to the throne. This act is done by Solomon in order to claim his status as David's successor.

---

do not fall under this umbrella include Taylor, *Formation*, 150ff.; Cranfield, *Mark*, 348; E. Schweizer, *The Good News according to Mark* (Richmond, Va.: John Knox, 1970), 227; W. L. Lane, *The Gospel of Mark: The English Text with Introduction, Exposition and Notes* (Grand Rapids: Eerdmans, 1974), 392; Evans, *Mark*, 140.

[53] LXX = ὑποζύγιον.
[54] LXX = πῶλον νέον.
[55] LXX omits this phrase.
[56] Zechariah's importance near the turn of the common era is discussed below.
[57] LXX = ἡμίονον.

This act symbolically distinguished Solomon from Adonijah. Both were heirs, but David placed Solomon on his own mule to symbolically endorse him as the rightful heir to his father's throne.[58] Furthermore, David had hoped to promote the notion that Solomon would be a greater king than his father. It is also important that David's endorsement of Solomon included the support of the prophet Nathan and Zadok the priest. They announced his new office with a shout and followed his procession. Lastly, Zadok the priest plays the crucial role of anointing Solomon.

Considering this narrative backdrop, the possibility must be considered that such a royal procession is a uniquely Solomonic act. Solomon was the first son of David to become like his father, and eventually supersede his father. Zechariah (and perhaps Jesus) drew upon this imagery in order to embody what was first achieved in the reign of Solomon. As David's original design intended, the act of riding a colt among shouts of royal adulation was a symbolic claim to be David's successor. Therefore, this act was Davidic *in a particularly Solomonic sense*. Zechariah was prophesying that Zerubbabel would sit on David's throne just like Solomon had.

This affinity with Solomon is of particular importance for Zechariah, because Zerubbabel is prophesied as the builder of the temple; this too is the responsibility of the Davidic king and is particularly Solomonic. Zechariah 6:12-13 reads as follows:

> Then say to him, "Thus says YHWH of hosts, 'Behold, a man whose name is Branch, for he will branch out from where he is; and he will build the temple of YHWH.' Indeed, he will build the temple of YHWH and it is he who will bear the honor and sit and reign. And there will be a priest at his throne and a council of peace between the two."

ואמרת אליו לאמר כה אמר יהוה צבאות לאמר הנה־איש צמח שמו
יצמח ובנה את־היכל יהוה והוא יבנה את־היכל יהוה והוא־ישא הוד
וישב ומשל על־כסאו והיה כהן על־כסאו ועצת שלום תהיה בין
שניהם

This text highlights the mutual relationship between the priest and the royal figure "Branch," no doubt following the lead of 1 Kings 1. Here also we are reminded of the relationship between the "one coming" and the priesthood in Psalm 118. Both texts emphasize the king's peaceable relationship with the priesthood.

---

[58] Contrast the unsuccessful processions of Absalom (2 Sam 18:9) and Mephibosheth (2 Sam 19:26); cf. Sanders, 179.

Such vegetation language is not uncommon in texts that refer to an eschatological Davidic figure.[59] This metaphor most likely connotes a sort of family-tree imagery, evoking the concept of lineage. The metaphor probably stems from 2 Samuel 7:12, where David is promised that his descendant, or "seed [זַרְעֲ]," will proceed [יֵצֵא] from him and establish his kingdom.[60] Zechariah 6:12-13 is interesting for several reasons, but what is particularly interesting at this point is that "Branch [צֶמַח]" is used as a name. As the phrase "his name [שְׁמוֹ]" indicates, the vegetation metaphor has evolved from a conceptual referent to a specific title. "Throne [כִּסֵּא]" (6:13) demonstrates the figure's royalty. The fact that he will "build the temple" shows that the promise to David concerning Solomon is being eschatologically recycled.

At this point Mark's lack of appeal to Zechariah is most curious, especially given the fact that Mark appeals to Zechariah in several other places in his narrative. Mark Black's doctoral dissertation demonstrated the pervasive influence of Zechariah upon Mark's Passion Narrative.[61] The many Markan phrases and concepts borrowed from Zechariah cannot be detailed here, but Marcus' summary of Mark 14's relationship to Zechariah 9–14 aptly exemplifies the narrative grid provided by Zechariah to much of the Passion Narrative:[62]

Mark		Zechariah
14:24	My blood of the covenant	9:11
14:25	That day, kingdom of God	14:4, 9
14:26	Mount of Olives	14:4
14:27	Strike the shepherd and sheep will be scattered	13:7
14:28	Resurrection	14:4
14:28	Restoration of scattered sheep	13:8-9

Elsewhere Mark borrows language directly from Zechariah (LXX). There can be little doubt that Mark's passion was heavily influenced by Zechariah. But Mark 11:8-11 seems to deviate from this pattern. There is no borrowed

---

[59] Cf. my previous discussion of Isaiah 11 (chap. 5) and below in the present chapter.

[60] In this passage YHWH promises to appoint a place for his people Israel and he "will plant them [נְטַעְתִּיו] . . ." (2 Sam 7:10). This serves to connect the Davidic covenant with Exodus 15:17, which also uses נטע; see D. Juel, *Messianic Exegesis: Christological Interpretation of the Old Testament in Early Christianity* (Philadelphia: Fortress, 1988), 65.

[61] M. C. Black, "The Rejected and Slain Messiah Who Is Coming with the Angels: The Messianic Exegesis of Zechariah 9-14 in the Passion Narratives" (Ph. D. diss.; Emory University, 1990); See Marcus, 153–64, for a summary and extension of Black's work.

[62] Marcus, chap. 8.

language from Zechariah as one might expect (cf. Matthew's use of Zech 9:9). Instead this passage hinges on Psalm 118. The affinity with Zechariah 9 can indeed be seen in that both have a royal figure riding amid adulation, but there is no evidence of a redactional attempt to highlight this affinity. Compare this caveat with the introductory Markan frame of the procession passage in Mark 11:2: "ἐφ' ὅν οὐδεὶς οὔπω ἀνθρώπων ἐκάθισεν."[63] Black suggests that this detail takes its cue from Zechariah 9:9 LXX, which describes the animal as a "πῶλον νέον" which can be literally rendered "new colt."[64] This vague connection is the closest conceptual allusion to Zechariah in Mark 11:1-11, and it is found in Mark's redactional introduction. There is simply no overt link between Zechariah 9 and the core of the material that Mark received.

Black is certain that "Mark was aware of the relationship between this story [of Jesus' procession] and Zech 9.9."[65] However, Ambrozic argued that the influence of scriptural precedents on Jesus' procession is to be found in pre-Markan tradition. He concluded that "it was the tradition as such which influenced the story; the working of the OT texts was only indirect."[66] Black admits, "The passage recalled (Zech 9.9), while acknowledged as messianic in contemporary literature, is nonetheless one of the most humble messianic images available; and even its use lies just beneath the text rather than in plain view."[67]

By not overtly appealing to Zechariah 9 or 1 Kings 1, Mark is either not aware of this connection or is content to leave the royal adulation implicit in his narrative as it is in Psalm 118. For this reason, it is more likely that the subtext of Mark betrays not what the evangelist hopes to portray but something that is embedded in the tradition that Mark has received. This suggests that Mark's mnemonic localization of the Passion Narrative within a Zechariah 9–14 framework did not originate with Mark. Rather, the evangelist has followed the lead of an interpretive trajectory that has understood Jesus' last week in light of Zechariah. But in the particular case of Jesus' procession, the significance of Jesus' act has not been highlighted in this way.

If, then, it is correct to say that there is an implicit political dimension akin to Zechariah in this narrative, it is necessary to analyze how Zechariah's royal categories were interpreted in the first century. This analysis is accomplished by discussing the messianic trajectory of Zechariah in the Qumran library.

---

[63] Notice the use of the double negative, a common trait of Mark's redaction, so V. Taylor, *The Gospel according to St Mark* (London: Macmillan, 1966), 46.
[64] M. C. Black, 163–64.
[65] M. C. Black, 163.
[66] A. Ambrozic, *The Hidden Kingdom: A Redaction-Critical Study of the References to the Kingdom in Mark's Gospel* (CBQMS 2; Washington, D.C.: CBQ Association of America, 1972), 37.
[67] M. C. Black, 168.

The Dead Sea Scrolls' Davidic Offspring

In order to appreciate better the function of the "Son of David" in the Jesus tradition, it is necessary to compare the form taken by similar titles/categories employed in the Dead Sea Scrolls. The present section suggests that "David" should be distinguished from the "Offspring of David" in that the texts of the Qumran library employ the former as a historical figure, while the latter is an eschatological figure. This discussion also sheds light on Zechariah's influence on messianic categories contemporary to the writing of the NT.

"Son of David" is used only once in the Dead Sea Scrolls.[68] This relative lack of use is striking, considering how many other Davidic referents are evidenced in this library. Among the undisputed Davidic referents are שרט, נשיא (כל) העדה, משוח ישראל, משיח, and of particular interest to the present discussion are צמח דויד and זרע דויד.[69] I focus here on the last two in this list (and cognates) as I am specifically interested in how the proper name "David" functions in Qumran messianism.

As discussed earlier in this text, *Psalm of Solomon* 17:23 contains the first titular mention of Son of David in a messianic context. This is certainly an important text to fill in the backdrop of the title. However, in order to take seriously the conceptual backdrop of our title, the hard and fast lines between Davidic titles and the exact phrasing of "Son of David" must be blurred. The fact that *Psalm of Solomon* 17:23 uses this exact phrase is helpful, as it is proof that the messianic application of "Son of David" was indeed pre-Christian. What cannot be inferred from this fact is that *Psalm of Solomon* 17 contains the first extant reference to a titular form of this expectation, because other Davidic titles in pre-Christian literature carry a similar eschatological significance. One such case has been seen previously in Zechariah 3:8 and 6:12 where Zerubbabel, a descendant of David, is called "Branch [צמח]."

The Dead Sea Scrolls' interest in David was largely due to the community's preoccupation with eschatological categories. In 2 Samuel 7:13, YHWH promises that David's son will have an everlasting kingdom. This language invited eschatological interpretation and, when viewed through lenses like Zechariah, took on a particularly messianic character. As mentioned above, 2 Samuel 7:12's mention of David's "seed [זרע]" contributed to a common vegetation metaphor.[70] The following texts exemplify this metaphor:

---

[68] As noted previously, the only use of the phrase "Son of David" in the Dead Sea Scrolls is 4Q398 f.11 13.1: "Solomon, Son of David."

[69] For a comprehensive list of the messianic referents at Qumran, see M. Abegg and C.A. Evans, "Messianic Passages in the Dead Sea Scrolls," in *Qumran-Messianism: Studies on the Messianic Expectations in the Dead Sea Scrolls* (ed. J. H. Charlesworth, H. Litchenberger, and G. S. Oegema; Tübingen: Mohr Siebeck, 1998), 191–203.

[70] Telford (*Barren Temple*, 137–41) surveys a large quantity of HB passages that relate to

There I will cause to sprout [אַצְמִיחַ] the horn of David. I have prepared a lamp for my anointed. (Ps 132:17)

In those days, at that time, I will cause a branch of righteousness [צְדָקָה צֶמַח] of David to spring forth [אַצְמִיחַ], and He shall execute justice and righteousness on the earth. (Jer 33:15; cf. 23:5)

ויצא חטר מגזע ישי ונצר משרשיו יפרה

Then a shoot will spring from the stem of Jesse, and a branch from his roots will bear fruit. (Isa 11:1)[71]

In the case of Psalm 132, the imagery is less explicit. But 132:17 demonstrates that the verbal use of צָמַח is an appropriate interpretation of 2 Samuel 7:13 (Ps 132:11 directly appeals to 2 Sam 7:13). Both Jeremiah and Isaiah extend the metaphor. This becomes a popular messianic category in the Dead Sea Scrolls. Consider the following phrases:

צמח דויד "branch of David" (4Q161 7-10 3.22; 4Q174 1-3 1.11; 4Q252 5.3-4, 4Q285 5 3; 5 4)

זרע דויד "seed of David" (4Q479 f1.4)

ויצא חוטר מגזע ישי "and a shoot shall come out of the stump of Jesse" (4Q285 f7.2)

ישי ונצר "sprout of Jesse" (4Q161 3.15)

Other messianic references to the Davidic figure include:

סוכת דו(י)ד "tent of David" (CD 7.14;[72] 4Q174 3.12,13)

יושב כסא דויד "one who sits on the throne of David" (4Q252 5.2)

What is common to all of the above is that (1) these references are indirect in nature (i.e., none appeal to "David" independently from circumlocutive language) and (2) all these references are eschatological categories. In the Qumran corpus, when David is referred to as a historical figure, he is simply called "David" (CD 5.2, 5; 1QM 11.2; 4Q174 3.7; 4Q177 1.7, 4:7; 4Q398 f11 13.1, f14 17ii:1; 4Q504f1 6-8). In such cases, he is not called the *son of*

---

metaphorical vegetation language and posits that the tree was often used a metaphor for an individual's or collective Israel's spiritual status. This probably stands behind the royal application of this metaphor. In the present section, I focus only on the application of this metaphor to Davidic figures (and their counterparts).

[71] Cf. also Ezek 17:3-4.
[72] CD 7.14 uses דוד.

Jesse or the *branch of* Jesse; there is no circumlocution employed. It seems then that circumlocutions are applied only when the category is specifically eschatological.

Given the consistency of the contexts where David is evoked, we may conclude that where David is referred to as an eschatological category, some circumlocution (such as vegetation language) will be employed. Conversely, where David is referred to as a historical figure, no circumlocution is employed. In these cases, the proper name stands alone. This variation is not due to the style of the individual authors because, as seen in CD and 4Q174, which contain both historical references and eschatological references, this formula holds true.

One possible reason for this circumlocution is reverence. After all, similar circumlocutions are used in Jewish literature when referring to YHWH. However, the analysis of other eschatological figures attested in the Dead Sea Scrolls dismisses this possibility. This is so because circumlocution seems to be distinctive of Davidic messianism.

For example, contrast the above Davidic language with 11Q13. This eschatological text predicts the return of Melchizedek as a liberator of Israel. Guided by imagery from Isaiah, the author expects this figure to defeat the sons of Belial and lead Israel in a type of new exodus. What is most intriguing about this figure is that Isaiah 61:2 is quoted, but rather than "proclaiming the year of YHWH's favor" this texts proclaims "the year of Melchizedek's favor" (11Q13 2.9). Considering the monotheistic source of this text, it is hard to imagine a more exalted depiction. 11Q13 2:11 makes a similar substitution for the divine name in its interpretation of Psalm 7:7-8. 11Q13 2.10 claims that Melchizedek is "god [אלוהים]" (spoken of in Ps 81:1) who pronounces judgment over all other gods.[73] No other expected figure in the Qumran library is venerated in such exalted categories. If the authors of the Dead Sea Scrolls were concerned about circumlocution out of reverence for an eschatological figure, one would expect 11Q13 to employ such language around Melchizedek's name. This strongly suggests that the circumlocution of David's name was not due to a YHWH-like reverence.

Once this possibility has been dismissed, it becomes more probable that the Davidic messiah was referred to indirectly because these texts are not referring to a David figure. Rather, following the lead of 2 Samuel 7, the Qumran community expected a messiah like David's offspring. 4Q174 1:10-13[74] supports this hypothesis:

---

[73] 11Q13 2:10 reads: אלוהים [נ]צב בע[ד]ת אל [בקרוב אלוהים ישפוט.

[74] K. E. Pomykala, *The Davidic Dynasty Tradition in Early Judaism: Its History and Significance for Messianism* (SBLEJL 7; Atlanta: Scholars Press, 1995), 192, represents the scholarly majority that dates this text to the late first century BCE or early first century CE.

> "And YHWH decl[ares] to you that He will make you a house," and that "I will raise up your offspring after you, and establish the throne of his kingdom [fore]ver. I will be a father to him, and he will be My son." This passage refers to the Branch of David, who is to arise with the Interpreter of the Law, and who will [arise] in Zi[on in the La]st Days, as it is written, "And I will raise up the tent of David that is fallen." This passage describes the fallen Branch of David, [w]hom He shall raise up to deliver Israel.[75]

This text conflates and exploits 2 Samuel 7:12, 14; Amos 9:11; and Zechariah 6:13. But 2 Samuel 7 is most prominently interpreted.[76] Although fragmentary, the text sustains a common eschatological focus throughout.[77] As such, it has the potential to illuminate Qumran's understanding of the Davidic messiah on several levels. I am here merely interested in the titles employed.

A closer look at this passage might provide a clue as to why Solomon's title was not employed more often in the Dead Sea Scrolls. Abegg and Evans observe that 4Q174 is the only mention of the Davidic messiah as "son."[78] Following 2 Samuel 7:14, the "Branch of David" will be a son to YHWH. Yet all of the passages that might indicate that this passage was originally about David's literal son (Solomon) have been removed. Pomykala writes:

> Missing from the quotation are the phrases stating that: 1) God will raise up David's seed when his days are fulfilled and he lies with his fathers; 2) this offspring will come from David's own body; and 3) this offspring will build a temple for God's name.[79] . . . Without these phrases the dynastic promise is freed from the moorings of its historical fulfillment so that it directly addresses the eschatological situation, which is the central concern of the author.[80]

As seen in my previous discussion on the "Prince of the Community" in 1QSb,[81] this author's expectation of the Davidic messiah was not constrained by typological frameworks. For the most part, the interpreters represented by the Dead Sea Scrolls were free to apply, conflate, and omit scriptural passages to conform to their eschatological ideals. It is possible that because "Son of

---

[75] Unless otherwise noted, I follow the translation of M. Wise, M. Abegg, and E. Cook, *The Dead Sea Scrolls: A New Translation* (San Francisco: HarperSanFrancisco, 1996). However, it should be noted that one would expect סוכה to be glossed "tent" in line 17.

[76] More to the point, 2 Samuel 7:11 is quoted immediately prior to this passage.

[77] G. J. Brooke, *Exegesis at Qumran: 4QFlorilegium in Its Jewish Context* (JSOTSup 29; Sheffield: JSOT Press, 1985), 144.

[78] Abegg and Evans, 199.

[79] Cf. Brooke, 111–12.

[80] Pomykala (194) echoes the previous observations of Juel, *Exegesis*, 67–68; cf. also Brooke, 111–12.

[81] See chap. 5; Abegg and Evans (194) note that all of the occurrences at Qumran of the נשיא (כל) העדה are messianic.

David" was traditionally applied to Solomon, the Qumran community has avoided the eschatological use of this title.

It is now necessary to look at the only Dead Sea Scroll that explicitly employs the title "Son of David." The fragment reads:

> [. . . the bles]sin[gs] came on [and] in the days of Solomon, the son of David [שלומוה בן דויד]. Indeed the curses [which] came in the d[ays of Jer]oboam the son of Nebat until the ex[i]le of Jerusalem and Zedekiah the king of Juda[h]. (4Q398 f11 13.1-2)

Although this text is too fragmentary to contribute to my thesis in any great way, two points are warranted. The first highlights what I noted previously in chapter 5: as should be expected, "Son of David" is specifically a Solomonic referent. The second point is more pertinent to my discussion in the present section: This indirect mention of David is not an eschatological referent; it is undoubtedly a historical reference. The author refers the blessings that came "*in the days of* Solomon, the son of David" (emphasis added).[82] Following the lines cited, several other historical references are mentioned. Lines 6-7 conclude, ". . . remember the kings of Israe[l] and consider their works carefully. For he who feared [the la]w was delivered from his troubles." This conclusion exhorts the remembrance of historical kings because much can be learned from the consequences of their historical attitudes toward the law. Thus, among the Dead Sea Scrolls, Son of David is not employed as an eschatological category. While this text does mention David indirectly, it is a direct reference to his historical son: Solomon.

I would cautiously suggest that Solomon typology was unattractive to the Qumran community in their effort to achieve a pure priesthood for the eschaton. 4Q398 shows that Solomon's title was known to the group, but this title is all but absent from the Dead Sea library. It is possible that because Solomon was the only king to perform priestly tasks (with divine endorsement), the Qumran community sought to underemphasize his legacy. Moreover, the title "Son of David" was made prominent by the Chronicler, who emphasized Solomon's jurisdiction over the temple and cultic matters.[83] The Qumran community sought to emphasize the opposite: the Davidic messiah was to be secondary to the priestly messiah. Thus, the author's conception of David's offspring is not as an antitype of Solomon. This might explain why the renewed temple[84] is built by YHWH for the Davidic figure and not vice versa (4Q174 1.1-6).

---

[82] 3Q398 f.11 13.1, emphasis added.
[83] W. Horbury, *Jewish Messianism and the Cult of Christ* (London: SCM Press, 1998), 45.
[84] For the sake of focus, I do not discuss whether this temple is metaphorical or literal. For representatives on either side of this argument, see D. Dimant, "4QFlorilegium and the Idea

This decreased role for the Davidic messiah is to be expected. Not only did the Qumran community want the Davidic messiah to have decreased jurisdiction over cultic matters, but this figure was to be of lesser rank in political matters as well.[85] As is well known, Qumran's messianism included multiple offices.[86] 4Q174 mentions two: the first is the branch of David; the second is the interpreter of the Law. Fitzmyer voices his initial surprise at this duality:

> Even though משיח was applied in post-monarchial times to a historical priest in Leviticus 4, it is a surprise to see a priestly figure become a part of the Qumran community's messianic expectations, because there is little in the Old Testament itself about a future "priest," unless Zech 6:13b is so understood.[87]

While Fitzmyer suggests this connection very cautiously, the evidence for Zechariah's influence on Qumran's messianism warrants a stronger argument. First, Zechariah 6:12-13 does indeed mention two eschatological offices under peaceful coexistence: Zerubbabel (or "Branch") and Joshua the high priest. Second, both figures are depicted as olive branches[88] and called "sons of anointing [בני־היצהר]" in 4:14.[89] The invitation toward messianic interpretation is obvious. Third, Zechariah 6:12 is the first time the vegetation metaphor becomes a messianic title foreshadowing the title "Branch of David."[90] Thus, Zechariah has the potential to illuminate at least three pecu-

---

of the Community as Temple," in *Hellenica et Judaica* (ed. A. Caquot, M. Hadas-Lebel, and J. Riaud; Leuven: Peeters, 1986), 165–86; and M. O. Wise, "4QFlorilegium and the Temple of Adam," *RevQ* 15 (1991–1992).

[85] Zimmermann comments on the reduced rank of the Davidic messiah in 4Q161: "In order to carry out a righteous justice the expected king relies on the teaching and the orders of the priests" (translated from *Messianische Texte aus Qumran: Königliche, priesterliche und prophetische Messiasvorstellungen in den Schriftfunden von Qumran* [WUNT 2.104; Tübingen: Mohr Siebeck, 1998], 71).

[86] See discussions in Collins, *The Scepter and the Star: The Messiahs of the Dead Sea Scrolls and Other Ancient Literature* (New York: Doubleday, 1995), chap. 4, and M. Abegg, "The Messiah at Qumran: Are We Still Seeing Double?" *DSD* 2 (1995): 125–44.

[87] Fitzmyer, *Dead Sea Scrolls*, 83.

[88] The vision of Zechariah 4 shows the temple as a lamp stand alongside two olive branches which pour out their oil.

[89] Collins, *Scepter*, 77.

[90] It is commonly argued that Qumran has adapted the vegetation language of Jeremiah, e.g., A. S. van der Woude, *Die Messianischen Vorstellungen der Gemeinde von Qumrân* (Assen: Gorcum, 1957), 171; Juel, *Exegesis*, 67; C. A. Evans, "Are the 'Son' Texts at Qumran Messianic?" (1998): 141; J. Laansma, *I Will Give You Rest* (WUNT 98; Tübingen: Mohr Siebeck, 1997), 225–26. There can be no doubt that the Jeremiah texts cited above also contributed to the "Branch" language. I do not wish to paint these two passages as mutually exclusive options.

liar features of Qumran's messianism. Still, while Zechariah seems to have spurred the imaginations of the Dead Sea interpreters, it obviously did not constrain their messianism to any great extent. Zechariah's royal messiah was a Solomonic figure who is expected to build the temple, and the priestly "messiah" seems to have a supporting role. As seen, Qumran departs from these ideas.[91]

As the next section returns to the NT, keep the following points in mind: (1) Some circles in the first century thought that Zechariah provided a precedent for dual messianism. (2) The messianic Davidic figure at Qumran should not be seen as an antitype of David or Solomon since there is a strict separation between eschatological and historical categories. (3) Scriptural precedents served to spur messianic ideas at Qumran but did little to constrain them. In what follows, I suggest that the evangelists (particularly Matthew) represent a more typological approach to the application of Scripture while betraying some affinity to what we have seen in this section.

Matthew's Zechariah Localization

F. F. Bruce catalogued eleven parallels between Zechariah and Jesus' passion spanning all four gospels.[92] To summarize these parallels, the following chart has set direct quotations in quotes, strong allusions in simple text, and echoes in italics.

Quote/Concept	Zechariah	Gospel
1. "Say to the Daughter of Zion, 'Behold, your king coming . . . mounted on a colt, the foal . . .!'"	9:9 + Isa 62:11[93]	Matt 21:4ff.
2. "King coming . . . seated on an ass's colt!"	9:9	John 12:14ff.
3. ". . . shall not look on him whom they have pierced"	12:10 + Exod 12:46	John 19:33ff
4. "I will strike the shepherd . . ."	13:7	Mark 14:27// Matt 26:31

---

[91] A more comprehensive treatment would have to consider the influence of Numbers 27:18-23 on Qumran's multiple offices as portrayed in the examples of Eleazar and Joshua.

[92] Bruce, "Book of Zechariah."

[93] This conflation with Isaiah 62:11 further confirms Matthew's interest in Isaiah as discussed in chap. 5.

Quote/Concept *(cont.)*	Zechariah *(cont.)*	Gospel *(cont.)*
5. Weighed out . . . 30 pieces of silver	11:12	Matt 26:15
6. Money cast down . . . used to buy field	11:13 + Jer 18:2	Matt 27:9ff
7. *The poor of the flock // little ones*	11:11 // 13:7	Luke 12:32
8. *My covenant blood*	9:11 + Exod 24:8	Mark 14:24 par.
9. *Temple Mount cleft?*	14:4	Mark 11:23// Matt 21:21
10. *Flowing of living water*	13:1 + Isa 44:3	John 7:38
11. *House of trade*[94]	*Tg. Zech* 14:21	John 2:16

As seen here, the first four parallels take the form of direct quotations. Taken together, examples five and six seem strongly influenced by Zechariah even though no direct quote is supplied. The next five represent faint echoes, perhaps too vague to be noticed individually. But given the weight of the previous six and the overall total, one is compelled to consider their merit.

Bruce concludes that there is enough evidence to suggest that the parallels to Zechariah in Jesus' passion originated in the mind of Jesus himself—that individual quotations should not be seen as "something isolated, but as part of Jesus' presentation of Himself as the good shepherd."[95] For the sake of focus, Bruce's interpretation of Jesus as the "shepherd King" will not be considered here. At this point it is necessary to assess whether Bruce's argument that traces Zechariah tradition back to Jesus can be sufficiently sustained.

Since it is upon the direct quotations that this argument is centered, I begin here and work outward to the more peripheral evidence. On the basis of the quotations alone, the dispersion of these quotations is unexpected. Numbers 1 and 2 originate independently in Matthew and John. The Fourth Evangelist also directly appeals to Zechariah 12:10 to interpret the physical-

---

[94] In this case, the key conceptual parallel is the Aramaic paraphrase "there shall no longer be a *trader* in the house of the YHWH on that day." Here the meturgeman has changed "Canaanite" to "trader." The late date of the written tradition cautions against any strong argument. Even so, it seems that there are two exegetical options available. The first places this tradition after the destruction of the temple. If this is so, *Tg. Zech* suggests that the Herodian temple was remembered as an institution corrupted by the abuse of trade. The second option is that the written tradition represents a much earlier sentiment that is contemporary to the issue at stake in Jesus' temple demonstration. Both options cast further light on the state of the temple shortly before its destruction.

[95] Bruce, "Book of Zechariah," 345.

ity of Jesus' death. It should be pointed out that in each of these cases, the Zechariah quotations derive not from the lips of Jesus but from the narrative interpreters of Jesus' actions. Mark 14:27 employs Zechariah 13:7 in the context of Jesus' prediction of his death and resurrection. Matthew follows suit. Such sayings are generally taken to be a result of post-Easter apologetic. This does not negate the possibility that Jesus foresaw his death (if only in a cause-effect sort of way) and had appealed to Zechariah in doing so. Yet the weight of scholarly opinion does not lend itself to Bruce's thesis thus far. What can be said is that the evangelists appeal to Zechariah with remarkable uniformity. What cannot be said is that there is enough evidence to trace this line of thought back to the mind of Jesus. This is confirmed by Matthew's employment of Zechariah in Judas' betrayal. Here again, it is the narrator who has interpreted the significance of the thirty pieces of silver. As far as the narrator is concerned, Jesus has no knowledge of this money or its significance.

As such, it is more probable that Matthew has followed Mark's lead in quoting Zechariah 13:7 and has taken this saying as a key for understanding the larger significance of the events of the passion. Noticing the many similarities between Mark's passion and Zechariah, Matthew has created something of a Zechariah matrix, which can be seen in Matthew's interpretation of Jesus' procession as the fulfillment of Zechariah 9:9. It can also be seen in Matthew's expansion of Mark 14:11 to include details from Zechariah 11:12-13. Bruce is then correct to quote Dodd on this matter:

> There is no reason to suppose that this belongs to the primitive corpus of testimonia, but we may well believe that Matthew was led to it because the whole passage of Zechariah was already recognized as a source of testimonies.[96]

In this way, Matthew has followed a refraction trajectory present in the tradition he has received and has expanded it.[97] Similarly the gospel of John has utilized Zechariah, not in matrix fashion, but as a resource for his theme of Jesus as the "good shepherd." The crucial difference between Matthew and John is the extent of their expansions and the extent of their creative license. In the case of John, the evangelist has probably inherited a shepherd metaphor uttered by Jesus (cf. Mark 6:34; Luke 12:32) and expanded this into a dominant literary theme. Matthew, on the other hand, follows Mark's lead

---

[96] C. H. Dodd, *According to the Scriptures: The Sub-Structure of New Testament Theology* (London: Collins, 1952), 62, as quoted in Bruce, "Book of Zechariah," 349.

[97] P. J. Achtemeier observes that in comparison to Matthew, Mark's procession account seems "unusually ambiguous" ("And He Followed Him: Miracles and Discipleship in Mark 10:46-52," *Semeia* 11 [1978]: 130). Matthew's account has thus taken steps to improve this ambiguity.

as far as events are concerned and uses the Zechariah matrix to supply details and thereby interpret these events.

As Matthew's account of Jesus' procession follows Mark, the evangelist reinforces the implicit typology with more explicit appeals.[98] In this way, Matthew continues the trajectory of typological localization implicit in Mark's narrative. This typological lens refracts the tradition in two ways. The first is narrativization: the process of refraction that takes place in storytelling. The second is instrumentalization: the reinterpretation of memories in order to serve the present better.

Jesus' procession was a public exhibition. As such, there were originally several personal memories of this event that first competed and then reinforced one another to become formalized into a socialized version of the event. Mark's account relayed a particular socialized version of the event. Upon Matthew's hearing of the story, the evangelist received a highly formalized account that was part of a narrative complex. It seems that Matthew's retelling took its interpretive cues from those implicit in Mark.

Matthew consciously rolled this trajectory forward by localizing the event within an already established category of significance, one with considerable momentum. By appealing to Zechariah directly, the evangelist placed the significance of Jesus' act within a potent and evocative memory vehicle. As attested in the Qumran library, messianic categories in the first century had an extremely strong magnetism, pulling (and conflating) disparate texts and traditions into conglomerates of eschatological expectation. Texts like 2 Samuel 7 invited associations with similar incarnations of familial expectation. Matthew's use of Zechariah 9:9 might be explained in such a way. The fact that the crowd's cry departs from the Psalm 118 formula to include, "Blessed is the coming kingdom of our ancestor David" (Mark 11:10) might have spurred memories of messianic proof-texts contained in this category. Therefore, Matthew's localization of Jesus' act within Zechariah 9:9 betrays instrumentalization and narrativization. But Matthew's use of Zechariah is different than that of the Dead Sea Scrolls in that the evangelist also seems constrained by this Zechariah framework, as fleshed out in what follows.

Matthew's account strays from Mark's with regard to its immediate telos. Mark's anticlimax is dropped altogether to include what becomes one of the most climactic moments of the narrative: Jesus' demonstration in the temple.

---

[98] D. A. Hagner writes: "Again in Matthew's use of Mark, we see close dependence but considerable abridgment together with free alteration for his own purposes, especially in the specific adaptations of Markan material with the OT citation in mind" (*Matthew 14–28* [WBC 33B; Dallas: Word, 1995], 592). Cf. N. A. Dahl, "The Passion Narrative in Matthew," in *The Interpretation of Matthew* (Edinburgh: T&T Clark, 1983 [1955]).

This is a textbook example of refraction by narrativization.[99] When memories are transformed into stories, they receive beginnings and endings. Moreover, the details included in these stories are so because they serve the telos of the story.[100] This happens along all stages of memory. In Matthew's case, the evangelist has taken the broader telos of the story and placed it in the immediate context of Jesus' procession.[101] The temple was, of course, both Jesus' final destination and the central reason that his symbolic act was effective. In both these ways, Matthew's broader telos is not radically different than Mark's. What Matthew does refract is Mark's immediate anticlimax. This is simply good storytelling. It should be noted, however, that Mark's placement of the fig tree incident (Mark 11:12-14, 20-26) was undoubtedly strategic. Mark has couched Jesus' temple action within a type of actualized parable. With this in mind, it is possible that Matthew's refraction (and subsequent redaction) comes closer to how the event was originally remembered. This is confirmed by Luke's corresponding climax.[102]

Given Zechariah's influence upon Matthew's interpretation, the evangelist's teleological emphasis is understandable. For Matthew, Jesus' royal office is linked with his relationship to the temple, and as such, Matthew places Jesus' demonstration in a more prominent location in his narrative. This shift is better explained when Matthew's use of Zechariah is examined.

As shown, Zechariah 9:9 mimics Solomon's original claim to the throne in 1 Kings 1:32-40. Zechariah employs this imagery because Zerubbabel's most important office is that of temple builder. The prophet portrays him as the antitype of Solomon in order to demonstrate his authority as the "Branch" of David spoken of in 2 Samuel 7. As the Dead Sea Scrolls attest, Zechariah's dual figures (priestly and royal) contributed to a dual messianism in the first century. Both figures were expected to lead Israel in the last days, and a large part of this was the expectation of a reestablished temple. This expectation concerning the temple illuminates Matthew's telos.

This point must be kept in mind when reading Matthew 21:2, 5, and 7. Here Matthew borrows from Zechariah by inventing dual animals. LXX Zechariah 9:9 reads:

---

[99] Mark, of course, also represents narrativized refraction. My point here is to say that Matthew's unique narrative has further refracted the story of the procession to conform accordingly.

[100] Also, Matthew omits the details of the fetching of the colt and its "unriddenness," perhaps because these details do not directly connect to either of the Scriptures to which Matthew has appealed; cf. M. C. Black, 170–71.

[101] Cf. Hagner, *Matthew 14–28*, 600.

[102] There is no need to suppose that Matthew and Luke are privy to an independent "procession source." Both seem to have refracted Mark's story by their own narrativization in order to correct Mark's anticlimax.

> Rejoice greatly, O daughter of Zion; proclaim aloud, O daughter of Jerusalem! Behold, the King is coming to you, just, and a Savior; he is meek and riding on an ass, and a young foal.
>
> Χαῖρε σφόδρα θύγατερ Σιων κήρυσσε θύγατερ Ιερουσαλημ Ἰδοὺ ὁ βασιλεύς σου ἔρχεταί σοι δίκαιος καὶ σῴζων αὐτός πραΰς καὶ ἐπιβεβηκὼς ἐπὶ ὑποζύγιον καὶ πῶλον νέον [חמור ועל־עיר בן־אתנות].

This passage interprets the Hebrew dual description of the same animal (a common feature of Hebrew parallelism) and creates two separate animals.[103] As such, Matthew has taken a poetic category and literalized it in his narrative.[104] Matthew emphatically emphasizes that Jesus rode upon both animals: "... and mounted upon a donkey, even upon the foal of a beast of burden [καὶ ἐπιβεβηκὼς ἐπὶ ὄνον καὶ ἐπὶ πῶλον υἱόν ὑποζυγίου]" (Matt 21:5). The double use of "upon" [ἐπὶ] suggests that Jesus was actually mounted upon both animals at the same time.[105] Thus Matthew's symbolism was meant to be overt; indeed, the absurdity of this scene demands a symbolic explanation.

This literalization is perhaps an extension of the first-century belief of dual messiahs as suggested by Zechariah and evidenced in the Dead Sea Scrolls. We have thus far seen that (1) Psalm 118 emphasizes the king's relationship with the temple establishment, (2) Zadok played a key role in Solomon's prototypical inaugural procession, (3) Zechariah describes both the king and the high priest as "anointed," and (4) Qumran's expectation of multiple messiahs was influenced by Zechariah. From this perspective, it is clear that Matthew followed suit with the first three of the above in placing Jesus' relationship to the temple establishment at center stage. Given that Zechariah was the dominant mnemonic paradigm at work in Matthew's interpretation, his literalization of the two animals might also have served to comment on Jesus' relationship with the temple establishment. In Zechariah, both Zerubbabel and Joshua were anointed, and each had a crucial role in reestablishing the temple; Zerubbabel took on Solomon's mantle of building the temple, while Joshua occupied Zadok's priestly office. This is most probably the paradigm that informed Matthew's interpretation of Jesus' relationship with the temple. But in Jesus' case, the high priest is absent and at odds with Zion's king.

---

[103] This detail probably does not have origins in memory, contra R. H. Gundry, *Matthew: A Commentary on His Literature and Theological Art* (Grand Rapids: Eerdmans, 1992), 409; and Hagner, *Matthew 14–28*, 594. Gundry's argument that the colt was accompanied by its mother for comfort is not convincing (*The Use of the Old Testament in St. Matthew's Gospel* [SNT 18; Leiden: Brill, 1967], 197–99).

[104] Ironically *Gos. Thom.* 47 reads, "Jesus said, 'A person cannot mount two horses or bend two bows'. . . ."

[105] My thanks to James Charlesworth for pointing this out in personal conversation.

What is not clear at this point is whether Matthew is portraying Jesus as filling both offices due to the absence of his counterpart, or whether the evangelist has merely intended to highlight the negligence of the high priest. If it is the former, Matthew's account serves as a defense against those who would begrudge Jesus both offices. If it is the latter, Matthew has demonstrated that Jesus made every effort to include the temple establishment in the coming kingdom; it was *their* decision to reject the Messiah, and so they ultimately excluded themselves. In either case, Matthew has ultimately portrayed Jesus as a singular Messiah.[106] If Matthew did indeed feel the need to address messianic duality (viz. Qumran ideology), he does so by highlighting that Jesus alone rode into Jerusalem on two animals.

By localizing his narrative within a Zechariah framework, Matthew has more than just garnished Mark's storyline with a few scriptural citations and allusions. Matthew has interpreted Jesus' significance by mnemonically associating his symbolic act with a historical type. According to Matthew, Jesus was the Davidic antitype predicted by Zechariah and first modeled by Solomon. It is in this sense that Matthew has employed the title "Son of David." Given the results of my previous chapter concerning Matthew's interest in this title, there can be little doubt that Matthew saw a connection between Jesus' procession and Solomon typology as mediated by Zechariah. In this way, Matthew probably saw his account to be an improvement of Mark's because Mark had not adequately drawn out the significance of Jesus' symbolic procession. While it was enough for Mark to relay the crowd's Davidic shout, Matthew takes this a step further and associates Jesus with the Solomonic title: Son of David.

According to Matthew 21:9, Jesus rides into Jerusalem amid the shouts, "Hosanna, Son of David! Blessed be he who comes in the name of the Lord! Hosanna in the Highest!" This is a departure from Mark in that "Son of David" is inserted in place of Mark's mention of "the kingdom of David our father!" As Matthew's agenda dictates, "Son of David" again finds a prominent position in his narrative. In this story, Jesus' procession leads to the temple, where Jesus will demonstrate his authority over it as the messianic Son of David. Zechariah again mnemonically guides Matthew's imagery. Jesus' authority over the temple is justified by the fact that he is typologically akin to the first Son of David, Solomon, who served as the prototype for Zechariah's prophecy. Unlike the Dead Sea Scrolls, Matthew has imported the context of Zechariah to inform Jesus' significance and not merely the imagery. This not only serves to strengthen Jesus' eschatological significance, but it also anchors him within an archetypal memory.[107]

---

[106] This anticipates my discussion of Psalm 110 in the following chapter.
[107] Having completed my look at Matthew's (synchronic) commemoration of the

The Procession in Historical Memory

Thus far, the present discussion has focused on interpretive trajectories. This study has traced the process of mnemonic refraction by localization: the categorization and alteration of memories within previous established lenses of tradition. We are now in a position to ask the following questions: What were the first memories of Jesus' procession into Jerusalem, and how might these account for the mnemonic trajectories that followed?

Wright, among others, has placed a great deal of weight on the fact that Jesus rode into Jerusalem on a colt.[108] Lane has pointed out that, since pilgrims traditionally entered the city on foot for such festivals, Jesus' mounting of a colt was a conscious royal appeal to Zechariah 9:9.[109] Surely, Mark seems to think that the details surrounding the procurement of this colt are important for the reader. But to make an argument for Jesus' original appeal to royal imagery perhaps places undue weight on the simple fact that Jesus mounted a colt and rode it. Are we justified to infer so much from this mounting?

Witherington observes that there is no other mention of Jesus riding an animal.[110] Furthermore, France's pith is appreciated, "Jesus walked all the way from Galilee, and surely did not need to ride a donkey for only the last two

---

procession, the present chapter has established the minimum elements required for triangulation. (1) Mark and Matthew evidence a particular interpretive trajectory and (2) the Fourth Gospel provides a separate but almost parallel trajectory. While it is not essential for my present purposes to give a full treatment of Luke's account, it should be noted that N. F. Marcos has argued that the procession was particularly Solomonic from Luke's perspective.

Marcos argued that Luke consciously imitated the LXX's account of 1 Kgs 1 rather than Zech 9 ("La unción de Salomón y la entrada de Jesús en Jerusalén: 1 Re 1,33-40/Lc 19,35-40," *Biblica* 68 [1987]: 89). He concludes, "Este fenómeno de imitación literaria que afecta tambien a otros evangelistas se ha puesto de manifesto particularmente en Lucas, hasta el punto de que su método de narrar la historia de Jesús ha podido ser calificado de la manera mas adecuada como de 'historiografía imitativa'" (96). Translated: "This phenomenon of literary imitation, which has been seen in other evangelists, has been manifested particularly in Luke, to the point that his narrative method in telling Jesus' story can be designated most adequately as 'imitative historiography.'" If Marcos is correct, Luke's interpretation might provide another distortion trajectory diverging away from Matthew's reading of Mark (cf. R. Hanig, "Christus als 'wahrer Salomo'" in der frühen Kirche," *ZNW* 84 [1993]: 112, 133–34). However, a fuller treatment of this thesis would have to account for Luke's omission of Solomon in his genealogy. Hence, the possibility remains that Luke did not intend to highlight Jesus as a Solomonic antitype (*pace* Marcos) and that the affinity between Jesus and Solomon was present in the tradition that Luke received (e.g., Luke 11:31 // Matt 12:42). If Hanig is correct that a Christology built upon Solomon typology circulated in the second century, there is remarkably little evidence for it. It seems more probable that such associations were made early and were later eclipsed by Son of God Christologies.

[108] Wright, *Jesus and the Victory of God* (Minneapolis: Fortress, 1996), 491ff.
[109] Lane, 393.
[110] Witherington, *Christology*, 106.

miles."¹¹¹ The act of riding a colt in Jerusalem therefore is abnormal on three levels. One, pilgrims usually walked. Two, Jesus is said to have ridden only in this instance. Three, Jesus rides only on the last leg of his journey. These three abnormalities give more credence to the special character of the act. That there was a traditionally established royal significance for riding into the city amid cheers of welcome only secures the likelihood that the act was not happenstance. This said, it is hard to imagine that simply mounting a colt would have attracted so much attention. In order for the proper symbolism to be evoked, there must have been some choreography involved. We might take seriously, then, Meier's suggestion that a small group of disciples prompted the crowd[112] (or as many as could be swayed).

This leads us to ask, how are we to imagine this so-called pomp? As seen above in Fitzmyer's discussion, the adulation "hosanna" was probably no more than a typical greeting offered to every pilgrim entering the city for a feast. It is more than likely that "hosanna" does not represent a royal adulation in and of itself. Witherington suggests that

> Jesus simply [was] accompanied by various pilgrims [. . .] singing the pilgrim songs, one of which is based on Ps. 118:26ff. and was certainly used during the Feasts of Tabernacles and Passover. (Psalm 118:26 may be no more than a greeting used to address pilgrims as they approach the holy city.)[113]

Sanders, very plausibly, suggests that shouting of "hosanna" and the shouting of "blessing" were antiphonal.[114] While Sanders' suggestion imagines a chorus shouting in staggered accord rather than in unison, another possibility exists. One might imagine a larger group of welcomers with no messianic agenda shouting "hosanna" (as was the custom), with a smaller group of Jesus' followers spinning the welcome in a messianic direction. It is more probable that Jesus and his disciples took the opportunity to reinterpret the ready-made appeal to Psalm 118 than it is to imagine an entire crowd coming to the same interpretation in unison. If this is so, the refraction of this memory within a Davidic/Solomonic category began in the minds of the first observers of the event.

---

[111] France, 296.
[112] Meier, "Elijah-like Prophet," 67.
[113] Witherington, *Christology*, 105; cf. Taylor, *St. Mark*, 456; I. H. Marshall, *Commentary on Luke* (Grand Rapids: Eerdmans, 1978), 715; D. Flusser, *Jesus* (Jerusalem: Magnes, 1998), 105.
[114] Sanders, 181–82; cf. Evans, *Mark*, 146. Horbury suggests that this chorus might betray an early Christian hymn that has been worked into the narrative (*Jewish Messianism*, 109). Looked at from a social memory perspective, song is an extremely effective mnemotechnique that facilitates the stability of a memory as it transitions from context to context. Thus, the possibility emerges that "Hosanna" represents both a Jewish festival ritual and an adapted Christian ritual.

Finally, consider Bruce's suggestion that the appeal to Zechariah tradition was historical before it was literary. As discussed, he demonstrated that allusions and direct quotes of Zechariah are prevalent in the Passion Narratives of all four gospels. While Bruce's conclusion that Zechariah typology existed in the mind of Jesus is difficult to defend, it is probable that this typology was present among Jesus' contemporaries. While it is extremely difficult to probe the historical mind of Jesus, it is not so difficult to establish early and widespread perceptions of Jesus.

Jesus' procession into Jerusalem is an apt case study for the present book because there is early and widespread evidence of typological interpretation that is not overtly manifested in the earliest synoptic account. Mark has made no literary attempt to draw out the significance of Jesus' action by an appeal to Zechariah, nor has he given any overt cues concerning Solomon typology. The typological significance of Jesus' procession seems to have first existed on the level of memory. That Mark's subtext betrays this typology is confirmed in the overt appeals to Zechariah by John and Matthew and Matthew's overt application of "Son of David."

In the minds of Jesus' disciples (and perhaps others), this was indeed a typological act. It was either choreographed by them or by Jesus himself. Given how influential Zechariah was at Qumran, the typology was specifically meant to demonstrate a claim of political leadership. But more importantly, the mimicry of Solomon's precedent as filtered through Zechariah was meant to elicit the endorsement and support of the temple priesthood.

In the story of Solomon, Zadok was included in the ceremony. Zechariah's "Branch" of David, Zerubbabel, was partnered with his co-anointed Joshua. Qumran's eschatology envisioned the coming of at least two messiahs, one to reestablish the priesthood and one to reestablish the Davidic line. Psalm 118 illustrates homogeny between the house of Aaron and the rest of Israel. Later Aramaic interpreters represent this as the relationship between David and the temple. The several historical and literary precedents catalogued by Catchpole typify a cultic destination and activity whether for good or ill. If Jesus' procession into Jerusalem evoked any of these precedents, this act would have been perceived as an invitation to the priesthood to acknowledge his claim as David's successor. It is improbable that the title "Son of David" was used of Jesus during this episode. Even so, Matthew's use of "Son of David" simply makes explicit a typology that can be deduced from the early and widespread memories of this event.

8

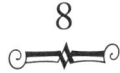

The "Son of David" Question

In Mark 12:35-37, Jesus poses a series of questions challenging the so-called scribal teaching concerning the Son of David.

> And Jesus answering *began* to say, as He taught in the temple, "How is it that the scribes say that the Christ is the son of David?" David himself said in the Holy Spirit, 'The Lord said to my lord, "Sit at my right hand, Until I put your enemies beneath your feet."' "David himself calls him 'Lord'; and so in what sense is he his son?" And the great crowd enjoyed listening to him.

> Καὶ ἀποκριθεὶς ὁ Ἰησοῦς ἔλεγεν διδάσκων ἐν τῷ ἱερῷ· Πῶς λέγουσιν οἱ γραμματεῖς ὅτι ὁ χριστὸς υἱὸς Δαυίδ ἐστιν; Αὐτὸς Δαυὶδ εἶπεν ἐν τῷ πνεύματι τῷ ἁγίῳ· Εἶπεν κύριος τῷ κυρίῳ μου· Κάθου ἐκ δεξιῶν μού ἕως ἂν θῶ τοὺς ἐχθρούς σου ὑποκάτω τῶν ποδῶν σου. Αὐτὸς Δαυὶδ λέγει αὐτὸν κύριον, καὶ πόθεν αὐτοῦ ἐστιν υἱός· Καὶ ὁ πολὺς ὄχλος ἤκουεν αὐτοῦ ἡδέως.

Because the questions presented in this passage remain ultimately unanswered by Jesus' audience, or Jesus himself, they have invited and continue to invite inference. The Son of David Question is Jesus' only mention of the title "Son of David" in the Gospels and therefore it is obviously pertinent to the present study. But it should be said from the outset that while a thorough analysis of this logion is required, the reader should not expect more than modest exegetical results. Due to the difficulties with respect to origin and meaning, the Son of David Question does little to clarify the question of Jesus' relationship to the title. Complicating matters further, Psalm 110 (quoted in this passage) presents several exegetical problems of its own. Indeed, the Son of David Question has often left exegetes and theologians with more problems concerning the title and solves very few. These are be detailed below, but it is not to say that the saying is of no value for the larger methodological aim of this book.

Over the course of this study, I have argued in favor of a historical method that traces the evidence of mnemonic refraction along redactional trajectories to postulate early and widespread perceptions of Jesus by his contemporaries. In the case of the Son of David Question, its value is found in that it is a historically indefinite test case for my proposed method. Because the origin of the saying is uncertain, it is necessary to approximate where the Son of David Question stands on its mnemonic trajectory. Moreover, this saying betrays certain ideological categories that were relevant in Jesus' historical context. For both of these reasons, the Son of David Question is historically important despite its ambiguity.

The present chapter is laid out as follows:

(1) The question of the origin of Mark 12:35-37 is discussed.
(2) Psalm 110 is analyzed for the purpose of tracing its trajectory(ies) of interpretation through the first century and beyond.
(3) The interpretation(s) of this psalm is measured against the trajectory of Davidic and messianic ideology(ies) that converged in or near the first century.
(4) Mark 12:35-37 is measured against the previous discussions with special emphasis upon pre-Markan tradition.

Mark 12:35-37 and the Problem of Origin

Scholarship is divided on the historical value of Mark 12:35-37. There are good reasons to think that this passage reflects a memory of an argument between Jesus and the Jerusalem leadership. There are also reasons to think that this story reflects an early, but invented, story that has placed Psalm 110 on the lips of Jesus. Both possibilities are given equal voice in what follows. Although my discussion of origin and "historicity" is more comprehensive than most commentators, I do not ultimately decide in favor of historicity or against it.

It is worth reiterating, however, that if one were to come to the conclusion that this passage is best explained as a product of invention, it would not necessarily render moot the discussion of the historical Jesus. If the story does represent early invention,[1] it is of value in that it provides a window to which

---

[1] By "early," I mean an invention story that circulated among the first generation of Jesus' followers. The importance of this lies in the idea of historical plausibility. If the invented story was used to interpret Jesus' significance within a category that does not seem plausible to those people who remembered his words and deeds, the story would have had difficulty being established in social memory. It is also worth acknowledging the possibility that invented stories about Jesus may have circulated during his lifetime (as sometimes happens with controversial figures). Again these stories would have only gained acceptance if they cohered with other "established" memories of Jesus.

interpretative categories had been employed to understand Jesus' significance and how. By locating these categories and analyzing their refractive effect(s), we gain insight into how memory stories of Jesus might have been interpreted at earlier stages of the Jesus tradition.

Conversely, if one were to come to the conclusion that this passage is a memory story, it would not necessarily render moot the discussion of refraction. As I have argued extensively in this book, all memories require interpretation and are therefore seen through refractive lenses. In the case of a memory story adapted by Mark's narrative, one should expect that Mark has employed interpretive categories that render the story meaningful to his post-Easter context. With this in mind, the discussion of origin aids my assessment of how best to apply these interpretive categories to Jesus' historical context.

In Favor of Memory

Bultmann argued that this saying was a product of an early Christian dispute over Jesus' Davidic descent. He supposed that the Son of David Question was invented by a small circle who denied Jesus' relationship with David.[2] While this theory has come under fire, it was more fully defended by Burger.[3] Burger argued that the Son of David Question represents a tradition whose purpose "was originally to disprove the Judaic understanding of Son of David being the messiah."[4]

Chilton exposes a weakness in this argument, averring that Bultmann's "hypothetical circle" would have held an ideology contrary to the theology of Matthew 1:6, 17, 20; Luke 1:27, 32, 3:31; Romans 1:3; 2 Timothy 2:8; and Revelation 5:5; 22:16. Because there are so many different strata representing unanimity on this point, Burger's thesis becomes highly difficult to defend. The lack of positive evidence for the existence of this hypothetical circle militates against Burger's imagination.[5] Brown also noticed this

---

[2] R. Bultmann, *History of the Synoptic Tradition* (trans. J. Marsh; New York: Harper, 1963), 145–46; cf. G. Schneider, "Die Davidssohgfrage (Mk 12.35-37)," *Bib* 53 (1972): 66–67; P. J. Achtemeier, "And He Followed Him: Miracles and Discipleship in Mark 10:46-52," *Semeia* 11 (1978): 115–45.

[3] C. Burger, *Jesus als Davidssohn: Eine traditionsgeschichtliche Untersuchung* (FRLANT 98; Göttingen: Vanderhoeck and Ruprecht, 1970), 52–59.

[4] Translated from Burger, 166.

[5] B. D. Chilton, "Jesus ben David: Reflections on the Davidssohnfrage," in *The Historical Jesus: A Sheffield Reader* (ed. C. A. Evans and S. E. Porter; Sheffield: Sheffield Academic Press, 1995), 195–96; contrarily, G. Voss has argued that Luke intentionally downplayed Jesus' physical descent from David in favor of a legal claim to Davidic office (*Die Christologie der lukanischen Schriften in Grundzügen* [StudNeot 2; Paris: Desclée de Brouwer, 1965], 67–68). M. L. Straus rightly points out that Voss' thesis cannot account for the use of Lukan language in Acts 2:30 and 13:23 (*The Davidic Messiah in Luke-Acts: The Promise and its Fulfillment in Luke Christology* [JSNT 110; Sheffield: Sheffield Academic Press, 1995], 126–29, esp. 128).

unanimity and noted that Jesus' Davidic descent does not seem to have been controversial in the earliest traditions.[6] Chilton argues that it is difficult to attribute this tradition to early church invention because although the titles "Son of David," "Messiah," and "Lord" are used in the passage, none of these are used in ways that are typical of NT usage. The distance between Lord (God) and lord (messiah) is very dissimilar to NT usage (cf. Mark 5:19-20, where Jesus' identity is in view). Furthermore, according to Chilton, the Son of David Question would seem to contradict both Matthean and Lukan genealogies, "and does not correspond to any theme which is emphasized in Mark." Chilton's observation of the atypical use of titles in this passage is not easily disputed and perhaps is the strongest reason to affirm an origin in early memory rather than invention. Chilton concludes that "the so-called Christological titles in the passage do not correspond very well to what we, on the basis of ordinary New Testament usage, might expect the early Church to have said of Jesus."[7]

Following Chilton, it is possible that this saying represents an early stage of memory and therefore does not typify the more christologically charged versions of these titles found in later traditions.[8] Chilton's observation might indicate that this tradition preserves a use of the title "Son of David" which has not yet been seen through the lens of christological refraction. One must grant that the evangelists included the tradition hoping to evoke a more fully developed Christology.[9] But since the theological statement being made on the lips of Jesus is ambiguous, one imagines an original context that predates the fully developed agenda(s) of Christology. Marcus writes:

> The apparent denial in Mark 12:35-37 that the Messiah is the son of David, therefore, represents a puzzling piece of christology that is at home neither in first-century Judaism, nor in first-century Christianity, nor in the flow of Mark's story.[10]

Perhaps the most difficult question to answer is why an invention of the early church would yield such little christological data. Evans argues that no

---

[6] R. E. Brown, *The Death of the Messiah: From Gethsemane to the Grave* (2 vols.; New York: Doubleday, 1994), 505–12; W. D. Davies and D. C. Allison Jr., *The Gospel according to Saint Matthew* (3 vols.; ICC; Edinburgh: T&T Clark, 1997 [1998]), 250, point out that *Barn* 12.10 is the first to play the title "Son of God" against the title "Son of David." Cf. *Ps.-Clem Hom* 18.13 and the *Dialogue of Adamantius* 4.46.

[7] Chilton, "Reflections," 194.

[8] J. A. Fitzmyer, *The Gospel according to Luke* (AB 28; New York: Doubleday, 1970), 1310.

[9] Burger, 116.

[10] Marcus, *The Way of the Lord: Christological Exegesis in the Gospel of Mark* (Louisville, Ky.: Westminster John Knox, 1992), 140.

"explicit affirmation of Christology is provided." He asks, "What has been clarified? What has the church gained? Casting doubt on the Davidic descent of the messiah is hardly what we should expect the church to have done."[11]

Before moving on to the factors that cast doubt on the saying's origin, one last point is warranted. The quotation formula that introduces Psalm 110:1 is an anomaly for the Markan Jesus. Nowhere else in Mark does Jesus cite Scripture by appealing to the authority of the Holy Spirit.[12] In addition, Mark 12:37's use of πόθεν instead of the more common πῶς[13] is atypical in Mark.[14] In these ways, the saying runs contrary to the editorial tendency of the evangelist. As I discuss below, several other indicators suggest that the Son of David Question is not a Markan creation. This, however, does not prove that the logion is derivative of memory, but it does suggest that, if the saying was invented, it was done so prior to Mark's composition.

In Favor of Invention

Chilton's statement that the saying does not thematically correspond to any of Mark's emphases is open to scrutiny. Telford has argued that one of Mark's principal motives was to promote a "Son of God" Christology at the expense of a more Jewish-political understanding of "Son of David."[15] Therefore, in contrast to Chilton's statement, the Son of David Question might serve to distance "Christ" from "Son of David," and if so it fits neatly into one of Mark's key agendas.[16] If one agrees with Telford that Mark had such an aim, it weakens Chilton's argument for historicity.

More problems of this nature surface when one considers the popularity of Psalm 110 among the NT writers. Taken together, Matthew 22:44;

---

[11] C. A. Evans, *Mark 8:27–16.20* (WBC 34B; Nashville: Thomas Nelson, 2001), 270; Cf. D. M. Hay, *Glory at the Right Hand: Psalm 110 in Early Christianity* (SBLMS 18; Nashville: Abingdon, 1973), 114, 158–59; Fitzmyer, *Luke*, 1310; and V. Taylor, *The Gospel according to St Mark* (London: Macmillan, 1966), 490–93; M. Hengel, *Studies in Early Christology* (Edinburgh: T&T Clark, 1995), 119–225, esp. 172–75.

[12] E. Lohmeyer, *Das Evangelium des Markus* (2 vols.; Göttingen: Vandenhoeck and Ruprecht, 1951), 262, argued that, elsewhere in the NT, when the Holy Spirit is appealed to in citation, the author does so for eschatological reasons (cf. Acts 1:16; 4:25; Heb 3:7; 9:8; 10:15; 1 Pet 1:21). This would seem to cohere with the internal discussion of messianic expectations within this pericope (discussed below).

[13] Cf. Matt 22:45; Luke 20:44.

[14] S. H. Smith, "The Son of David Tradition in Mark's Gospel," *NTS* 42 (1996): 536.

[15] W. R. Telford, *The Theology of the Gospel of Mark* (Cambridge: Cambridge University Press, 1999), 35–54; F. Hahn, *The Titles of Jesus in Christology: Their History in Early Christianity* (trans. Knight and Ugg); London: Lutterworth, 1969 [1963]), 13–15, previously argued that this saying is a result of a Hellenistic community attempting to support the notion that Jesus was not only the Son of David but also the Son of God.

[16] Telford, *Mark*, 36–37.

26:64; Mark 12:36; 14:62; Luke 20:42; 22:69; Acts 2:33-35; Romans 8:34; 1 Corinthians 15:25, 27; Ephesians 1:19-22; Hebrews 1:3, 13; 5:5-10; 8:1; 10:13[17] suggest that Psalm 110 was a potent memory vehicle that carried the early church's conception of an exalted Christ.[18] Bultmann argued that the use of this quote assumes Jesus' status as Messiah (and perhaps even his preexistence).[19] That this psalm was placed on the lips of Jesus for this reason must remain a possibility. Furthermore, the quote of Psalm 110 is dependent upon the Septuagint.[20]

Mark 12:36	Psalm 109:1 LXX
εἶπεν κύριος τῷ κυρίῳ μου· κάθου ἐκ δεξιῶν μου, ἕως ἂν θῶ τοὺς ἐχθρούς σου **ὑποκάτω** τῶν ποδῶν σου.	εἶπεν **ὁ** κύριος τῷ κυρίῳ μου κάθου ἐκ δεξιῶν μου ἕως ἂν θῶ τοὺς ἐχθρούς σου **ὑποπόδιον** τῶν ποδῶν σου.

The agreement is not perfect (set in bold above),[21] but close enough to suggest dependence. Marcus suggests that the use of "under" instead of the LXX's "footstool" is due to conflation with Psalm 8:7 LXX: "You have subordinated all things under [ὑποκάτω] his feet."[22] This suggests that the pericope was conceptualized in Greek thought.[23] Adding more support to this argument, Marcus draws attention to the chiastic structure of this pericope.

---

[17] For a survey and treatment of these passages and later apostolic witness concerning Ps 110, see Hengel, *Studies in Early Christology*, 119–225.

[18] Cf. also Acts 5:31; 7:55; Heb 12:2; 1 Pet 3:22.

[19] Bultmann, *History*, 136–37.

[20] F. Hahn, 114; R. Pesch, *Das Markusevangelium* (2 vols.; HTKNT; Freiburg: Herder, 1991), 254; Davies and Allison, *Matthew*, 250.

[21] Pesch, *Markusevangelium*, 254.

[22] Marcus, 130; Hay (35–36) demonstrated that the coupling of these verses is common in early Christianity.

[23] Gnilka argued for an origin in Hellenistic Jewish Christianity for an altogether different reason. He contended that Jesus' Davidic sonship is curiously relativized in Mark 12:35-37. According to him, it is "difficult to integrate into Palestinian/Jewish Christianity where genealogies were created in order to protect it" (translated from *Das Evangelium nach Markus* [2 vols.; Zürich: Berzinger, 1978], 2:169). This argument is only convincing if one agrees with Gnilka's premise concerning the origin of the genealogies.

Καὶ ἀποκριθεὶς ὁ Ἰησοῦς ἔλεγεν διδάσκων ἐν τῷ ἱερῷ·	A
Πῶς λέγουσιν οἱ γραμματεῖς ὅτι ὁ χριστὸς υἱὸς Δαυίδ ἐστιν;	B
αὐτὸς Δαυίδ εἶπεν ἐν τῷ πνεύματι τῷ ἁγίῳ·	C
Εἶπεν κύριος τῷ κυρίῳ μου· Κάθου ἐκ δεξιῶν μου, ἕως ἂν θῶ τοὺς ἐχθρούς σου ὑποκάτω τῶν ποδῶν σου.	D
αὐτὸς Δαυὶδ λέγει αὐτὸν κύριον,	C′
καὶ πόθεν αὐτοῦ ἐστιν υἱός;	B′
Καὶ ὁ πολὺς ὄχλος ἤκουεν αὐτοῦ ἡδέως.	A′

In this way, the lines are arranged to highlight the quotation of Psalm 110:1 which is the keystone. Such structure lends support to the argument that the Son of David Question was originally authored in Greek. But the possibility remains that Mark (or an earlier memory) has simply restructured a saying inherited from an earlier stage of oral tradition. Marcus writes:

> What is Mark's direct role in shaping this passage? It seems essentially to be limited to fashioning the frame of the passage, Mark 12:35a, 37c. Mark 12:35a, "and answering Jesus said, teaching in the Temple," is replete with Markan vocabulary. The word "teaching," for example, indicates a favorite theme of Markan redactional verses, and the mention of the Temple links our passage with the overlapping redactional framework of the entire section 11:27–13:1. As for v. 37c, "large crowd" is a characteristic term for Markan redaction.[24]

Marcus concludes that aside from the redactional frame, "the rest of the passage seems to be basically traditional."[25] But as we have just seen, the bulk of "the rest of the passage" seems dependent upon the Septuagint. In sum, the introductory and closing remarks, the scriptural citation and the overall structure look to have originated in Greek. So the possibility remains that this logion was invented by a Greek speaker for a Hellenistic audience.

All considered, the origin of the Son of David Question remains elusive. Chilton's argument for dissimilarity and tradition contrary to the tendency of the evangelists does not ultimately convince that this logion has an origin in

---

[24] Marcus, 131.
[25] Marcus, 131.

early memory. On the other hand, this logion is not easily explained as early Christian invention. Accordingly, the Son of David Question provides the present study with an opportunity to apply my proposed method to a historically indefinite test case.

Refraction and Mark 12:35-37

Crucial to my proposed application of memory refraction is the idea of continuity. I have previously discussed how memory most naturally functions as a translator that renders perceptions of the past intelligible to the frameworks of the present. I have argued that a perceived continuity between former perceptions and new perceptions is essential for maintaining both personal and social stability. A breach in one's perceived mnemonic continuity has the capacity to cause identity crisis and a disassociation from the new social framework that has dramatically negated the integrity between past and present.

When applied to the Jesus tradition, the principle of continuity militates against a dramatic breach between Jewish-Christian Christology(ies) at the time of Mark's authorship and the Jewish messianism(s) contemporary to the historical Jesus. Mark's presentation of the Jesus tradition is best seen as the stabilization of a refraction trajectory connecting the social-frameworks of Mark's community to significant (i.e., self-defining) memories of Jesus. Mark's story, stories, and sayings of Jesus must lie somewhere along this trajectory.

Because the Son of David Question is historically indefinite (i.e., it seems to repel easy classification with either social framework but seems at least partially intelligible to both), I would argue that this particular saying represents a middle stratum between early memories of Jesus and later Christian invention. In order for this to be the case, two things must be demonstrated: (a) that the Son of David Question was intelligible both to a pre-Christian, Jewish framework and to a christological framework and (b) that there is evidence of mnemonic refraction which enables us to chart a plausible course between the two frameworks.

Perhaps the biggest difficulty for those who argue for the historicity of the Son of David Question is its use of Psalm 110:1. We have seen that this text was one of the most popular in the NT and that the Markan citation seems to betray Greek authorship. But when this discussion is approached from the paradigm of memory refraction, another possibility emerges. This quotation of Psalm 110:1 might betray what memory theorists call conventionalization.

Conventionalization is the process of memory refraction whereby memories tend to conform to sociotypical experiences. In the case of Scripture quotation, if a text has been memorized it will tend to evoke a more formal citation. For instance, in contemporary, popular Christianity, John 3:16 is often memorized in the King James Version. This verse is so popular in some circles that when read aloud from other (newer) versions, the reader is inclined to use the more familiar words "begotten," "believeth," and "perish" in place of the alternate words provided by the text before them. The same could be said for the Lord's Prayer in liturgical recitation. More contemporary versions are often printed for congregations in order to be read from aloud, but even so, the phrases "who art in Heaven" and "thy kingdom" tend to be spoken aloud in place of the phrases "who is in Heaven" and "*your* kingdom." In such cases, the more familiar expressions tend to dominate one's memory and thus have the capacity to refract.

The fact that Psalm 110 was so popular in early Christianity and that (the tradition known now as) the Septuagint was largely their translation of choice makes it probable that the Son of David Question was refracted along the lines of conventionalization. As this saying was passed down, it might have attracted a memorized form of Psalm 110:1. This does not necessarily support an origin in memory rather than invention; it merely weakens the argument for invention on the basis of affinity to the Septuagint. The Son of David Question may or may not have originated in Greek, but in either case, one should expect a conventionalized citation as the saying was localized within a framework where Psalm 110 was well known and often cited.

Another manifestation of mnemonic refraction evident in the Son of David Question is that of narrativization. Narrativization is the tendency for memories to be refracted through the constraints of storytelling. This category of refraction no doubt overlaps with the previously discussed category. But here I specifically call attention to the chiastic formation of the Son of David Question, that which Marcus calls a "beautifully arranged" structure.[26] Marcus' comment is perhaps telling of why chiasms were mnemonically important for oral cultures. The fact that they can be recognized for the elegance of their form[27] speaks to the possibility that they had the capacity to reinforce narrative mnemonically. In other words, chiasms make oral narratives easier to remember.

If we are to take seriously the notion that the Jesus tradition existed in oral tradition for any period of time, the role of narrativization cannot be underestimated. While this certainly applied to the larger narrative of Mark, I am here concerned with the refractive effect that this had on the Son of David Question as an individual unit. As emphasized in previous chapters, the restructuring of memories to conform to the conventions of storytelling most often occurs on a subconscious level. But as Dunn has recently pointed out, it is necessary to take inventory of the kind of memories that

---

[26] Marcus, 130.
[27] Especially in the case of shorter, simple chiasms: e.g., ABCBA.

are represented in the Jesus tradition. Memories of Jesus were transformative both for individuals and groups, and there is a strong likelihood that they were formally memorized for oration. As such, we should not expect them to have functioned casually.[28]

Perhaps then narrative structures also played a more strategic role in the memorization of individual units. I have previously described the nature and function of mnemotechniques (or memory vehicles; see chap. 2). One might think of the examples of rhyme and song as common techniques used in memorization. It is possible that the imposition of a chiasm upon a story or logion functioned in similar fashion.[29] By memorizing the Son of David Question along the lines of chiastic structure, the story would have maintained a high degree of stability in the retelling. As such, the Son of David Question might betray a kind of mnemotechnique utilized by ancient orators.

One last observation on memory refraction should be made with regard to distanciation. As discussed in chapter 2, distanciation is the most simple and prevalent form of memory selection. It is the tendency for memories to become vague or for details to be forgotten. This observation is relevant to Gagg's suggestion that the Son of David Question is only a fragment of a longer conflict story.[30] Gagg saw in Mark 12:35-37 an abbreviated conflict story that stemmed from a situation in the life of Jesus but did not obtain its Markan form until the pre-questions of Jesus' adversaries were left out. If Gagg was correct, this passage betrays a formalized kind of distanciation in which a larger story has been lost in favor of a more mnemonically stable chiastic structure—or perhaps, merely in favor of a more pithy form of the story.

In sum, analysis of the Son of David Question yields a number of possible mnemonic refractions which suggest that Mark 12:35-37 stands somewhere along a trajectory between the earliest memories of Jesus and the fully developed commemoration of Jesus by the early church. And because of the subject matter, this text provides a window to the thought world in which "Son of David" developed along a messianic trajectory and branched out in the direction of Christology. Therefore it is necessary to establish the pre-Christian

---

[28] J. D. G. Dunn, "History, Memory, and Eyewitnesses," *JSNT* 2b, no. 4 (2004): 478.

[29] Cf. the discussion of chiasms in J. D. Harvey, *Listening to the Text: Oral Patterning in Paul's Letters* (ETS Studies 1; Grand Rapids: Baker, 1998), chaps. 5, 13. Harvey's work is ultimately concerned with the larger structures and patterns in Paul's letters, but he effectively lays a background for oral and aural patterns utilized in Hellenism (e.g., Homer). He analyzes chiastic structure alongside other patterns such as ring composition, inclusio, etc.

[30] R. P. Gagg, "Jesus und die Davidssohnfrage: Zur Exegese von Markus 12:35-37," *TZ* 7 (1951): 18–30; Gagg's suggestion was picked up by C. E. B. Cranfield, *The Gospel according to St. Mark* (CTGC; Cambridge: Cambridge University Press, 1963), 381–82 and Schneider, "Davidssohnfrage," 68; and more recently by Davies and Allison, 250.

trajectory that provided the relevant point of departure. The following section analyzes Psalm 110 in order to determine where this psalm stands along this trajectory and its eventual attraction by the Jesus tradition.

Psalm 110

Over the course of this book, I have argued for the importance of locating the trajectory(ies) of any Scriptures in which the stories of Jesus have been localized. I have argued that the fundamental virtue of this approach is that, once located, such texts can be expected to have typologically refracted the memories of Jesus by his contemporaries, and (subsequently) such refractions can be historiographically charted. This, of course, presupposes that specific incidences of pre-Christian usage can be found and that noticeable refraction has taken place.

Unfortunately, not every text in the HB has a discernable (and chartable) life between its oldest recognizable form and its NT usage. In such cases, to speak of a trajectory on which Jesus' connection with the tradition is located might be misleading. Yet, as is often the case, there is enough intertextuality in the HB that such texts often betray ideas that have been previously developed in other passages. In this way, a tradition that does not demonstrate a history of interpretation prior to the first century often demonstrates the development of other traditions and therefore does indeed represent a refraction trajectory.

Psalm 110 is such a text as it draws upon (and uniquely develops) several Hebrew concepts that hearken to other precedents in the HB. Psalm 110 reads:

> A Psalm of David.
>
> 1. YHWH says to my lord: "Sit at my right hand until I make your enemies a stool for your feet."
>
> 2. YHWH will stretch forth your strong scepter from Zion, "Rule in the midst of Your enemies."
>
> 3. Your people will volunteer freely in the day of your power; In holy array, from the womb of the dawn, your youth are to you as the dew.
>
> 4. YHWH has sworn and will not change His mind, "You are a priest forever according to the order of Melchizedek."
>
> 5. YHWH is at your right hand; he will shatter kings in the day of his wrath.
>
> 6. He will judge among the nations, he will fill them with corpses; he will shatter the chief men over a broad country.

7. He will drink from the brook by the wayside; therefore he will lift up his head.[31]

לדוד מזמור
נאם יהוה לאדני שב לימיני עד־אשית איביך הדם לרגליך
מטה־עזך ישלח יהוה מציון רדה בקרב איביך
עמך נדבת ביום חילך בהדרי־קדש מרחם משחר לך טל ילדתיך
נשבע יהוה ולא ינחם אתה־כהן לעולם על־דברתי מלכי־צדק
אדני על־ימינך מחץ ביום־אפו מלכים
ידין בגוים מלא גויות מחץ ראש על־ארץ רבה
מנחל בדרך ישתה על־כן ירים ראש

Psalm 110 does not have a history of interpretation prior to the first century. This is especially odd given the apparent popularity of Psalm 110 in early Christianity and later rabbinic messianic[32] interpretations.[33] One explanation for this is that Psalm 110's composition was relatively late. The date of composition for Psalm 110 is disputed to such an extent that the debate represents a spectrum of possibilities spanning almost a thousand years. Hardy was among those scholars who considered this psalm to have its origins in the historical reign of King David.[34] According to Mettinger, the psalm was produced during Solomon's reign.[35] Yet there is evidence that this psalm was composed in

---

[31] 110:7 has defied confident interpretation. L. C. Allen calls the verse enigmatic but eventually suggests that the "reference may be to a ritual drinking from the Gihon spring as a sacramental means of receiving divine resources for the royal task" (*Psalms 101–150* [WBC 21; Nashville: Thomas Nelson, 2002], 118). M. Dahood called this verse "baffling" and attempts to "prescind" from the MT vocalization in order to make sense of it (*Psalms III: 101–150* [AB 17A; Garden City, N.Y.: Doubleday, 1970], 119). I here follow the lead of the NASB.

[32] E. J. Kissane, who assigned late authorship, argued that Psalm 110 was initially composed with a messianic agenda and was interpreted as such from the start ("The Interpretation of Psalm 110," *ITQ* 21 [1954]: 103–14); cf. J. L. McKenzie, "Royal Messianism," *CBQ* (1957): 36. This view has been recently challenged by H. Bateman, "Psalm 110:1 and the New Testament," *Bibliotheca Sacra* 149 (1992): 447–50; and S. Gillingham, "The Messiah in the Psalms: A Question of Reception History and the Psalter," in *King and Messiah in Israel and the Near East* (ed. J. Day; JSOTSup 270; Sheffield: Sheffield Academic Press, 1998), 212–15.

[33] Hay provided a fairly comprehensive treatment of how Ps 110 was interpreted in both Christian and rabbinic literature and concluded that there is no single dominant interpretive commonality except that the lord is often thought to refer to the Messiah; cf. D. Juel, *Messianic Exegesis: Christological Interpretation of the Old Testament in Early Christianity* (Philadelphia: Fortress, 1988), 137–39.

[34] E. R. Hardy, "The Date of Psalm 110," *JBL* 64 (1945): 385–90; cf. F. L. Horton, *The Melchizedek Tradition: A Critical Examination of the Sources to the Fifth Century A.D. and the Epistle to the Hebrews* (SNTSMS 30; Cambridge: Cambridge University Press, 1976), 34.

[35] T. N. D. Mettinger, *King and Messiah: The Civil and Sacral Legitimation of the Israelite*

the postexilic period,[36] perhaps in Hellenistic Judaism. Callimachus relays a Greek mythological parallel in *Hymn to Apollo* 29. Apollo is said to have been seated at the right hand of Zeus (cf. Ps 110:1), and in verses 67-68, Apollo is praised for always keeping his oath (cf. Ps 110:4).[37] But it is also possible that the Greek hymn borrowed from an earlier mythology akin to that manifested in Psalm 110.[38] Furthermore the fact that the psalm has been authored in Hebrew might suggest a pre-Hellenistic date.

Treves argued that the psalm was composed in the Maccabean period by deciphering an acrostic from the initial letters of the divine voice that spells out "Simon is terrible (or awe-inspiring)": שמען אים.[39] If correct, the reference is to Simon Maccabeus (142–135 BCE), who followed his brother Jonathan in claiming both the offices of king and high priest. Psalm 110:4 states that "YHWH has sworn and will not change his mind. 'You are a priest forever according to the order of Melchizedek.'" Similar to the language in 110:4, Simon was said to be "high priest into eternity [ἀρχιερέα εἰς τὸν αἰῶνα]" (1 Macc 14:41).[40] Note the similar claims to (1) priesthood by a royal figure and (2) to eternal tenure. But Treves' supposed acrostic is not ultimately convincing,[41] and it is not necessary that the psalm was composed

---

Kings (ConBOT Series 8; Lund: Gleerup, 1976), 259; cf. H. J. Kraus, *Psalmen* (BKAT 15; Neukirchen: Neukirchener Verlag des Erziehungsvereins, 1959), 755; J. A. Fitzmyer, *The Semitic Background of the New Testament* (Grand Rapids: Eerdmans, 1997), 225.

[36] E.g., M. Rehm, *Der königliche Messias im Licht der Immanuel-Weissagungen des Buches Jesaja* (Kevekaer: Butzon and Bercker, 1968), 329–31; G. Gerleman, "Psalm cx," *VT* 31 (1981): 1–19.

[37] M. Treves, "Two Acrostic Psalms," *VT* 15 (1965): 87.

[38] J. W. Hilber, "Psalm CX in the Light of Assyrian Prophecies," *VT* 53, no. 3 (2003): 353–66, has recently revived the suggestion of H. Gunkel (*Die Psalmen* [Göttingen: Vandenhoeck and Ruprecht, 1926], 481–83) that Psalm 110 contains several parallels with Assyrian prophetic oracles (Hilber counts twelve). This argument reopens the possibility that this psalm was composed as early as the seventh century BCE.

[39] Treves, 86; cf. M. Fishbane, *Biblical Interpretation in Ancient Israel* (Oxford: Oxford University Press, 1985), 464. Previously, several commentators acknowledged the first word of the acrostic, "Simon." For a discussion of earlier versions of this thesis, see R. H. Pfeiffer, *Introduction to the Old Testament* (London: Adam and Charles Black, 1952), 630.

[40] Treves, 85; He neglected to mention that the Maccabees also closely aligned themselves with Phinehas (1 Macc 2:54) who is also given an eternal priest covenant (Num 25:12-13). See A. Schofield and J. C. Vanderkam, "Were the Hasmoneans Zadokites?" *JBL* (2005): 74–75. This does not necessarily negate the possibility of their appeal to Melchizedek tradition, but it does demand that the Melchizedek connection served as a secondary reinforcement. For a more comprehensive answer to Treves, see J. W. Bowker, "Psalm CX," *VT* 17 (1967): 31–41.

[41] In order for the acrostic to work, one has to begin with the first character of the divine voice (thus the middle of the first verse) rather than the first character of the first verse. Furthermore it is not entirely clear that the divine voice is continued throughout the psalm since there is a shift from first to third person (see discussion in E. S. Gerstenberger, *Psalms Part 2 and Lamentations* [FOTL 15; Grand Rapids: Eerdmans, 2001], 263).

in the Maccabean period to have been used by the Maccabees.[42] While a late date may explain the absence of Psalm 110's overt use until Christian and rabbinic literature, such a supposition must remain inconclusive.

Where Treves' treatment of Psalm 110 is most compelling is in his observation that Psalm 110 would have been especially helpful to those wishing to claim both royal and sacral offices. While there are biblical precedents that militate against Aaronic duty being done by someone other than a descendant of Aaron,[43] Melchizedek (both king and priest endorsed by YHWH) provides an alternative. This further supports 1 Maccabees 14:41's allusion to Psalm 110:4. While it is not crucial to the present study to prove that Simon appealed to this verse, it provides a possible precedent for how Psalm 110 might have been applied in Jesus' context. What is presently important is to recognize that Psalm 110 uniquely relates the dual offices of king and high priest. There are extremely few passages in the HB that suggest the merger of these offices. With this in mind, a discussion of intertextuality proves important in what follows.

What most interests HB scholarship about Psalm 110 is the problem presented by 110:4. Bracketing 110:4, the psalm is royal from start to finish, promising continued military dominance. The fact that there is a mention of priestly office amid the graphic depiction of military victory has led many to wonder whether the psalmist had one or two figures in mind.[44] For my own purposes, it suffices to observe that for later interpreters, it was an option to interpret Psalm 110 as a description of a single figure who holds both the offices of king and priest. The Epistle to the Hebrews confirms that this interpretation was a live possibility in early Christianity. The author of

---

[42] If one supposes that Psalm 110 was utilized by the Maccabees (perhaps for the coronation of Simon; so Cranfield, *Mark*, 381), it might explain why the Qumran library contains no mention of the psalm. The absence of Psalm 110 in the Dead Sea Scrolls is striking given its triumphant character and its explicit mention of (the highly revered) Melchizedek. It has long been assumed that the Qumran community was opposed to the Maccabean (non-Zadokite) claim to the high priesthood; see J. C. VanderKam, *The Dead Sea Scrolls Today* (Grand Rapids: Eerdmans, 1994), 103; H. Burgmann, *Der "Sitz im Leben" in den Josuafluchtexten in 4Q379 22 II und 4QTestimonia* (Krakow: Enigma, 1990); J. A. Fitzmyer, *Dead Sea Scrolls and Christian Origins* (Grand Rapids: Eerdmans, 2000), 253–54. With this in mind, it seems reasonable that, if this psalm was employed for the enthronement of Simon (or one of his kin), it would have been unpopular with the "sons of Zadok" at Qumran. This, of course, is an argument from silence, but for Qumran to completely ignore a text that was elsewhere interpreted messianically is perplexing and warrants modest speculation.

[43] Cf. the demise of Uzziah in 2 Chronicles 26:18; 27:2.

[44] See the discussions of H. H. Rowley, "Melchizedek and Zadok (Gen 14 and Ps 110)," in *Festschrift für Alfred Bertholet* (Tübingen: J. C. B. Mohr, 1950), 461–72; C. C. Broyles, *Psalms* (Peabody, Mass.: Hendrickson, 1999), 415; and R. G. Haney, *Text and Concept Analysis in Royal Psalms* (Series in Biblical Literature 30; New York: Peter Lang, 2002), 119.

Hebrews interprets Jesus' significance by applying both Psalm 110:1 (Heb 1:3, 13; 10:12; 12:2) and Psalm 110:4 (Heb 7:17-21).[45] So if one does not find the connection between the Hasmoneans and Psalm 110 convincing, the application of Psalm 110 in Hebrews is uncontroversial. Later rabbinic interpretations also support this interpretation.[46] The meturgeman (i.e., the Targumic interpreter) understood this psalm to refer to a single figure but was uncomfortable assigning both offices to him. In the Targums, the sacral elements have been removed from Psalm 110 in favor of purely royal language. Targum Psalm 110:4 reads:

> YHWH has sworn and will not repent, that you are *appointed leader in the age to come* [מתמני לרבא לעלמא], because of the merit that you were a *righteous king* [מלך זכי].

There is no attempt here to separate the two offices by applying each to a different figure. Instead the meturgeman simply eliminates the second office and with it the name of Melchizedek. Therefore, while this interpretation disagrees with the dual-office messianism held by the author of Hebrews, both agree that Psalm 110 refers to only one figure.

The fact that none of the Dead Sea Scrolls quote Psalm 110[47] might indicate that the Qumran community was uncomfortable with the psalm's

---

[45] Furthermore, the author of this epistle is comfortable applying to Jesus royal language (Ps 2:7) alongside sacral language (Ps 110:4). Indeed the author employs the titles "Son" (cf. Ps 2:7) and "High Priest" (Ps 110:4) with equal frequency, see V. C. Pfitztner, *Hebrews* (Nashville: Abingdon, 1997), 38.

[46] It is apparent that Psalm 110 became an extremely popular messianic proof-text in rabbinic thought. Texts such as *Sanh* 38b, *Gen.Rab* 85.9, and *Num.Rab* 18.23 suggest that Ps 110 was commonly thought to be instructive of the coming Messiah's character and office. Midrashic teaching on Psalm 110:4 (given by R. Eleazar ben Pedat ca. 250 CE) instructs that what the Lord tells to David, "to the messiah also it shall be said." This is important for two reasons. Here the rabbi supposes that 110:4 was written originally to David suggesting a merging of royal and sacral offices. It also teaches that the Messiah will be divinely endorsed for priestly office in similar fashion. *Numbers Rabbah* 18.23 makes a connection between Psalm 110 and the "Rod of Aaron for the House of Levi (Num 17.8)." Psalm 110 is referenced, and then the claim is made that this messianic staff is the same one that every king would hold until the destruction of the temple.

[47] I am unconvinced by those who argue that 11QMelch echoes Psalm 110. Marcus (133) argues to this end, concluding that "the combination of themes found in both documents (Melchizedek, exaltation to God's right hand, divine Kingship, victory of enemies, and judgment) is too close to be fortuitous." Cf. B. Witherington III, *The Gospel of Mark: A Socio-Rhetorical Commentary* (Grand Rapids: Eerdmans, 2001), 333.

On the contrary, it is because there are so many conceptual similarities between these texts that are *not* derived from Psalm 110 that the absence of a direct quote or allusion is puzzling. 11QMelch directly quotes both Psalm 82:1 and Psalm 7:6. The text borrows the idea of divine kingship and judgment from the former and the idea of victory over enemies from the latter.

application of dual offices as well. Because the Qumran community saw a division of these offices,[48] perhaps this psalm was unattractive. This possibility would further suggest that the single-figure interpretation was the dominant application of this psalm among Jesus' contemporaries. Because there is no explicit first-century application of Psalm 110 to support a two-figure paradigm, one could argue that such a reading was simply not an available possibility. My own conclusion is more modest, however. I only posit that Psalm 110 invited many to suppose that a single figure could legitimately hold both royal and sacral offices. It is probable that this interpretation was spurred by the traditional precedents evoked by the psalm.

The appeal to Melchizedek[49] in 110:4 is telling of the general purpose of the psalm. Here the psalmist appeals to the figure described in Genesis 14:18-20 as both a king and priest. This lends support to the idea that the original psalmist appealed to this unique precedent to justify a single figure holding both offices. This case is strengthened further by the observation that the appeal to Melchizedek is typological in nature. Fitzmyer writes, "Whatever the puzzling Hebrew phrase [על־דברתי מלכי־צדק] means, no one has ever suggested that it be understood in terms of hereditary succession."[50] This, of course, is due to the fact that the king-priest mentioned in Genesis 14 has neither recorded lineage nor progeny. Indeed, one of the reasons that Melchizedek intrigued later interpreters was his mysterious possession of both offices and yet, apparently, he was endorsed by "God Most High" (Gen 14:18).[51] What Psalm 110:4 shows is that, in some cases, divine endorsement trumps proper lineage. This is most likely why Hyrcanus took the title "High priest of God Most High [θεοῦ ὑψίστου]" (*Ant* 16.163).[52]

Also, while the 11QMelch figure is exalted, there is no mention of Psalm 110's "right hand" language (contra Marcus). It must be kept in mind that 11QMelch is an interpretation that frequently incorporates and conflates direct quotations. In fact, the ratio of quotes per sentence is virtually 1:1. There are several places where a direct quote or allusion to Psalm 110 is warranted but absent. Instead the author chooses to quote a myriad of other texts. Because of this, the relationship between Psalm 110 and 11QMelch can be best characterized as parallel but independent interpretive trajectories.

[48] However, there is a possible exception in 4Q266.

[49] Dahood (112) avoided the use of the proper name in favor of the etymologically literal "legitimate king," but most translators favor the use of the proper name.

[50] Fitzmyer, *Semitic Background*, 225.

[51] It is possible that this enigma invited the "eternal" aspect of the Melchizedek tradition. Having come from nowhere and having returned in the same way, the "righteous king of Salem" invited a great deal of speculation for later interpreters (cf. Heb 7:3). However, it is more likely that Psalm 110:4 refers to eternal office as an extension of the underlying canvas provided by 2 Samuel 7. This is discussed further below.

[52] The LXX of Genesis 14:18 reads, "Μελχισεδεκ . . . ἱερεὺς τοῦ θεοῦ τοῦ ὑψίστου."

The psalmist is not claiming that his priest is a descendant of Melchizedek. Rather, Melchizedek is the archetypal high priest with no other claim to the office except divine endorsement. Psalm 110's priest embodies certain characteristics that are reminiscent of Melchizedek. Specifically, the priest is divinely endorsed, and he enjoys eternal tenure. In these two ways, the Psalm 110 priest is of the same type as Melchizedek. Moreover, if indeed this psalm only refers to a single figure, a third characteristic is shared: both figure the psalmist's king and Melchizedek hold the dual offices of king and priest. But the first attribute is the most important. From divine endorsement flows the office(s) and perpetuity. Essentially Psalm 110 is a divine endorsement of the same type that YHWH first offered to Melchizedek. Fitzmyer points out that the author of Hebrews similarly interprets Psalm 110:4 as "[according to the likeness of Melchizedek] κατὰ τὴν ὁμοιότητα Μελχισέδεκ" (Heb 7:15).[53] The phrase "according to the likeness of" is clearly the language of typology.[54]

In the case of Psalm 110, the psalmist is not merely appealing to a precedent; he is not saying, "*God has made this kind of endorsement before, so it must be legitimate to affirm a similar case.*" The appeal is much stronger; it asserts that God is acting now like he has acted before. The priesthood claimed in 110:4 is typologically defined by Melchizedek, not merely a legitimating reference.

At this point it is important to grant that there is no necessary dichotomy between claim to office via lineage and claim via typological appeal. One can easily imagine instances where it might be advantageous to evoke both.[55] Certainly there is a great deal of weight carried in the claim of Davidic lineage. Although Idumean, Herod claimed to be of David's line through Jewish-Babylonian descent in an attempt to strengthen his claim to be "King of the Jews."[56] But the claim of Davidic descent would not have been enough (after all, there were many descendants of David[57]); in order to substantiate such a claim, one had to embody the characteristics promised to David's heir.[58]

---

[53] Fitzmyer, *Semitic Background*, 226, asks, "Does the Peshitta reflect this in Ps 110:4 or preserve its own ancient interpretation: badmûteh deMelkîzedeq, 'in the likeness of Melchizedek'?" While it is not within the scope of this study to answer his question, it is important to note that the rabbinic testimony corroborates the interpretative trajectory on which Hebrews stands.

[54] B. F. Westcott, *Epistle to the Hebrews: The Greek Text with Notes and Essays* (London: Macmillan, 1889), 183–86.

[55] I have previously demonstrated that Zerubbabel (from David's family tree; he is literally named "Branch") further strengthened his bid for the throne by typologically mimicking Solomon's historic ride into Jerusalem (Zech 9).

[56] J. Neusner, *A History of the Jews in Babylonia* (Leiden: Brill, 1965), 35.

[57] Hillel, Judah the Prince, Ḥiyya, and Huna are all said to be of Davidic descent without any messianic claim.

[58] With this in mind, one should consider Herod's rebuilding of the temple a politically advantageous act as it served to align him with the promise of 2 Samuel 7:13. Cf. also Simon's rededication of the temple (1 Macc 13:51).

Of primary importance is the perception that this particular descendant of David is the one endorsed by YHWH in 2 Samuel 7. It was not enough to be a descendant of David; such appeals must be typologically modeled after the specific characteristics first promised of Solomon. In similar fashion, Psalm 110 is a typological appeal that presupposes YHWH's promise to David in 2 Samuel 7. So while Fitzmyer is correct that the appeal to Melchizedek is not an appeal to lineage, Psalm 110 is also undoubtedly Davidic in a typological sense.

The most prominent typological characteristic of Psalm 110:4 is Melchizedek's eternal office. It is also the characteristic least easily construed from Genesis 14. This aspect of the divine endorsement echoes 2 Samuel 7:13: "He shall build a house for my name, and I will establish the throne of his kingdom forever." Because the appeal to Melchizedek has been localized within a royal psalm, the Genesis 14 allusion has been reinforced with Davidic language.[59] That this is a specific allusion to the Davidic covenant is confirmed by the preamble: "YHWH has promised and will not change his mind." In this way, Psalm 110:4 references a covenant previously oathed and mnemonically appropriate for an enthronement ceremony.[60] Notice the conceptual links to the Davidic covenant present in Psalm 110: (1) David, (2) enthronement, (3) eternal tenure, (4) rest from enemies, (5) promise of progeny, (6) divine oath. With these several points of coherence in mind, there can be little doubt that the reference to a previous divine oath recalls the Davidic covenant.[61] But what is unique about the allusion in Psalm 110:4 is that a priestly office is being reinforced with language originally attributed to David's heir.

One aspect of the Davidic covenant that is not present in Psalm 110 is the promise to build the temple. It is possible that this cultic aspect of 2 Samuel 7 has been reformulated. In the Davidic covenant, David's son is expected to build the temple and thus enjoy eternal tenure. These two concepts are juxtaposed in 2 Samuel 7:13.[62] In Psalm 110:4, there is no mention of building the temple, but a cultic promise remains linked with the promise of eternal tenure. The Davidic heir is promised eternal sacral jurisdiction over the

---

[59] The reference to enthronement in 110:1 likely hearkens back to this promise, as 2 Samuel 7:13 uses throne imagery.

[60] Contrast this with Psalm 2:7: "I will surely tell of the decree of YHWH: he said to me. . . ." This preamble makes no reference to a previous divine endorsement; it is self-referential.

[61] Mettinger (*King and Messiah*, 258–59), however, took a slightly different approach. He suggested that 2 Sam 7 drew upon and crystallized concepts previously manifested in Psalm 110. While this remains a possibility (if one is willing to grant Mettinger's early date), he was mistaken that this psalm uses "son of God" language (258). Unfortunately, this mistake occupied a central place in his treatment of Psalm 110.

[62] On the intentional reciprocity of 7:13, see chap. 5.

temple cult. In light of this, Psalm 110:4 should not be seen as a parenthetical reference to priestly office in an otherwise royal psalm. Rather it is an extension of the Davidic covenant to include sacral duty. This argument is further supported in what follows. This dramatic addition to the royal job description is perhaps unexpected but, as is discussed, not without precedent.

Psalm 110 echoes 2 Samuel 7:11: "I will give you rest from all your enemies."[63] This is seen metaphorically in the footstool (v. 1) and scepter (v. 2) and then reinforced in 110:5-6. The graphic depiction of "filling the nations with corpses" and "shattering kings" may well be a summary of 2 Samuel 8 which recounts David's defeat of several foreign armies and kings. This possibility becomes more likely when the last verse of this chapter is considered, ". . . and the sons of David became priests [ובני דוד כהנים היו]" (2 Sam 8:18). This detail has puzzled interpreters of 2 Samuel,[64] but for our purposes, it serves to better illuminate Psalm 110:4.

If the psalmist's conceptual undergirding extends from the popular 2 Samuel 7 to the less celebrated chapter 8, it might explain why a mention of priestly office was warranted in the first place. Perhaps the Davidic king of Psalm 110 has taken on the mantle of these first "sons of David" who were priests (thus inviting the explicit appeal to Melchizedek for affinity's sake). If so, Psalm 110 is at the same time a typological and an ancestral appeal. It is important to note that while some of David's sons were priests, only one of them was both king and priest; Solomon alone provides a (legitimate[65]) royal/sacral precedent.

Solomon acts out this priestly office in 1 Kings 3:4 by offering "one thousand burnt offerings" before building the temple. Then more officially in 1 Kings 8, Solomon offers sacrifices during the dedication of the temple. In this rare exception to the rule,[66] Solomon acts as priest as he officiates on Israel's behalf over the altar with the peace offering, burnt offering, with oxen, sheep, and grain (in exaggerated quantities).[67] Solomon offers these sacrifices before (1 Kgs 8:5) and after (8:62-64) his prayer of dedication, wherein he claims

---

[63] McKenzie, 35–36; Kraus, 763–64; Fitzmyer, *Semitic Background*, 225; The echo of Psalm 2 is also unmistakable: see Haney, 122.

[64] E.g., G. Wenham, "Were David's Sons Priests?" *ZAW* 87 (1975); Anderson, *2 Samuel*, 137–38.

[65] Saul (1 Sam 13:8-14), Adonijah (1 Kgs 1:9), Uzziah (2 Chr 26:16-21), and Ahaz (2 Kgs 16:13-14; 2 Chr 28:1-5) all attempt to conflate these offices to their own peril.

[66] A. P. Ross, *Holiness to the LORD: A Guide to the Exposition of the Book of Leviticus* (Grand Rapids: Baker, 2002), 199.

[67] V. Fritz, *1 & 2 Kings: A Continental Commentary* (trans. A. Hagedorn; Minneapolis: Fortress, 2003), 100–10; M. J. Mulder, *1 Kings*, vol. 1. *Kings 1–11* (trans. J. Vriend; Leuven: Peeters, 1998), 451.

the fulfillment of the Davidic covenant.[68] Thus, the extension of the Davidic covenant to include sacral duty was rare (only seen with Solomon[69]), but not unprecedented.

Psalm 110, then, is drawing upon a linear tradition that is built upon YHWH's seminal promise to David and its prototypical fulfillment in Solomon. This tradition undergirds the thought-world on which this royal psalm is based. When read in this light, the overt typological appeal to Melchizedek can be seen as a cohesive part of this structure. The psalmist, much like the author of 1 Kings 8, seems to have seen in the Davidic covenant a legitimation of the king's sacral duty. The psalmist typologically reinforced this concept by appealing to the archetypical priest-king of Genesis 14:18. This interplay between the conceptual undergirding of Psalm 110 and the overt typology of Psalm 110:4 helps to explain why the mention of a second (priestly) office was warranted amid a royal psalm. What at first glance looked to be a sacral parenthesis in an otherwise royal poem can be better understood as an expected feature in light of 2 Samuel 8:18, and 1 Kings 3:4 and 8:5, 62-64.

In the present section, I have followed an admittedly thin thread backward from the Maccabees to Solomon to Melchizedek. It is thin because precedents for priest-kings are extremely rare in the HB. But this has been necessary because Psalm 110 is specifically interested in legitimating a royal figure according to the likeness of Melchizedek. It is impossible to know with any certainty where Psalm 110 stands in relationship to Solomon or Simon, but there is a strong likelihood that the psalmist has appealed to and extended the Davidic covenant to include priestly office. This extension is given pri-

---

[68] 1 Kings 8:16-27 is especially pertinent in that Solomon's prayer of dedication claims that his dedication of the temple is the fulfillment of the Davidic covenant with specific emphasis upon the fulfillment of 2 Samuel 7:13a. This passage in 1 Kings 8 directly alludes to 2 Samuel 7 in several respects and includes the following request placed upon the lips of Solomon: "Now therefore, Oh God of Israel, let your word, I pray, be confirmed which you have spoken to your servant, my father David" (1 Kgs 8:26). In this supplication, Solomon calls upon YHWH to fulfill his end of the Davidic covenant. One might see this text in parallel to Psalm 110:4 where the psalmist assures the Davidic king that "YHWH has promised and will not change his mind." In 1 Kings 8:26, the appeal takes the form of supplication; in Psalm 110:4, the appeal takes the form of reaffirmation. It is not necessary to argue that either text was drawing from the other; this parallel simply demonstrates that the proper establishment of the temple cult involved an appeal to the Davidic covenant. It was important for all parties involved to legitimate their activity by localizing it within YHWH's promise to David.

[69] W. Horbury, *Jewish Messianism and the Cult of Christ* (London: SCM Press, 1998), 44–46, has argued that, as Solomon's legacy increases in Chronicles to include sacral jurisdiction, the notion of a "dual" leadership in Israel diminishes. While texts like Leviticus 4:3 suggest two anointed figures, the Chronicler envisages a clear sacral hierarchy, with Solomon as chief over the chief priest.

mary authoritative weight in the appeal to Melchizedek. So while it is perhaps less important to link Psalm 110 to Solomon and the Maccabees, it is more important to recognize that the central feature that made Psalm 110 distinct and memorable was its legitimation of kingship and high priesthood in a single text. This essential feature is further corroborated by the psalm's possible relationship to these other precedents. If it can be granted that Psalm 110 provided dual legitimation, it is necessary to keep this in mind when reading Mark. Mark quotes Psalm 110 twice, both times within a temple context. Moreover, Mark has used these quotes to highlight Jesus' conflict with the temple establishment.

Psalm 110 in Markan Context

There are narrative indications that the Son of David Question is not of Markan origin. The present section argues that Mark 12 is a compilation of related sayings and that 12:35-37, in particular, is pre-Markan. Mark's implementation of the Son of David Question is then measured against Mark's larger narrative and christological agendas in order to analyze how and to what extent this pericope has been refracted within this localization. Having already touched upon this above, I focus here on the immediate context of the Son of David Question in Mark 12 and the evangelist's climactic trial scene in Mark 14. There are several reasons to see these two passages as mutually interpretative, but the central reason is that these two passages place Psalm 110 on the lips of Jesus. By devoting brief attention to the trial narrative, light may be shed on Mark's attraction to this psalm.

Immediate Context: "The Scribes" Sayings

The verse that directly precedes the Son of David Question emphasizes a narrative conclusion. At the end of Jesus' conversation with the scribe (12:28-34), Mark concludes by saying: "When Jesus saw that he had answered intelligently, he said to him, 'You are not far from the kingdom of God.' After that, no one would venture to ask him any more questions" (12:34). Several observations concerning this verse are pertinent to the present section. The first is that the phrase "And after that, no one would venture to ask Him any more questions [καὶ οὐδεὶς ἐτόλμα αὐτὸν ἐπερωτῆσαι]" denotes an end to Jesus' reception of questions; this much might be obvious. The more important observation is that the phrase seems to connote an end to dialogue in the temple precincts. In Mark's context, however, the temple dialogue is picked up again in the next verse (12:35). This narrative incongruity might be explained by reading a shift in the speaking roles; in the immediately preceding pericopes Jesus was being questioned, whereas in the Son of David Question he becomes the questioner.[70] But this reading presumes a certain rhetorical rigidity (a lack of give-and-take) between the parties, where each is assigned a particular role. Instead I think it is more natural to read such dialogues with fluidity, where each party is free to take on either role. With this in mind, the best reading of 12:34 is that of a narrative conclusion which implies an end to dialogue and not merely a reversal of speaking roles.

It is also important to observe the general mood in this pericope as compared with its immediate context. Jesus' debate with the Sadducees in 12:18-27 demonstrates a decidedly hostile mood.[71] As seen above, Jesus' discussion with the scribe immediately prior to the Son of David Question concludes with the complimentary statement: "When Jesus saw that he had answered intelligently, He said to him, 'You are not far from the kingdom of God'" (v. 34). Verse 12:35 proceeds with contempt toward scribal teaching and yet "the large crowd enjoyed listening to him" (12:37). Does this statement presume that there were no scribes present to argue? If this logia-sequence was Mark's creation, one must either assume that the scribe mentioned previously in 12:34 has left or that he agrees with Jesus on this point. Mark 12:38-40 militates against the latter solution as Jesus moves from attacking a scribal teaching to a diatribe about the character of the scribes. The most plausible solution is that Mark has here acted as a collector of tradition rather than an original composer.

It seems as if Mark was unconcerned with the shifts of mood in his narrative and is more concerned with topical arrangement. This kind of narrative arrangement likely betrays mnemonic reinforcement; sayings concerning the scribes have been mnemonically categorized together. Mark (or previous oral memory) remembered Jesus' criticism of the scribes "who devour widows' houses" (12:40) and intentionally has placed this criticism in a temple treasury setting.[72] Since this memory was previously reinforced by other sayings concerning the scribes (perhaps they were previously memorized in this way), these other sayings were evoked from memory alongside Mark 12:41-44. Simply put, one saying concerning the scribes called to mind the others.[73]

---

[70] Evans, *Mark*, 276.

[71] Mark 12:24 reads: "Is this not the reason you are mistaken, that you neither understand the scriptures nor the power of God?" Mark 12:27 concludes with, "you are greatly mistaken."

[72] There are historical questions concerning the identity of the scribes, but what is key in this discussion is the fact that Jesus associates the scribes with the other religious leaders in 12:38-39. Thus, in Mark's context, this saying serves as a launching point to lament the widow's offering (12:41-44).

[73] Perhaps complementary to this observation is the suggestion by Marcus (145–46) that the evangelist has placed the Shema saying immediately prior to the Son of David Question lest there be any charge that Jesus' exaltation undermined monotheism.

Since the sayings located in Mark 12 cannot be placed confidently in the historical setting of the temple, it is necessary to question the intended setting of the Son of David Question. Mark 12:35 specifies that Jesus' use of Psalm 110 is meant to be understood in a temple setting. It is possible that this detail was attached to the tradition that Mark received.[74] It is also possible that this detail is a product of Markan redaction.[75] The new pericope begins, "And Jesus answering began to say as he taught in the temple. . . ." Since the setting of the immediate context (all of Mark 12) is clearly the temple precincts, the introduction to the pericope might be seen as unnecessarily redundant. The larger narrative context necessitates a temple setting. Therefore this detail might have been attached to the Son of David Question in its pre-Markan form. On the other hand, the vocabulary in 12:35a is common to Mark.[76] It is possible that the evangelist has repeated the setting for emphasis. In my estimation, the most plausible answer is the first: the Son of David Question was associated with the temple before Mark's redaction as indicated by the redundant setting detail provided in Mark 12:35a. Because of this, the evangelist has associated Psalm 110 with Jesus' conflict with the Jerusalem temple establishment. This might be confirmed in that the Markan Jesus only appeals to this psalm one other time, and it is during Jesus' trial before the Sanhedrin where Jesus' relationship with the temple is at center stage.[77]

Larger Context: The Trial Narrative

It is often noted that Jesus' trial hinges on Jesus' confession to the charge of being "the Christ, the Son of the blessed [ὁ χριστὸς ὁ υἱὸς τοῦ εὐλογητοῦ]" (Mark 14:61). But, as Chilton has pointed out, the simple claim of messiahship would not have necessarily warranted the charge of blasphemy or sedition.[78] With this in mind, it is helpful to observe Mark's conceptual links between (a) Jesus' conflict with the temple establishment, (b) the title χριστός, and (c) the use of Psalm 110 that is present in both 12:35-37 and 14:55-64. By examining how Mark has linked these concepts in his trial narrative, we

---

[74] K. L. Schmidt, *Der Rahmen der Geschichte Jesu: literarkritische Untersuchungen zur ältesten Jesusüberlieferung* (Berlin: Trowitzsch, 1919), 289; Taylor, *St. Mark*, 490.

[75] Gnilka points to "the mention of the teaching of Jesus and of the temple" as evidence that that 12:35a is a product of Markan redaction (translated from Markus, 2:169); cf. Marcus, 131–32.

[76] Marcus, 131.

[77] Following the scholarly consensus, I do not take Mark 16:19 to be original to Mark's narrative. It is, however, interesting that the "final redactor" of Mark has used the language of Psalm 110 to convey Jesus' ultimate telos.

[78] Chilton, "Jesus ben David," 211; contra W. L. Lane, *The Gospel of Mark: The English Text with Introduction, Exposition, and Notes* (Grand Rapids : Eerdmans, 1974), 536.

are better able to estimate how the evangelist has localized the Son of David Question within his larger narrative.

In Mark's trial scene, two key themes converge and find clarity. Jesus' conflict with the temple establishment climaxes and Jesus' true identity is conveyed.[79] Because of this, neither theme can be properly understood apart from the other. Jesus' true identity is cast in antithesis to the true identity of the temple establishment. That Jesus' stance concerning the temple is at center stage is made clear by Mark 14:58. Jesus is accused of having predicted the temple's destruction and restitution.[80] Mark is careful to point out that this accusation represents an inconsistency on the part of the false witnesses.[81] This detail (while not explicitly denying that Jesus made such a claim) speaks to Jesus' innocence in contrast to the guilt of his accusers and the general illegitimacy of the trial.[82] This point is further illuminated in Jesus' dialogue with the Markan high priest.

After a period of silence on Jesus' part, "the high priest was questioning him, and saying to him, 'Are you the Christ, the Son of the Blessed?'" Notice here the circumlocution for the name of God and the affinity of this confession with Mark 1:1: ". . . Christ, the Son of God". Mark has thus placed his central confession of Jesus' identity on the lips of his chief antagonist.[83] Compare this with the similar "Son of God" confessions on the lips of the demon in Mark 3:11 and the Roman centurion in Mark 15:39.[84] Peter's "Christ" confession in Mark 8:29-33 also follows this motif. Here Peter confesses "you are the Christ" but is in the same context rebuked as "Satan (Accuser)." It is then no coincidence that Peter's denial of Jesus antithetically mirrors[85] the confession of Mark's high priest (14:54, 66-72).

---

[79] M. Hooker, *The Son of Man in Mark* (London: SPCK, 1967), 163; J. D. Kingsbury, *The Christology of Mark* (Philadelphia: Fortress, 1983), 162.

[80] This is revisited below.

[81] Mark employs χευδομαρτυρέω twice (15:56-57).

[82] J. B. Green argued that this contrast is part of Mark's agenda to paint Jesus as the righteous sufferer of the psalms (e.g., Ps 22, 31, 34, 35, and 69), who was innocent, accused falsely, but would eventually be vindicated by God. This paradigm also explains Jesus' initial silence at the trial (14:61) and the mocking and abuse that Jesus receives after the trial (14:65). Both elements are featured in these psalms (*The Death of Jesus: Tradition and Interpretation in the Passion Narrative* [WUNT 2:33; Tübingen: Mohr Siebeck, 1988], 317–18). Green follows the earlier leads of C. H. Dodd, *According to the Scriptures: The Sub-Structure of New Testament Theology* (London: Collins, 1952), 97–98, and B. Lindars, *New Testament Apologetic: The Doctrinal Significance of the Old Testament Quotations* (Philadelphia: Westminster, 1962): 89–93. Cf. also Juel, *Exegesis*, 89–116; and J. Painter, *Mark's Gospel* (London: Routledge, 1997), 195.

[83] D. Juel, *Messiah and Temple: The Trial of Jesus in the Gospel of Mark* (SBLDS 31; Missoula, Mont.: Scholars Press, 1973), 47–48.

[84] Cf. also Mark 15:2, 18, 32 concerning the title "King of the Jews."

[85] E. Schweizer, *Mark*, 320, 332; Witherington, *Mark*, 386–87.

Jesus' positive affirmation of the high priest's question is then clarified with a conflation of Daniel 7 and Psalm 110: "I am; and you shall see[86] the Son of Man sitting at the right hand of Power, and coming with the clouds of heaven" (Mark 14:62).[87] Berger correctly described this quote in terms of ironic juxtaposition.[88] His exegesis of Mark's trial scene drew out the relationship between the charge of blasphemy against Jesus (14:64) and the actual blasphemy committed by the judicial counsel against God's agent. He helpfully compared this judicial reversal to the final words of the martyrs in the context of their Roman trial in 2 Macc 7:34-36:

> But you, unholy wretch, you most defiled of all men, do not be elated in vain and puffed up by uncertain hopes, when you raise your hand against the sons of Heaven. You have not yet escaped the judgment of the almighty, all-seeing God. For our brothers after enduring a brief suffering have drunk of everlasting life under God's covenant; but you, by the judgment of God, will receive just punishment for your arrogance.

In this way, the accused/judged claims ultimate victory in that he will be vindicated by God as he is among the "sons of Heaven." The key idea here is that one cannot condemn YHWH's sons[89] without bringing down reciprocal judgment.[90] Berger concluded that Jesus' self-identification as the figure of Daniel 7 and Psalm 110 served to condemn all those who would condemn him. In this way, "the proclamation of the son of man is a judicial indictment."[91] Jesus' scriptural pronouncement shows him to be the true judge,

---

[86] N. Perrin argued that "you shall see" echoes Zechariah 12:10 ("Mark 14:62: The End Product of a Christian Pesher Tradition?" *NTS* 12 [1965]: 150–55).

[87] Juel (*Messianic Exegesis*, 168) suggested that Psalm 80 provides a precedent for the merger of the conceptual spheres manifested in Psalm 110 and Daniel 7: "Let your hand be upon the man of your right hand; upon the son of man whom you have made strong for yourself" (80:17; emphasis added to highlight the key concepts paralleled in Ps 110:1 and Dan 7:13). The targum of Psalm 80 interprets this verse messianically. Hay (26) suggested that the authorship of Daniel 7 was conceptually dependent upon Psalm 110.

[88] K. Berger, "Die Königlichen Messiastraditionen des Neuen Testaments," *NTS* 20 (1984): 1–44, 18–19; cf. Hooker, 171.

[89] It is fascinating that both trials appeal to the idea of divine sonship (and circumlocute the divine name). Perhaps this betrays a protective aspect of divine sonship whereby a true son of God may not be harmed. The most likely solution is that this is an extension of the collective concept of sonship often applied to Israel as opposed to their oppressors (cf. Exod 4:22-23). It is also interesting to note that in Q, the true "sons of the Most High [υἱοὶ ὑψίστου]" love their enemies (Matt 12:45 // Luke 6:35) and promote peace (Matt 5:9) in the midst of persecution.

[90] Note the similar ideas of reciprocal judgment found in Q: Matt 7:1 // Luke 6:37 (cf. Rom 2:1); Matt 12:41–42 // Luke 11:31-32; Matt 12:27 // Luke 11:19.

[91] Translated from Berger, 19.

while the Markan high priest is judged to be false.[92] Conflated within this context, Psalm 110 is to be read in similar fashion.[93] Psalm 110 is here used as an indictment against the Jerusalem temple establishment, in that by identifying himself with Psalm 110, Jesus has claimed authority over the temple and its cult.[94] It is in antithesis to the false authority of the high priest that Jesus is "Christ, the Son of God."

As seen in the previous discussion of Psalm 110, what made this psalm distinctive and memorable was its rare legitimation of a priest-king not of Aaronic descent. It is no coincidence that Mark has placed this psalm on the lips of Jesus as he claims to be God's true wielder of temple authority at the expense of the established high priest.[95] The tearing of the high priest's garments likely foreshadows the tearing of the sanctuary curtain in Mark

---

[92] To better support Berger's conclusion, it will be helpful to recall the thesis of J. Theisohn, *Der auserwählte Richter: Untersuchungen zum traditionsgeschtlichtem Ort der Menschensohngestalt der Bilderreden des Äthiopischen Henoch* (SUNT; Göttingen: Vandenhoeck and Ruprecht, 1975), 112. His thesis was that the title "Son of Man" is best measured against the expection for an eschatological judge. Theisohn qualifies this by suggesting that this expectation overlaps with the expectation of eschatological royal and priestly figures. It is in this qualification that we are most helped in our discussion of Mark's trial narrative. Jesus' jurisdiction over the temple cult, and/or his authority as eschatological judge, extends from the general conception of kingdom authority. This explains why the appeal to the authority of the Danielic figure has been conflated with the royal-priestly text of Psalm 110. Cf. the thesis of Horbury (*Jewish Messianism*, 65): "One should not search for an abstract unifying principle of messianic hope, but should recognize that the various concepts surrounding the messianic figure are essentially those which surrounded the Davidic king." Horbury here follows the work of H. Riesenfeld, *Jésus transfiguré: l'arrière-plan du récit évangélique de la Transfiguration de Notre-Seigneur* (Copenhagen: Hakan Ohlsson, 1947), 54–83.

[93] Cf. Hooker, 169–70.

[94] Thus clarity is also given to Jesus' statement concerning the destruction and restitution of the temple. Mark's Jesus does have authority over the temple, but his claim to this authority has been misunderstood.

[95] C. H. T. Fletcher-Louis has argued that Daniel 7's Son of Man should be understood as the cultic mediator between God and Israel and in this way bears a close resemblance to the high priest's temple function ("The High Priest as Divine Mediator in the Hebrew Bible: Dan 7.13 as a Test Case," *SBLSP* 36 [1997]: 161–93). It is not within the scope of the present section to argue that Daniel's Son of Man is (or is not) a high priestly figure, nor is it necessary to do so. For my present argument, it is enough to observe that Psalm 110 speaks directly of a high priestly figure and that Mark has used this psalm to support Jesus' authority. This reading of Psalm 110 may or may not support Fletcher-Louis' reading of Daniel 7. So while I am sympathetic to his more recent treatment of Psalm 110 (Fletcher-Louis, "Jesus as the High Priestly Messiah," *JSHJ* 4, no. 2 [2006]: 173–74), I remain cautious as to what this treatment presupposes of Daniel 7's Son of Man. Fletcher-Louis' emphasis on the cultic aspects of the Son of Man might be tempered by the possibility that "at the time of the first Jewish War the idea of Son of Man had already undergone a symbiosis with the Earthly national aims of expectation around the royal Son of David (4 Ezra 13:1-13; Syr. Bar 53:1-3, 7b-11)" (translated from U. B. Müller, *Messias und Menschensohn in jüdischen Apokalypsen und in der Offenbarung des Johannes* [Studien zum Neuen Testament Band 6; Gütersloh: Gütersloher Verlagshaus, 1972], 310).

15:38.⁹⁶ Mark thus opens this scene by pointing backward to Jesus' misunderstood statement concerning the destruction of the temple and closes it by pointing forward to the rending of the temple's curtain.

Jesus' identity is thus revealed in direct relationship to the temple cult. The Markan Jesus, in contrast to the corrupt temple establishment, is the true mediator between humanity and God. His fate and the fate of the temple are tied together. This makes Mark's use of Psalm 110 especially appropriate to both contexts in Mark's passion.

Mark's "Son of David" Question

Caution is warranted as we return to the Son of David Question from this vantage point. While my brief treatment of Mark's trial narrative has perhaps helped to clarify Mark's agenda with regard to some of the key concepts emphasized in Mark 12:35-37, it must be acknowledged that several important christological elements of the trial narrative are absent in the Son of David Question. I have already mentioned the overlap which includes "Son of David," Christ, Psalm 110, and the temple each within a setting of conflict. With this in mind, it is highly probable that the evangelist has included the Son of David Question in his narrative to develop certain themes that come to fruition in the trial narrative (what I have referred to as "narrativization"). But it is also necessary to acknowledge that the trial focuses on the titles "Son of Man," and "Son of the Blessed" (= God); directly quotes Daniel 7:13; and manifests Mark's antagonist confession motif. Furthermore, the Son of David Question serves to distance Jesus from a particular (or limited) understanding of the Messiah, while the association between scriptural precedents in the trial narrative is inclusive of multiple concepts and titles.⁹⁷ Finally, the Son of David Question hinges on Jesus' wordplay between "Lord" and "lord"; this title is altogether absent in the trial scene.⁹⁸ In sum, the Son

---

⁹⁶ Hooker, 357. Hooker's literary argument is strengthened by recent observations by Fletcher-Louis ["High Priestly Messiah," 159–60] that the garments of the high priest represent the glory of God (Exod 28:2, 40; Sir 50:11; *2 En* 22:8). With this in mind, the significance of the high priest's garments was especially linked with the purpose of the sanctuary.

⁹⁷ Juel (*Messianic Exegesis*, 166) correctly concluded that "promises of the coming Son of Man [in Mk 13 and 14] serve as validation of Jesus' claim to be the true Christ, the Son of God. The point of the sayings is not that Jesus is Son of Man, as opposed to something else, but that everyone will witness his public vindication." Cf. Juel, *Messiah and Temple*, 77–95, esp. 85ff..

⁹⁸ Κύριος does not feature prominently in Mark. Aside from Titus and the Johannine Epistles, Κύριος (and cognate inflections) occur less frequently in Mark than any in other NT book (1.38 occurrences per one thousand words). Mark only uses the root eighteen times (cf. Matthew's 80; Luke's 105; Acts' 107; John's 52). Furthermore, Mark does not use the titular form with any uniformity. It is often used to refer to YHWH, echoing the LXX's rendering of the tetragrammaton (Mark 1:3; 11:9; 12:11, 29). But it is also used of Jesus, connotative of

of David Question touches upon enough subjects of interest to Mark that he has adapted it into his narrative, but his interest is limited to developing certain aspects of the tradition. It seems that Mark's interest in the Son of David Question was in its use of Psalm 110 and not because he had any particular interest in the title "Son of David." Thus, in order to observe how the Son of David Question fits into Mark's narrative agenda, it will be more fruitful to focus on Psalm 110.

We are now in a position to come to a conclusion concerning Mark's use of Psalm 110 and his aim for including the Son of David Question. If the Markan Jesus was utilizing Psalm 110 to make a claim of sacral authority, such a claim would have been perceived as a threat by the Jerusalem temple establishment. Jesus' appeal to the Psalm 110 figure while he taught in the temple would have undermined the authority of the contemporary temple establishment. Hahn argued that Mark 12:37's "πόθεν αὐτοῦ ἐστιν υἱός" should be interpreted as "In what sense is he his son?"[99] While this interpretation is based upon an argument of connotative value, it might capture the emphasis of the question. Jesus has asked his opponents to specify in what sense the Messiah is David's son. This suggests that the office of the Messiah was open to interpretation; it could be debated.

The use of Psalm 110 implies how the Markan Jesus envisaged the Messiah and his relationship to the temple. The Messiah was more than a royal figure; the Messiah would also have cultic jurisdiction. Therefore, Jesus' interpretation of messianic office was threatening to the current priesthood. Mark confirms this in his trial narrative.

Historical Analysis

Jesus and the Temple-Saying

My discussion of Psalm 110 has brought to the fore Jesus' relationship to the temple and its priesthood. With this in mind, it is helpful to compare the Son of David Question with historical memories that clearly speak to this relationship. Jesus' Temple-Saying (Mark 14:56-59; cf. John 2:18-21) is especially relevant in this respect.

"master" or "rabbi" (7:28); it is used by Jesus to refer to YHWH (5:19; 13:20); and it is used by Jesus of himself to claim authority (2:28). It is also notable that Mark's appendix contains the only occurrence in the Gospels of "Lord Jesus [κύριος Ἰησοῦς]" (16:19) and does so in connection with Psalm 110. Luke does not employ this title until the beginning of Acts.

[99] F. Hahn, 252; Cranfield, *Mark*, 382.

It is not advisable (nor possible) to broadly describe a national Jewish sentiment toward the temple and priesthood. It is, however, necessary to observe that there was a longstanding Jewish sentiment that considered the temple to have been defiled by its ministers and no longer suitable to house the presence of God. Ezekiel 8–10 describes the glory/presence of God departing from the temple. Because of this, the prophet believes that a new temple is required in order for God's glory to return (Ezek 43:1-12). Ezekiel 40–48 is the prophet's final vision of a new and eternal heavenly temple, Jerusalem, and theocracy. Malachi echoes a similar criticism of the temple priesthood (see especially Mal 2) and expects an eschatological messenger to come and purify the "sons of Levi" (Mal 3:1-3).

Upon this foundation the *Testament of Levi* makes a similar critique of the earthly priesthood and expects an eschatological priest to come and establish a new temple from heaven. The author writes of the priest in this way: "The heavens shall be opened, and from the temple of glory and sanctification shall come upon him" (*T. Levi* 17:10). Use of *Testament of Levi* to establish a Jewish interpretive trajectory is complex, however, because it has been substantially redacted by a Christian editor. Yet, fortunately, 4Q541 preserves a comparatively large fragment (9, Col. 1) of *Testament of Levi* which confirms that the pre-Christian version expected this eschatological figure to reestablish an effective temple cult. This document expects the figure to make atonement for his generation and enact God's commands on earth as they have been issued in heaven. The fragment does not specifically preserve the statement of 17:10 that speaks of the heavenly "temple of glory," but 4Q541 confirms enough about this figure to take seriously the possibility that the pre-Christian version was extending the trajectory of Ezekiel 40–48. Part of this extension includes the belief that the eschatological temple would be ushered in by a specific figure. This belief comes not from Ezekiel, but from texts like Zechariah.[100]

As discussed in the previous chapter, Zechariah 6:12 expects "Branch (Zerubbabel)" to rebuild the temple. The Targum of Zechariah interprets this messianically by inserting the title "Messiah" in place of the name "Branch." The belief that the Messiah would rebuild the temple is also attested in *Targum Isaiah* 53:5. Elsewhere YHWH himself is expected to build the temple (11QTemple 29:7-10; cf. 2 Bar 4:3). These beliefs do not necessarily contradict each other if the Messiah is seen as God's agent on the Earth. One could say that YHWH's metaphorical "hands" are the literal actions of the Messiah.[101] Indeed, this metaphor is made explicit in the rabbinic interpretation of Solomon's first temple construction:

---

[100] Cf. Evans, *Mark*, 445.
[101] This, after all, is the sense given in Psalm 110:2 where YHWH extends the king's scepter.

> But when He [YHWH] came to build the temple, He did it, as is done, with both of His hands, as it is said, 'The sanctuary [מִקְדָשׁ], Oh Lord, which your hands have established.'" (*Mek.* on Exod 15:17-21)

The rabbi is not supposing that YHWH instead of Solomon built the temple; he is merely giving proper credit to God for Solomon's temple.

To summarize, there was a well-established voice in the HB that criticized Jerusalem's priesthood and believed that the temple was ineffective in its ultimate purpose. This voice was given a specific shape by Ezekiel, who depicted YHWH's presence forsaking the temple until a new temple of heaven was erected in the eschaton. This trajectory was extended to include an eschatological figure. Some circles, like those represented by *Testament of Levi* (cf. 4Q541), envisioned this figure as a priest who would usher in the temple of heaven and sanctify his people. Other circles, like those represented by the Targums of Zechariah and Isaiah (cf. Zech 6:12) emphasized the role of the Davidic messiah as the temple builder. Still others, like those represented by 11QTemple and 2 Baruch, believed that YHWH himself would build the eschatological temple.[102]

Important to my discussion of memory is the eschatological character of these traditions. These texts not only represent possible mnemonic categories, these eschatological voices were intended to project forward and provide an interpretive grid by which later realities might be measured. Social frameworks effect perceptions in varying degrees depending upon how central the framework is to the society's worldview.

In the first century some communities were extremely eschatologically minded, some less. Those who were inclined to interpret contemporary events in eschatological ways were also inclined to associate specific characters, regimes, problems, victories, and salvations of the past with those of the present. It is possible that fervent expectation for a new temple and an incorrupt priesthood acted as a catalyst for dissatisfaction with the contemporary temple and temple establishment. And, of course, the reverse is true; dissatisfaction and disillusionment with the first-century temple establishment called to mind such texts and thus spurred eschatological hopes. The spiraling character of mnemonic localization provides continuity between perceptions of the past and present (see chap. 4). In the case of eschatological social frames, this continuity has the capacity to collapse into a single histori-

---

[102] Cf. also Tob 14; *1 En* 91; Rev 21:1-3. The last of these reads: "Then I saw a new heaven and a new earth; for the first heaven and the first earth passed away, and there is no longer sea. And I saw the holy city, a new Jerusalem, coming down out of Heaven from God, made ready as a bride adorned for her husband. And I heard a loud voice from the throne, saying, 'Behold, the tabernacle of God is among men, and he will dwell among them, and they shall be his people, and God himself will be among them!'"

cally defining moment, one where traditional categories, future hopes, and present realities collapse into one climactic event. The expectations for a new temple from heaven, a new kingdom of God, a righteous and wise ruler, and so on, seem to have the markings of such mnemonic categories. Theissen correctly sees this as the backdrop for Jesus' claim concerning the destruction and rebuilding of the temple.[103]

Having already touched upon the Markan context of the Temple-Saying, it now serves to compare this synchronic frame (Mark) with another (John). Directly following Jesus' temple demonstration, the Fourth Gospel includes the following interaction and interpretation:

> The Jews then said to him, "What sign do you show us as your authority for doing these things?" Jesus answered them, "Destroy this temple, and in three days I will raise it up." The Jews then said, "It took forty-six years to build this temple, and you will raise it up in three days?" But he was speaking of the temple of his body. So when he was raised from the dead, his disciples remembered that he said this; and they believed the scripture and the word which Jesus had spoken. (John 2:18-22)

Here the evangelist places on Jesus' lips a saying remarkably similar to what Mark's "false witnesses" accuse Jesus of saying.[104] But the interpretation of this saying is opposite. Thatcher has recently drawn from John 7:37-39 and 20:22 to label this kind of commemoration "pneumatic memory" and describes it as "a complex reconfiguration of past experience" in light of new interpretations of Scripture that had been prompted by the Holy Spirit.[105] In doing so, he argues that John's gospel was, by nature, a commemoration of how the community's religious experience interacted with their memories of Jesus. This approach to Johannine commemoration is very close to my own concerns. John has commemorated the Temple-Saying according to his particular christological agenda.[106] In this case, the refractive effects of the mnemonic process are acutely recognizable.

---

[103] Cf. G. Theissen, "Die Tempelweissagung Jesu," *TZ* 32 (1976): 158.

[104] Mark 14:56-59: "For many were giving false testimony against him, but their testimony was not consistent. Some stood up and began to give false testimony against him, saying, 'We heard Him say, "I will destroy this temple made with hands, and in three days I will build another made without hands."' Not even in this respect was their testimony consistent."

[105] T. Thatcher, "Why John Wrote a Gospel: Memory and History in an Early Christian Community," in Memory, Tradition and Text: Uses of the Past in Early Christianity (Semeia 52; Leiden: Brill, 2005), 84–85; He concludes, "Because John does not view memory as a mental archive of information but rather as a complex spiritual experience, it seems unlikely that he would [write a Gospel] in order to preserve traditional material about Jesus for later review and recitation."

[106] That the Jerusalem temple represented the presence/glory of YHWH and the locus for

Mark and John represent two diverging refraction trajectories. Mark aims to show that Jesus never made such a claim concerning the temple's destruction and rebuilding (or if he did, he had been misunderstood[107]); to claim otherwise is to testify falsely. In contrast, John aims to show that Jesus did indeed speak of rebuilding the temple but takes the saying metaphorically (the temple's reinstitution represents Jesus' resurrected body). In this way, Mark 14 and John 2 are heavily redacted accounts that run in separate directions. Furthermore, it is highly probable that these stories represent refraction trajectories that share the same mnemonic point of departure—namely, the perception that Jesus made a claim similar to what Mark's false witness accused Jesus of saying in 14:58.[108]

This does not necessarily speak to the historicity of Mark's trial narrative. More likely, Mark has placed these statements on the lips of his characters in response to an early and widespread memory of Jesus' claim. Nonetheless, we may positively assert that Jesus was remembered (by his followers and his adversaries) to have made such a claim.

If this is so, we may conclude that Jesus was perceived by many as the temple-building Messiah and/or the eschatological priest associated with the mnemonic categories surveyed above. In either case, Jesus' claim would have been perceived as a stance of opposition to the current temple establishment and an aim to usher in the eschatological temple of heaven. In Michael Wise's opinion:

> it is felicitous to see here a messianic declaration in which Jesus clears the way for the Temple of the eschaton. Such a declaration would be in keeping with the negative attitudes toward the Temple [in previous and contemporary Judaism], and would look forward to a new Temple and, presumably, a new Jerusalem.[109]

If so, there is perhaps no better example in the Gospels of a discrepancy between saying and interpretation. John's interpretive shift plainly illustrates

---

Israel's worship is well known. But for the Johannine community, Christ occupied this locus. Beasley-Murray comments that, in Johannine theology, "The glory of God and the presence of God are revealed in the only Son and his redemptive acts; it is in and through him that mankind experiences that presence, is transfigured by that glory, and offers a worship worthy of his name" (*John* [WBC 36; Nashville: Thomas Nelson, 1999], 42).

[107] Indeed, logia such as Mark 11:23 and 13:1-2 constrain Mark from completely denying that Jesus might have made such a claim. Such sayings also allow us to appeal to the criterion of multiple forms as well as multiple attestation.

[108] Sanders, *Judaism*, 71–76; M. Dibelius hypothesized that the entire trial narrative was invented around this accusation, which itself is of pre-Passion origin (*From Tradition to Gospel* [London: Ivor Nicholson and Watson, 1934], 182–93).

[109] Wise, "Temple," 816.

the disparity between Jesus' original preaching and later preaching about Jesus. And yet John 2:19 includes Jesus' saying all the same. There has been no attempt to place the Johannine interpretation on the lips of Jesus. Sanders rightly asserts, "John 2:19 shows how deeply embedded in the tradition was the threat of destroying and the promise of rebuilding the temple. It was so firmly fixed that it was not dropped, but rather interpreted."[110] So while Thatcher is correct to say that John's gospel was not written "in order to preserve traditional material about Jesus for later review and recitation,"[111] such material is evident and available for analysis nonetheless. Moreover, it has been prominently displayed in this pericope. The memory has been framed by the commemoration.

Returning to the Son of David Question from this vantage point allows us to measure the refractions evident in Mark's narrativization against a particularly important aspect of Jesus' ministry that originated in historical memory.

Jesus and the Son of David Question

Many interpreters who are unconvinced that the Son of David Question is meant to deny Jesus' Davidic descent prefer to state that the title "Son of David" was simply "not adequate"[112] to describe the Messiah.[113] This point of view generally argues that the saying does not deny Jesus' Davidic descent as much as it portrays the Messiah as being much more than just David's son. According to Mark, of course, Jesus is Son of God, Son of Man, and so on. However, it is seldom suggested how exactly these titles ought to be distinguished. If the title "Son of David" did not quite capture the full sense of Jesus' messianic office, what is this fuller sense? The lack of an appeal to a superior title makes this argument tenuous. It is sometimes suggested that there is an implied appeal to the "greater" titles "Son of Man"[114] or "Son of God."[115] While this is most probably what Mark has in mind, it is less

---

[110] Sanders, *Jesus and Judaism* (London: SCM Press, 1985), 72–73.

[111] Thatcher, 85.

[112] Cranfield, 383.

[113] Taylor, *St. Mark*, 490–93; Pesch, *Markusevangelium*, 2:249–57; Marcus, 139–44; R. E. Watts, *Isaiah's New Exodus in Mark* (Grand Rapids: Baker Academic, 2000 [1997]), 287–89; Witherington, *Mark*, 333; Evans, *Mark*, 275–76.

[114] T. Eskola, *Messiah and the Throne* (Tübingen: Mohr Siebeck, 2001), 180, concludes, "The point of Jesus' speech is evident. The messiah cannot be merely a political earthy king. He must be a heavenly ruler who shall also be David's Lord, not his son and subordinate. Therefore . . . the Son of Man is actually identified with the son of David." Lohmeyer (Markus, 263) similarly suggested that Son of Man ideology was intended by Mark but that Jesus himself did not associate himself with the Son of Man.

[115] Telford (*Mark*, 36–37) argues that the Son of David Question is drawing a distinction

probable that this was the original implication of the pre-Markan setting of the Son of David Question. Neither of these titles is mentioned in the pericope, and the distance created between "Lord" and "lord" suggests a less developed Christology.

Perhaps a better solution is one that takes into account (1) the concepts uniquely developed in Psalm 110, (2) the setting provided within the Son of David Question pericope, (3) the setting provided by the larger Markan context, and (4) the direction taken by later NT developments. I contend that following this trajectory betrays a continuous development of related ideas.

We saw above that Psalm 110 is unique in that it takes those obscure traditions which have conflated royal and sacral offices and developed them into a typological depiction of enthronement. The royal figure in Psalm 110 is divinely endorsed to wield sacral authority. It seems no coincidence then that Mark has placed Jesus' quote of Psalm 110 in a temple setting. Furthermore, the logion itself (internally) provides a temple context for the saying (Mark 12:35), presenting the possibility that the pre-Markan tradition also supposed a temple setting. So by all accounts, the Son of David Question is meant to be interpreted in light of its temple context. This link between the presumed context and the unique subject matter of Psalm 110 has been given very little consideration in previous discussions of Mark 12:35-37. However, when the Son of David Question is seen in this light, the possibility arises that Jesus' quote has made a messianic claim to sacral authority.

The fact that the Son of David Question portrays "David" calling the Messiah "lord" highlights the belief that the Messiah will supersede David. Jesus' interpretation of Psalm 110 argued that the Messiah promised to David would be his superior. It is likely that this messianic interpretation flows from the same fountainhead common to the other forms of Davidism previously discussed. The promise to David in 2 Samuel 7 was that his son would be given authority to do what was beyond David's authority, namely, to have jurisdiction over the building of the temple.[116] Thus, the Davidic covenant promised that his son would supersede David in this specific respect. As I have argued, Psalm 110 extends the Davidic covenant to include priesthood as well. When one follows the lead of this trajectory, it is possible to suggest how exactly the Messiah was to be David's superior. According to Psalm 110,

---

between a Gentile concept of Son of God and the Jewish concept of political messiah. Indeed, the title "Son of God" certainly superseded Son of David in early Christianity. But building from my previous argument for mnemonic continuity, I am opposed to painting the two frameworks in such a stark contrast in cases of uncertain origin. Moreover, if one is to follow Telford's thesis, one has to grant that the Son of David Question represents a fully developed Markan Christology. My argument thus far has yielded results to the contrary.

[116] The context of 2 Samuel 7 places David's inability to build the temple at center stage.

the Davidic king (unlike David) would have divinely endorsed authority over both the kingdom and the temple.

Given this context, it is possible that Jesus' appeal to Psalm 110 was meant to emphasize his divinely endorsed authority in and over the temple as Messiah. With Psalm 110 in mind, it is not necessary to understand such a claim as negation of political authority; according to the psalmist, the two need not be mutually exclusive. This coheres well with Daube's observation that the Son of David Question bears the markings of rabbinic haggadah (cf. Nid. 69b-71a);[117] this might suggest that "the intention of Jesus would have been to suggest the ultimate correctness of both alternatives."[118] The Son of David Question would, in this way, represent a belief that Jesus was messianic in the dual sense promoted by Psalm 110: both royal and sacral.[119]

Mark has followed the lead of many of these elements as he has located the Son of David Question within his narrative. But the simple act of including the pericope within his narrative has refracted its telos and endowed certain internal subjects with thematic significance. The subjects "Christ," "Psalm 110," and so on have been localized within a narrative framework that is particularly interested in the christological development of these subjects. In this way, (some of) the subjects under discussion in the pre-Markan form of the Son of David Question are set to work thematically. Therefore, there are two ways to read the Son of David Question: (1) as a contributor of Markan themes and (2) as an isolated discussion.

As seen in my discussion of Mark's larger context, the problem involved in attempting the first reading is that some of the subjects under discussion in the Son of David Question (such as the definition of the title "Son of David") are of less interest to Mark's Christology. It seems Mark is more interested in developing the concepts at work in Psalm 110. I would argue that Mark has included this saying, not to clarify the title, but to clarify that Jesus ought to be understood in light of Psalm 110.

Because the Son of David Question did not serve as the guiding mnemonic framework of Mark's themes, the evangelist has left some of the subjects in

---

[117] D. Daube, *The New Testament and Rabbinic Judaism* (London: Athlone, 1956), 163–64.

[118] S. H. Smith, 535; cf. Schneider, "Davidssohnfrage," 68.

[119] This is remarkably similar (but not identical) to how the author of Hebrews utilizes Ps 110: In this later context, Christ is also the high priest like Melchizedek. The difference between these passages is that Hebrews has carried this refraction trajectory to a particular christological extreme. Hebrews 9 argues that Christ's priestly authority extends to the heavenly temple; the Son of David Question merely implies that the messiah will have sacral jurisdiction (that Jesus was applying this title to himself is only implied). For this reason, it is correct to assert that these two passages stand along parallel trajectories but that Hebrews represents a more fully developed sphere of christological refraction.

this discussion underdeveloped. Unless there is some acknowledgment of this, the reader will be frustrated by Mark's contentedness to introduce certain subjects without further explanation. Contrast this with the trial narrative that does indeed serve as a more directive framework whereby certain thematic developments are guided and given their narrative meaning(s). Mark's trial narrative is among a handful of gravitational hubs that attract and propel his narrative elements.[120] Within this narrative context, the telos of the Son of David Question in Mark's narrative is guided and refracted. Mark's interest in the Son of David Question revolves around his portrayal of an exalted and vindicated Christ. Because Psalm 110 is a prominent subject and because Jesus' use of this psalm sets him in opposition to the temple establishment, Mark has used the Son of David Question to propel themes that find climax in his trial narrative. A byproduct of this telos is that the significance of "Son of David" has been marginalized.

This acknowledgment leads to the second reading, which also is problematic. By granting that Mark is relatively uninterested in the development of "Son of David," further analysis of "Son of David" involves an attempt to prescind from Mark's narrative context. This is problematic because it is impossible to read a passage in total isolation. No tradition is conceived or passed down apart from some mnemonic context. Thus, in order to isolate the Son of David Question from Mark's narrative, one must postulate the now-lost mnemonic frame by which the tradition was originally given meaning. As indicated in the first section of the present chapter, the original context of the Son of David Question must remain indefinite. Thus, our second reading presents two possibilities: (a) the Son of David Question was invented by one of Mark's predecessors to combat a misunderstanding of Jesus' relationship to the title "Son of David" or (b) the Son of David Question represents a memory of Jesus attempting himself to qualify the messianic expectation associated with the title "Son of David."

In either case it is highly probable that the Son of David Question originated in relationship to a historical perception of Jesus. The only remaining question is whether this perception was remembered by one of Jesus' contemporaries. While this must remain inconclusive, we can conclude with relative certainty that the Son of David Question betrays conceptual links with mnemonic categories available to Jesus' contemporaries. In this way, this pericope does indeed aid our discussion of Jesus' historical context.

My contention is that both readings are necessary for exegesis and historical inquiry. As demonstrated, a strictly literary reading is ultimately frustrated

---

[120] I here specifically refer to theme, but this "hub" is also directive of plot, characterization, etc. as discussed above.

because Mark is not strictly a narrator; he is a narrator of received tradition and therefore does not give his full attention to every detail that he has included in his narrative. On the other hand, a strictly "historical" reading is frustrated by passages (such as ours) that defy confident historical postulation. It is therefore necessary to measure pericopes against their synchronic narrative context as well as their diachronic development. As my discussion of the Son of David Question has attempted to demonstrate, it is in the relationship between these contexts that historical Jesus research is most fruitful.

Conclusion

As briefly discussed, early and widespread memories of Jesus considered him to have claimed divinely endorsed authority to destroy the present temple to make way for the temple of heaven. While the Son of David Question might not have originated in early memory, it does confirm two important aspects of the historical Jesus: (1) Jesus' perceived rank and mission stood in direct opposition to the Jerusalem temple establishment; (2) Jesus' perceived rank and mission were hinged upon his authority over the Jerusalem temple. My exegesis of Psalm 110 in conjunction with the temple context of the Son of David Question has shown that the Markan portrayal of Jesus is that of a messiah characterized by both of the above aspects.

The Son of David Question is of pre-Markan origin and seems to have extended these historical perceptions of Jesus, albeit in a highly refracted form. This refraction has localized Jesus' significance within the exegesis of Psalm 110. When applied christologically, this psalm painted Jesus as having royal and sacral jurisdiction. In this way, the Son of David Question propels the interpretive trajectory of Psalm 110 in a distinctly christological direction. While the saying does not represent a fully developed Christology as does Hebrews, it looks to be a midpoint along this trajectory. Therefore "Son of David" is best understood to be a title employed not by the earliest memories of Jesus but rather a mnemonic frame employed by later Christianity to assimilate pre-Christian memories of Jesus into more fully developed Christology. "Son of David" thus provided the necessary mnemonic continuity between the historical Jesus and the Christology of early Christianity.

9

Concluding Analysis

In chapter 4, I presented my theory of historiography as I discussed the essential relationships between history, memory, and typology. In order to illustrate my theory and proposed method, I provided an admittedly superficial treatment of the John the Baptist tradition. I am now in a position to return to my theoretical argument upon the foundation of the more thorough exegesis demonstrated over the course of this study concerning the title "Son of David."

The Mnemonic Cycle

An excellent example of the mnemonic cycle can be seen in the Son of David Question. In Mark 12:35-37, Jesus challenges a teaching concerning the Son of David by offering a new perspective on Psalm 110.

Figure 9.1
The Mnemonic Cycle

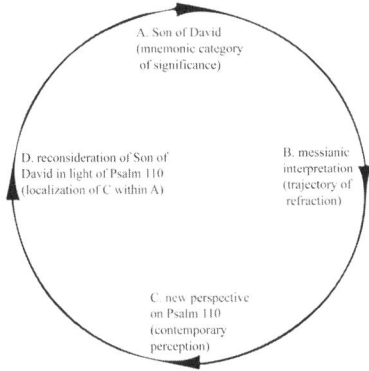

Jesus' first question presupposes that a particular mnemonic frame (A) is already in place: "How is it that the scribes say that the Messiah is the Son of David?" (12:35). As I have argued, Mark is more interested in endowing Jesus' significance with concepts from Psalm 110 than he is in clarifying the significance of the title "Son of David." As such, "Son of David" does not act as the dominant mnemonic framework in this case. This question presupposes that Son of David was a well-known category (A) and that it was subject to messianic interpretation (B),[1] but Jesus' use of Psalm 110 (C) demonstrates the inadequacy of the previous category. C, in this case, thus acts as the dominant category, and A receives the larger portion of refraction (D); A must be realigned accordingly.

Because the previous category (A) does not ultimately control the new perception, this cycle does not necessarily demonstrate typological interpretation. The Markan Jesus argues that the Messiah cannot so easily be categorized as Son of David as evidenced by Psalm 110.[2] As Mark has inherited this tradition, he has used it to emphasize the importance of Psalm 110. As such, he refracts this tradition to serve better his present interests concerning Jesus' sacral authority. (Notice here that Mark redacts the tradition very minimally. Even so, the new narrative context of this tradition requires it to be reframed mnemonically. Thus literary redaction is not always required to assess the memory refraction at work in the passing of tradition. Literary device simply mimics what is natural to the mnemonic process. The historian should expect that memory refraction is at work on all levels of interpretation and not just those that manifest literary redaction.)

As shown in my discussion of the contrasting interpretations of Isaiah 11 by *Psalm of Solomon* 17 and 1QSb 5, typology requires that the scriptural category (A) play a more constraining role in the mnemonic localization (see chap. 5). In contrast, the Son of David Question demands that the previous category (Son of David) is diminished by the "superior" messianic interpretation provided by Psalm 110. If this new perspective on Psalm 110 is to be taken seriously, Mark's audience must reconsider how "Son of David" fits into this new paradigm (cf. 12:37). In this way, both Psalm 110 and "Son of David" are refracted by instrumentalization: the tendency for memories to be reinterpreted to serve the present better (see chap. 2). As argued, Mark's interest in Psalm 110 was hinged on his agenda to show Jesus' authority over

---

[1] Indeed, the presupposition behind Jesus' first question suggests that it was uncontroversial to interpret Psalm 110 messianically. In all likelihood, the previous category of significance (A) invited common patterns of refraction.

[2] Eventually, the author of Hebrews employs Psalm 110 as category A and localizes Jesus' significance (C) therein. This is an apt example of typological refraction and also demonstrates how new interpretations (if memorable) tend to become mnemonic categories of significance. But at this point, my interest is limited to a synchronic analysis of Mark.

the temple and the priesthood. Such refraction follows the lead of the issues at stake in Psalm 110. In this way, we see that Mark's use of the Son of David Question anticipates Jesus' appeal to Psalm 110 during his trial before the high priest (see chap. 8).

Thus far, no discussion of historical memory has been offered; this has been an entirely synchronic analysis. This mnemonic cycle has simply illustrated how mnemonic refraction most commonly functions when previous categories are reconsidered in light of new interpretations.

The Typological Cycle

I have compared Mark's nontypological use of "Son of David" with that of Matthew (see chap. 6). Matthew 12:22-23 represents a Matthean addition to the Beelzebul controversy concerning Son of David: "Then a demon-possessed man who was blind and mute was brought to Jesus, and he healed him, so that the mute man spoke and saw. All the crowds were amazed, and were saying, 'This man cannot be the Son of David, can he?'" This suggestion of Jesus' identity is couched between an appeal to Isaiah 42 and a competing interpretation of Jesus' actions by the Pharisees. With this framework in mind, consider the following figure:

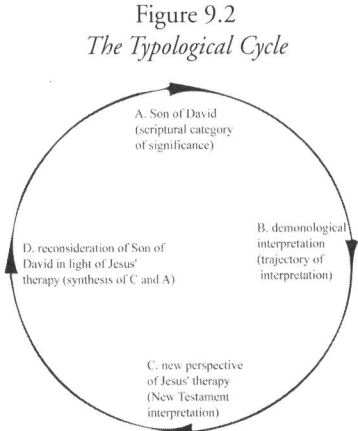

Figure 9.2
The Typological Cycle

As argued in chapter 4, typology is primarily a manifestation of the mnemonic process and not necessarily a literary device. This is further demonstrated in my subsequent diachronic analysis. However, as illustrated by Matthew's synchronic framework, typology is also a literary device that naturally follows the mnemonic cycle. So, as illustrated here, Matthew's commemoration of Jesus' therapeutic ministry is essentially similar to the mnemonic process. The key difference is that Matthew's commemoration typologically refracts Jesus' significance. Unlike Mark's use of the title, Matthew imports a mnemonic framework with the title "Son of David" and thus allows this framework to guide his own narrative. Thus, Matthew, keenly interested in legitimating Jesus' ministry via scriptural precedents, interprets several of Jesus' healings as Davidic/Solomonic. I have also argued that Matthew has used Isaianic therapy passages in a similar way: they are not simply proof-texts; such passages impose meaning upon Matthew's Jesus and guide the structure of his narrative.

I have argued that Matthew's adaptation of Markan tradition betrays an apologetic against accusations much like those leveled by the Pharisees in Matthew 12:24: "But when the Pharisees heard this, they said, 'This man casts out demons only by Beelzebul the ruler of the demons.'" By viewing Jesus' significance through an apologetic Son of David lens, Matthew has undoubtedly refracted the Jesus tradition. But equally important is that, from Matthew's perspective, his interpretation has provided a corrective; he has "correctly" reinforced Jesus' therapeutic significance from a Jewish-Christian perspective.

Diachronic Continuity

In comparing Matthew's use of "Son of David" to that of Mark, my discussion has inevitably moved from synchronic to diachronic analysis. Indeed, comparing Matthew to Mark is nothing new to NT studies. What this book has tried to emphasize is that the refractions that occur from one mnemonic cycle to the next (most often) maintain continuous patterns of refraction, what I have referred as refraction trajectories. With this in mind, consider Figure 9.3. The Jericho healing enters Mark's commemorative interests very modestly (A→B). The fact that Bartimaeus calls Jesus "Son of David" is incidentally included. Indeed, the title is only used one other time in Mark (12:35-37) and does little to clarify the title's significance. In Mark's narrative world (C), the category "Son of David" is less subject to redaction simply because Mark does not offer much interpretation as to how it should be applied to Jesus, if at all. Due to the prominence of Mark's other agendas (D), Bartimaeus' plea is isolated (A2) and relatively undeveloped (B2).

I have previous clarified that a simple spiral does not adequately illustrate the complex oral and literary progress from Mark to Matthew. It is not my intention to oversimplify the larger relationship between the two books. What I have demonstrated in Figure 9.3 is the refraction from Mark 10:46-52 to Matthew through the analysis of a single pericope and subsequent theme. As such, B3 is not meant to represent a single mnemonic cycle, but a longer continuum of cycles that are not made manifest until Matthew's commemoration of this tradition (B5).

It is important to reemphasize that while Matthew has refracted his received tradition (B), this refraction has not taken the form of dramatic

Figure 9.3
The Diachronic Continuity of Historical Memory

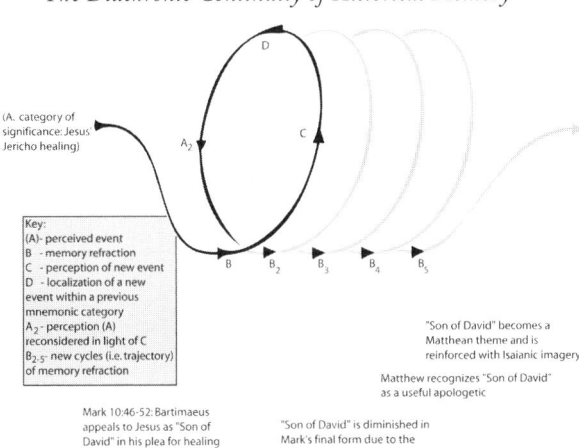

shifts. To the point, Matthew's therapeutic apologetic follows the lead of what he has found implicit in Mark 10:46-52. What began as a therapeutic context for the title has been refracted further in this direction. Moreover, Matthew has not invented this application of "Son of David"; he stands as the beneficiary of a long trajectory of interpreters who have refracted Solomon's and David's legacy along these lines. Consider Figure 9.4, an expansion of the previous diagram:[3]

Figure 9.4
The Refraction Trajectory of the Solomon-the-Exorcist Tradition

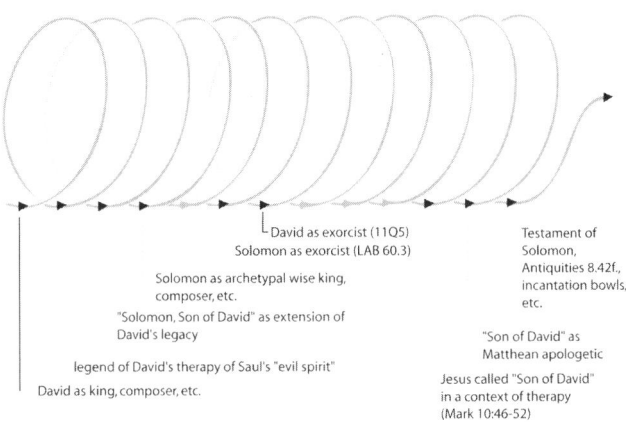

[3] I emphasize again that, with this spiral, I am following the single thread of a much larger complex of tradition. Indeed, each cycle attracts and localizes categories from many other spirals with conceptual kinship.

This figure illustrates much of chapter 6, but it also highlights a key point made in chapter 5. The reader will be reminded that Solomon's legacy was first and foremost an extension of his father's; with "Son of David," the Chronicler coins a title that embodies both the promise to David and the fulfillment of this promise in Solomon. Thus, it is not surprising to find that the Solomon-the-exorcist tradition caused a reconsideration of David's legacy. Moreover, because of the cyclical character of mnemonic localization, it is difficult to tell which of these figures attracted demonological speculation first.

In light of Figure 9.4, I reiterate here four points that have been important for the present study:

1. As a title, "Son of David" was a Solomonic referent (a) from its first use by the Chronicler, (b) through its use as a sapiential pseudonym/archetype, (c) as it was employed in *Psalm of Solomon* 17, (d) as it was employed in the Dead Sea Scrolls, and (e) as it was employed in the *Testament of Solomon*.[4] Given this continuity, Matthew's use of the title should be seen along this trajectory.
2. My second point speaks more directly to my primary historiographical thesis: the shift from Solomon as the archetypal wise king to exorcist par excellence is a dramatic refraction. In social memory terminology, one could say that Solomon tradition underwent a dramatic relocalization as it was reinforced by demonological categories. Having said this, it is crucial to recognize that this refraction is first evidenced several hundred years after Solomon's legacy first took shape. I must reiterate that within the first generation[5] of a historical memory (especially those with significant impact), refractions happen incrementally and continuously. Each refraction must be rendered intelligible to the previous mnemonic cycle and to the one that follows. With this in mind, I return to Matthew's refraction of the Jesus tradition.
3. By expanding Figure 9.3 to show how it related to the longer Solomon-the-exorcist tradition (Figure 9.4), I have demonstrated that Matthew's apologetic refraction follows the lead of a much longer trajectory. Thus, by refracting Mark, Matthew has predictably moved

---

[4] It is noteworthy that the *T. Sol.* eventually attracted Christian interest. This further demonstrates how the novum (Jesus as exorcist) can round the mnemonic cycle to (re)inform the previous category (Solomon as exorcist)—the Jesus and Solomon tradition are both refracted in the process.

[5] As discussed in chap. 2, social memory theorists generally grant two to three generations before a "crisis of memory" occurs.

this larger continuum forward. Yet Matthew rarely refracts Mark's tradition in dramatic fashion. This is so because such refractions have been spurred and constrained by the social memory established by the first interpretations of Jesus by his contemporaries. In this way, refractions to the Jesus tradition were subject to the constraints of the first categories employed during Jesus' historical ministry.

4. Finally, Figure 9.4 has left a noticeable gap between the pre-Christian traditions and "Son of David" as it first appears in Mark 10. Indeed, a more complete model would show many gaps along a much longer trajectory. I have underscored this gap so that I might point out that such typological interpretations of Jesus most probably stand somewhere along this trajectory. As I argued in chapter 6, Bartimaeus' typological interpretation of Jesus as "Son of David" betrays an interpretation contemporary to Jesus' context. In making such a connection, Bartimaeus locates Jesus' significance along this larger scriptural trajectory.

The fact that this detail was included in Mark's narrative suggests that Bartimaeus was not alone in his interpretation of Jesus. While Mark may not have chosen to develop this interpretation, it has been remembered in the Jesus tradition because some group of rememberers found it interesting, clarifying, appropriate, and so on.

No doubt, Mark represents a refracted version of this account, which is further distorted by Matthew. After all, each cycle does not represent a new perception (cf. Figure 9.3 movement C), but a refraction of that perception (cf. Figure 9.3 movement B2). Because of these refractions historical memory is chartable. Such diachronic analysis suggests that Solomon/David typology was an interpretation that preceded the more formalized literary manifestations of this typology. However, I have argued that distinguishing a memory-story from literary invention requires closer comparison of the refraction tendencies of related synchronic cycles (see chap. 6).

Historical Memory

I have made judicious use of authenticity criteria. The application of such criteria has been one step among several to postulate historical memory. I have argued that, while the assessment of origin by no means exhausts the historian's task, it is necessary to attempt to distinguish tradition that originated in memory from that which originated in invention. Yet even in cases where a story's origin is doubted, I have argued that the evidence of refraction represented by such a story is valuable for charting interpretive trajectories. Thus, while the origin of Mark 12:35-37 is inconclusive, it confirms Mark's interest in Psalm 110 and his disinterest in Son of David, and helps to confirms Jesus' historical tension with the Jerusalem temple establishment. Because Mark's interpretive tendencies can be seen, such analysis provides the historian with a means of charting such refraction.

Memory refraction is most prevalent on the subconscious level. However, typological refraction tends to be more recognizable as it involves overt comparisons between significant mnemonic categories and especially impressionable new perceptions. This is seen most clearly in Jesus' procession toward the temple and procession to the temple. Figure 9.5 draws largely from the analysis of chapter 7.

Figure 9.5
The Refraction Trajectory of Solomonic Processions

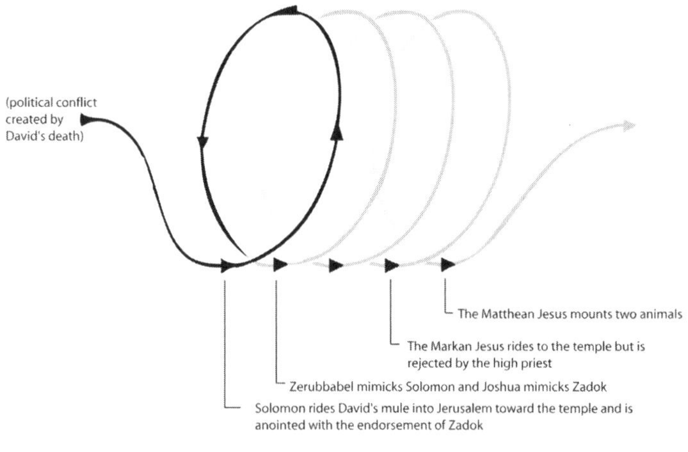

(political conflict created by David's death)

- The Matthean Jesus mounts two animals
- The Markan Jesus rides to the temple but is rejected by the high priest
- Zerubbabel mimicks Solomon and Joshua mimicks Zadok
- Solomon rides David's mule into Jerusalem toward the temple and is anointed with the endorsement of Zadok

Much like Figure 9.4, a dual typology sets this trajectory in motion. In order to set Solomon apart from all other would-be claimants to his throne, David choreographs Solomon's anointment procession. In this way, Solomon is explicitly modeled after David. In 1 Kings 1, Solomon is set upon David's mule, hailed as king, and anointed by Zadok the high priest (1 Kgs 1:39). Shouting to YHWH, this procession supplicates, "make his throne greater than the throne of my lord King David!" This narrative is reenacted by Zerubbabel and Joshua (who is also anointed). As argued, the emphasis in both cases is on the homogeny between the high priest and the Davidic heir. This is especially important for Zerubbabel as he is given the Solomonic task of rebuilding the temple.

This narrative background has been underemphasized in many previous studies on Jesus' procession. But when seen along this trajectory, the absence of an endorsement by the high priest in Jesus' procession demands to be recognized. That there should have been a cohesive relationship between Jesus and the Jerusalem temple establishment is highlighted by Mark's inclusion of Psalm 118, which emphasizes this relationship. This further confirms that Jesus' procession mnemonically evoked scriptural precedents that emphasized the relationship between the anointed king and the priesthood. Moreover, I have argued that the appeal to Psalm 118 is best explained as historical memory rather than invention. Considering this trajectory and the themes evoked and echoed by Psalm 118, it is most probable that at least some of Jesus' contemporaries interpreted his actions as a scriptural mimic.

What this discussion demonstrates is that typological imitation is an act of narrative refraction. I have argued that, in this case, this "narrativization" colored the first memories of Jesus' historical act. Consider Figure 9.6:

Figure 9.6
Mnemonic Triangulation of Jesus' Procession

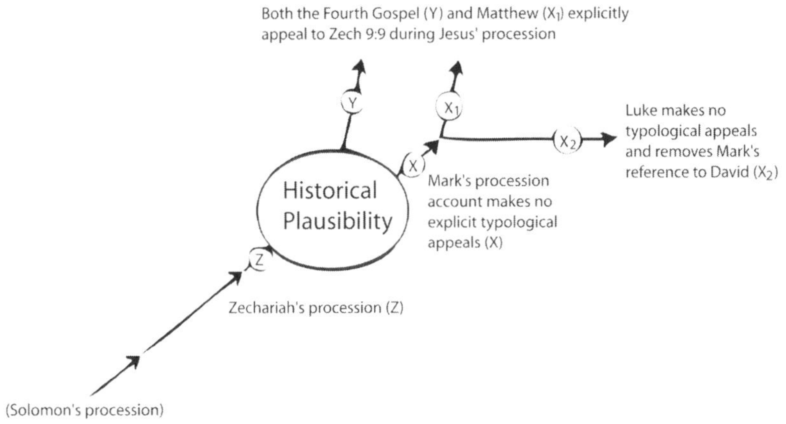

Both the Fourth Gospel (Y) and Matthew (X_1) explicitly appeal to Zech 9:9 during Jesus' procession

Luke makes no typological appeals and removes Mark's reference to David (X_2)

Mark's procession account makes no explicit typological appeals (X)

Historical Plausibility

Zechariah's procession (Z)

(Solomon's procession)

This figure illustrates what I have referred to as mnemonic triangulation. Trajectory Z represents a linear projection of Figure 9.5 above. Trajectories X and Y represent the mnemonic refractions evidenced in the narratives of John and Mark. As shown, Mark makes no explicit typological appeal (X). Although some have argued that Mark and Luke (X2) betray implicit typologies, all agree that they diverge from John (Y) in their nonuse of Zechariah 9:9.

What is most important for my present argument is the fact that both John (Y) and Matthew (X1) independently provide a direct quotation of Zechariah 9:9. This warrants the application of multiple attestation (IV.2.2), but more importantly, it provides two separate trajectories that seem to have been propelled by the same mnemonic sphere. Thus, the most plausible explanation for this is that the typological interpretation of Jesus' procession originated in historical memory and not by literary invention. While Mark employs Zechariah imagery elsewhere, he does not do so in this instance. However, his account contains enough implicit cues that Matthew has recognized this typological significance of Jesus' act and refracted this tradition to include both a quote of Zechariah and the Solomonic title "Son of David."

Conclusion

Over the course of this book, I have attempted to demonstrate that the first perceptions of Jesus were bent and distorted through the mnemonic process like light is bent and distorted through a lens. Indeed, memory requires interpretation and thus is a refractive process.

The historical Jesus is the memorable Jesus; he is the one who set refraction trajectories in motion and who set the initial parameters for how his memories were to be interpreted by his contemporaries. If this is so, then the historian does not "find" Jesus in spite of the refractions of the evangelists. Rather, the historian discerns his historical presence and impact on the basis of these refractions. It is because these refractions exist that we can confidently postulate the mnemonic sphere in which the memories of Jesus were located.[6]

Building from this, my primary thesis, the key results of my work have been threefold. (1) When history is thought in terms of memory refraction, the dichotomy between historical fact and historical interpretation dissolves.[7] (2) When the mnemonic process is related to typological interpretation, the false dichotomy between history and typology dissolves.[8] (3) When typology is thought of as a kind of memory refraction (narrativization), the title "Son of David" exemplifies how a mnemonic category can develop typologically and be charted accordingly. In these ways, I consider the present work to be both a hermeneutical corrective and a historiographical advance in historical Jesus research.

---

[6] Contra Sanders (see chap. 1).
[7] Contra Crossan and Lüdemann (see chap. 1).
[8] Contra Goulder (see chap. 1).

Bibliography

Abegg, M. "The Messiah at Qumran: Are We Still Seeing Double?" *DSD* 2 (1995): 125–44.

——— and C. A. Evans. "Messianic Passages in the Dead Sea Scrolls." Pages 191–203 in *Qumran-Messianism: Studies on the Messianic Expectations in the Dead Sea Scrolls*. Edited by J. H. Charlesworth, H. Litchenberger, and G. S. Oegema. Tübingen: Mohr Siebeck, 1998.

Aberbach, M. "The Historical Allusions of Chapters IV, XI, and XIII of the *Psalms of Solomon*." *JQR* 41 (1959): 379–96.

Achtemeier, P. J. "And He Followed Him: Miracles and Discipleship in Mark 10:46-52." *Semeia* 11 (1978): 115–45.

Ackroyd, P. R. *The Second Book of Samuel*. Cambridge: Cambridge University Press, 1977.

Aitkins, W. E. M. "Beelzebul." *JBL* (1912): 34–53.

Allen, L. C. *Psalms 101–150*. WBC 21. Nashville: Thomas Nelson, 2002.

Allison, D. C., Jr. *The Intertextual Jesus: Scripture in Q*. Harrisburg, Pa.: Trinity, 2000.

Allison, H. E. *Lessing and the Enlightenment*. Ann Arbor: University of Michigan Press, 1966.

Alt, A. "Solomonic Wisdom." Pages 102–12 in *Studies in Ancient Israelite Wisdom*. Edited by J. L. Crenshaw. New York: Ktav, 1976.

Altizer, T. J. J. "The Self-Saving of God." Pages 427–43 in *The Blackwell Companion to Postmodern Theology*. Edited by G. Ward. Oxford: Blackwell, 2006 [2001].

Ambrozic, A. *The Hidden Kingdom: A Redaction-Critical Study of the References to the Kingdom in Mark's Gospel*. CBQMS 2. Washington, D.C.: CBQ Association of America, 1972.

Anderson, A. *2 Samuel*. WBC 11. Dallas: Word, 1989.

Anderson, H. *The Gospel of Mark*. London: Oliphants, 1976.

Assmann, A. *Zeit und Tradition: Kulturelle Strategien der Dauer*. Beiträge zur Geschichtskultur 15. Köln: Böhlau, 1999.

Assmann, J. "Ancient Egyptian Antijudaism: A Case of Distorted Memory." Pages 365–78 in *Memory Distortion*. Edited by D. Schachter. Cambridge, Mass.: Harvard University Press, 1995.

———. "Collective Memory and Cultural Identity." *New German Critique* 65 (1995): 125–33.

———. *Das kulturelle Gedächtnis: Schrift, Erinnerung und politische Identität in frühen Hochkulturen.* Munich: Beck, 1992.

———. *Moses the Egyptian: The Memory of Egypt in Western Monotheism.* Cambridge, Mass.: Harvard University Press, 1997.

———. *Religion and Cultural Memory: Ten Studies.* Translated by R. Livingstone. Stanford: Stanford University Press, 2006 [2000].

———. *Religion und kulturelle Gedächtnis: Zehn Studien.* Munich: Beck, 2000.

Atkinson, K. *I Cried to the Lord: A Study of the Psalms of Solomon's Historical Background and Social Setting.* JSJSup 84. Leiden: Brill, 2004.

———. "On the Herodian Origin of Militant Davidic Messianism at Qumran: New Light from *Psalm of Solomon* 17." *JBL* 3 (1999): 435–60.

Aune, D. E. "Magic in Early Christianity." *ANRW* 2.23.2 (1980): 1507–57.

Barnett, P. W. "The Jewish Sign Prophets—AD 4–70: Their Intentions and Origin," *NTS* 27 (1981): 679–97.

Barth, K. *Der Römerbrief.* Zürich: Theologischer Verlag, 1922.

Barton, S. C. *The Spirituality of the Gospels.* London: Holy Trinity Church, 1992.

Bateman, H. "Psalm 110:1 and the New Testament." *Bibliotheca Sacra* 149 (1992): 447–50.

Bauer, D. R. "Son of David." Pages 766-69 in *Dictionary of Jesus and the Gospels.* Edited by J. B. Green and S. McKnight. Downers Grove, Ill.: InterVarsity, 1992.

Bauer, W. *A Greek-English Lexicon of the New Testament and Other Early Christian Literature.* Translated by W. F. Arndt and F. W. Gingrich. Chicago: University of Chicago Press, 1979 [1958].

Beasley-Murray, G. R. *John.* WBC 36. Nashville: Thomas Nelson, 1999.

Becker, M. "4Q521 und die Gesalbten." *RevQ* 18 (1997): 73–96.

Bennema, C. "The Sword of the Messiah and the Concept of Liberation in the Fourth Gospel." *Biblica* 86 (2005): 35–58.

Berger, K. "Die Königlichen Messiastraditionen des Neuen Testaments." *NTS* 20 (1984): 1–44.

Berquist, J. K. *Judaism in Persia's Shadow: A Social and Historical Approach.* Minneapolis: Fortress, 1995.

Betz, H. D. "Legion." Pages 507–8 in *Dictionary of Deities and Demons in the Bible.* Edited by K. van der Toorn, B. Becking, and P. van der Hoorst. Leiden: Brill, 1999.

Beuken, W. A. M. *Jesaja 1–12.* Herders Theologischer Kommentar zum Alten Testament. Freiburg: Herder, 2002.

Black, M. *An Aramaic Approach to the Gospels and Acts.* Oxford: Clarendon, 1967.

Black, M. C. "The Rejected and Slain Messiah Who Is Coming with the Angels: The Messianic Exegesis of Zechariah 9–14 in the Passion Narratives." Ph.D. diss. Emory University, 1990.

Blenkinsopp, J. *Sage, Priest, Prophet: Religious and Intellectual Leadership in Ancient Israel.* Louisville, Ky.: Westminster John Knox, 1995.

Bock, D. C. *Studying the Historical Jesus.* Grand Rapids: Baker Academics, 2002.

Bockmuehl, M. "New Testament *Wirkungsgeschichte* and the Early Christian Appeal to Living Memory." In *Memory and Remembrance in the Bible and Antiquity.* Edited by L. T. Stuckenbruck, S. C. Barton, and B. G. Wold. Tübingen: Mohr Siebeck, 2007.

———. "A 'Slain Messiah' in 4Q Serekh Milhamah (4Q245)?" *TynBul* 43 (1992): 155–69.

———. *This Jesus.* Downers Grove, Ill.: InterVarsity, 1994.

Borg, M. J. *Conflict, Holiness and Politics in the Teachings of Jesus.* Studies in the Bible and Early Christianity 5. New York: Mellen, 1984.

Bornkamm, G., G. Barth, and H. J. Held. *Überlieferung und Auslegung im Matthäusevangelium.* WMANT 1. Neukirchen: Neukirchener Verlag, 1960.

Bousset, W., and H. Gressmann. *Die Religion des Judentums im spät-hellenistischen Zeitalter.* HNT 3. Tübingen: Mohr Siebeck, 1926.

Bowker, J. W. *Jesus and the Pharisees.* Cambridge: Cambridge University Press, 1973.

———. "Psalm CX." *VT* 17 (1967): 31–41.

Bowman, J. "David, Jesus and the Son of David and Son of Man." *Abr-Nahrain* 27 (1989): 1–22.

———. "Exorcism and Baptism." Pages 249–63 in *A Tribute to Arthur Voorbus: Studies in Early Christian Literature and its Environment.* Edited by R. H. Fischer. Chicago: Lutheran School of Theology, 1977.

———. "Solomon and Jesus." *Abr-Nahrain* 23 (1984–1985): 1–13.

Braaten, C. E. Introduction to *The So-called Historical Jesus and the Historic Biblical Christ*, by M. Kähler. Philadelphia: Fortress, 1964.

Braun, R. L. *1 Chronicles.* WBC 14. Waco, Tex.: Word, 1986.

———. "Solomon, the Chosen Temple Builder: The Significance of 1 Chronicles 22, 28 and 29 for the Theology of Chronicles." *JBL* 95 (1976): 581–90.

———. "Solomonic Apologetic in Chronicles." *JBL* 92 (1973): 503–16.

Brooke, G. J. *Exegesis at Qumran: 4QFlorilegium in Its Jewish Context.* JSOTSup 29. Sheffield: JSOT Press, 1985.

Brown, R. E. *The Birth of the Messiah: A Commentary on the Infancy Narratives in Matthew and Luke.* Garden City, N.Y.: Doubleday, 1979.

———. *The Death of the Messiah: From Gethsemane to the Grave.* 2 vols. New York: Doubleday, 1994.

———. *The Gospel According to John.* Garden City, N.Y.: Doubleday, 1966.

Broyles, C. C. *Psalms.* Peabody, Mass.: Hendrickson, 1999.

Bruce, F. F. "The Book of Zechariah and the Passion Narrative." *BJRL* 43 (1960–1961): 336–53.

———. *New Testament History.* Garden City, N.Y.: Doubleday, 1971 [1969].

Brueggemann, W. *First and Second Samuel.* Louisville, Ky.: Westminster John Knox, 1990.

———. *Isaiah 1–39.* Louisville, Ky.: Westminster John Knox, 1998.

———. *Solomon: Israel's Ironic Icon of Human Achievement.* Columbia: University of South Carolina Press, 2005.

Bultmann, R. *Das Evangelium des Johannes*. Göttingen: Vandenhoeck and Ruprecht, 1941.

———. *Die Geschichte der synoptischen Tradition*. Göttingen: Vandenhoeck and Ruprecht, 1961.

———. *Existence and Faith*. London: Hodder and Stoughton, 1961.

———. *The Gospel of John*. Oxford: Blackwell, 1971.

———. *History and Eschatology: The Presence of Eternity*. New York: Harper and Bros, 1957.

———. *History of the Synoptic Tradition*. Translated by J. Marsh. New York: Harper, 1963.

———. "Is Exegesis Without Presuppositions Possible?" Pages 242–48 in *The Hermeneutics Reader*. Edited by K. Mueller-Vollmer. Oxford: Basil Blackwell, 1985. Repr. from TZ 13 (1957).

———. *Jesus*. Berlin: Deutsche Bibliothek, 1926.

———. *Jesus Christ and Mythology*. New York: Scribner's and Sons, 1958.

———. *Jesus and the Word*. New York: Scribner's, 1934 [1926].

———. *Kerygma and Myth*. London: SCM Press, 1953.

———. *Myth in the New Testament*. London: SCM Press, 1952.

———. "New Testament and Mythology." Pages 1–44 in *Kerygma and Myth*. Edited by E. Bartsch. New York: Harper and Row, 1953.

———. *Primitive Christianity*. New York: Meridian Books, 1956.

———. "The Problem of Demythologizing." Pages 248–55 in *The Hermeneutics Reader*. Edited by K. Mueller-Vollmer. Oxford: Basil Blackwell, 1985. Repr. from *Glauben und Verstehen: Gesammelte Aufsätze*, vol. 4. Tübingen: Mohr Siebeck, 1965.

———. "The Significance of the Old Testament for the Christian Faith." Pages 8–35 in *The Old Testament and the Christian Faith*. Edited by B. W. Anderson. New York: Harper and Row, 1963.

———. *Theologie des Neuen Testaments*. Tübingen: Mohr Siebeck, 1948.

———. *Theology of the New Testament*. Translated by K. Grobel. New York: Scribner's and Sons, 1951–1955.

Burger, C. *Jesus als Davidssohn: Eine traditionsgeschichtliche Untersuchung*. FRLANT 98. Göttingen: Vandenhoeck and Ruprecht, 1970.

Burgmann, H. Der *"Sitz im Leben" in den Josuafluch-texten in 4Q379 22 II und 4QTestimonia*. Krakow: Enigma, 1990.

Burke, P. *Eyewitnessing: The Uses of Images as Historical Evidence*. London: Reaction Books, 2001.

———. "History as Social Memory." Pages 97–114 in *Memory: History, Culture, and the Mind*. Edited by T. Butler. Oxford: Blackwell, 1989.

Burkitt, F. C. *The Gospel History and Its Transmission*. Edinburgh: T&T Clark, 1906.

Burrows, E. *The Gospel of the Infancy and Other Biblical Essays*. Bellarmine Series 6. London: Burns, Oates and Washbourne, 1940.

Byrskog, S. *Jesus the Only Teacher: Didactic Authority and Transmission in Ancient*

Israel, Ancient Judaism, and the Matthean Community. Stockholm: Almqvist and Wiksell, 1994.

Caird, G. B. "Jesus and Israel: The Starting Point for New Testament Christology." Pages 58–68 in *Christological Perspectives: Essays in Honor of Harvey K. McArthur*. Edited by R. F. Berkey and S. A. Edwards. New York: Pilgrim, 1982.

———. *The Language and Imagery of the Bible*. Grand Rapids: Eerdmans, 1997 [1980].

Carlson, R. A. *David, The Chosen King: A Traditio-Historical Approach to the Second Book of Samuel*. Uppsala: Almquist and Wicksell, 1964.

Carlston, C. E. "A Positive Criterion of Authenticity." *Biblical Research* 7 (1962): 33–44.

Carr, D. "Narrative and the Real World: An Argument for Continuity." *History and Theory* 25 (1986): 117–31.

———. *Time, Narrative and History*. Bloomington: Indiana University Press, 1976.

Carr, E. H. *What Is History?* London: Penguin, 1987.

Carson, D. A. *The Gospel according to John*. Grand Rapids: Eerdmans, 1991.

Cartledge, T. W. *1 & 2 Samuel*. SHBC 7. Macon, Ga.: Smyth and Helwys, 2001.

Casey, M. *Aramaic Sources of Mark's Gospel*. SNTSMS 102. Cambridge: Cambridge University Press, 1998.

Cassirer, E. *The Philosophy of the Enlightenment*. Translated by F. Koellen and J. Pettigrove. Boston: Beacon, 1951 [1932].

Catchpole, D. R. "The 'Triumphal' Entry." Pages 319–35 in *Jesus and the Politics of His Day*. Edited by E. Bammel and C. F. D. Moule. Cambridge: Cambridge University Press, 1984.

Ceci, S. J. "False Beliefs." Pages 91–125 in *Memory Distortion*. Edited by D. Schachter. Cambridge, Mass.: Harvard University Press, 1995.

Charles, R. H. *The Book of Enoch or 1 Enoch*. Oxford: Clarendon, 1912.

Charlesworth, J. H. "The Concept of the Messiah in the Pseudepigrapha." *ANRW* 2.19.1 (1979): 188–218.

———. "Solomon and Jesus: The Son of David in Ante-Markan Traditions (Mk 10:47)." Pages 125–51 in *Biblical and Humane: A Festschrift for John F. Priest*. Edited by L. B. Elder, D. L. Barr, and E. S. Malbon. Atlanta: Scholars Press, 1996.

———. "The Son of David: Solomon and Jesus (Mark 10.47)." Pages 72–87 in *The New Testament and Hellenistic Judaism*. Oxford: Arden, 1995.

Childs, B. S. *Isaiah*. Louisville, Ky.: Westminster John Knox, 2001.

Childs, H. *The Myth of the Historical Jesus and the Evolution of Consciousness*. SBLDS 179. Atlanta: SBL, 2000.

Chilton, B. D. "Commenting on the Old Testament." Pages 122–40 in *It Is Written: Scripture Citing Scripture: Essays in Honour of Barnabas Lindars*. Edited by D. A. Carson and Williamson H. Cambridge: Cambridge University Press, 1988.

———. "Exorcism and History: Mark 1:21-28." Pages 253–71 in *Gospel Perspectives* 6. Sheffield: JSOT, 1976.

———. "Jesus ben David: Reflections on the Davidssohnfrage." Pages 192–218 in *The Historical Jesus: A Sheffield Reader.* Edited by C. A. Evans and S. E. Porter. Sheffield: Sheffield Academic Press, 1995.

———. *Pure Kingdom: Jesus' Vision of God.* Grand Rapids: Eerdmans, 1996.

Clements, R. E. "Solomon and the Origins of Wisdom in Israel." *Perspectives in Religious Studies* 15, no. 4 (1988): 23–36.

Coggan, F. D. "Note on the Word Hosanna." *ExpTim* 52 (1940–1941): 76–77.

Cohn-Sherbok, D. "An Analysis of Jesus: Arguments Concerning the Plucking of Grain on the Sabbath." *JSNT* 2 (1979): 31–41.

Collingwood, R. G. *The Idea of History.* Oxford: Oxford University Press, 1956.

———. *Philosophy and Religion.* London: Macmillan, 1916.

Collins, J. J. *The Apocalyptic Imagination: An Introduction to the Jewish Matrix of Christianity.* New York: Crossroad, 1984.

———. *Apocalypticism in the Dead Sea Scrolls.* New York: Routledge, 1997.

———. "A Herald of Good Tidings: Isaiah 61:1-3 and Its Actualization in the Dead Sea Scrolls." Pages 225–40 in *The Quest for Context and Meaning: Studies in Biblical Intertextuality.* BIS 28. Edited by C. A. Evans and S. Talmon. Licdcn: Brill, 1997.

———. "'He Shall Not Judge By What His Eyes See': Messianic Authority in the Dead Sea Scrolls." *DSD* 2 (1995): 145–64.

———. *Jewish Wisdom in the Hellenistic Age.* Louisville, Ky.: Westminster John Knox, 1997.

———. "The Nature of Messianism in the Light of the Dead Sea Scrolls." Pages 199–217 in *The Dead Sea Scrolls in Their Historical Context.* Edited by T. H. Lim. Edinburgh: T&T Clark, 2000.

———. *The Scepter and the Star: The Messiahs of the Dead Sea Scrolls and Other Ancient Literature.* New York: Doubleday, 1995.

———. "The Works of the Messiah." *DSD* 1 (1994): 98–112.

Conybeare, F. C. *Philostratus: Life of Apollonius of Tyana.* LCL 16, 17. London: Macmillan, 1912.

———. "The Testament of Solomon." *JQR* 11 (1898): 1–45.

Copleston, F. *A History of Philosophy.* New York: Doubleday, 1963.

Coser, L. A. Introduction to *On Collective Memory,* by M. Halbwachs. Chicago: University of Chicago Press: 1992.

Cranfield, C. E. B. *The Gospel according to St. Mark.* CTGC. Cambridge: Cambridge University Press, 1963.

Creed, J. M. *The Gospel according to St. Luke.* London: Macmillan, 1942.

Cross, F. M. *Canaanite Myth and Hebrew Epic: Essays in the History of the Religion of Israel.* Cambridge: Harvard University Press, 1973.

Crossan, J. D. *The Birth of Christianity: Discovering What Happened after the Execution of Jesus.* Edinburgh: T&T Clark, 1998.

———. *The Historical Jesus: The Life of a Mediterranean Jewish Peasant.* San Francisco: HarperSanFrancisco, 1992.

———. "Redaction and Citation in Mark 11:9-10 and 11:17." *BR* 17 (1972): 33–50.

———. "Why Is Historical Jesus Research Necessary?" Pages 7–37 in *Jesus 2000 Years Later*. Edited by J. H. Charlesworth and W. P. Weaver. Harrisburg, Pa.: Trinity, 2000.

Cullman, O. *The Christology of the New Testament*. Translated by S. Guthrie and C. Hall. London: SCM Press, 1963 [1957].

———. *The Earliest Christian Confessions*. Translated by J. Reid. London: Lutterworth, 1949 [1943].

———. *Salvation in History*. Translated by S. G. Sowers. London: SCM Press, 1967 [1965].

Dahl, N. A. "The Passion Narrative in Matthew." Pages 53–68 in *The Interpretation of Matthew*. Edited by G. Stanton. Edinburgh: T&T Clark, 1983 [1955].

———. "The Problem of the Historical Jesus." Pages 81–111 in *Jesus the Christ: The Historical Origins of Christological Doctrine*. Edited by D. Juel. Minneapolis: Fortress, 1962.

Dahood, M. *Psalms III: 101–150*. AB 17A. Garden City, N.Y.: Doubleday, 1970.

Daube, D. *The New Testament and Rabbinic Judaism*. London: Athlone, 1956.

Davenport, G. L. "The Anointed of the Lord in *Psalms of Solomon* 17." Pages 67–92 in *Ideal Figures in Ancient Judaism: Profiles and Paradigms*. Edited by J. J. Collins and G. W. E. Nickelsburg. Chico, Calif.: Scholars Press, 1980.

Davidson, M. J. *Angels at Qumran: A Comparative Study of 1 Enoch 1-36, 72-108 and Sectarian Writings from Qumran*. Sheffield: Sheffield Academic Press, 1992.

Davies, S. L. *Jesus the Healer: Possession, Trance, and the Origin of Christianity*. New York: Continuum, 1995.

Davies, W. D., and D. C. Allison Jr. *The Gospel according to Saint Matthew*. 3 vols. ICC. Edinburgh: T&T Clark, 1997 [1988].

Dawes, G. W. *Introduction to the Historical Jesus Quest: A Foundational Anthology*. Leiden: Deo, 1999.

Delcor, M. "Melchizedek from Genesis to the Qurmran Texts and the Epistles to the Hebrews." *JSJ* 1–3 (1972): 115–32.

Denton, D. L, Jr. *Historiography and Hermeneutics in Jesus Studies: An Examination of the Work of John Dominic Crossan and Ben F. Meyers*. JSNTSup 2 and 2. London: T&T Clark International, 2004.

Dibelius, M. *From Tradition to Gospel*. Translated by B. Woolf. London: Ivor Nicholson and Watson, 1934.

Dilthey, W. "The Development of Hermeneutics." In *Dilthey: Selected Writings*. Edited by H. P. Rickman. Cambridge: Cambridge University Press, 1976.

Dimant, D. "4QFlorilegium and the Idea of the Community as Temple." Pages 165–86 in *Hellenica et Judaica*. Edited by A. Caquot, M. Hadas-Lebel, and J. Riaud. Leuven: Peeters, 1986.

———. "Pseudonymity in the Wisdom of Solomon." Pages 243–55 in *La Septuaginta en la investigacion contemporanea*. Madrid: Instituto Arias Montano, 1985.

———. "The Qumran Manuscripts: Contents and Significance." Pages 23–55 in *Time to Prepare the Way in the Wilderness*. Edited by D. Dimant and H. Schiffman. Leiden: Brill, 1995.

Dirksen, P. *1 Chronicles*. Leuven: Peeters, 2005.

Dodd, C. H. *According to the Scriptures: The Sub-Structure of New Testament Theology*. London: Collins, 1952.

———. *Historical Traditon in the Fourth Gospel*. Cambridge: Cambridge University Press, 1963.

Dodds, E. R. *The Ancient Concept of Progress and Other Essays in Greek Literature and Belief*. Oxford: Clarendon, 1973.

Downing, F. G. "Magic and Scepticism in and around the First Christian Century." Pages 86–99 in *Magic in the Biblical Word: From the Rod of Aaron to the Ring of Solomon*. Edited by T. E. Klutz. London: T&T Clark, 2003.

Duling, D. C. "The Eleazar Miracle and Solomon's Magical Wisdom in Flavius Josephus's *Antiquitates Judaicae* 8.42-49." *HTR* 78 (1985): 1–25.

———. "Matthew's Plurisignificant 'Son of David' in Social Science Perspective: Kinship, Kingship, Magic and Miracle." *BTB* 22 (1992): 99–116.

———. "The Promises to David and Their Entrance into Christianity—Nailing Down a Likely Hypothesis." *NTS* 20 (1974): 55–77.

———. "Solomon, Exorcism and the Son of David." *HTR* 68 (1975): 235–52.

———. "The Therapeutic Son of David: An Element in Matthew's Christological Apologetic." *NTS* 24 (1977–1978): 392–410.

Dunn, J. D. G. "All That Glistens Is Not Gold: In Quest of the Right Key to Unlock the Way to the Historical Jesus." Pages 131–62 in *Der historische Jesus: Tendenzen und Perspektiven der gegenwärtigen Forschung*. Edited by J. Schröter and R. Brucher. BZNW 114. Berlin: De Gruyter, 2002.

———. *Christology in the Making: A New Testament Inquiry into the Origins of the Doctrine of the Incarnation*. Grand Rapids: Eerdmans, 1989 [1980].

———. "History, Memory and Eyewitnesses." *JSNT* 26, no. 4 (2004): 473–87.

———. "Jesus in Oral Memory." Pages 84–145 in *Jesus: A Colloquium in the Holy Land*. Edited by D. Donnelly. London: Continuum, 2001.

———. *Jesus Remembered*. Grand Rapids: Eerdmans, 2003.

———. *Jesus and the Spirit*. Grand Rapids: Eerdmans, 1975.

———. *A New Perspective on Jesus: What the Quest for the Historical Jesus Missed*. Grand Rapids: Baker Academic, 2005.

———. *Romans*. Dallas: Word, 1988.

———. "Social Memory and the Oral Jesus Tradition." In *Memory and Remembrance in the Bible and Antiquity*. Edited by L. T. Stuckenbruck, S. C. Barton, and B. G. Wold. Tübingen: Mohr Siebeck, 2007.

———, and G. H. Twelftree. "Demon-Possession and Exorcism in the NT." *Churchman* 94 (1980): 210–25.

Edwards, R. A. *The Sign of Jonah in the Theology of the Evangelists and Q*. Studies in Biblical Theology Second Series 18. Naperville, Ill.: Allenson, 1971.

Eissfelt, O. *The Old Testament: An Introduction*. Translated by P. R. Ackroyd. Oxford: Blackwell, 1965.
Ellis, E. E. Preface to *Typos: The Typological Interpretation of the Old Testament in the New*, by L. Goppelt. Grand Rapids: Eerdmans, 1982.
Ernst, J. *Das Evangelium nach Markus*. Regensburg: Pustet, 1981.
Eskola, T. *Messiah and the Throne*. Tübingen: Mohr Siebeck, 2001.
Evans, C. A. "Are the 'Son' Texts at Qumran Messianic?" Pages 135–53 in *Qumran-Messianism: Studies o the Messianic Expectations in the Dead Sea Scrolls*. Tubingen: Mohr Siebeck, 1998.
———. "The Baptism of John in a Typological Context." Pages 44–70 in *Dimensions of Baptism*. Edited by F. M. Cross and S. E. Porter. JSNTSup. Sheffield: Sheffield Academic Press, 2002.
———. *Jesus*. Grand Rapids: Baker, 1992.
———. "Jesus' Action in the Temple: Cleansing or Portent of Destruction?" *CBQ* 51 (1989): 237–70.
———. "Jesus and the 'Cave of Robbers': Towards a Jewish Context for the Temple Action." *BBR* 3 (1993): 93–110.
———. "Jesus and the Dead Sea Scrolls from Qumran Cave 4." Pages 91–100 in *Eschatology, Messianism and the Dead Sea Scrolls*. Edited by C. A. Evans and P. W. Flint; Grand Rapids: Eerdmans, 1997.
———. *Jesus and His Contemporaries*. AGJU 25. Leiden: Brill, 1995.
———. "The Jewish Gospel Tradition." Pages 241–77 in *Jewish Believers in Jesus: A History from Antiquity to the Present*. Vol. 1: *Antiquity (ca. 30-500 C.E.)*. Edited by R. Hvalvik and O. Skarsaune. Peabody, Mass.: Hendrickson, 2007.
———. *Mark 8:27–16:20*. WBC 34B. Nashville: Thomas Nelson, 2001.
———. "Typology and First-Century Exegesis." Pages 862–65 in *Dictionary of Jesus and the Gospels*. Edited by J. Green and S. McKnight. Downers Grove, Ill.: InterVarsity, 1992.
Fairbairn, P. *The Typology of Scripture*. 2 vols. New York: Funk and Wagnalls, 1876.
Farmer, W. R. *The Synoptic Problem*. New York: Macmillan, 1964.
Fenton, J. C. *Saint Matthew*. Baltimore: Pelican, 1963.
Fentress, J., and C. Wickham. *Social Memory*. Oxford: Blackwell, 1992.
Fergusson, D. *Bultmann*. Collegeville, Minn.: Liturgical Press, 1992.
Fickett, H. *Conversations with Jesus*. Colorado Springs: Piñon Press, 1999.
Fishbane, M. *Biblical Interpretation in Ancient Israel*. Oxford: Oxford University Press, 1985.
Fisher, L. R. "Can This Be the Son of David?" Pages 82–97 in *Jesus and the Historian, Ernest Cadman Colwell Festschrift*. Philadelphia: Westminster, 1968.
Fitzmyer, J. A. *The Dead Sea Scrolls and Christian Origins*. Grand Rapids: Eerdmans, 2000.
———. *The Gospel according to Luke*. AB 28. New York: Doubleday, 1970.
———. "More About Elijah Coming First." *JBL* 104 (1985): 292–94.
———. *The Semitic Background of the New Testament*. Grand Rapids: Eerdmans, 1997.

———. "The Son of David Tradition and Mt. 22.41-46 and Parallels." Pages 113–26 in *Essays on the Semitic Background of the Old Testament*. London: Geoffery Chapman, 1971.

———. *A Wandering Aramaean*. Eerdmans: Grand Rapids, 1997 [1979].

Fletcher-Louis, C. H. T. "The High Priest as Divine Mediator in the Hebrew Bible: Dan 7.13 as a Test Case." *SBLSP* 36 (1997): 161–93.

———. "Jesus as the High Priestly Messiah." *JSHJ* 4, no. 2 (2006): 155–75.

Flusser, D. *Jesus*. Jerusalem: Magnes, 1998.

Fox, M.V. *Proverbs 1–9*. AB 18A. New York: Doubleday, 2000.

France, R. T. *Matthew: Evangelist and Teacher*. London: Academie, 1989.

Franklyn, P. N. "The Cultic and Pious Climax of Eschatology in the *Psalms of Solomon*." *JSJ* 18 (1987): 1–17.

Fredericks, D. C. *Qoheleth's Language: Re-evaluating Its Nature and Date*. Lewiston, Me.: Mellen, 1988.

Freedman, D. N. "The Chroniclers Purpose." *CBQ* 23 (1961): 436–42.

Frey, J. "Different Patterns of Dualistic Thought in the Qumran Library: Reflections of Their Background and History." Pages 275–336 in *Legal Texts and Legal Issues: Proceedings of the Second Meeting of the International Organization for Qumran Studies, Cambridge 1995, Published in Honour of Joseph M. Baumgarten*. STDJ 23. Edited by M. Bernstein, F. G. Martínez, and J. Kampen. Leiden: Brill, 1997.

Fritz, V. *1 & 2 Kings: A Continental Commentary*. Translated by A. Hagedorn. Minneapolis: Fortress, 2003.

Frye, N. *The Great Code: The Bible and Literature*. New York: Harcourt Brace Jovanovich Pardes Ilana, 1982.

Fuchs, A. *Sprachliche Untersuchungen zu Matthüas und Lukas: Ein Beitrag zur Quellenkritik*. Rome: Biblical Institute Press, 1971.

Gadamer, H. G. *Philosophical Hermeneutics*. Translated by D. E. Linge. Berkeley: University of California Press, 1976.

———. "The Problem of Language in Schleiermacher's Hermeneutic." *JTC* 7 (1970): 68–95.

———. *Truth and Method*. New York: Continuum, 2004 [1960].

Gagg, R. P. "Jesus und die Davidssohnfrage: Zur Exegese von Markus 12:35-37." *TZ* 7 (1951): 18–30.

Gakuru, G. *An Inner-Biblical Exegetical Study of the Davidic Covenant and the Dyanastic Oracle*. Mellen Biblical Press Series 58. Lewiston, Maine: Mellen, 2000.

Garrett, S. R. *The Demise of the Devil: Magic and the Demoniac in Luke's Writings*. Minneapolis: Fortress, 1989.

Gaston, L. "Beelzebul." *TZ* 18 (1962): 247–55.

Gedi, N., and Y. Elam. "Collective Memory—What Is It?" *History and Memory* 8 (1996): 30–50.

Gerhardsson, B. *Memory and Manuscript: Oral Tradition and Written Transmission in Rabbinic Judaism and Early Christianity*. Lund: Gleerup, 1961.

Gerleman, G. "Psalm cx." *VT* (1981): 1–19.

Gerstenberger, E. S. *Psalms Part 2 and Lamentations*. FOTL 15. Grand Rapids: Eerdmans, 2001.
Gibbs, J. M. "Purpose and Pattern in Matthew's Use of the Title 'Son of David.'" *NTS* 10 (1963–1964): 446–64.
Gibson, J. "Jesus' Refusal to Produce a 'Sign' (Mark 8.11-13)." Pages 271–99 in *The Historical Jesus: A Sheffield Reader*. Edited by C. A. Evans and S. E. Porter. Sheffield: Sheffield Academic Press, 1995.
Gilbert, M. "Wisdom Literature." Pages 2:283–320 in *Jewish Writings of the Second Temple Period*. Edited by M. E. Stone. Philadelphia: Fortress, 1984.
Gillingham, S. "The Messiah in the Psalms: A Question of Reception History and the Psalter." Pages 209–37 in *King and Messiah in Israel and the Near East*. Edited by J. Day. JSOTSup 270. Sheffield: Sheffield Academic Press, 1998.
Ginzberg, L. *Legends of the Jews*. Philadelphia: Jewish Publication Society, 1908-1938.
Glasswell, M. E. "The Relationship between John and Mark." *JSNT* 23 (1985): 99–115.
Glover, T. R. *The Jesus of History*. New York: Associated Press, 1919.
Gnilka, J. *Das Evangelium nach Markus*. 2 vols. Zürich: Benzinger, 1978.
Gold, M. "Adoption: A New Problem for Jewish Law." *Judaism* 36 (1987): 443–50.
Goldstein, J. A. *I Maccabees*. AB. Garden City, N.Y.: Doubleday, 1976.
Goodacre, M. S. *Goulder and the Gospels: An Examination of a New Paradigm*. JSNTSup 133. Sheffield: Sheffield Academic Press, 1996.
Goppelt, L. Typos: *The Typological Interpretation of the Old Testament in the New*. Translated by Donald H. Madvig. Grand Rapids: Eerdmans, 1982 [1964].
Goulder, M. "On Putting Q to the Test." *NTS* 24 (1978): 218–34.
———. *The Psalms of the Return (Book V, Psalm 107–150)*. JSOTSup 258. Sheffield: Sheffield Academic Press, 1998.
———. *Type and History in Acts*. London: SPCK, 1964.
Grabbe, L. L. *Wisdom of Solomon*. Sheffield: Sheffield Academic Press, 1997.
Grappe, C. "Jésus exorciste à la lumière des pratiques et des attentes de son temps." *RB* 110 (2003): 178–96.
Gray, G. B. *The Book of Isaiah*. ICC. Edinburgh: T&T Clark, 1969.
Gray, R. *Prophetic Figures in Late Second Temple Jewish Palestine: The Evidence from Josephus*. Oxford: Oxford University Press, 1993.
Grayston, K. "Exorcism in the NT." *Epworth Review* 2 (1975): 90–94.
Green, J. B. *The Death of Jesus: Tradition and Interpretation in the Passion Narrative*. WUNT 2:33. Tübingen: Mohr Siebeck, 1988.
Grenz, S. J. *A Primer on Postmodernism*. Grand Rapids: Eerdmans, 1996.
Gundry, R. H. *Mark: A Commentary on His Apology for the Cross*. Grand Rapids: Eerdmans, 1992.
———. *Matthew: A Commentary on His Literary and Theological Art*. Grand Rapids: Eerdmans, 1982.
———. *The Use of the Old Testament in St. Matthew's Gospel*. SNT 18. Leiden: Brill, 1967.

Gunkel, H. *Die Psalmen*. Göttingen: Vandenhoeck und Ruprecht, 1926.

———. *An Introduction to the Psalms: The Genres of the Religious Lyric of Israel*. Translated by J. Nogalski. Macon, Ga.: Mercer University Press, 1998 [1933].

Gunn, D. A. *The Fate of King Saul*. JSOTSup 14. Sheffield: JSOT Press, 1980.

Hagner, D. A. *Matthew 1–13*. WBC 33A. Dallas: Word, 1993.

———. *Matthew 14–28*. WBC 33B. Dallas: Word, 1995.

Hahn, F. *The Titles of Jesus in Christology: Their History in Early Christianity*. Translated by Knight and Ogg. London: Lutterworth, 1969 [1963].

Hahn, R. R. "The Community of the Pious: The Social Setting of the *Psalms of Solomon*." *SR* 17 (1988): 169–89.

Halbwachs, M. *On Collective Memory*. Translated by Lewis A. Coser. Chicago: University of Chicago Press, 1992.

———. *The Collective Memory*. Translated by F. J. Ditter Jr. and V. Y. Ditter. New York: Harper and Row, 1980.

———. *La Topographie des Evangiles en Terre Sainte. Etude de mémoire collective*. Paris: Presses universitaires de France, 1941.

———. *Les Cadres sociaux de la mémoire*. Paris: F. Alcan, 1925.

Haney, R. G. *Text and Concept Analysis in Royal Psalms*. Series in Biblical Literature 30. New York: Peter Lang, 2002.

Hanig, R. "Christus als 'wahrer Salomo' in der frühen Kirche." *ZNW* 84 (1993): 111–34.

Hardy, E. R. "The Date of Psalm 110." *JBL* (1945): 385–90.

Harnack, A. *The Sayings of Jesus*. Translated by J. R. Wilkenson. London: Williams and Norgate, 1908.

Harrington, D. J. *The Gospel of Matthew*. Sacra Pagina 1. Collegeville, Minn.: Liturgical Press, 1991.

Harvey, J. D. *Listening to the Text: Oral Patterning in Paul's Letters*. ETS Studies 1. Grand Rapids: Baker, 1998.

Hatina, T. R. *In Search of a Context: The Function of Scripture in Mark's Narrative*. JSNTSup 232. Sheffield: Sheffield Academic Press, 2002.

Hay, D. M. *Glory at the Right Hand: Psalm 110 in Early Christianity*. SBLMS 18. Nashville: Abingdon, 1973.

Hays, R. B. *Victory over Violence: The Significance of N.T. Wright's Jesus for New Testament Ethics*. Downers Grove, Ill.: InterVarsity, 1999.

Hearon, H. "The Story of 'the Woman who Anointed Jesus' as Social Memory: A Methodological Proposal for the Study of Tradition as Memory." Pages 79–97 in *Memory, Tradition, and Text: Uses of the Past in Early Christianity*. Leiden: Brill, 2005.

Heidegger, M. *Being and Time*. Translated by J. M. Macquarrie and E. Robinson. London: SCM Press, 1962 [1927].

———. *Sein und Zeit*. Tübingen: Max Niemeyer, 1961 [1927].

Held, H. J. "Matthew as Interpreter of the Miracle Stories." Pages 165–299 in *Tradition and Interpretation in Matthew*. Edited by G. Bornkamm, G. Barth, and H. J. Held. London: SCM Press, 1963 [1960].

Hempel, C. G. "The Function of General Laws in History." *The Journal of Philosophy* 39 (1942): 35–48.
Hengel, M. *Die Zeloten: Untersuchungen zur Jüdischen Freiheitsbewegung in der Zeit von Herodes I. bis 70 N. Chr.* Leiden: Brill, 1961.
———. *Judaism and Hellenism*. Translated by J. Bowden. Minneapolis: Fortress, 1974.
———. *Studies in Early Christology*. Edinburgh: T&T Clark, 1995.
———. *Victory over Violence: Jesus and the Revolutionists*. Translated by David Green. Philadelphia: Fortress, 1973 [1971].
Hertzberg, H. W. *I & II Samuel: A Commentary*. Translated by J. Bowden. London: SCM Press, 1964 [1960].
Hilber, J. W. "Psalm CX in the Light of Assyrian Prophecies." *VT* 53, no. 3 (2003): 353–66.
Hildebrandt, W. *An Old Testament Theology of the Spirit of God*. Peabody, Mass.: Hendrickson, 1995.
Hiley, D. R., J. F. Bohman, and R. Shusterman. *Introduction to The Interpretive Turn: Philosophy, Science, Culture*. Edited by D. R. Hiley et al. Ithaca: Cornell University Press, 1991.
Hodges, H. A. *Wilhelm Dilthey*. London: Routledge and Kegan Paul, 1969.
Hogan, C. L. *Healing in the Second Temple Period*. NTOA 21. Göttingen: Vandenhoeck and Ruprecht, 1992.
Hollenbach, P. "Jesus, Demoniacs, and Public Authorities: A Socio-Historical Study." *JAAR* 49 (1988): 567–88.
Holmberg, B. "Questions of Method in James Dunn's Jesus Remembered." *JSNT* 26 (2004): 445–57.
Holm-Nielsen, S. *Die Psalmen Salomos*. JSHRZ 4.2. Gütersloh: Gütersloher Verlagshaus, 1977.
Hooker, M. *The Gospel According to Mark*. Peabody, Mass.: Hendrickson, 1991.
———. *The Son of Man in Mark*. London: SPCK, 1967.
Horbury, W. *Herodian Judaism and the New Testament*. WUNT 193. Tübingen: Mohr Siebeck, 2006.
———. *Jewish Messianism and the Cult of Christ*. London: SCM Press, 1998.
———. "The Twelve and the Phylarchs." *NTS* 32 (1986): 503–27.
Horsley, R. A. *Jesus and the Spiral of Violence: Popular Jewish Resistance in Roman Palestine*. San Francisco: Harper and Row, 1987.
———. "Prominent Patterns in the Social Memory of Jesus and Friends." Pages 57–78 in *Memory Tradition and Text: Uses of the Past in Early Christianity*. Edited by A. Kirk and T. Thatcher. Semeia 52. Leiden: Brill, 2005.
———, and J. S. Hanson. *Bandits, Prophets and Messiahs: Popular Movements at the Time of Jesus*. San Francisco: Harper and Row, 1985.
Horton, F. L. *The Melchizedek Tradition: A Critical Examination of the Sources to the Fifth Century A.D. and the Epistle to the Hebrews*. SNTSMS 30. Cambridge: Cambridge University Press, 1976.
Hubbard, D. A. "Songs of Solomon." Pages 1120–21 in *New Bible Dictionary*. Edited by J. D. Douglas et al. Downers Grove, Ill.: InterVarsity, 1996.

Hull, J. M. *Hellenistic Magic and the Gospel Tradition.* London: SCM Press, 1974.
Humboldt, W. von. "On the Historian's Task." Pages 5–23 in *The Theory and Practice of History.* Edited by G. G. Iggers and H. von Moltke. New York: Bobbs-Merrill, 1973.
Hume, D. *An Enquiry Concerning Human Understanding.* Oxford: Oxford University Press, 1961.
Hurst, L. D. "The Neglected Role of Semantics in the Search for the Aramaic Words of Jesus." *JSNT* 28 (1986): 63–80.
Hurtado, L. W. "Christ." Pages 106–17 in *Dictionary of Jesus and the Gospels.* Edited by J. Green and S. McKnight. Downers Grove, Ill.: InterVarsity, 1992.
———. "The Gospel of Mark: Evolutionary or Revolutionary Document." Pages 196–214 in *The Synoptic Gospels.* Edited by C. A. Evans and S. E. Porter. Sheffield: Sheffield Academic Press, 1995.
Hutton, P. *History as an Art of Memory.* Hanover, N.H.: University Press of New England, 1993.
Hübner, H. "Clean and Unclean (NT)." In volume 6 of *Anchor Bible Dictionary.* Edited by D. N. Freedman. Garden City, N.Y.: Doubleday, 1992.
———. "Die Weisheit Salomons." In *Das Alte Testament Deutsch: Apokryphen.* Edited by O. Kaiser and L. Perlitt. Göttingen: Vandenhoeck and Ruprecht, 1999.
Iggers, G. G. *Historiography in the Twentieth Century.* Hanover, N.H.: Wesleyan University Press, 1997.
———. Introduction to *The Theory and Practice of History*, by L. von Ranke. Edited by G. G. Iggers and H. von Moltke. New York: Bobbs-Merrill, 1973.
Iser, W. *The Range of Interpretation.* New York: Columbia University Press, 2000.
Jacobson, H. *A Commentary on Pseudo-Philo's Liber Antiquitatum Biblicarum.* 2 vols. Leiden: Brill, 1996.
Jeffers, A. *Magic and Divination in Ancient Palestine and Syria.* Leiden: Brill, 1996.
Jenkins, K. *Re-thinking History.* London: Routledge, 1991.
Jeremias, J. *The Parables of Jesus.* London: SCM Press, 1963.
Johnson, S. I. "The Testament of Solomon from Late Antiquity to the Renaissance." Pages 35–49 in *The Metamorphosis of Magic from Late Antiquity to the Early Modern Period.* Edited by J. Bremmer and J. Veenstra. Leuven: Peeters, 2002.
Johnstone, W. *1 and 2 Chronicles.* JSOTSup 253. Sheffield: Sheffield Academic Press, 1997.
Jones, G. *Bultmann: Towards a Critical Theology.* Oxford: Polity, 1991.
Jones, G. H. *The Nathan Narratives.* JSOTSup 80. Sheffield: Sheffield Academic Press, 1990.
Jonge, M. de. "The Expectation of the Future in the Psalms of Solomon." Pages 3–27 in *Jewish Eschatology, Early Christian Christology and the Testaments of the Twelve Patriarchs: Collected Essays of Marinus de Jonge.* NTSup 63. Leiden: Brill, 1991.
———. *Outside the Old Testament.* Cambridge: Cambridge University Press, 1985.
———. "The Use of the Word 'Annointed' in the Time of Jesus." *NovT* 8 (1966): 132–48.

———. "Χρίω." Pages 511–17 in *TDNT* IX. Edited by G. Kittel. Grand Rapids: Eerdmans, 1965.
Juel, D. *Messiah and Temple: The Trial of Jesus in the Gospel of Mark.* SBLDS 31. Missoula, Mont.: Scholars Press, 1973.
———. *Messianic Exegesis: Christological Interpretation of the Old Testament in Early Christianity.* Philadelphia: Fortress, 1988.
Kaiser, O. *Isaiah 1–12: A Commentary.* Philadelphia: Westminster, 1972.
Kalluweettil, P. *Declaration and Covenant.* AnBib 88. Rome: Biblical Institute Press, 1982.
Kammen, M. "Some Patterns and Meanings of Memory Distortion in American History." Pages 329–45 in *Memory Distortion.* Edited by D. Schachter. Cambridge, Mass.: Harvard University Press, 1995.
Karrer, M. *Der Gesalbte: Die Grundlagen des Christustitels.* Göttingen: Vandenhoeck and Ruprecht, 1991.
Kautzsch, E. *Grammatik des Biblisch-aramäichen mit einer kritischen Erörterung der aramäichen Wörter im Neuen Testament.* Leipzig: F. C. W. Vogel, 1884.
Keck, L. E. "Toward the Renewal of New Testament Christology." *NTS* 32 (1986): 362–77.
Kee, H. C. *Medicine, Miracle and Magic in the New Testament Times.* SNTS 55. Cambridge: Cambridge University Press, 1986.
Keightley, G. M. "The Church's Memory of Jesus: A Social Science Analysis of 1 Thessalonians." *BTB* 17 (1987): 149–56.
Kelber, W. *The Oral and the Written Gospel: The Hermeneutics of Speaking and Writing in the Synoptic Tradition, Mark, Paul, and Q.* Philadelphia: Fortress, 1983.
Kingsbury, J. D. *The Christology of Mark.* Philadelphia: Fortress, 1983.
———. *Matthew: Structure, Christology, Kingdom.* Philadelphia: Fortress, 1975.
———. "The Title 'Kyrios' in Matthew's Gospel." *JBL* 94 (1975): 246–55.
———. "The Title "Son of David" in Matthew's Gospel." *JBL* 95 (1976): 591–602.
Kinman, B. *Jesus' Entry into Jerusalem: In the Context of Lukan Theology and the Politics of His Day.* AGJU 28. Leiden: Brill, 1995.
Kirk, A. "Social and Cultural Memory." Pages 1–24 in *Memory, Tradition, and Text: Uses of the Past in Early Christianity.* Edited by A. Kirk and T. Thatcher. Semeia 52. Leiden: Brill, 2005.
———, and T. Thatcher. "Jesus Tradition as Social Memory." Pages 25–42 in *Memory, Tradition, and Text: Uses of the Past in Early Christianity.* Edited by A. Kirk and T. Thatcher. Semeia 52. Leiden: Brill, 2005.
———, eds. *Memory, Tradition, and Text: Uses of the Past in Early Christianity.* Leiden: Brill, 2005.
Kissane, E. J. "The Interpretation of Psalm 110." *ITQ* (1954): 103–14.
Klauck, H.-J. The Religious Context of Early Christianity. Edited by J. M. G. Barclay, J. Marcus, and J. Riches. *Studies of the New Testament and Its World.* Edinburgh: T&T Clark, 2000 [1995–1996].

Klausner, J. *Jesus of Nazareth: His Life, Times and Teaching*. London: George Allen and Unwin, 1925.

———. *The Messianic Idea in Israel: from Its Beginning to the Completion of the Mishnah*. Translated by W. F. Stinespring. London: George Allen and Unwin, 1956 [1902].

Klein, R. W. *2 Samuel*. WBC 10. Dallas: Word, 1983.

Klutz, T. E. "The Archer and the Cross." Pages 219–44 in *Magic in the Biblical Word: From the Rod of Aaron to the Ring of Solomon*. Edited by T. E. Klutz. London: T&T Clark, 2003.

Knox, W. L. *Sources for the Synoptic Gospels,* Vol. 1: *St. Mark*. Cambridge: Cambridge University Press, 1953.

Kraus, H. J. *Psalmen*. BKAT15. Neukirchen: Neukirchener Verlag des Erziehungsvereins, 1959.

Kruse, H. "David's Covenant." *VT* 35 (1985): 139–64.

Kähler, M. *Der sogenannte historische Jesus und der geschichtliche, biblische Christus*. Munich: Deichert and Leipzig, 1896.

Laansma, J. *I Will Give You Rest*. WUNT 98. Tübingen: Mohr Siebeck, 1997.

Lampe, G. W. H. "Reasonableness of Typology." Pages 9–38 in *Essays on Typology*. Edited by G. W. H. Lampe and K. J. Woollcombe. London: SCM Press, 1957.

Lane, W. L. *The Gospel of Mark: The English Text with Introduction, Exposition and Notes*. Grand Rapids: Eerdmans, 1974.

Langdon, E. *Essentials of Demonology: A Study of Jewish and Christian Doctrine, Its Origins and Development*. London: Epworth, 1949.

Lange, A. "The Essene Position on Magic and Divination." Pages 377–435 in *Legal Texts and Legal Issues: Proceedings of the Second Meeting of the International Organization for Qumran Studies, Cambridge 1995, Published in Honour of Joseph M. Baumgarten*. Edited by M. Bernstein et al. STDJ 23. Leiden: Brill, 1997.

Larcher, C. *Le Livre de la Sagesse ou la Sagesse de Salomon*. 3 vols. Nouvelle série 1. Paris: Gabalda, 1983.

Le Donne, A. "Theological Memory Distortion in the Jesus Tradition: A Study in Social Memory Theory." PAGES 163–77 in *Memory and Remembrance in the Bible and Antiquity*. Edited by L. T. Stuckenbruck, S. C. Barton, and B. G. Wold. Tübingen: Mohr Siebeck, 2007.

Le Goff, J. *History and Memory*. New York: Columbia University Press, 1992 [1977].

Lessing, G. E. *Gesammelte Werke*. Edited by P. Rilla. 10 vols. Berlin: Aufbau Verlag, 1954–1958.

———. "On the Proof of the Spirit and of Power." Pages 51–56 in *Lessing's Theological Writings*. Edited by H. Chadwick. London: William Clowes and Sons, 1956.

Levin, Y. "Jesus, 'Son of God' and 'Son of David.'" *JSNT* 28, no. 4 (2006): 415–42.

Lietzmann, H. *From Constantine to Julian: A History of the Church*. Vol. 3. Translated by B. L. Woolf. London: Lutterworth, 1950.

Lindars, B. *New Testament Apologetic: The Doctrinal Significance of the Old Testament Quotations*. Philadelphia: Westminster, 1962; 89–93.

Loader, W. R. G. "Son of David, Blindness, Possession, and Duality in Matthew." *CBQ* 44 (1982): 570–85.
Lohmeyer, E. *Das Evangelium des Markus*. 2 vols. Göttingen: Vandenhoeck and Ruprecht, 1951.
———. *Gottesknecht und Davidsohn*. FRLANT 61. Göttingen: Vanderhoek and Ruprecht, 1953.
Lohse, E. "υἱὸς Δαυίδ." Pages 478–88 in *TDNT* 8.
———. "Der König aus Davids Geschlecht. Bemerkungen zur messianischen Erwartung der Synagoge." Pages 337–45 in *Abraham unser Vater. Festschrift für Otto Michel*. Leiden: Brill, 1963.
———. "Hosianna." *NovT* 6 (1963): 113–19.
Lonergan, B. "Cognitional Structure." Pages 205–21 in *Collection: Papers by Bernard Lonergan*. Toronto: University of Toronto, 1988.
———. *Insight: A Study of Human Understanding*. New York: Harper and Row, 1978.
———. *Method in Theology*. London: Darton, Longman and Todd, 1972.
Lövestam, E. "Jésus Fils de David chez les Synoptiques." *Studia Theologica* 28 (1974 [1972]): 97–109.
Lowenthal, D. *The Past Is a Foreign Country*. Cambridge: Cambridge University Press, 1985.
Lüdemann, G. *Jesus After 2000 Years: What He Really Said and Did*. Translated by J. Bowden. London: SCM Press, 2000.
Lustick, I. S. "History, Historiography, and Political Science: Multiple Records and the Problem of Selection Bias." *American Political Science Review* 90, no. 3 (1996): 605–18.
Luz, U. *Matthew 8–20: A Commentary*. Minneapolis: Augsburg Fortress, 2001.
Lydall, F. *Slaves, Citizens, Sons: Legal Metaphors in the Epistles*. Grand Rapids: Academie, 1984.
Lyons, J. *Language, Meaning, and Context*. London: Fontana, 1981.
MacMullen, R. *Enemies of the Roman Order: Treason, Unrest and Alienation in the Empire*. Cambridge, Mass.: Harvard University Press, 1966.
Macquarrie, J. *An Existentialist Theology: A Comparison of Heidegger and Bultmann*. London: SCM Press, 1965 [1955].
Maloney, E. C. *Semitic Interference in Marcan Syntax*. SBLDS 51. Missoula, Mont.: Scholars Press, 1980.
Mann, C. S. *Mark*. AB 27. Garden City, N.Y.: Doubleday, 1986.
Manson, T. W. "The Cleansing of the Temple." *BJRL* 33 (1950/1): 271–82.
———. *The Sayings of Jesus*. London: SCM Press, 1947.
Marcos, N. F. "La unción de Salomón y la entrada de Jesús en Jerusalén: 1 Re 1,33-40/Lc 19,35-40." *Biblica* 68 (1987): 89–97.
Marcus, J. *The Way of the Lord: Christological Exegesis in the Gospel of Mark*. Louisville, Ky.: Westminster John Knox, 1992.
Marshall, I. H. *Commentary on Luke*. Grand Rapids: Eerdmans, 1978.
———. *The Gospel according to Luke: A Commentary on the Greek Text*. Exeter: Paternoster Press, 1978.

Marwick, A. *The New Nature of History*. Chicago: Lyceum, 2001.
Matera, F. J. *The Kingship of Jesus: Composition and Theology in Mark 15*. SBLDS 66. Chico, Calif.: Scholars Press, 1982.
Mays, J. L. *Psalms*. Louisville, Ky.: Westminster John Knox, 1994.
McCarthy, D. J. "II Samuel 7 and the Structure of the Deuteronomic History." *JBL* 84 (1965): 131–38.
McCasland, S. V. *By the Finger of God: Demon Possession and Exorcism in Early Christianity in Light of Modern Views of Mental Illness*. New York: Macmillan, 1951.
McCown, C. C. *The Testament of Solomon*. Leipzig: J. C. Hinrich, 1922.
McEleney, N. J. "Authenicating Criteria and Mark 7:1-23." *CBQ* 34 (1972): 431–60.
McKenzie, J. L. "Royal Messianism." *CBQ* 19 (1957): 25–52.
Meier, J. P. "From Elijah-like Prophet to Royal Davidic Messiah." Pages 45–83 in *Jesus: A Colloquium in the Holy Land*. Edited by D. Donnelly. London: Continuum, 2001.
———. *A Marginal Jew: Rethinking the Historical Jesus*. 4 vols. New York: Doubleday, 1991.
Mettinger, T. N. D. *The Dethronement of Sabaoth*. ConBOT 18. Lund: Wallin and Dalholm, 1982.
———. *King and Messiah: The Civil and Sacral Legitimation of the Israelite Kings*. ConBOT 8. Lund: Gleerup, 1976.
Meyer, B. F. *Critical Realism and the New Testament*. Princeton Theological Monograph Series 17. Allison Park, Pa.: Pickwick, 1989.
Michaelis, W. "Die Davidssohnschaft Jesu als historisches und kerygmatisches Problem: Beiträge zum Christusverständnis in Forschung und Verkündigung." Pages 317–30 in *Der historische Jesus und der kerygmatische Christus*. Edited by H. Ristow and K. Matthiae. Berlin: Evangelische Verlag, 1962.
Miller, J. *One, by One, by One: Facing the Holocaust*. New York: Simon and Schuster, 1990.
Miller, R. J. "The (A)historicity of Jesus' Temple Demonstration: A Test Case in Methodology." Pages 235–52 in SBLSP 30. Edited by E. H. Lovering. Atlanta: Scholars Press, 1991.
Montgomery, J. A. *Aramaic Incantation Texts from Nippur*. Philadelphia: University of Pennsylvania Museum Publications, 1913.
Mournet, T. *Oral Tradition and Literary Dependency: Variability and Stability in the Synoptic Tradition and Q*. WUNT 195. Tübingen: Mohr Siebeck, 2005.
Mowinckel, S. "Israelite Historiography." *ASTI* 2 (1963): 4–26.
———. *The Psalms in Israel's Worship*. Grand Rapids: Eerdmanns, 2004 [1962].
Moxter, M. "Erzählung und Ereignis: Über den Spielraum historischer Repräsentation." Pages 67–88 in *Der historische Jesus: Tendenzen und Perspektiven der gegenwärtigen Forschung*. Edited by J. Schröter and R. Brucher. BZNW 114. Berlin: De Gruyter, 2002.
Mueller-Vollmer, K. *The Hermeneutics Reader*. New York: Continuum, 1985.

Mulder, M. J. *1 Kings*. Vol. 1: *1 Kings 1–11*. Translated by J. Vriend. Leuven: Peeters, 1998.
Müller, U. B. *Messias und Menschensohn in jüdischen Apokalypsen und in der Offenbarung des Johannes*. Studien zum Neuen Testament Band 6. Gütersloh: Gütersloher Verlagshaus, 1972.
Mullins, T. Y. "Jesus, the 'Son of David.'" *AUSS* 29 (1991): 117–26.
Murphy-O'Connor, J. "John the Baptist and Jesus: History and Hypotheses." *NTS* 36 (1990): 359–74.
Myers, C. *Binding the Strong Man: A Political Reading of Mark's Story of Jesus*. Maryknoll, N.Y.: Orbis, 1988.
Namer, G. *Mémoire et société*. Paris: Méridiens Lincksieck, 1987.
Neirynck, F., J. Delobel, et al. *Jean et les synoptiques: examen critique de l'exégèse de M.-E. Boismard*. BETL 49. Louvain: University Press, 1979.
Neugebauer, F. "Die Davidssohnfrage (Mark xii 35-7 parr.) und der Menschensohn." *NTS* 21 (1974): 81–108.
Neusner, J. *A History of the Jews in Babylonia*. Leiden: Brill, 1965.
Nickelsburg, G. W. E. *George W. E. Nickelsburg in Perspective: An Ongoing Dialogue of Learning*. Vol. 1. Leiden: Brill, 2003.
———. *Jewish Literature between the Bible and the Mishnah: A Historical and Literary Introduction*. Philadelphia: Fortress, 1981.
Nietzsche, F. *The Genealogy of Morals*. Edited by W. Kaufmann. Translated by C. Diethe. Garden City, N.Y.: Doubleday, 1956 [1887].
———. *The Will to Power*. Translated by W. Kaufmann and R. J. Hollingdale. London: Weidenfeld and Nicolson, 1967 [1901].
Nineham, D. E. *The Gospel of St. Mark*. Pelican New Testament Commentaries. New York: Penguin, 1963.
Nitzan, B. *Qumran Prayer and Religious Poetry*. Translated by Chipman. Leiden: Brill, 1994.
Nock, A. D. "Paul and the Magus." Pages 164–88 in *The Beginnings of Christianity. Part 1: The Acts of the Apostles*. Edited by F. Jackson and K. Lake. London: Macmillan, 1920–1933.
Nolan, B. M. *The Royal Son of God: The Christology of Matthew 1-2 in the Setting of the Gospel*. Orbis Biblicus et Orientalis 23. Fribourg: Biblical Institute of the University of Fribourg, 1979.
Nora, P. "Between Memory and History: Les Lieux de mémoire." *Representations* 26 (1989): 7–25.
———. *Les Lieux de mémoire*. Paris: Gallimard, 1984.
———. *Realms of Memory: Rethinking the French Past*. New York: Columbia University Press, 1996.
Nordheim, E. von. "König und Tempel: Der Hintergrund des Tempelbauverbotes in 2 Samuel vii." *VT* 27 (1977): 434–53.
Norris, C. *Spinoza and the Origins of Modern Critical Theory*. Oxford: Basil Blackwell, 1991.

Novakovic, L. *Messiah, the Healer of the Sick: A Study of Jesus as the Son of David in the Gospel of Matthew.* WUNT 170. Tübingen: Mohr Siebeck, 2003.
Oegema, G. S. *The Anointed and His People: Messianic Expectations from the Maccabees to Bar Kochba.* JSPSup. Sheffield: Sheffield Academic Press, 1998.
Oppenheim, A. L. "Man and Nature in Mesopotamian Civilization." Pages 634–66 in *Dictionary of Scientific Biography.* Edited by C. C. Gillespie. New York: Scribner's and Sons, 1978.
Osborne, G. R. *The Hermeneutical Spiral.* Downers Grove, Ill.: InterVarsity, 1991.
Oswalt, J. N. *The Book of Isaiah: Chapters 1–39.* Grand Rapids: Eerdmans, 1986.
Paffenroth, K. "Jesus as Anointed and Healing Son of David in the Gospel of Matthew." *Biblica* 80 (1999): 547–54.
Painter, J. *Mark's Gospel.* London: Routledge, 1997.
———. *Theology as Hermeneutics: Rudolf Bultmann's Interpretation of the History of Jesus.* Sheffield: Almond Press, 1987.
Pannenberg, W. "Hermeneutics and Universal History." *Journal for Theology and Church* 4 (1967): 122–52.
Pao, D. W. *Acts and the Isaianic New Exodus.* Grand Rapids: Baker Academic, 2002 [2000].
Parker, D. *The Living Text of the Gospels.* Cambridge: Cambridge University Press, 1997.
Parkinson, G. H. R., ed. *Leibniz: Philosophical Writings.* London: J. M. Dent, 1973.
Parry, D., and E. Tov. *The Dead Sea Scrolls Reader.* 2 vols. Leiden: Brill, 2004.
"Passion of Christ." Pages 625–29 in *Dictionary of Biblical Imagery.* Edited by L. Ryken, J. Wilhoit, and T. Longman III. Downers Grove, Ill.: InterVarsity, 1998.
Patsch, V. H. "Der Einzug Jesu in Jerusalem: ein historischer Versuch." *ZTK* 68 (1971): 1–26.
Patte, D. *The Gospel according to Matthew: A Structural Commentary on Matthew's Faith.* Philadelphia: Fortress, 1987.
Pelikan, J. *Jesus through the Centuries: His Place in the History of Culture.* New Haven: Yale University Press, 1985.
Perrin, N. "Mark 14:62: The End Product of a Christian Pesher Tradition?" *NTS* 12 (1965): 150–55.
Pesch, R. *Das Markusevangeliem.* 2 vols. HTKNT. Freiburg: Herder, 1991.
Peters, J. *Finding the Historical Jesus.* London: Collins, 1965.
Pfeiffer, R. H. *Introduction to the Old Testament.* London: Adam and Charles Black, 1952.
Pfitztner, V. C. *Hebrews.* Nashville: Abingdon, 1997.
Plummer, A. *The Gospel according to St. Luke.* ICC. New York: Charles Scribner's Sons, 1903.
Polkow, D. "Method and Criteria for Historical Jesus Research." Pages 336–56 in *Society of Biblical Literature 1987 Seminar Papers.* Edited by K. H. Richards. SBLSP. Atlanta: Scholars Press, 1987.
Polt, R. *Heidegger: An Introduction.* London: Routledge, 1998.
Pomykala, K. E. *The Davidic Dynasty Tradition in Early Judaism: Its History and*

Significance for Messianism. Society of Biblical Literature Early Judaism and Its Literature 7. Atlanta: Scholars Press, 1995.
Porter, S.E. *The Criteria for Authenticity in Historical Jesus Research.* JSNTSup 131. Sheffield: Sheffield Academic Press, 2000.
———. "Did Jesus Ever Teach in Greek?" *TynBul* 44, no. 2 (1993): 199–235.
Poythress, V. S. "Is Romans 1:3-4 a Pauline Confession after All?" *ExpTim* (1975–1976): 180–83.
Preus, S. *Spinoza and the Irrelevance of Biblical Authority.* Cambridge: Cambridge University Press, 2001.
Puech, É. "Une Apocalypse Messianique (4Q521)," *RevQ* 15 (1992) : 475–519.
———. "11QPsAp(a): Un ritual d'exorcismes. Essai de reconstruction." *RevQ* 14 (1990): 377–408.
———. *Qumrân Grotle 4.XXII.* DJD 25. Oxford: Clarendon, 1998.
Pusey, E. B. *An Historical Enquiry into the Probable Causes of the Rationalist Character Lately Predominant in the Theology of Germany.* London: C. and J. Rivington, 1828.
Rad, G. von. "The Beginnings of Historical Writing in Ancient Israel." Pages 176–204 in *The Problem of the Hexateuch and Other Essays.* New York: McGraw-Hill, 1966.
Rae, M. *History and Hermeneutics.* Edinburgh: T&T Clark, 2006.
Ranke, L. von. *The Theory and Practice of History.* Edited by G. G. Iggers and H. von Molke. New York: Bobbs-Merrill, 1973.
Rehm, M. *Der königliche Messias im Licht der Immanuel-Weissagungen des Buches Jesaja.* Kevekaer: Butzon and Bercker, 1968.
Ricoeur, P. "The Hermeneutical Function of Distanciation." *Philosophy Today* 17, no. 2 (1973): 129–41.
———. *Interpretation Theory: Discourse and the Surplus of Meaning.* Fort Worth: Texas Christian University Press, 1976.
Riesenfeld, H. *The Gospel Tradition and Its Beginnings: A Study in the Limits of "Formgeschichte."* London: A. R. Mowbray, 1961 [1957].
———. *Jésus transfiguré: l'arrière-plan du récit évangélique de la Transfiguration de Notre-Seigneur.* Copenhagen: Hakan Ohlssohn, 1947.
Robbins, V. K. "The Healing of Blind Bartimaeus (10:46-52) in the Marcan Theology." *JBL* 92 (1973): 224–43.
Robinson, J. M. *A New Quest of the Historical Jesus.* London: SCM Press, 1959.
———, P. Hoffmann, and J. S. Kloppenborg. *The Sayings of the Gospel Q in Greek in English.* Leuven: Peeters, 2001.
Rosen, D., and A. Salvesen. "A Note on the Qumran Temple Scroll 56:15-18 and *Psalm of Solomon* 17:33." *JJS* 38 (1987): 99–101.
Ross, A. P. *Holiness to the Lord: A Guide to the Exposition of the Book of Leviticus.* Grand Rapids: Baker, 2002.
Rost, L. *The Succession to the Throne of David.* Translated by M. Rutter and D. Gunn. Sheffield: Almond Press, 1982 [1926].
Rowley, H. H. "Melchizedek and Zadok (Gen 14 and Ps 110)." Pages 461–72 in *Festschrift für Alfred Bertholet.* Tübingen: J. C. B. Mohr, 1950.

Saachi, P. *Jewish Apocalyptic and Its History.* Translated by William J. Short. Sheffield: Sheffield Academic Press, 1990.

Sanders, E. P. *The Historical Figure of Jesus.* London: Penguin, 1993.

———. *Jesus and Judaism.* London: SCM Press, 1985.

———. *Pauls and Palestinian Judaism: A Comparison of Patterns of Religion.* Philadelphia: Fortress, 1977.

Sanders, J. A. "A New Testament Hermeneutic Fabric: Psalm 118 in the Entrance Narrative." Pages 177–90 in *Early Jewish and Christian Exegesis.* Edited by C. A. Evans and W. F. Stinespring. Atlanta: Scholars Press, 1987.

Saucy, M. *The Kingdom of God in the Teachings of Jesus in 20th Century Theology.* Dallas: Word, 1997.

Schachter, D. "Memory Distortion: History and Current Status." Pages 1–46 in *Memory Distortion.* Edited by D. Schachter. Cambridge, Mass.: Harvard University Press, 1995.

Schalit, A. *König Herodes: Der Mann und sein Werk.* Studia Judaica 4. Berlin: de Gruyter, 1969.

Schleiermacher, F. D. E. *Hermeneutics, The Handwritten Manuscripts.* Translated by J. Duke and J. Forstmann. Missoula, Mont.: Scholars Press, 1977.

———. *Hermeneutik, Nach den Handschriften neu herausgegeben und eingeleitet von Heinz Kimmerle.* Heidelberg: Karl Winter Universitätverlag, 1959.

Schmidt, K. L. *Der Rahmen der Geschichte Jesu: literarkritische Untersuchungen zur ältesten Jesusüberlieferung.* Berlin: Trowitzsch, 1919.

Schmithals, W. *Das Evangelium nach Markus.* 2 vols. OTNT 1–2. Gütersloh: Mohn, 1979.

Schneider, G. "Die Davidssohnfrage (Mk 12.35-37)." *Bib* 53 (1972): 65–90.

———. "Zur Vorgeschichte des christologischen Prädikats 'Sohn Davids.'" *TTZ* 80 (1971): 247–53.

Schofield, A., and J. C. Vanderkam. "Were the Hasmoneans Zadokites?" *JBL* (2005): 73–87.

Schröter, J. "Die Frage nach dem historischen Jesus und der Charakter historischer Erkenntnis." Pages 207–54 in *The Sayings Source Q and the Historical Jesus.* Edited by A. Lindemann. Leuven: Leuven University Press, 2001.

———. "Von der Historizität der Evangelien: Ein Beitrag zur gegenwärtigen Diskussion um den historischen Jesus." Pages 163–212 in *Der historische Jesus: Tendenzen und Perspektiven der gegenwärtigen Forschung.* Edited by J. Schröter and R. Brucher. BZNW 114. Berlin: De Gruyter, 2002.

Schudson, M. "Dynamics of Distortion in Collective Memory." Pages 346–64 in *Memory Distortion.* Edited by D. Schachter. Cambridge, Mass.: Harvard University Press, 1995.

Schuller, E. M. *Non-Canonical Psalms from Qumran: A Pseudepigraphic Collection.* Atlanta: Scholars Press, 1987.

Schüpphaus, J. *Die Psalmen Salomos: Ein Zeugnis Jerusalemer Theologie und Frömmigkeit in der Mitte des vorchristlichen Jahrhunderts.* Leiden: Brill, 1977.

Schürer, E. *The History of the Jewish People in the Age of Jesus Christ (175 B.C.–A.D. 135).* 3 vols. Edited by G. Vermes et al. Edinburgh: T&T Clark, 1973–1987.

Schwartz, B. "The Social Context of Commemoration: A Study in Collective Memory." *SF* 61, no. 2 (1982): 374–402.
Schweitzer, A. *The Quest of the Historical Jesus: A Critical Study of the Progress from Reimarus to Wrede*. Translated by W. Montgomery. London: Adam and Charles Black, 1952.
Schweizer, E. *The Good News according to Mark*. Richmond, Va.: John Knox, 1970.
———. *The Good News according to Matthew*. Philadelphia: Westminster, 1975.
Scott, J. M. *Adoption as Sons of God*. WUNT 48. Tübingen: Mohr Siebeck, 1992.
Senior, D. *The Gospel of Matthew*. Nashville: Abingdon, 1997.
Shekan, P. W. "A Single Author for the Whole Book of Proverbs." Pages 15–26 in *Studies in Israelite Poetry and Wisdom*. Washington, D.C.: Catholic Biblical Association, 1971.
Smith, C. W. F. *The Paradox of Jesus in the Gospels*. Philadelphia: Westminster, 1969.
Smith, M. *Jesus the Magician: Charlatan or Son of God?* San Francisco: Harper and Row, 1978.
Smith, S. H. "The Son of David Tradition in Mark's Gospel." *NTS* 42 (1996): 523–39.
Solomon, R. C. *Continental Philosophy since 1750: The Rise and Fall of the Self*. Oxford: Oxford University Press, 1988.
Sorensen, E. *Possession and Exorcism in the New Testament and Early Christianity*. WUNT 157. Tübingen: Mohr Siebeck, 2002.
Spinoza, B. *The Chief Works*. Translated by R. H. M. Elwes. New York: Dover, 1951.
———. "Tractatus Theologico-Politicus." Pages 5–26 in *The Historical Jesus Quest: A Foundational Anthology*. Edited by G. W. Dawes. Leiden: Deo Publishing, 1999 [1670].
Stanton, G. *The Gospels and Jesus*. Oxford: Oxford University Press, 2002 [1989].
———. "Jesus of Nazareth: A Magician and False Prophet Who Deceived God's People?" Pages 164–80 in *Jesus of Nazareth Lord and Christ: Essays on the Historical Jesus*. Edited by J. Green and M. Turner. Grand Rapids: Eerdmans, 1994.
———. "The Origin and Purpose of Matthew's Gospel: Matthean Scholarship from 1945 to 1980." Pages 1889–1951 in *ANRW*. Edited by H. Temporini and W. Haase. Berlin: de Gruyter, 1985.
———. "The Origin and Purpose of Matthew's Sermon on the Mount." Pages 181–92 in *Tradition and Interpretation in the New Testament: Essays in Honor of E. E. Ellis*. Grand Rapids: Eerdmans, 1987.
———. Review of G. Lüdemann, *Jesus after 2000 Years: What He Really Said and Did*. *JTS* 54 (2003): 422–23.
Stein, R. H. "The 'Criteria' for Authenticity." Pages 225–63 in *Gospel Perspectives: Studies of History and Tradition in the Four Gospels*, vol. 1. Edited by R. H. France and D. Wenham. Sheffield: JSOT Press, 1980.
———. *Jesus the Messiah: A Survey of the Life of Christ*. Downers Grove, Ill.: InterVarsity, 1996.
Stone, M. E. "The Concept of the Messiah in IV Ezra." Pages 295–312 in *Studies in the History of Religions* 14. Leiden: Brill, 1968.

———. *Fourth Ezra*. Hermeneia. Minneapolis: Fortress, 1990.
Straus, Mark L. *The Davidic Messiah in Luke-Acts: The Promise and Its Fulfillment in Luke Christology.* JSNT 110. Sheffield: Sheffield Academic Press, 1995.
Strauss, D. F. *The Life of Jesus Critically Examined.* London: SCM Press, 1946 [1892].
Strawson, P. "The Incoherence of Empiricism II." *Proceedings of the Aristotelian Society* 66 (1992): 139–62.
Stuckenbruck, L. T. "Messianic Ideas in the Related Literature of Early Judaism: An Assessment and Prospects for Further Study." PAGES 9–113 in *The Christ and Christs in the Old and New Testaments*. Edited by S. E. Porter. Grand Rapids: Eerdmans, 2007.
Stuckenbruck, L. T., S. C. Barton, and B. G. Wold, eds. *Memory and Remembrance in the Bible and Antiquity.* Tübingen: Mohr Siebeck, 2006.
Suggs, M. J. "Wisdom of Solomon 2:10-15: A Homily Based on the Fourth Servant Song." *JBL* (1957): 26–33.
Suhl, A. "Der Davidssohn im Matthäus-Evangelium." *ZNW* (1968): 57–59.
———. *Die Funktion der alttestamentlichen Zitate und Anspielungen im Markusevangelium.* Güttersloh: Gerd Mohn, 1965.
Tate, M. "King and Messiah in Isaiah of Jerusalem." *RevExp* 65, no. 4 (1968): 409–21.
Taylor, J. E. *The Immerser: John the Baptist within Second Temple Judaism.* Grand Rapids: Eerdmans, 1997.
Taylor, V. *Formation of Gospel Tradition.* London: Macmillan, 1953.
———. *The Gospel according to St Mark.* London: Macmillan, 1966.
———. *The Life and Ministry of Jesus.* London: Macmillan, 1955.
Telford, W. R. *The Barren Temple and the Withered Tree.* JSNTSup 1. Sheffield: JSOT Press, 1980.
———. *The Theology of the Gospel of Mark.* Cambridge: Cambridge University Press, 1999.
Thatcher, T. "Why John Wrote a Gospel: Memory and History in an Early Christian Community." Pages 79–97 in *Memory, Tradition, and Text: Uses of the Past in Early Christianity.* Edited by A. Kirk and T. Thatcher. Semeia 52. Leiden: Brill, 2005.
Theisohn, J. *Der auserwählte Richter: Untersuchungen zum traditionsgeschichtlem Ort der Menschensohngestalt der Bilderreden des Äthiopischen Henoch.* SUNT. Göttingen: Vandenhoeck and Ruprecht, 1975.
Theissen, G. "Die Tempelweissagung Jesu." *TZ* 32 (1976): 144–58.
———. *Miracle Stories of the Early Christian Tradition.* Edinburgh: T&T Clark, 1983.
Theissen, G., and A. Merz. *The Historical Jesus: A Comprehensive Guide.* Minneapolis: Fortress, 1998.
Theissen, G., and D. Winter. *The Quest for the Plausible Jesus: The Question of Criteria.* Translated by M. Eugene Boring. Louisville, Ky.: Westminster John

Knox, 2002. Originally titled *Die Kriterienfrage in der Jesusforschung*. Fribourg: University Press, 1997.
Thiselton, A. C. "Hermeneutics." Pages 293–97 in *New Dictionary of Theology*. Edited by S. Ferguson, D. Wright, and J. I. Packer. Downers Grove, Ill.: InterVarsity Press, 1988.
———. *New Horizons in Hermeneutics*. Grand Rapids: Zondervan, 1992.
———. *The Two Horizons: New Testament Hermeneutics and Philosophical Description with Special Reference to Heidegger, Bultmann, Gadamer, and Wittgenstein*. Exeter: Paternoster, 1980.
Tolstoy, L. *War and Peace*. Translated by Rosemary Edwards. London: Harmondsworth, 1971.
Torijano, P. A. *Solomon the Esoteric King: From King to Magus, Development of a Tradition*. JSJSup 73. Leiden: Brill, 2002.
Torrey, C. C. *Our Translated Gospels*. London: Hodder and Stoughton, 1936.
Treves, M. "Two Acrostic Psalms." *VT* 15 (1965): 81–90.
Trumbower, J. A. "The Role of Malachi in the Career of John the Baptist." Pages 28–41 in *The Gospels and the Scriptures of Israel*. Edited by C. A. Evans and W. R. Stegner. JSNTSup. Sheffield: Sheffield Academic Press, 1994.
Trunk, D. *Der messianische Heiler: eine redaktions-und religionsgeschichtliche Studie zu den Exorzismen im Matthäusevangelium*. Freiburg: Herder, 1994.
Turner, H. E. W. *Historicity and the Gospels*. Oxford: A. R. Mowbray, 1963.
Twelftree, G. H. *Jesus the Exorcist: A Contribution to the Study of the Historical Jesus*. Peabody, Mass.: Hendrickson, 1993.
———. *Jesus the Miracle Worker: A Historical and Theological Study*. Downers Grove, Ill.: InterVarsity, 1999.
VanderKam, J. C. *The Dead Sea Scrolls Today*. Grand Rapids: Eerdmans, 1994.
Van Seters, J. *In Search of History*. New Haven: Yale University Press, 1983.
Vasina, J. *Oral Tradition as History*. Madison: University of Wisconsin Press, 1985.
Veijola, T. *Die Ewige Dynastie: David und die Enstehung seiner Dynastie nach der deuteronomistischen Darstellung*. Helsinki: Suolmalainen Tideakatemia, 1975.
Verhey, A. *Remembering Jesus: Christian Community, Scripture, and the Moral Life*. Grand Rapids: Eerdmans, 2002.
Vermes, G. *Jesus in His Jewish Context*. Minneapolis: Fortress, 2003.
———. *Jesus the Jew: A Historian's Reading of the Gospels*. Minneapolis: Fortress, 1981.
———. "The Oxford Forum for Qumran Research Seminar on the War Rule from Cave 4 (4Q285)." *JJS* 43 (1992): 85–94.
Vico, G. *The Autobiography of Giambattista Vico*. Translated by M. H. Fisch and T. G. Bergin. New York: Cornell University Press, 1944.
Voss, G. *Die Christologie der lukanischen Schriften in Grundzügen*. StudNeot 2. Paris: Desclée de Brouwer, 1965.
Vögtle, A. "Der Spruch vom Jonaszeichen." Pages 103–36 in *Synoptische Studien: Alfred Wikenhauser zum siebzigsten Geburtstag am 22*. München: Karl Zink Verlag, 1953.

———. "Die Genealogie Mt 1,2-16 und die matthäische Kindheitgeschichte." *BZ* 8 (1965): 45–58.
Wahlen, C. *Jesus and the Impurity of Spirits in the Synoptic Gospels.* WUNT 2.185. Tübingen: Mohr Siebeck, 2004.
Walker, R. C. S. "Contingency." Pages 650–52 in *Routledge Enclyclopedia of Philosophy.* London: Routledge, 1998.
Wallace, D. *Greek Grammar, Beyond the Basics.* Grand Rapids: Zondervan, 1996.
Watchel, N. "Memory and History." *History and Anthropology* 2, no. 2 (1996): 207–24.
Watts, J. D. W. *Isaiah 1–33.* WBC 24. Waco, Tex.: Word, 1985.
Watts, R. E. *Isaiah's New Exodus in Mark.* Grand Rapids: Baker Academic, 2000 [1997].
Wegner, P. D. *An Examination of Kingship and Messianic Expectation in Isaiah 1–35.* Lewiston, Maine: Mellen Biblical Press, 1992.
Weinfeld, M. "The Covenant of Grant in Israel and the Ancient Near East." *JAOS* 90 (1970): 184–203.
———. *Deuteronomy and the Deuteronomist School.* Oxford: Clarendon, 1972.
Weiser, A. *The Psalms: A Commentary.* Translated by H. Hartwell. London: SCM Press, 1962 [1959].
Weiss, J. *Jesus' Proclamation of the Kingdom of God.* Translated by David Holland. Minneapolis: Fortress, 1971.
Weissberg, L. Introduction to *Cultural Memory and the Construction of Identity.* Edited by D. Ben-Amos and L. Weissberg. Detroit: Wayne State University Press, 1999.
Wellhausen, J. *Die Pharisäer und die Sadducäer.* Greifswald: L. Bamberg, 1874.
Wenham, G. "Were David's Sons Priests?" *ZAW* 87 (1975): 79–82.
Wessel, L. P. *G. E. Lessing's Theology: A Reinterpretation.* The Hague: Mouton, 1977.
Westcott, B. F. *Epistle to the Hebrews: The Greek Text with Notes and Essays.* London: Macmillan, 1889.
Whiston, W. *The Works of Josephus.* Peabody, Mass.: Hendrickson, 1987.
White, H. *Metahistory.* Baltimore: Johns Hopkins University Press, 1973.
Wilcox, M. "The Promise of the 'Seed' in the New Testament and Targumim." *JSNT* 5 (1979): 2–20.
Wildberger, H. *Isaiah 1–12.* Minneapolis: Fortress, 1991 [1972].
Winston, D. *Wisdom of Solomon.* AB 43. Garden City, N.Y.: Doubleday, 1979.
Wise, M., M. Abegg, and E. Cook. *The Dead Sea Scrolls: A New Translation.* San Francisco: HarperSanFrancisco, 1996.
Wise, M. O. "The Eschatological Vision of the Temple Scroll." *JNES* 49 (1990): 155–73.
———. "4QFlorilegium and the Temple of Adam." *RevQ* 15 (1991–1992): 103–32.
———. "Temple." Pages 810–16 in *Dictionary of Jesus and the Gospels.* Edited by

J. Green, S. McKnight, and I. H. Marshall. Downer's Grove, Ill.: InterVarsity, 1992.
Witherington, B., III. *The Christology of Jesus*. Minneapolis: Fortress, 1990.
———. *The Gospel of Mark: A Socio-Rhetorical Commentary*. Grand Rapids: Eerdmans, 2001.
———. *The Jesus Quest: The Third Search for the Jew of Nazareth*. Downers Grove, Ill.: InterVarsity Press, 1995.
———. *New Testament History: A Narrative Account*. Grand Rapids: Baker, 2001.
Wollheim, R. "On Persons and Their Lives." Pages 299–321 in *Explaining Emotions*. Edited by R. Rorty. Berkeley: University Press, 1980.
Woollcombe, K. J. "The Biblical Origins and Patristic Development of Typology." Pages 39–75 in *Essays on Typology*. Edited by G. W. H. Lampe and K. J. Woollcombe. SBT 22. London: SCM Press, 1957.
Woude, A. S. van der. *Die Messianischen Vorstellungen der Gemeinde von Qumrân*. Assen: Gorcum, 1957.
Wright, A. T. *Origin of Evil Spirits: The Reception of Genesis 6:1-4 in Early Jewish Literature*. WUNT 198. Tübingen: Mohr Siebeck, 2005.
———. "Prayer and Incantation in the Dead Sea Scrolls." Pages 75–88 in *Studies in Jewish Prayer*. Edited by R. Hayward and B. Embry. Oxford: Oxford University Press, 2005.
Wright, N. T. *Jesus and the Victory of God*. Minneapolis: Fortress, 1996.
———. *The New Testament and the People of God*. Minneapolis: Fortress, 1992.
Yamauchi, E. M. "Aramaic Magic Bowls." *JAOS* 85, no. 4 (1965): 551–23.
———. "Magic or Miracle? Diseases, Demons and Exorcisms." Pages 89–183 in *Gospel Perspectives*, vol. 6, *The Miracles of Jesus*. Edited by D. Wenham and C. Blomberg. Sheffield: JSOT, 1986.
Zerubavel, Y. "The Historical, the Legendary and the Incredible: Invented Tradition and Collective Memory in Israel." Pages 105–25 in *Commemorations: The Politics of National Identity*. Edited by J. R. Gillis. Princeton, N.J.: Princeton University Press, 1994.
———. *Recovered Roots: Collective Memory and the Making of Israeli National Tradition*. Chicago: University of Chicago Press, 1995.
Zimmermann, J. *Messianische Texte aus Qumran: Königliche, priesterliche und prophetische Messiasvorstellungen in den Schriftfunden von Qumran*. WUNT 2.104. Tübingen: Mohr Siebeck, 1998.

Scripture Index

Old Testament

Genesis
6:1-4	142
14:18	236
16:4	102
20:12	140
20:17-18	140
30:4	102
38:2	102
49:10	126

Exodus
12:46	211
15:17	99
22:18	154

Leviticus
19:26	154
19:31	154
20:6-27	154

Numbers
24:27	126

Deuteronomy
12	99
17:16-17	120, 129
18:10-11	154
31:1-6	99

Joshua
13:3	166

Judges
16:1	102

1 Samuel
10	111
10:6	111
11:6	111
14	111
16	154
16:4-16	154
16:13	111
16:14-23	152
16:18	155
16:23	155

2 Samuel
5:3-10	172
7	82, 94–112, 116, 121, 156, 207, 254
7:1	99
7:5, 7	97–98
7:8-17	97–98
7:10	99
7:11	99
7:12	153
7:12-13	205
7:12-14	102, 208
7:13	98–99, 144, 206, 237, 238, 240
7:14-15	99, 102, 104
7:15	102, 155
12	103

12:12-14	102–3	2:13-15	79
13:1	96	5	140
14:17	124	5:10	79–80
14:20	124	7:12	203
16:22	102	9:13	196
17:14	105		
22:9	113	1 Chronicles	
		10–29	103
1 Kings		17	82, 105
1	204	17:11-14	103–4
1:32-40	194–202, 218	22	103
1:34	191	22:1-19	103
1:39	266	22:7-10	99
2:45	121	28-29	103
3	121, 149–52, 156		
3:4	239	2 Chronicles	
3:9	111, 135	1:1	106
3:5-15	113	6:42	110
3:11	107, 111	11:18	96, 103
3:16-28	113	30:26	103, 106–7
3:22	99	35:3	103, 106
3:28	107, 111, 114		
3–4	149	Nehemiah	
3–5	107, 116	13:26	102
4:29-34	107, 149		
5:3	99	Job	
5:9	107, 111	1–2	154
5:12	107		
8	99, 239	Psalms	
8:5	239	2	128, 239
8:62-64	239	2:7	238
8:16-27	240	2:9	120, 125
8:18	99	7:6	235
8:23	102	7:7-8	207
8:26	240	8:7	226
10:10	109	18:8	113
10:22	109	22	244
11:34-36	100	31	244
22:17	107	33:6	112
30:1	107	34–35	244
31:1	108	47:18	112
		69	244
2 Kings		71:1	108
2	78–79	72	108–10, 112, 116–17, 120–21
2:8	80		

72:1-3	111–12, 117	11:6-8	135
72:2	117	11:6-10	118–19
72:4	114	11:11-16	118–19
72:8-12	112	11:13-14	118–19
72:10	109	13:4	134
72:16	109	13:17	134
72:18-19	109	35:5	140
80	245	35:5-6	140–44, 163, 188
91	142, 153	42:4	166
110	123, 217, 221–57, 259–61, 266	49:2	113
		53:4	140
118	191, 196–204, 267	56:7	171
118:22-29	197	56:7-10	173
118:25-26	192, 199	61	145
132:11-12	109	61:1-2	142, 163, 173
		61:1-3	144
Proverbs		62:11	211
1:1	106	66:20	125
25:15	112		

Qoheleth (Ecclesiastes)
1:1   106–8

Jeremiah
7:11	171
23:15	206
33:15	206

Isaiah
9	113
9:4	113
9:6-7	120
9:7	113, 118–19
9:17	113
10	110
10:13	111
10:21	111
10:22–11:5	118
10:33-34	134
11:1	82, 94, 101, 116, 118–19, 110–35, 156, 203, 206, 260
11:1-9	110, 112–13
11:2	111, 118–19, 126, 135
11:2, 4	111–14, 117–19
11:4	118–19, 123–29, 135
11:5	128
11:4-5	111, 116, 118–19, 126
11:6-7	127–28

Ezekiel
17:3-4	206
23:44	102, 249
43:1-12	249

Daniel
7	245–46
7:13	247

Hosea
6:5	113, 124

Amos
9:11	208

Micah
4:13	126

Zechariah
3:8	203, 204

4	203	9:36	173
6:12	191, 194–96, 200–20, 267	10:8	164
6:12-13	211–12, 245	10:25	168, 177
6:13	203	11:2	144
9	211–13	11:2-6	164
9:9	194–220, 237, 266	11:4-5	145
9:11	208, 210	11:5	160, 163
11:11-13	212–13	11:7-9	68, 85
12:9	202–3, 210	11:10	69
12:10	205, 210, 249, 250	11:12-15	78, 85
12:46	210	11:14	84
13:7	205	12:18-21	166
13:7-9	211–12	12:22	160
14:4	203, 212	12:22-23	261
14:11	212	12:22-28	165, 177
14:21	212	12:23-24	170
		12:24	168, 262
Malachi		12:24-28	164
1:2	102	12:24-39	171
3:1	69–70, 78, 85–86	12:27	245
4:5-6	78–79, 85, 113	12:33	157
		12:41-42	245
New Testament		12:45	245
Matthew		13:51	161
1-2	95	14:14	173
1:1	157, 187	15:14	160, 170
1:6	223	15:21-28	165
1:20	157, 223	15:22	157
3:5	145	15:22-28	168
3:11-12	144	15:22	164
4:18	160	15:22-28	176
5:9	245	15:25	164
7:1	245	15:29-31	163
7:32	164	15:30-31	160
8:16	164	15:32	173
8:28	160	17:15	164
8:28-34	162	17:19	164
8:31	164	18:19-20	160
9:18	160	20:29-34	157–64, 177
9:27	157	20:30	160
9:27-31	157–64	20:30-31	157
9:27-28	164	20:30-33	164
9:30	163	20:34	163, 173
9:33-34	164	21:1, 7	160

21:2	215	8:22-26	162, 176
21:5	215–16	8:29-33	244
21:9	157, 191, 199, 211, 217	10:46	178, 198, 212
21:12	171	10:46-52	157, 164, 177, 213, 262
21:13	171		
21:14	160	10:47	177
21:14-16	171	10:47-48	188
21:15	157, 170	10:50	178
21:21	212	10:51	178
22:40	160	11:2	196, 204
22:22-45	225	11:1-6	193
22:41-46	157	11:1-11	191–200, 204
23:16-26	188	11:9-11	177
26	172	11:10	214
26:15	212	11:12-14	215
26:16-26	160, 170	11:17	196
26:31	211	11:7-11	193, 196
26:60	160	11:20-26	215
27:21	160	11:23	212
27:9	212	11:8	192
		11:8-11	203
Mark		11:9	247
1:1	199, 244	11:9-10	192, 196–200
1:3	247	11:23	252
1:32-33	164	12	241
1:43	161	12:11	247
3:10-11	164	12:27	242
3:11	244	12:28-34	241
3:17	178	12:29	247
3:21-27	177	12:34	241–42
5:8-10	162	12:35	227, 241–43, 254, 260
5:19	248	12:35-37	119, 157, 177, 179, 221–57, 259, 262, 266
5:19-20	224		
5:41	178	12:36	226
6:13	164	12:37	225, 227, 242, 248, 260
6:34	213	12:38-40	242
7:1-23	88	12:36	226
7:3	95	12:37	225, 227, 242, 248, 260
7:11	178	12:41-44	242
7:24	176	12:42	178
7:25	169	13:1-2	252
7:27	168	13:20	248
7:31-37	163	14	241
7:34	178	14:11	213

14:24-28	203	1 Corinthians	
14:27	211, 213	15:25-27	226
14:54-72	244		
14:55-64	243	Galatians	
14:56-59	248, 251	3:16	99
14:58	244, 252		
14:62	226, 245	Ephesians	
15:2	244	1:19-22	226
15:16-42	178		
15:18	244	2 Timothy	
15:32	244	2:8	186, 223
15:38	247		
15:39	244	Hebrews	
		1:3	125, 226, 235
Luke		5:5-10	226
3:15-17	144	7:3	236
3:17	145	7:15	237
7:24-26	68, 85	7:17-21	235
7:27	69	10:12	235
11:14	165	10:13	226
11:14-22	177	12:2	235
		13	226, 235
John			
1:28	80, 85	James	
1:19-21	84	3:8	112
2:16	212		
2:18-22	251	Revelation	
2:19	253	3–5	143
7:38	212	3:19-21	143
8:24	151	5:5	223, 143
9:1-12	163	21:1-3	250
10:40	80, 85	22:16	223
12:12-15	193		
12:14	211	**Septuagint**	
19:33	211	LXX Gen 14:18	236
		LXX Exod 23:20	171
Acts		LXX 2 Sam 7:11, 13	99
2:33-35	226	LXX 2 Sam 7:12	153, 156
		LXX 1 Kgs 1	218
Romans		LXX 1 Kgs 4:32	107, 149
1:3	223	LXX Tob	14
1:3-4	186–87	LXX Ps 8:7	226
2:1	245	LXX Ps 71:1	108
8:34	226	LXX Ps 71:4	114

LXX Ps 109:1	226	21:6	112
LXX Ps 117:25	198	53:1-3	246
LXX Prov 22:17	301, 107		
LXX Sir 45:25	197	1 Enoch	
LXX Sir 48:10-11	80	8:3	151
LXX Isa 11:4	112, 135	91	250
LXX Isa 35:5	163		
LXX Isa 61:1-2	163	*Liber antiquitatum biblicarum* (Ps.-Philo)	
LXX Zech 9:9	201, 204, 2:15	1:187-88	152

OT Apocrypha

		60	148, 156
4 Ezra (2 Esdras)		60:1-3	152–54, 263
11:38–12:3	124	64:1	152
12:32-33	125		
13	125	*Psalms of Solomon*	
13:1-13	246	1–2	105
13:8-13	123–24	2:26-27	134
		17	82, 94, 96, 101–10, 114–45, 156, 170, 260, 264
Judith			
16:5	112		
		17-18	116–17
1 Maccabees		17:3	134
4:19-25	194	17:4	120, 133
5:45-54	194	17:4-6	143
10:86	194	17:5	118–19, 121, 133
13:49-51	194	17:6	118–19
13:51	237, 245	17:8	121
14:41	223–24	17:10	120
		17:17-18	118–19
2 Maccabees		17:19	118-19
4:21-22	194	17:21	95, 118–21, 133
7:34-36	245	17:20-24	114–16
10:1-7	192	17:23-24	118–19, 125, 135
		17:25	121
Wisdom of Solomon		17:26	118-19
7	148	17:28	118-19
7:16-20	151	17:29	117, 119
7:17-21	150	17:10	118–19
18:15	124	17:16-19	133
		17:31	118–19
OT Pseudepigrapha		17:32-34	122
2 Baruch		17:33	118–19, 129
4:3	249	17:33-34	135
7b-11	246	17:34-45	129

17:35-36	135	1QapGen	
17:36	121	20.16-21	142
17:37	117–19	20.28-29	142
17:40	118–19	1QS	
17:44	118–19	3.6	167
18	115	3.18-19	167
18:7	117–19	1QSa	
18:8	118–19	2 4b-9	174
		1QSb	123–31, 208
Sibylline Oracles		5	123, 260
3:767-802	119	5.24-29	126
		5.20	126
Testament of Levi		5.25	127
17:10	249–50	5.26	128
		5.27	153
Testament of Solomon		5.27-29	127–28
1:5	149	5.29	129
1:7	146–47	4Q	
1:17	147	4Q161	119, 123
2:2	148	4Q161 3.15	206
2:8	146	4Q161 7-10	206
2:8-3:6	166	4Q174	123, 207, 208, 210
6:1-11	166	4Q174 1.1-6	206, 209
6:12	146	4Q174 1.10-13	207–8
8:42	263	4Q174 3.7	206
12:3	147	4Q174 3.12, 13	206
12:5	146	4Q177 1.7	206
9:6	148	4Q177 4.7	206
11:2	148	4Q242	142
12:4-5	148	4Q245	129
13:7	148	4Q246	123
20:1	147	4Q252 5.2-4	206
		4Q266	236
Dead Sea Scrolls		4Q285 5	206
CD	207	4Q285 f7	123, 129
5.2	206	4Q285 f7.2	206
5.5	206	4Q286 f7 2.1-6	167
7.14	206	4Q398 f11 13.1	206, 209
15 15b-17a	174	4Q398 f14 17ii.1	206
4QDa 8 1.6-7	174	4Q479 f1.4	206
1QM		4Q504 f1 6–8	206
1.5	123	4Q521	142–46, 188
7.1-7	174	4Q521 l.7	143
11.2	206	4Q541	250

4Q541 9.1	249	**Early Christian Literature**	
11Q		Didache	
11QTemp	250	10:6	199
11QTemp 29.7-10	249		
11QTemp 56.15-18	129	Origen	
11Q5	263	Cels.1:28	179
11Q5 27.10	142		
11Q11	142–56	Suetonius	
11Q11 2.2-4	153	*Vesp.* 7:2-3	163
11Q13	144, 207, 236		
11Q13 2.18	145	**Nag Hammadi Tractates**	
11Q13 2.4-19	145	*Gos.Thom.* 47	216
11Q13 2.9-11	207		
		Other Hellenistic Writings	
Rabbinic Literature and Prayers		Flavius Philostratus	
Mekilta de Rabbi Ishmael		1.26	182
on Exodus 15:17-21	249–50	4.45	183
Midr.Ps. 110	123	Callimachus	
Gen.Rab. 85.9	235	*Hymn to Apollo* 29	223
Num.Rab. 18.23	235		
Pesiq.Rab. 15	153	Josephus	
Sanh. 38b	235	*Antiquities*	
Sota. 47a	132	8.42f.	148, 150, 152
Ta'an. 23a	132	11.325-39	194
Mo'ed Qat. 16b	196	12.312	194
b.Bat. 8.6	185	12.348-49	194
b.Ber. 16b	185	13.304-6	194
b.Git. 68a	149	16.12-15	194
b.Sanh. 43a	179	17.194-239	194
b.Sanh. 107b	179	*Jewish War*	
		1.110	133
Targumim		1.114	134
Tg. Ps.J. Gen 49:11	122	1.194-239	194
Tg. Isa 53:5	249	2.136	151
Tg. Zech 14:21	212	7.185	151

Author Index

Abegg, M., 101, 208, 210
Achtemeier, P.J., 213, 223
Ackroyd, P.R., 115, 155
Allen, L.C., 232
Allison, D.C., 139, 163, 166, 168–72, 177, 185, 187, 224, 226, 230
Anderson, A., 97–99, 156, 185, 239
Assmann, A., 60
Assmann, J., 44, 46, 47, 50–54, 61, 73–74
Atkinson, K., 115, 122–23, 127, 129, 130
Aune, D.E., 138, 141, 167

Bauer, D.R., 95, 122
Beasley-Murray, G.R., 252
Berger, K., 138, 146–47, 152, 164, 168, 169, 245, 246
Beuken, W.A.M., 110, 113
Black, M., 90–91,
Black, M.C., 203–4, 215
Blenkinsopp, J., 108
Bockmuehl, M., 61, 129, 165
Bornkamm, G., 162
Bowker, J.W., 170, 233
Bowman, J., 147
Braaten, C.E., 34
Braun, R., 103, 104, 105
Brooke, G.J., 208
Brown, R.E., 107, 185–88, 223–24
Bruce, F.F., 132, 135, 192, 200, 211–13, 220
Brueggemann, W., 103, 105–7, 111
Bultmann, R., 17, 29, 32, 33, 34, 35, 36, 37, 38, 39, 43, 65, 71, 176, 186, 192, 223, 226
Burger, C., 95, 100, 137–39, 157, 161, 197–98, 223–24
Burke, P., 46, 55–56, 59, 77
Byrskog, S., 12

Caird, G., 1
Carlson, R.A., 98
Carr, D., 63
Carson, D.A., 88
Cartledge, T.W., 155
Casey, M., 90
Catchpole, D.R., 194, 195, 200, 220
Charles, R.H., 128
Charlesworth, J.H., 122, 139, 144–49, 152, 164, 167, 178–79
Childs, B.S., 111, 135
Childs, H., 6, 10–11
Chilton, B.D., 138, 139, 223–27, 243
Clements, R.E., 107
Collingwood, R.G., 7, 18, 35, 43
Collins, J.J., 80, 101, 122, 126, 127, 143, 145, 210, 213, 244
Coser, L.A., 41–42, 45, 67
Cranfield, C.E.B., 169, 200–201, 230, 234, 248, 253
Creed, J.M., 200
Cross, F.M., 80, 98
Crossan, J.D., 3, 6, 27, 62, 175–76, 196, 268
Cullman, O., 186

Dahl, N.A., 76, 214
Dahood, M., 232, 236
Daube, D., 255
Davies, W.D., 139, 163, 166, 168, 170, 172, 177, 185, 187, 224, 226, 230
Denton, D.L., 6, 8–10, 27, 62, 139
Dibelius, M., 252
Dilthey, W., 7, 10, 18, 30, 35, 39
Dimant, D., 107, 150, 209
Dodd, C.H., 213, 244
Duling, D.C., 106, 138, 146–47, 152–53, 157, 161, 164, 189
Dunn, J.D.G., 11–13, 23, 47, 60–64, 71, 73, 76, 165, 177, 186, 188, 229, 230, 248

Elam, Y., 46, 54, 60
Ernst, J., 197
Evans, C.A., 80, 89, 131, 139, 143–44, 192–94, 196–201, 205, 208, 210, 219, 223–25, 242, 249, 253

Fentress, J., 46, 49–55, 59
Fishbane, M., 194, 233
Fisher, L.R., 137–38, 149
Fitzmyer, J.A., 90, 95, 104, 110, 144, 198–99, 210, 219, 224–25, 233–39
Fletcher-Louis, C.H.T., 246–47
Flusser, D., 73, 219
Fox, M.V., 107–8

Gadamer, H.G., 19, 28–29, 32, 71
Gakuru, G., 98–99
Gedi, N., 46, 54, 60
Gerhardsson, B., 12
Gibbs, M., 161–64, 188
Gilbert, M., 150
Gnilka, J., 161, 196, 226, 243
Goodacre, M.S., 89
Goppelt, L., 131
Goulder, M., 2–3, 89, 268
Grabbe, L.L., 150
Gray, G.B., 113
Grayston, K., 138
Green, J.B., 244
Gundry, R.H., 95, 174, 177–78, 197, 216
Gunkel, H., 109, 223
Gunn, D.A., 155–56

Hagner, D.A., 161, 214–16
Hahn, F., 137, 225, 226, 248
Halbwachs, M., 41–54, 59–61, 67, 70, 87
Haney, R.G., 234, 239
Harrington, D.J., 172
Harvey, J.D., 230
Hatina, T.R., 199
Hay, D.M., 225–26, 232, 245
Hearon, H., 13

Heidegger, M., 10, 11, 17, 29–34, 39, 67, 70–71
Held, H.J., 162
Hengel, M., 115, 122, 151, 225–26
Hildebrandt, W., 111, 155
Holmberg, B., 11, 63
Hooker, M., 200, 244–47
Horbury, W., 73, 112, 124, 209, 219, 240, 246
Horsley, R.A., 13, 175
Humboldt, W., 27–28
Hutton, P., 43–44, 47, 56, 67
Hübner, H., 151, 175

Iggers, G.G., 26–28
Iser, W., 29, 71

Jenkins, K., 7–8
de Jonge, M., 115, 117, 122, 132, 134
Juel, D., 76, 99, 123, 203, 208, 210, 232, 244–47

Kaiser, O., 113, 151
Kammen, M., 46, 50–51
Kautzsch, E., 198
Kee, H.C., 140, 175
Keightley, G.M., 13
Kelber, W., 12
Kingsbury, J.D., 169–70, 172, 185, 188, 244
Kinman, B., 192, 195
Kirk, A., 12, 60
Klutz, T.E., 141, 146
Kraus, H.J., 233, 239
Kähler, M., 33–34

Laansma, J., 99, 210
Lane, W.L., 95, 201, 218, 243
Le Donne, A., 12, 41
Le Goff, J., 45–49
Lessing, G.E., 17, 22–27, 38, 76, 143, 166, 169, 200, 209, 219
Levin, Y., 185–88
Lindars, B., 244

Loader, W.R.G., 138, 157, 160–61, 188
Lohmeyer, E., 106, 196, 225, 253
Lohse, E., 95, 100, 199
Lonergan, B., 8–10
Lövestam, E., 138–39, 146–47, 152, 165
Luz, U., 148, 160–64

Macquarrie, J., 34, 37–38
Marcos, N.F., 218
Marcus, J., 123, 175, 182, 200, 203, 224–29, 235–36, 242–43, 253
Marshall, I.H., 219
Mays, J.L., 109
Meier, J.P., 88–89, 139, 180, 185–86, 189, 193, 213, 219, 223
Mettinger, T.N.D., 232, 238
Meyer, B.F., 6, 8–11, 27, 30, 67, 106, 196, 225, 253
Mournet, T., 12
Moxter, M., 61, 75
Müller, U.B., 122, 124–25, 129–31, 134, 246

Nuegebauer, F., 95
Neusner, J., 237
Nickelsburg, G.W.E., 128, 134
Nietzsche, F., 52
Nitzan, B., 153
Nock, A.D., 140
Nolan, B.M., 95, 115, 139
Nora, P., 45–54, 57, 60, 72, 88, 139, 197–98
Novakovic, L., 139, 142–45, 147, 151–53, 164–67

Oegema, G.S., 119, 126, 188–89, 205
Oswalt, J.N., 112

Paffenroth, K., 172–73
Pannenberg, W., 28
Pao, D.W., 119
Perrin, N., 245
Pesch, R., 196–97, 226, 253

Polkow, D., 87
Pomykala, K.E., 102, 105, 129, 134, 207–8
Porter, S.E., 87, 51, 91, 122, 139, 223
Puech, É., 142–43, 153

von Ranke, L., 17, 26–28, 33, 38
Ricoeur, P., 29, 31–32, 52, 61, 67, 71
Robbins, V.K., 138
Robinson, J.M., 176

Saachi, P., 102, 138
Sanders, E.P., 4–7, 73–75, 181, 252–53, 263, 268
Sanders, J.A., 199, 200, 202, 219
Schachter, D., 50
Schleiermacher, F.D.E., 10, 17, 28–32, 39, 67, 83
Schmidt, K.L., 243
Schneider, G., 96, 223, 230, 255
Schröter, J., 61, 63, 75–76
Schudson, M., 46, 49–52
Schwartz, B., 45–47, 60–61
Senior, D., 171
Smith, M., 138, 142, 167, 180–81, 225, 255
Sorensen, E., 140, 148, 154–55, 164, 166, 174–75
Stanton, G., 6, 138, 140, 167, 180
Stone, M.E., 124–25, 150–51, 179
Stuckenbruck, L.T., 108, 122, 124, 183

Taylor, V., 192, 197, 201, 204, 219, 225, 243, 253
Telford, W.R., 200, 205, 225, 253–54
Thatcher, T., 12, 60, 251, 253
Theisohn, J., 117, 246
Theissen, G., 23, 74, 76–77, 141, 163–64, 169, 251
Thiselton, A.C., 29, 33, 36, 71
Torijano, P.A., 96, 103, 108, 116–17, 121
Trumbower, J.A., 80
Trunk, D., 168–72, 176, 182

Twelftree, G.H., 138, 147, 171, 174
Watts, J.D.W., 111
Watts, R.E., 119, 253
Weiser, A., 109
Weissberg, L., 45, 47
White, H., 62–63
Wildberger, H., 111, 113, 128, 135
Wise, M.O., 208, 210, 239–40, 251–52, 264
Witherington, B., 6–7, 95, 194–95, 200, 218–19, 235, 244, 253

van der Woude, A.S., 115, 126, 131, 210
Wright, N.T., 9–10, 73, 165, 167, 175, 218
Wright A.T., 142, 153, 155

Yamauchi, E.M., 137–38

Zerubavel, Y., 46, 50, 56–61, 77
Zimmermann, J., 96, 119, 126–30, 143, 210

Subject Index

Apollonius of Tyana, 182–83
authenticity criteria, 87–91

Bultmann, R., 32–39

critical realism, 9–10

Davidic covenant, 97–106
Davidic descent, 185–89
demonology, 146–57
Dunn, J.D.G., 11–13, 64, 76

exorcism as therapy, 164–67

Halbwachs, M., 41–46, 48
Heidegger, M., 30–34
hermeneutical circle, 28–32; *see also* hermeneutical spiral
hermeneutical spiral, 71–86, 262–64
historie vs. geschichte, 33–36
how to get the most out of this book, xiii

Lessing, G.E., 22–27

magic, 179–83
Melchizedek, 234–41

memory distortion, 50–52; *see also* memory refraction
memory refraction, 13–14, 50–59, 66–77, 215, 228–31
memory vs. commemoration, 60–63
messianic dualism, 196–220
metaphorical blindness, 173–74
mnemonic continuity, 70–77, 228–31, 262
mnemonic cycle, 65–70, 259–60
militaristic vs. non-militaristic messianism, 122–27

narrativization, 52–59, 62–64, 213–17
Nora, P., 45–47, 60–61

von Ranke, L., 26–28, 33, 38

Sanders, E.P., 4–7, 73–75, 252–53, 268
Schleiermacher, F.D.E., 28–32
Schröter, J., 61, 63, 75–76
Schudson, M., 46, 49–52
Solome, Queen, 132–36
Spinoza, B., 18–22, 35
synchronic vs. diachronic analysis, 70–75, 79, 91, 257, 261–65

Theissen, G. and D. Winter, 74–77
triangulation, 85–86, 267–68
typology, toward a definition of, 2–5, 77–80, 93, 261–62
typology vs. other kinds of eschatology, 123–32

vegetation language, 205–11
violent metaphors, 112

Winter, D. and G. Theissen, 74–77